The Future of Punishment

OXFORD SERIES IN NEUROSCIENCE, LAW, AND PHILOSOPHY

SERIES EDITORS

Lynn Nadel, Frederick Schauer, and Walter P. Sinnott-Armstrong

Conscious Will and Responsibility
Edited by Walter P. Sinnott-Armstrong and Lynn Nadel

Memory and Law
Edited by Lynn Nadel and Walter P. Sinnott-Armstrong

Neuroscience and Legal Responsibility
Edited by Nicole A. Vincent

A Primer on Criminal Law and Neuroscience
Edited by Stephen J. Morse and Adina L. Roskies

The Future of Punishment
Edited by Thomas A. Nadelhoffer

The Future of Punishment

Edited by Thomas A. Nadelhoffer

OXFORD
UNIVERSITY PRESS

OXFORD
UNIVERSITY PRESS

Oxford University Press is a department of the University of Oxford.
It furthers the University's objective of excellence in research, scholarship,
and education by publishing worldwide.

Oxford New York
Auckland Cape Town Dar es Salaam Hong Kong Karachi
Kuala Lumpur Madrid Melbourne Mexico City Nairobi
New Delhi Shanghai Taipei Toronto

With offices in
Argentina Austria Brazil Chile Czech Republic France Greece
Guatemala Hungary Italy Japan Poland Portugal Singapore
South Korea Switzerland Thailand Turkey Ukraine Vietnam

Published in the United States of America by
Oxford University Press
198 Madison Avenue, New York, NY 10016

Library of Congress Cataloging-in-Publication Data
The future of punishment / edited by
Thomas A. Nadelhoffer.
pages cm.—(Oxford Series in Neuroscience, Law, and Philosophy)
ISBN 978-0-19-977920-8 (hardback : alk. paper)—
ISBN 978-0-19-977935-2 (e-book) 1. Criminal justice, Administration of—Moral and ethical aspects. 2. Punishment—Moral and ethical aspects. 3. Responsibility. 4. Free will and determinism. I. Nadelhoffer, Thomas, editor of compilation.
HV7419.F885 2013
364.601—dc23
2012029161

9 8 7 6 5 4 3 2 1
Printed in the United States of America
on acid-free paper

CONTENTS

ACKNOWLEDGMENTS

For starters, I would like to thank all of the contributors to the volume for their willingness to participate in the project. It was a pleasure working with such a stellar group of researchers from a variety of fields on the exciting issues discussed herein. I would also like to thank all of the people who graciously agreed to review the chapters and provide the authors with invaluable feedback—Joseph Campbell, Douglas Husak, Robert Kane, Anders Kaye, Eddy Nahmias, Saul Smilansky, Tamler Sommers, Neal Tognazzini, Manuel Vargas, and two additional anonymous referees. Working with such a talented group of authors and referees was a true delight.

I would also like to thank Dickinson College for allowing me to take a 2-year leave of absence to be a postdoctoral fellow with the MacArthur Foundation Law and Neuroscience Project—which afforded me the time to work on this volume. During my tenure as a postdoctoral fellow, I was fortunate enough to talk about many of the issues discussed in this volume with Michael Gazzaniga, Gideon Yaffe, Joshua Greene, Michael Moore, and a number of other leading neuroscientists, psychologists, legal theorists, and philosophers. It was an ideal setting for thinking through the relationship between recent advances in the sciences of the mind and our traditional views concerning the nature and limits of human agency and responsibility.

I also owe a special thanks to Walter Sinnott-Armstrong. Not only was he one of the co-directors of the Law and Neuroscience Project, but he has also been a very supportive mentor and friend. The time I spent working with him at Duke University's Kenan Institute for Ethics was as rich and rewarding as it was stimulating. Finally, I would like to thank Peter Ohlin and Oxford University Press for the opportunity to work on this volume.

CONTRIBUTORS

Eyal Aharoni (Ph.D.) is a postdoctoral researcher with appointments in the Psychology Department at the University of New Mexico and The Mind Research Network for Neurodiagnostic Discovery in Albuquerque, New Mexico. He has served as a fellow for the MacArthur Foundation's Law and Neuroscience Project. His research investigates motives for punishment, moral reasoning, psychopathy, and aggression, and their implications for criminal and legal decision making.

Michael Louis Corrado (J.D., Ph.D.) is the Arch T. Allen Distinguished Professor of Law and Professor of Philosophy at the University of North Carolina at Chapel Hill. He is the author of a number of books, including *The Analytic Tradition in Philosophy, Justification and Excuse in the Criminal Law, Comparative Constitutional Review*, and two forthcoming books, *Preventive Detention in American Law*, and *Comparative Criminal Law*. He is the former editor of *Law and Philosophy*, and the convener of the conference series, The Future of Adversarial Systems.

Farah Focquaert (Ph.D.) is a Research Fellow at the Bioethics Institute Ghent, Ghent University. She was a Visiting Research Fellow at the Center for Cognitive Neuroscience, Dartmouth College and a visiting scholar at the Department of Criminology and the Center for Neuroscience and Society at the University of Pennsylvania. She is a Research Fellow of the Research Foundation Flanders and a member of the Moral Brain research group. Her work focuses on ethical issues surrounding neuromodulation research and treatment for neuropsychiatric conditions. Her recent work seeks to integrate our advancing neurobiological knowledge on the criminal brain in the current ethical debates on moral responsibility, and the punishment and prevention of criminal behavior.

Alan J. Fridlund (Ph.D.) is an Associate Professor in the Department of Psychology at the University of California Santa Barbara. His research interests in social and clinical psychology lie in human ethology (especially nonverbal communication), neuroethology, psychopathology, and sexology. He won the Distinguished Early Career Contribution Award of the Society for Psychophysiological Research, and was a member of the Faculty in Experimental Psychopathology at the University of Pennsylvania. He is the author of *Human Facial Expression: An Evolutionary View* (1994), and the coauthor of the introductory text, *Psychology* (6th ed., 2003).

John Martin Fischer (Ph.D.) is Distinguished Professor and Chair of the Department of Philosophy at the University of California, Riverside, where he has held a University of California President's Chair (2006–10). He has written extensively on such topics as freedom of the will, moral responsibility, death, immortality, meaningfulness of life, and issues in normative ethics. He is the author of *The Metaphysics of Free Will* (1994); with Mark Ravizza, *Responsibility and Control: A Theory of Moral Responsibility* (1998); and with Kane, Pereboom, and Vargas, *Four Views on Free Will* (2007). He is the author of three recent collections published by Oxford University Press: *My Way: Essays on Free Will and Moral Responsibility* (2006); *Our Stories: Essays on Life, Death, and Free Will* (2009); and *Deep Control: Essays on Free Will and Value* (2011).

Andrea Glenn (Ph.D.) is a Postdoctoral Research Fellow in the Department of Child and Adolescent Psychiatry at the Institute of Mental Health in Singapore. She received her Ph.D. in Psychology from the University of Pennsylvania. Her research focuses on understanding the biological factors that contribute to antisocial behavior and psychopathic personality traits, and developing interventions that take biological factors into consideration. She is interested in the implications of this type of research for the legal system, including the use of neuroscience evidence in the determination of criminal responsibility and punishment.

Geoffrey Goodwin (Ph.D.) is an assistant professor in the Department of Psychology at the University of Pennsylvania. Dr. Goodwin's research is situated at the intersection of cognitive and social psychology. His work spans a variety of issues in moral psychology, including whether people think of their moral beliefs as objective facts, or alternatively as subjective preferences; how people place value on different human lives; how people perceive moral character in others, and how that affects their attitudes and judgments; what drives the motivation to punish acts of harm or wrongdoing (including those carried out by nonhumans, e.g., animals); and what predicts whether people are willing to take "neuroenhancement" technologies that aim to improve aspects of their psychological functioning. In addition, he has an ongoing program of research on mental models in deductive reasoning and concept learning.

Dena Gromet (Ph.D.) is a postdoctoral fellow with The Risk Management and Decision Processes Center, The Wharton School, University of Pennsylvania. Dr. Gromet's research is primarily concerned with investigating how people react to harmful events, wrongdoing, and decisions that involve risk. She has published articles and book chapters on situational and dispositional factors that influence people's responses to criminal harms and injustices, and their support for punitive and reparative methods of responding to these events.

Neil Levy (Ph.D.) is an Australian Research Council Future Fellow, based at the Florey Neuroscience Institutes, Melbourne, Australia. He is also Director of Research at the Oxford Centre for Neuroethics and the editor in chief of the journal *Neuroethics*. He has published widely on many topics in philosophy, including bioethics, applied philosophy, continental philosophy, free will, and empirical approaches to ethics. He has written several books, including *Moral Relativism* (2002), *Neuroethics: Philosophical Challenges for the 21*st *Century* (2007), and *Hard Luck: How Luck Undermines Freedom* (2011).

Alfred R. Mele (Ph.D.) is the William H. and Lucyle T. Werkmeister Professor of Philosophy at Florida State University and director of the Big Questions in Free Will Project (2010–13). He is the author of *Irrationality* (1987), *Springs of Action* (1992), *Autonomous Agents* (1995), *Self-Deception Unmasked* (2001), *Motivation and Agency* (2003), *Free Will and Luck* (2006), *Effective Intentions* (2009), and *Backsliding* (2012). He also is the editor or coeditor of *Mental Causation* (1993), *The Philosophy of Action* (1997), *The Oxford Handbook of Rationality* (2004), *Rationality and the Good* (2007), and *Free Will and Consciousness: How Might They Work?* (2010).

Stephen J. Morse (J.D., Ph.D.) is Ferdinand Wakeman Hubbell Professor of Law, Professor of Psychology and Law in Psychiatry, and Associate Director of the Center for Neuroscience and Society at the University of Pennsylvania. Trained in both law and psychology at Harvard, Dr. Morse is an expert in criminal and mental health law whose work emphasizes individual responsibility and the relation of the behavioral and neurosciences to responsibility and social control. Professor Morse was Co-Director of the MacArthur Foundation Law and Neuroscience Project and he co-directed the Project's Research Network on Criminal Responsibility and Prediction. He is currently a member of the MacArthur Foundation Research Network on Law and Neuroscience. He is coeditor with Adina Roskies of *A Primer on Law and Neuroscience* (forthcoming), and is currently working on a book, *Desert and Disease: Responsibility and Social Control*. Professor Morse is a founding director of the Neuroethics Society and a Trustee of the Bazelon Center for Mental Health Law. Before joining the Penn faculty, he was the Orrin B. Evans

Professor of Law, Psychiatry and the Behavioral Sciences at the University of Southern California.

Nancey Murphy (Ph.D.) is professor of philosophy at Fuller Seminary in Pasadena, California. She is the author of 10 books, most recently *Did My Neurons Make Me Do It? Philosophical and Neurobiological Perspectives on Moral Responsibility and Free Will* (with W. S. Brown). She has coedited 12 books, including *Evolution and Emergence: Systems, Organisms, Persons* (with W. R. Stoeger). Her research interests include contemporary Anglo-American philosophy; philosophy of science; and philosophy of mind, neuroscience, and Christian anthropology.

Thomas Nadelhoffer (Ph.D.) is an Assistant Professor in the Philosophy Department at the College of Charleston. He specializes in the philosophy of mind and action, moral psychology, and the philosophy of law—which were the focus of his research during his time as a postdoctoral fellow with the MacArthur Foundation Law and Neuroscience Project. He also recently coedited *Moral Psychology: Historical and Contemporary Readings* (2010) with Eddy Nahmias and Shaun Nichols.

Eddy Nahmias (Ph.D.) is an Associate Professor in the Philosophy Department and the Neuroscience Institute at Georgia State University. He specializes in philosophy of mind and cognitive science, free will, moral psychology, and experimental philosophy. He is currently working on a book, *Rediscovering Free Will: Autonomy and Responsibility in the Age of the Mind Sciences.*

Shaun Nichols (Ph.D.) is Professor of Philosophy at the University of Arizona, where he directs a research group on experimental philosophy. He has published widely at the intersection of philosophy and psychology, including a book on moral judgment, *Sentimental Rules* (2004), as well as several articles in experimental philosophy on free will, responsibility, and cultural diversity. He is also coeditor (with Joshua Knobe) of *Experimental Philosophy* (2008).

Michael S. Pardo (J.D.) is the Henry Upson Sims Professor of Law at the University of Alabama School of Law. He writes and teaches in the areas of evidence, criminal procedure, civil procedure, and jurisprudence. He is the author of several articles in these areas and a coauthor of *Evidence: Text, Problems, and Cases* (2011). He is currently writing a book on law and neuroscience with Dennis Patterson.

Dennis Patterson (J.D., Ph.D.) holds the Chair in Legal Theory and Legal Philosophy at the European University Institute. He is also Board of Governors Professor of Law and Philosophy at Rutgers University and Professor of International Trade and Legal Theory at Swansea University, Wales (UK). He is the author and editor of numerous books on legal theory, international trade, and commercial law, and is currently at work on a book on law and neuroscience with Michael Pardo.

Derk Pereboom (Ph.D.) is Professor of Philosophy at Cornell University. He received his Ph.D. from the University of California Los Angeles in 1985, and taught at the University of Vermont before moving to Cornell. He is the author of *Living Without Free Will* (2001) and *Consciousness and the Prospects of Physicalism* (2011), and a coauthor of *Four Views on Free Will* (with Robert Kane, John Martin Fischer, and Manuel Vargas, 2007). He has published articles on free will, philosophy of mind, philosophy of religion, and history of modern philosophy.

Adrian Raine (Ph.D.) is the Richard Perry University Professor in the Departments of Criminology, Psychiatry, and Psychology at the University of Pennsylvania. His research interests include the neurobiology of violence, psychopathic and antisocial behavior, schizotypal personality, brain imaging, psychophysiology, neurochemistry, neuropsychology, and behavioral and molecular genetics. He has published five books and more than 200 journal articles and book chapters.

Chandra Sekhar Sripada (M.D., Ph.D.) is Assistant Professor of Philosophy and Psychiatry at the University of Michigan, Ann Arbor. His research lies at the intersection of philosophy and the behavioral and brain sciences. Specific topics of interest include decision making in psychiatric disorders (especially ADHD and substance use disorders), mechanisms of self-control and willpower, free will and moral responsibility, and intentional action. His recent papers have appeared in journals in philosophy (*Philosophy and Phenomenological Research, Philosophical Studies*) and the sciences (*Proceedings of the National Academy of Sciences, Biological Psychiatry*).

Walter Sinnott-Armstrong (Ph.D.) is Chauncey Stillman Professor of Practical Ethics in the Philosophy Department and the Kenan Institute for Ethics at Duke University. He has served as vice-chair of the Board of Officers of the American Philosophical Association and co-director of the MacArthur Project on Law and Neuroscience. He publishes widely in normative moral theory, meta-ethics, applied ethics, moral psychology and neuroscience, philosophy of law, epistemology, informal logic, and philosophy of religion.

INTRODUCTION[1]

THOMAS A. NADELHOFFER

When it comes to the relationship between free will, responsibility, and punishment, and recent advances in neuroscience, genetics, and cognate fields, some people believe that there is already a revolution underfoot. Others are perhaps understandably more conservative in their assessment. According to the former view, as scientists continue to demystify the mind by identifying the mechanisms that undergird both normal and abnormal human behavior, the traditional picture of free will and moral agency could be torn asunder. According to the latter view, although recent and future advances in the biosciences will surely shed new and interesting light on how the human mind works, our traditional views of agency and responsibility both will and should remain largely intact. Needless to say, it is a very exciting time for researchers who are interested in issues at the crossroads of science, philosophy, and the law. Only time will tell whether those who counsel revolution, or those who defend the traditional picture of agency and responsibility, are largely correct.

The goal of the present volume is to provide philosophers, neuroscientists, psychologists, and legal theorists with an opportunity to examine the cluster of related issues that will need to be addressed as we struggle to come to grips with the picture of human agency that is being pieced together by researchers in the biosciences. Each contributor was asked to shed light on the important issues they take to be essential when it comes to the future of punishment and retribution. Given the complexity and breadth of both the empirical and conceptual issues that arise in this context, contributors understandably cover a lot of ground. In addition to exploring the sorts of issues that have traditionally been discussed when it comes to free will and punishment, this volume also contains several exciting new articles on the relevance (or lack thereof) of advances in the biosciences to our conceptions of agency and responsibility.

1. I would like to thank the contributors for providing me with abstracts of their chapters, which served as the templates for the summaries of their work contained in the following pages.

Although some contributors defend the philosophical status quo, others advocate no less than a total revaluation of our fundamental beliefs about moral and legal responsibility. As such, this volume not only exposes the reader to some cutting-edge research on the thorny relationship between traditional theories of agency and responsibility and recent and future scientific advances, but it also provides the reader with an introduction to some of the long-standing debates in action theory and the philosophy of law concerning the justification of punishment more generally.

Historically, theories of punishment have been divided into two general groups—namely, theories that try to justify punishment in terms of its positive consequences and theories that try to justify punishment in terms of justice, moral desert, and retribution. According to consequentialist theories, if punishment is going to be justified, it must be shown that the utility that results from punishing offenders outweighs the pain that we must inevitably inflict in exacting punishment. In their attempts to justify both the institution and the implementation of punishment, consequentialists can appeal to a wide range of potentially positive benefits produced by punishing wrongdoers, including:

1. *General deterrence*—punishing in order to deter other would-be offenders from committing similar offenses
2. *Incapacitation*—punishing in order to prevent the offender from committing similar crimes while he is being detained or treated
3. *Rehabilitation and moral education*—punishing in order to rehabilitate or reeducate the offender
4. *Communication*—punishing in order to communicate or express disapproval of an action
5. *Norm reinforcement*—punishing in order to highlight and reassert the importance of social values and norms.

In each of these cases, the prima facie moral badness of punishment is offset by the benefits that it produces. However, in the event that punishment fails to produce these positive consequences either in general or in a particular case, it loses its moral legitimacy. Either way, the moral propriety of punishment is entirely a function of the consequences of punishment.

Retributivist theories of punishment reject this consequentialist approach. According to retributivism, punishment is not justified in terms of some future benefit.[2] Rather, retributivists believe that "punishment institutions in general are justified by the giving of just deserts" and that "the punishment of each

2. For a thorough taxonomy of the varieties of retributivism, see Cottingham (1979).

offender is justified by the fact that he or she deserves it" (Moore 1997, 155). On this noninstrumentalist view, if an agent is morally responsible for breaking a moral norm, then that person deserves to be punished—that is, harmed—even if the harm produces no (other) benefits. Consider a case in which an agent is morally responsible for stealing (which we can take as violating a moral norm). Now imagine that there are two treatments that can be administered to the wrongdoer, and the treatments generate exactly the same consequential benefits (e.g., deterrence, incapacitation, rehabilitation). One of the treatments involves harming the wrongdoer, and the other doesn't. Provided that the harm is "proportional" to the wrong, the proponent of retributivism must opt for the former, whereas the proponent of consequentialism must opt for the latter. Indeed, according to retributivists, it is morally appropriate to inflict harm on offenders even if this yields no positive consequences at all. Consider, for instance, the following famous thought experiment from the prominent retributivist Immanuel Kant:

> Even if a civil society were to dissolve itself by common agreement of all its members (for example, if the people inhabiting an island decided to separate and disperse themselves around the world), the last murderer remaining in prison must first be executed, so that everyone will duly receive what his actions are worth and so that the blood guilt thereof will not be fixed on the people because they failed to insist on carrying out the punishment; for if they fail to do so, they may be regarded as accomplices in this public violation of legal justice. (1785, 102)

According to pure retributivists such as Kant, giving offenders the appropriate dose of harm is both necessary and sufficient for justified punishment.[3] Of course, if punishing the morally deserving happens to yield positive side effects such as deterring crime or rehabilitating the offender, these consequences may be welcomed by the retributivist as a "happy surplus" (Moore 1997, 89), but they do not constitute any part of the justifying aim of punishment for the pure retributivist.

Although the debate between consequentialists and retributivists has received the lion's share of attention in the philosophy of punishment literature, most of the recent research exploring the relationships among free will, responsibility,

3. Pure retributivism is to be distinguished from mixed theories of punishment, which include both consequentialist and retributive elements. For instance, according to the mixed retributivism one finds in Rawls (1956) and Hart (1968), while the *institution* of punishment is to be justified in consequentialist terms, the actual *implementation* of punishment in particular cases is to be justified in retributive terms. For present purposes, however, we are going to limit our attention to pure theories of both consequentialism and retributivism.

and advances in the biosciences has focused on the impact that these advances have on the traditional notions of moral desert that undergird retributive theories. After all, on the surface, there is no obvious incompatibility between punishment per se and discoveries in neuroscience, genetics, social psychology, and cognate fields. Indeed, if anything, as we learn more about the nature and limits of human agency, we will presumably be in a better position to ensure that punishment is implemented in ways that yield positive consequences for both offenders and society more generally. However, if advances in the biosciences undermine our traditional pictures of free will and responsibility as some suggest, then these advances would thereby undermine the moral desert required by retributive theories of punishment.

For this reason, the future of retributivism in the wake of the scientific progress being made in understanding the biopsychosocial determinants of crime is one of the central focuses of the present volume. But before we can assess the compatibility of retributivism with these gathering empirical challenges, we must first focus our attention on the conceptual and theoretical foundations of retributivism. After all, if retributivism isn't independently a workable theory of punishment, then we need not worry ourselves with whether retributivism is compatible with recent advances in the biosciences. As such, the first two chapters of the volume explore the nature and limits of retributive theories of punishment more generally rather than exploring the aforementioned compatibility question.

For instance, in the first chapter, John Martin Fischer's goal is to develop a distinctive way of understanding the structure of retributivist theories of punishment. In particular, he develops an approach to retributivism that he believes enables retributivists to respond to an important objection to their view according to which retributivism implies that whenever someone deserves to suffer, the state should seek to bring it about that the individual does indeed suffer (to the appropriate degree). In specifying the suggested structure of retributivism, Fischer follows H.L.A. Hart in distinguishing different questions about punishment—for example, What justifies the general practice of punishment? Which offenders are apt targets of punishment? How severely may we punish?—questions that Fischer believes call for a more nuanced, layered approach. By linking a broadly Strawsonian account of moral responsibility with a desert-based account of justified punishment, Fischer tries to shed light on these and related questions.

Next, Shaun Nichols argues that recent empirical work confirms what many have long believed—namely, that ordinary people endorse and act on the basis of norms of retributive justice. However, as Nichols correctly points out, norms of retributive justice are notoriously difficult to justify. This leads many philosophers to reject the legitimacy of those norms. Other philosophers attempt to justify retributivism by adverting to some objective moral footing (e.g., Kant, Moore). Nichols assumes for the sake of argument that morality is not objective, and he proceeds to argue that retributive norms nevertheless form part of a set of norms that do not need justification. Of course, as Nichols acknowledges, this does not mean that retributivism should stand, all things considered. To determine whether we should ultimately preserve our retributive norms will depend on a number of other factors, including both the expected utilities and our other core values—which are issues that Nichols explores along the way.

However, not all of the contributors to the volume are as comfortable with retributivism as Fischer and Nichols. For these theorists, rather than retributively focusing on giving offenders their just deserts, we should focus instead on detecting and preventing crime and rehabilitating offenders. For instance, in the third chapter, Derk Pereboom argues that his brand of free will skepticism—that is, hard incompatibilism—rules out retributive justifications of punishment. Moreover, he claims that alternative justifications, such as certain moral education and deterrence theories, are compatible with hard incompatibilism but fall to independent moral objections. Pereboom nevertheless thinks that free will skepticism is compatible with other ways of responding to criminal behavior, specifically preventative detention, rehabilitation, and the alteration of relevant social conditions, and he argues that these methods are morally justifiable and sufficient for good social policy.

In the next chapter, Michael Corrado takes Pereboom's hard incompatibilism as a starting point. According to Corrado, one of the most difficult challenges for Pereboom and other skeptics is adequately addressing the common objections to the therapeutic/incapacitative approach to crime control that is often associated with free will skepticism. Corrado suggests that responding to this challenge requires the hard incompatibilist to (1) find a way to distinguish between those who have traditionally been found responsible for their crimes and those who have been found not to be responsible, and (2) justify the infliction of intentionally harsh treatment on at least some of those who fall into the first category. The overall goal of Corrado's chapter is to develop a theory that satisfies both of these requirements.

In short, both Pereboom and Corrado push a revolutionary agenda whereby our traditional theories of agency and responsibility, as well as our traditional approaches to crime and punishment, ought to be replaced by new approaches that allegedly better comport with the gathering scientific data concerning the nature and limits of human cognition and behavior. However, as we saw earlier, not all researchers embrace the skepticism that drives the views that council revolution. Indeed, the authors of the next three chapters in the volume criticize these radical views on the grounds that they are purportedly based on mistaken conceptions of the criminal law or conceptual confusions concerning the relationships between agency, responsibility, and recent scientific advances. On this view, recent advances in the biosciences are fully compatible with the traditional picture of agency and responsibility.

Stephen J. Morse, for instance, argues that the criminal law is a thoroughly folk psychological enterprise that is completely consistent with the truth of determinism or universal causation. According to Morse, although criminal law doctrine and practice is fully consistent with metaphysical libertarianism—a view that he acknowledges may be common among lay persons and legal decision makers alike—this position is extremely implausible in the modern, scientific age. As such, Morse claims that if determinism or something quite like it is true, as he assumes it is, then only compatibilism can provide a secure basis for criminal responsibility. So, the goal of Morse's chapter is to demonstrate not only that compatibilism provides an accurate positive account of criminal law but also that compatibilist criminal law is normatively desirable.

Next, Michael Pardo and Dennis Patterson adopt a similar stance towards the neuroskepticism that permeates much of the recent work on the relationship between neuroscience and criminal responsibility. For instance, according to the provocative work by Joshua Greene and Jonathan Cohen, neuroscience will purportedly reveal that criminal defendants are not morally responsible for their actions and that this revelation will thereby undermine retributivist justifications for criminal punishment and challenge our traditional picture of agency and responsibility more generally. In their chapter, Pardo and Patterson discuss several serious problems with this kind of neuroskepticism. On their view, neuroscientific discoveries will not lead to the sorts of radical changes predicted by Greene and Cohen. However, even if neuroskepticism about free will and responsibility took hold, Pardo and Patterson claim that it would not be the product of neuroscientific insight but rather the result of unwarranted and problematic inferences that we purportedly ought to resist.

Finally, Nancey Murphy similarly tries to allay the worry that contemporary findings in the cognitive neurosciences call moral and legal responsibility into question. Using Alasdair MacIntyre's account of morally responsible action as a backdrop, Murphy tries to show that rather than *explaining away* free will and moral responsibility, recent advances in the cognitive neurosciences actually help *explain*, and thereby justify, belief in responsibility. According to Murphy, an agent is capable of moral responsibility if she has the capacity to evaluate that which moves one to act in light of some concept of the good. The central goal of Murphy's chapter is to provide a cognitive-science analysis of the intellectual and affective capacities that purportedly *enable* morally responsible action. Murphy also briefly discusses some of the neural systems and structures that are taken to subserve these responsibility-enabling capacities. On the basis of this analysis, Murphy goes on to address some of the arguments by neuroscientists such as Benjamin Libet and John-Dylan Haynes that are taken to call free will into question. Finally, Murphy explores some of the implications of her view when it comes to the role and justification of punishment. On her view, a restorative rather than retributive justice system has great potential for enhancing moral (and therefore legal) responsibility.

Whereas Pereboom and Corrado push a revolutionary agenda, Morse, Pardo, Patterson, and Murphy all try to stave off the skeptical worries that motivated the attempt to reevaluate our traditional picture of agency, responsibility, and punishment. The debate between these two camps is focused primarily on the normative question concerning whether we ought to change our beliefs about agency and responsibility and revise our punitive practices. However, as I mentioned at the outset, there is a related descriptive issue that merits close consideration as well—namely, what effect advances in the biosciences are likely going to have on people's views concerning agency and responsibility. Here, the question is not whether people's views *ought* to change, but rather whether they are likely to *actually* change.

Addressing this descriptive question calls for controlled and systematic empirical investigation of folk intuitions concerning both the nature of free will and responsibility and the perceived relationship between these notions and recent scientific advances. In order to address the descriptive issue at hand, we need data concerning both how people ordinarily conceptualize free will, responsibility, and punishment and how their views are likely to be shaped and influenced by scientific advances. The next three chapters in the volume each sheds light on these two distinct but related issues in different ways.

For instance, Alfred Mele explores the scientific arguments for the nonexistence of free will. As Mele correctly points out, these skeptical arguments often appeal to neuroscientific data to support empirical propositions that are then conjoined with a proposition about the meaning of "free will" to yield the conclusion that free will is an illusion. In his recent book, *Effective Intentions*, Mele argued that various empirical propositions put forward for this purpose are not warranted by the evidence offered to support them. It might be replied that the only empirical proposition needed in this connection is that substance dualism is false, because free will depends on the existence of immaterial minds or souls. This theoretical proposition about free will seems to have more adherents among present-day neuroscientists and biologists than among present-day philosophers. But Mele points out that the fact that one is a neuroscientist or biologist (or both) does not give one any special insight into what the expression "free will" means. Some may say that the same is true when one is a philosopher—or, more specifically, a philosopher who has written a lot about free will. So, Mele tries to shed light on this issue by building on recent work in experimental philosophy that explores folk intuitions about free will and moral responsibility. More specifically, he looks for evidence concerning whether mainstream use of "free will" makes substance dualism a necessary condition for having it. In light of the preliminary findings from some new studies, Mele concludes that scientists who have assumed that people are folk dualists about free will are mistaken. As such, Mele concludes that the scientific arguments that free will is an illusion ultimately fail.

In the next chapter, Thomas Nadelhoffer, Dena Gromet, Geoffrey Goodwin, Eddy Nahmias, Chandra Sripada, and Walter Sinnott-Armstrong explore the potential influence that advances in neuroscience may have on legal decision makers, and they present the findings from some recent studies that probe folk intuitions concerning the relationships among neuroscience, agency, responsibility, and mental illness. In examining this descriptive question, Nadelhoffer and colleagues first familiarize the reader with some of the early research in experimental philosophy on people's intuitions about agency and responsibility. They proceed to focus on a more specific issue—namely, whether people respond to explanations of human behavior framed in neuroscientific terms differently than they respond to explanations framed in more traditional folk psychological terms. Having set the stage, Nadelhoffer and colleagues next discuss some new findings which suggest that explanations of criminal behavior that are couched in neural terms appear to make people less punitive than explanations couched in mental terms, especially in the context of mental illness. Finally, the authors offer what they take to be the best explanation of these differences in people's intuitions—namely, when people are presented with neural explanations of human behavior, they tend to think that the agent's "deep self" (the values and beliefs they identify with) is somehow left out of the causal loop or bypassed, which in turn mitigates the agent's responsibility. In short, Nadelhoffer and colleagues suggest that it is bypassing of the deep self, and not determinism per se, that seems to be motivating people's concerns when it comes to the relationships between neuroscience, agency, and responsibility.

Next, Eyal Aharoni and Alan Fridlund explore folk intuitions about punishment more generally. The motivating question they address is: Why do individuals so willingly risk the enforcement of punishment of moral offenders? A satisfying explanation for moralistic punishment should consider possible incentives that could have reliably motivated individuals to incur the risks of punishment over the course of our evolution. Conceivably, moralistic punishment evolved to protect our social investments, namely individuals whose welfare was appraised to be beneficial to us in the future. In their chapter, Aharoni and Fridlund review empirical support for this reciprocity-based social capital theory, examining whether (1) third parties punish more on behalf of victims displaying signs of high value, and (2) individuals who systematically undervalue others' welfare are actually less punitive. Finally, Aharoni and Fridlund consider some implications of this punitive response for criminal punishment policy.

When it comes to our punitive policies, one issue that understandably garners a lot of attention is how we ought to respond to offenders who arguably have impaired cognition and behavior, such as drug addicts and psychopaths. Here, the issue isn't whether punishment and retribution are ever justified. Rather, the issue is whether it makes sense to punish certain groups of individuals who manifest abnormal psychologies. In his contribution, Neil Levy focuses on the punishment of addicts. Levy's starting point is the recent work by Gene Heyman, which suggests that addiction is a disorder of choice. According to Heyman, the gathering data on addiction suggests that addicts respond to incentives to use drugs, in the same way as nonaddicts. Levy believes that this claim generates a puzzle: Why are addicts often unresponsive to costs—legal penalties, impairment of relationships, loss of job or health, and so on—that seem sufficient motivation to abstain? In trying to resolve this puzzle, Levy argues that although addicts are responsive to incentives, this responsiveness is patchy. On his view, addicts are relatively insensitive to delayed and uncertain punishments. Instead, they are more responsive to rewards than punishments. Addicts can be motivated to change their behavior by incentives, positive and negative. As such, Levy suggests that the most effective response to addiction may involve the imposition of swift and certain, but relatively light, penalties, coupled with rewards for abstention. According to Levy, there is a philosophical upshot to the recent empirical work on addiction—namely, this research indicates that the common philosophical view that capacities are perfectly general-purpose must be rethought. In short, Levy believes that negative and positive rewards are not treated alike by the brain, and are differentially motivating for the addict—which are factors that we must take into consideration when trying to figure out whether it makes sense to punish addicts.

Finally, Farah Focquaert, Andrea Glenn, and Adrian Raine provide a detailed overview of the recent neurobiological findings on psychopathy and discuss how these might bear on moral responsibility. For example, psychopaths may suffer from brain impairments in regions that underlie emotional processing—regions that are necessary for moral development in normal individuals. Next, Focquaert and colleagues argue that a similar neurobiological approach might apply to other cases, such as individuals with antisocial personality disorder and those with substance abuse. On their view, even if one is not willing to give up on the notion of truly voluntary behavior, there remains a wealth of scientific data that urges us to reconsider our current approach to crime and punishment. In the last section of their chapter, the authors argue for a different approach that involves (a) the abandonment of massive incarceration as a solution to crime; (b) the guaranteed personal, physical, and mental well-being of incarcerated individuals; and (c) the integration of choice in terms of an offender's punishment and rehabilitation trajectory. According to Focquaert and colleagues their proposed changes to the criminal justice system not only reflect a more long-term approach to criminal behavior and recidivism but also have the potential to positively change our society and improve the safety of all its members.

Both the chapter by Levy and the chapter by Focquaert and colleagues nicely illustrate the fact that making progress on a policy issue such as whether to punish addicts or psychopaths requires not only good empirical research but also careful philosophical theorizing. Just as we have to carefully consider both the gathering data concerning folk intuitions about free will, agency, and responsibility and the gathering data about abnormal behaviors and disorders such as psychopathy and addiction when we are thinking about the limits of punishment, we have to pay close attention to the theoretical foundations of our views as well. It is for this reason that the contributors to this volume cover so much ground. Indeed, I think the work contained in this volume nicely illustrates the importance of interdisciplinary research when it comes to the future of punishment and retribution. Not only do we need better empirical evidence concerning the nature and limits of human agency as well as evidence concerning how people understand human agency but we also need more sustained philosophical reflection concerning the complex relationship between the gathering data and our traditional views on these fronts.

I hope that this volume will inspire other researchers to reach across disciplinary boundaries in their attempts to shed light on how we ought to think about punishment in the wake of the astonishing advances being made by researchers in the biosciences. It will be exciting to see how the thorny debates discussed in this volume play themselves out in the years to come.

PART ONE

Defending Retributivism

1

Desert and the Justification of Punishment

JOHN MARTIN FISCHER

INTRODUCTION

I explore in this chapter certain aspects of the relationship between desert and the justification of punishment. Various philosophers have thought that there are decisive counterexamples to approaches to the justification of punishment that rely crucially on desert. I argue that, whereas these counterexamples may well show that certain simple desert-based approaches to the justification of punishment are inadequate, they do not show the inadequacy of more nuanced and sophisticated desert-based theories. A goal of the paper is to lay out—and motivate—what I take to be the most promising desert-based approach to the justification of punishment. Of course, the literature on retributivist approaches to punishment and, specifically, on desert-based retributivism is voluminous, and I do not seek to give anything close to a comprehensive treatment of the literature (or associated issues) here. Rather, I shall home in on certain specific critiques of desert-based retributivism, and I shall use David Boonin's recent book, *The Problem of Punishment*, as a focal point for my discussion.[1] Although I find it useful to use Boonin's discussion as a framework, my real goal is to articulate a plausible desert-based approach to the justification of punishment that can withstand various counterexamples in the literature and also be independently motivated (i.e., motivated by considerations apart from the—admittedly welcome—efficacy in avoiding the counterexamples to other desert-based approaches).

1. David Boonin, *The Problem of Punishment* (New York: Cambridge University Press, 2008).

David Boonin's *The Problem of Punishment* is a comprehensive and highly impressive treatment of various proposed justifications of punishment. In the end, Boonin concludes that none of these proposals works, and thus that punishment—as opposed to, say, compulsory victim restitution—is not justified. The book is both penetrating and compendious. It is helpful both in posing the challenge (the "problem of punishment") in a clear and compelling way and in pointing out various ways in which the leading strategies for answering the challenge fall short.

In Boonin's view, punishment should be defined as "authorized intentional reprobative retributive harm" (p. 26). When we punish, we do not simply harm, but we also *intend* that the target individual be harmed. The retributive requirement is as follows: "to be a legal punishment, an act must involve intentionally harming someone because he previously did a legally prohibited act, which means that he is responsible for having done the act and that he had no valid legal excuse for doing so" (p. 17). The reprobative requirement is the essential element of condemnation (p. 22).

One might say that the problem of punishment is, roughly speaking, the problem of providing an adequate justification of punishment, so conceived (i.e., conceived as authorized intentional reprobative retributive harm). Boonin explains the problem of punishment nicely, as follows:

> Since it is considerably more difficult to justify intentionally harming someone than it is to justify merely foreseeably harming her, the problem of punishment is even greater than it might at first seem: we must explain not only why the line between offenders and nonoffenders is morally relevant at all but, in particular, how it can be important enough to justify not merely harming those on one side of the line but intentionally harming them. Punishment, in short, involves the states treating some of its citizens in ways that it would clearly be wrong to treat others. The problem is to explain how this can be morally permissible.[2]

In Boonin's view, the relevant justification must show that punishment, *rather than compulsory victim restitution*, is justified (morally permissible). An important feature of Boonin's book is to highlight compulsory victim restitution as an alternative to punishment and thus to point out that a justification of punishment must show how it is to be preferred (morally) to compulsory victim restitution. A focus on compulsory victim restitution might seem at once more humane to the criminal (insofar as it does not necessarily involve intentional harm or reprobation) and to the victim (insofar as it throws into relief the need to make the victim whole, insofar as possible).

2. Boonin, *The Problem of Punishment*, p. 28.

RETRIBUTIVISM

Despite the appeal of compulsory victim restitution, many philosophers are disposed to think that punishment, and not merely compulsory victim restitution, is fully justified. Insofar as we think that offenders are morally responsible for what they do, it is plausible that they are appropriate targets for what Boonin calls "reprobative" attitudes, such as indignation and resentment. Punishment can be thought of as at least in part a symbolic expression of such essentially reprobative attitudes.[3] A world without such attitudes might at first seem appealing, but upon more careful consideration would appear to lack important features of our interpersonal human relationships—features that help to give these relationships the rich texture they have, and without which life might be significantly different and, arguably, less attractive.[4]

There are, of course, various ways of seeking to justify punishment. Perhaps the most basic way to divide these approaches is by distinguishing (very roughly speaking) "forward-looking" and "backward-looking" strategies. The forward-looking approaches are typically called "consequentialist," and the backward-looking approaches, "deontological" or, more specifically within the context of the discussion of the justification of punishment, "retributivist." There are various different versions of both consequentialist and retributivist accounts of the justification of punishment. Also, although it will work for my purposes here, I should note that the distinction between forward-looking and backward-looking approaches is far too crude to capture adequately all of the various approaches to offering a justification of punishment. For example, according to various views—such as restorative or reconciliatory approaches—punishment is justified by backward-looking considerations but has specific forward-looking aims.[5]

3. Joel Feinberg, "The Expressive Function of Punishment," in J. Feinberg, ed. *Doing and Deserving* (Princeton, NJ: Princeton University Press, 1970), pp. 95–118.

4. Peter Strawson, "Freedom and Resentment," *Proceedings of the British Academy* 48 (1962), pp. 1–25. For discussion of Strawson's important and influential views, see Michael McKenna and Paul Russell, eds., *Perspectives on P. F. Strawson's "Freedom and Resentment"* (Aldershot, UK: Ashgate Press, 2008).

5. We might also have a theory of punishment that is in some ways parallel to certain approaches to the tort law, according to which we are concerned with assigning the responsibility for "paying" justly, and therefore we require the guilty/responsible to pay, rather than the innocent. Here the purpose is to spread the "damage" more justly, not to maximize well-being. So, we look backward to decide who is guilty/deserving, but our goal is forward looking. A contractualist approach to punishment is likely to take this form. See also D. M. Farrell, "Deterrence and the Just Distribution of Harm," *Social Philosophy and Policy* 12 (1995), pp. 220–240. I am indebted to Justin Coates and Saul Smilansky here.

Boonin describes the general form of retributism as follows:

> The retributivist [approach] … is essentially backward-looking. It claims that committing an offense in the past is sufficient to justify punishment now, whether or not this will produce any beneficial consequences in the future.[6]

Perhaps the most salient and straightforward versions of retributivism make essential reference to desert; put somewhat simply, the idea here is that punishing individuals who have violated a law is permissible because such individuals *deserve* to be punished.[7] Whereas some philosophers would make the invocation of desert a defining feature of retributivism, I follow Boonin in taking it that retributivism is essentially a backward-looking approach to the justification of punishment, where retributivism can include backward-looking approaches that are not best characterized in terms of desert.[8] Some non–desert-based forms of retributivism might invoke considerations involving the forfeiture of rights, fairness, trust, and debt.[9]

BOONIN'S CRITIQUE OF DESERT-BASED RETRIBUTIVISM

I wish to focus my attention in this chapter on desert-based forms of retributivism, and I shall use David Boonin's discussion as a route into the issues. Boonin distinguishes two general strategies for interpreting the structure of desert-based approaches to addressing the problem of punishment. The first strategy is (employing Boonin's term) the Argument from Cases. Here, the proponent of a desert-based justification of punishment begins by invoking various cases in which he alleges that most people will have the intuition that the individuals *deserve* punishment. The proponent of the Argument from Cases

6. Boonin, *The Problem of Punishment*, p. 85.

7. Two influential defenders of desert-based retributivism are Michael S. Moore and Stephan Kershnar: Michael S. Moore, "The Moral Worth of Retribution," in Michael Murphy, ed., *Punishment and Retaliation*, Third Edition (Belmont, CA: Wadsworth, 1987), pp. 94–130, and "Justifying Retributivism," *Israel Law Review* 27 (1993), pp. 15–49; Stephan Kershnar, "A Defense of Retributivism," *International Journal of Applied Philosophy* 14 (2000), pp. 97–117; and *Desert, Retribution, and Torture* (Lanham, MD: University Press of America, 2001).

8. John Cottingham identifies nine theories of punishment that have been called "retributivist" in: "Varieties of Retribution," *Philosophical Quarterly* 29 (1979), pp. 238–246. Nigel Walker identifies even more such approaches in: *Why Punish? Theories of Punishment Reassessed.* (Oxford, UK: Oxford University Press, 1993).

9. Boonin considers such versions of retributivism in *The Problem of Punishment*, pp. 103–154.

extrapolates to a general answer to the problem of punishment—an answer he believes to comport best with our considered judgments about the cases. The second approach starts with a more general moral principle, such as a principle of rights or fairness, and derives from it a more specific principle of retributive justice.

The best way to interpret the Argument from Cases is to take it to say that, upon reflection (involving consideration of a range of cases), we would judge that punishment is justified because criminals *deserve* to be punished. Slightly more carefully, the claim is that the state ought, all things considered, to punish criminals at least in part because they *deserve* to be punished. Here, the idea is that considerations of desert play a significant role in the total set of considerations on the basis of which it is true that the state ought, all things considered, to punish criminals.

Boonin objects to this desert-based approach to the justification of punishment by contending first that it would not allow for punishing certain morally innocent persons, whereas an adequate theory of punishment should imply that such individuals ought to be punished. Boonin further objects that the desert-based approach will require the punishment of certain morally but not legally guilty individuals, whereas an adequate theory of punishment would not permit punishment of such persons.

Consider, first, Boonin's contention that the desert-based approach would not allow the punishment of certain morally innocent persons, contrary to what we would think proper in the cases in question. He claims that "there are people who break a just and reasonable law but who do not morally deserve to suffer. Such cases give rise to the 'not punishing the guilty objection.'"[10] Boonin says:

> One kind of case that gives rise to this problem involves people who do acts that are illegal but not immoral. This may be because the act that the law forbids is never in itself an immoral act, or it may be because although the act is generally immoral, it is not so in a particular case. A person who uses her car to drive a friend to the emergency room even though her car has not passed a required emissions test, for example, is clearly violating the law but is just as clearly behaving morally. A person who steals a car to drive a friend to the emergency room clearly breaks the law, but at least in the case in which the friend will otherwise die and the owner of the car will not be significantly harmed by the theft (the owner, for example, has two other cars sitting in his driveway), it again seems clear that the act is not morally wrong.[11]

10. Boonin, *The Problem of Punishment*, p. 94.

11. Boonin, *The Problem of Punishment*, p. 94.

Boonin goes on to state:

> Unavoidably, therefore, there will be cases in which an act is not immoral even though it violates a just and reasonable law. But if an act is not immoral, then the person who performs it does not deserve to suffer for it. And if the person does not deserve to suffer for it, then the desert-based retributivist position cannot justify the claim that the state has the moral right to punish him for doing it. Such cases, therefore, establish that desert-based retributivism cannot draw the line between those who may be punished and those who may not in the place that the defender of punishment must draw it.[12]

Boonin also contends that there can be cases in which an illegal act is objectively immoral, but in which the agent does not deserve to suffer because he or she acted from unobjectionable (even admirable) motives. Boonin says:

> If the person does the act from an unobjectionable or even admirable motive, then I, at least, see no force at all to the claim that the world would be a better place in a morally relevant sense if he suffers for what he did. And so, once again the move from breaking a just and reasonable law to deserving to suffer proves unwarranted.[13]

Here Boonin gives a series of examples with characters whose names—for some mysterious reason—are those of TV's Three Stooges. (Even the infamous Fourth Stooge, Shemp, makes an appearance.) But perhaps it will suffice simply to have before us the initial, "simple" case:

> Larry has recently moved into a new neighborhood where all the houses look alike. The only way he recognizes his own house is by the large birdbath on the front lawn. One day while he is at work, his wife meets their next-door neighbor and gives her the birdbath as a token of friendship. When Larry gets home late at night, he reasonably believes that the house with the birdbath in front is his, and as he walks up the sidewalk, he sees a young woman trying to get into the house. When he demands to know what she is doing, she responds that she does not speak English. Having heard that several houses in the area had recently been broken into by a woman claiming to speak no English, Larry prevents her from going into the house. As it turns out, however, the woman is not a burglar and

12. Boonin, *The Problem of Punishment*, p. 94.

13. Boonin, *The Problem of Punishment*, p. 98.

> is simply trying to get into her own home. Objectively, therefore, Larry's act is clearly wrong. But it seems extremely unlikely that anyone would respond to the situation by saying that Larry deserves to suffer for having done this objectively wrong act. And the reason for this is simple: although objectively the woman had every right to go into the house she was trying to enter, Larry sincerely and non-negligently believed that she did not. Since he acted in good faith on the mistaken belief that she had no right to enter the house, his act does not cast him in a bad light, so we do not think that he deserves to suffer for what he did.[14]

Boonin's view is that this and the other cases in the series are cases "in which the practice of punishment dictates that the state should have the right to punish and the desert-based retributivist solution will be unable to account for this."[15]

Boonin has thus far argued that there are cases in which our practice of punishment should involve punishing individuals who are not deemed suitable for punishment by the desert-based approach. He also argues that, in some cases, certain individuals who do not break any relevant law nevertheless morally deserve to suffer; but since they have broken no (relevant) law, it would be impermissible to punish them, despite the fact that they morally deserve to suffer. As Boonin puts it, "For just as there are people who break the law and do not deserve to suffer, there are surely people who do not break the law but do deserve to suffer."[16]

Here is an example of the sort of case Boonin has in mind:

> Imagine, for example, that the laws regarding spousal abuse are drawn up according to your specifications. They draw the line between behavior that is legally forbidden and behavior that is legally permitted precisely where you think it should justly and reasonably be drawn. Now consider a man who familiarizes himself with the law and does everything he can to make his wife miserable without crossing that line. If he is legally allowed to scream at her, he screams at her. If he is allowed to cheat on her, he cheats on her. In any way that he is allowed to embarrass, belittle, degrade, and insult her, he does, and with relish. He refrains from beating or raping her, but only because he is afraid of the legal consequences. Or consider the racist who does everything she is legally permitted to do to insult black people. If she is legally allowed to play racist songs, she does. If she is allowed to throw a party celebrating the fact that hundreds of black people died in an

14. Boonin, *The Problem of Punishment*, pp. 96–97.

15. Boonin, *The Problem of Punishment*, p. 97.

16. Boonin, *The Problem of Punishment*, p. 99.

> earthquake, she does. She refrains from burning crosses on people's laws if she must, and she avoids lynching black people only because she is afraid of being caught.[17]

Boonin contends that these people are legally innocent and thus properly immune from punishment, even though they morally deserve to suffer for their behavior. Thus, again, the theory that seeks to explain the justification of punishment in terms of desert seems to be in trouble.

Boonin's cases here are similar to cases put forward to support the same contention by David Dolinko.[18] Here's one of Dolinko's cases:

> Consider, for example, Lear, a rich man with two sons, Jeremy and Howard. Jeremy truly loves Lear and has always treated him with affection and respect, even caring for him (at great personal sacrifice) during Lear's final illness. Howard, on the other hand, is a reprobate who has spent his time drinking, gambling, and chasing women, neglecting his father (for whom, in truth, he feels little regard) almost completely. Perversely, however, Lear has always felt a sneaking admiration for Howard while secretly despising Jeremy as a priggish, unimaginative, overly repressed bore. (This is grossly inaccurate, and unfair to Jeremy, but Lear at some level always wished he himself could have boldly defied the constraints of propriety and convention, as he believes Howard has.) Lear's will leaves Jeremy a comparative pittance and bequeaths the bulk of the estate to Howard. Surely we might well agree that Jeremy deserved to inherit the estate while Howard deserved to be cut out of the will. Yet the state, acting through its judiciary, will not on that account set aside Lear's will and hand over to Jeremy that which he, rather than Howard, deserves. To do so would violate Howard's *right* to the estate, a right he possesses despite deserving to inherit nothing. As Joel Feinberg has noted, "a person's desert of X is always a reason for giving X to him, but not always a conclusive reason," because "considerations irrelevant to his desert can have overriding cogency in establishing how he ought to be treated on balance."[19]

Dolinko's point, as applied to punishment, is that even if someone deserves to suffer for his behavior, it does *not* follow that the state may permissibly cause him to suffer for it. Desert does not *suffice* for the state's being justified in taking

17. Boonin, *The Problem of Punishment*, p. 99.

18. David Dolinko, "Some Thoughts about Retributivism," *Ethics* 101 (1991): 537–559.

19. Dolinko, p. 544. The quotation from Feinberg is from Joel Feinberg, "Justice and Personal Desert," in his *Doing and Deserving* (Princeton, NJ: Princeton University Press, 1970), p. 60.

action of the relevant sort. Boonin is in agreement with Dolinko here; both would insist that desert does not suffice for the state's causing the individual to suffer.

DISCUSSION OF BOONIN'S CRITIQUE

The "Not Punishing the Guilty" Objection

Let's begin with Boonin's example of someone who drives illegally in order to take a friend to the emergency room, when the friend would (probably) die if he weren't taken to the hospital immediately. We can use the version of the example in which the individual steals someone else's car for the purpose at hand. Let us stipulate that doing so is necessary for getting the friend to the hospital in time to save his life, that so behaving is against the law but morally permissible under the circumstances. Objectively speaking, using the car in these circumstances is not only permissible, but it also is the right thing to do. Given this, we can agree with Boonin that the individual should not, all things considered, be made to suffer (or pay) for taking the car in order to help his friend.

It is not clear, however, exactly what Boonin thinks this sort of example shows about the desert-based approach to the justification of punishment. As quoted earlier, he says, "And if the person does not deserve to suffer for [the relevant behavior], then the desert-based retributivist position cannot justify the claim that the state has the moral right to punish him for doing it. Such cases, therefore, establish that desert-based retributivism cannot draw the line between those who may be punished and those who may not in the place that the defender of punishment must draw it." But perhaps what is crucial here is a distinction between the state's having the right to punish and its being, all things considered, permissible for the state to punish in the given circumstances. I'm inclined to think that the state does have the right to punish here; but it is one thing to have a right to engage in certain behavior and quite another thing for it to be permissible (or right), all things considered, to exercise that right.[20]

A desert-based theorist might say that, given that the law in question is a just and reasonable law, anyone who violates it deserves to suffer for doing so. This desert claim explains why the state has the right to punish. But whether the state ought, all things considered, to exercise that right in a particular context will depend on further moral considerations. In the case in question, those considerations—the fact that the only way to save the friend's life is to use the

20. One need not invoke a right of the state's here. Using an alternative conceptual framework, one might say that the state has a *pro tanto* reason to punish in such cases but that it is outweighed (or mitigated) by other sorts of considerations.

car, the fact that the car's owner has other cars available, and so forth—imply that the state ought not, all things considered, to exercise its right to punish in this context. Of course, this does not entail that the owner should not be compensated for any inconvenience he is caused. Obviously, however, this point pertains more to compulsory victim restitution than to punishment per se.

The example is similar in many respects to Feinberg's famous "cabin case."[21] In this case, the only way to save your life is to break into a cabin that is owned by someone else. (Perhaps there has been a terrible storm, you are in danger of freezing to death, and the cabin owner is not currently in the cabin or nearby.) It seems perfectly permissible to break into the cabin, despite the fact that the cabin owner has a right to determine who shall enter the cabin; after all, he has property rights over the cabin. Further, even if the owner were monitoring the situation using some sort of security camera and he could intervene somehow to prevent you from entering the cabin, that would *not* be morally permissible. It would not be permissible, under the circumstances, for the owner to *exercise* his property rights, and it would be perfectly permissible for you to infringe his property rights. As Judith Thomson has argued, such an infringement would not be a *violation* of his property rights, that is, it would not be an *unjustified infringement* of his property rights. Similarly with Boonin's car case. And in both cases, some sort of restitution is owed the owners; one must, after all, apologize and compensate the owner of the cabin. But, again, as Boonin has forcefully argued, compulsory victim restitution is one thing, and punishment is another.

The same analysis appears to apply to the series of cases beginning with Larry's preventing the young woman from entering her own house. Boonin's conclusion was that "the practice of punishment dictates that the state should have the right to punish and the desert-based retributivist solution will be unable to account for this." Again, it seems to me that the desert-based approach can explain the fact that the state has the right to punish, even though it may be, all things considered, wrong, in the particular circumstances, to exercise the right in question. The desert theorist can appeal to the distinction between possessing a right and it being morally permissible, all things considered, to *exercise* that right, and Boonin's examples seem to elide the distinction (or presuppose that there is no such distinction).

Finally, I am not even sure that Boonin himself would think that a justified system of punishment would imply that the state has a right to punish in the cases we have been discussing. Recall Boonin's account of the retributive requirement on punishment: "to be a legal punishment, an act must involve intentionally harming someone because he previously did a legally prohibited

21. Joel Feinberg, "Voluntary Euthanasia," *Philosophy and Public Affairs* 7 (1978), p. 102.

act, which means that he is responsible for having done the act and that he had no valid legal excuse for doing so." Presumably, it is plausible that the individuals in the cases under discussion—the car case, the cabin case, the case of Larry—have valid legal excuses (duress, nonculpable ignorance, and so forth). Indeed, I am inclined to think that an obvious way to respond to Boonin's examples is to say that the relevant individuals have excuses and thus the state does not even have a (defeasible) right to punish them. On this approach, the examples would not even constitute prima facie counterexamples to desert-based retributivism because they would not be cases in which the state has a right to punish.

Boonin thus faces a dilemma. Either the individuals involved have valid legal excuses, in which case the state does not have a right to punish them, or the state has a defeasible right to punish them. In neither instance do we have examples in which the state has a right to punish but desert-based retributivism cannot account for this right.

The "Punishing the Innocent" Objection

Boonin contends that in his examples presented earlier of the abusive spouse and the racist, the individuals in question deserve to suffer for their reprehensible behavior, but they may not be permissibly *punished* because they have not broken the law. Similarly, in Dolinko's example given previously, Jeremy deserved the inheritance, whereas Howard deserved to be cut out of the will (according to Dolinko); but it does not follow that the state may permissibly overturn Lear's will. Here are more cases from Dolinko:

> Imagine, for example, a wealthy and callous individual whose inherited fortune allows him to lead a life of leisure and who dismisses poor people as lazy good-for-nothings whose poverty is their own fault. Surely one might believe that this fellow *deserves* to lose his money and learn first-hand what poverty is like and how hard it is to escape it—*without* necessarily believing that it would be morally permissible to bring about this result by theft or confiscation. Likewise, imagine a knowing apologist for a brutally oppressive regime; I may believe she *deserves* to experience first-hand the suffering she so blandly condones, yet *not* believe it would be morally permissible to torture her.[22]

The first thing to say about all of these cases is that it is not at all clear that the relevant claims about desert are true. Dolinko claims that Jeremy deserved to

22. David Dolinko, "Three Mistakes of Retributivism," *UCLA Law Review* 39 (1992): 1624–1657. The quotation is from p. 1629.

inherit the estate whereas Howard did not; but it is not at all obvious that gifts of this sort can be deserved (in the relevant sense). They might be more or less appropriate or fitting, but this is not to say that they can be deserved. Also, we might say that the wealthy person and the apologist are callous and complacent, and that maybe some relevant experience would shake them out of their unfortunate attitudes, but it is not clear that they "deserve" to suffer for these attitudes (in the relevant sense of "desert"). Perhaps the apologist "deserves" to suffer in the sense of "poetic justice," but that is hardly the sense of desert at issue. In what follows, however, I will put aside these worries and concede the desert claims, for the sake of the discussion.

I agree with Boonin and Dolinko that an individual's deserving to suffer for some behavior does not provide a sufficient condition for it being permissible for the state to cause him (or her) to suffer for the behavior in question. This shows that the Argument from Cases, understood as Boonin interprets it, is problematic. But I do not think that the proponent of a desert-based approach needs to adopt the Argument from Cases, interpreted as simply moving from "an individual deserves to suffer for his behavior in this case" to "the state would be justified in imposing that suffering in this and similar cases." A simple-minded desert-based approach must be rejected; but this leaves room for a more nuanced approach that appeals to desert at a basic level. In developing a more nuanced desert-based approach, it is crucial to distinguish among different questions about punishment.[23]

One question is about what Joel Feinberg called "the moral limits of the criminal law"—it is a question about when exactly—under what circumstances—the government may permissibly interfere with personal liberty.[24] This question asks when a state may legitimately make certain behavior illegal; a closely related question (and I shall assimilate it to the first) concerns when a state is morally justified in applying sanctions against certain behavior.

There are various well-known approaches to providing an answer to this first question. One such approach takes its cue from John Stuart Mill's Harm Principle, according to which a state has a good (although not necessarily decisive) reason to prohibit (and punish) behavior likely to cause harm to others.[25]

23. The following material relies heavily upon: John Martin Fischer, "Punishment and Desert: A Reply to Dolinko," *Ethics* 117 (2006), pp. 109–118.

24. Joel Feinberg presents a compendious analysis in his four-volume work, *The Moral Limits of the Criminal Law: Harm to Others* (New York: Oxford University Press, 1984); *Offense to Others* (New York: Oxford University Press, 1985); *Harm to Self* (New York: Oxford University Press, 1986); *Harmless Wrongdoing* (New York: Oxford University Press, 1988).

25. John Stuart Mill, *On Liberty*; Joel Feinberg describes the Harm Principle as follows:"It is always a good reason in support of penal legislation that it would probably be effective in preventing (eliminating, reducing) harm to persons other than the actor (the one prohibited from

The Harm Principle can be supplemented by some sort of Offense Principle.[26] Various other principles purport to specify under what circumstances it is permissible for the state to consider the prohibition and punishment of behavior.[27]

It is important to note that the various Liberty-Limiting Principles specify good reasons for the state to prohibit and punish, but that these reasons need to be put on the scales with countervailing reasons (reasons against state regulation) in a standard sort of "balancing test."[28] Thus, combining the Harm and Offense Principles can give an answer to the first question only when supplemented by a further analysis; that it, this combination can specify a (putatively) good reason for state intervention, which would need to be balanced against other considerations. Additionally, a Liberty-Limiting Principle, or combination of such principles, can *rule out* certain behavior as subject to legitimate state regulation. So, the Harm Principle (for example) sets limits to the actions that may be considered for social regulation. Actions that fall into the self-regarding sphere are immediately removed from such consideration, whereas actions that fall into the other-regarding sphere, that is, actions that invade the interests of others, are open to being considered for regulation. It may still be the case that society is not justified, all things considered, in regulating and punishing such actions. For John Stuart Mill, what determines whether society is justified in regulating behavior is a standard balance of interests test (or utilitarian calculation) of whether the interests served in making them criminal outweigh the interests served in letting people perform them without threat of legal punishment.[29]

Suppose one develops some sort of answer to the first question; this gives one's view about the moral limits of the criminal law. Now notice that one can

acting) *and* there is probably no other means that is equally effective at no greater cost to other values." (Feinberg, *Harm to Others*, p. 26)

26. Feinberg describes the Offense Principle as follows:"It is always a good reason in support of a proposed criminal prohibition that it is probably necessary to prevent serious offense to persons other than the actor and would probably be an effective means to that end if enacted." (Feinberg, *Harm to Others*, p. 26; for a detailed discussion, see Feinberg, *Offense to Others*.)

27. For a helpful summary, see Feinberg, *Harm to Others*, pp. 26–27; these principles are discussed at length in Feinberg's four-volume work, *The Moral Limits of the Criminal Law*.

28. This is clearly the approach taken by Feinberg. I am indebted to both John Deigh and Gerald Dworkin for helpfully highlighting the importance of this point (in personal correspondence).

29. Consequently, there could be other-regarding actions that deserved to be punished but that society was nonetheless not justified in making criminal because, on balance, the interests served by doing so were outweighed by the interests served by not doing so. An example might be adultery in which the offending spouse did not have his wife's or her husband's consent to break their vows. For this way of formulating the point as well as the example, I am (again) grateful to John Deigh.

ask about the moral justification of this answer—one can ask why it is morally permissible for the state to inflict punishment in those circumstances specified in the answer to the first question. Let's say (just for simplicity's sake) that the answer to the first question includes some sort of combination of the Harm and Offense Principles (supplemented by other considerations in a suitable balancing test, as specified previously). We can now ask what justifies the state in punishing those actions that run afoul of this combination of the Harm and Offense Principles (as supplemented by the balancing test); that is, we can ask why it is morally permissible for the state to punish those who violate these principles, so understood. Of course, just as there are various possible answers to the first question, there are various possible answers to the second question. One answer would be some sort of consequentialism. Another answer would posit an ineliminable residual retributivism. It would claim that someone who has, for example, harmed another and thus violated another's rights, in circumstances in which the balancing test yields the judgment that social regulation is justified, *deserves* to be punished.

It is important to see that the two questions are distinct (although obviously related). The first question could be called the *when question*, whereas the second question could be called the *why question*. Roughly speaking, the when question is a first-order question about under what circumstances the government may apply sanctions to behavior, whereas the why question is a second-order question about the justification of the answer to the when question. I contend that it is a mistake to conflate the two, or to suppose that the when question's answers are mere eliminable intermediate principles that are perhaps useful rules of thumb that help us to achieve the answer to the why question. It would be a mistake to suppose that we adopt, for example, the Harm Principle (suitably supplemented) as an answer to the question of what the moral limits of the criminal law are as a convenient rule of thumb or *means* to accomplishing the more basic goal of bringing it about that individuals get what they deserve.

Rather, the idea is that when someone, for example, fails to act in accordance with the Harm Principle (as supplemented by the balancing test), he thereby violates someone's rights (or, alternatively, invades or thwarts someone's interests). When an individual violates someone's rights in this way (or related ways—specified by one's answer to the first question), then *by virtue of so behaving,* he deserves to be treated in certain ways (to be punished). Taking this approach to the structure of the argument, it is *not* supposed that whenever someone deserves to be in a certain condition or to be treated in a certain way, it is permissible for someone else or the state to bring it about that he is in that condition or is treated in that way. Rather, the view is that when someone violates another's rights of a certain sort, then *by virtue of this,* he *deserves* to be treated in ways that would otherwise violate his rights.

It should be evident how the approach I have sketched would handle the examples presented by Boonin and Dolinko. These cases would present problems for a view according to which our answer to the first question was some sort of rule of thumb designed to facilitate in the general project of the state's ensuring that people get whatever they morally deserve. Once the two questions are distinguished and the structure of the desert-based view is highlighted, we can see that the examples are quite irrelevant to the desert-based approach, construed as I have suggested. After all, the individuals described have not violated others' rights not to be harmed or offended in the ways that indicate the moral limits of the criminal law, and thus it would not have been thought that they deserve punishment *for so behaving*. Note that, even though the combination of the Harm and Offense Principles in itself only gives a good reason for state intervention (which needs to be supplemented by a balancing test, as discussed earlier), it does *rule out* state intrusion into what is deemed the self-regarding sphere (morally unattractive as it may be).

Return to the various principles that purport to specify an answer to the first question. One such principle is the principle of Legal Moralism. Joel Feinberg defines Legal Moralism (in the broad sense) as follows: "It can be morally legitimate for the state to prohibit certain types of action that cause neither harm nor offense to anyone, on the grounds that such actions constitute or cause evils of other ('free-floating') kinds."[30] Of course, as in our discussion of the Harm and Offense Principles, the Legal Moralist believes that the fact that some action would be morally evil is a good reason for state intervention, but not necessarily a decisive reason. If one were to adopt Legal Moralism as an answer to the first question (or part of such an answer), then presumably one might respond to all of Boonin's and Dolinko's cases differently. Presumably, a Legal Moralist could indeed think that the state's role in all of these cases is precisely to ensure that people get what they deserve (given that the balancing test is met). But note that most of us would reject the principle of Legal Moralism as an answer to the first question. Indeed, it may be that the force of the examples comes from our tendency to reject Legal Moralism as an answer to the first question, rather than from a rejection of retributivism as such (construed as an answer to the second question).

In his classic treatment of punishment and responsibility, H. L. A. Hart not only emphasized that we should not necessarily expect there to be one answer to the question of the justification of punishment, but he also distinguished different questions.[31] Hart says:

30. Joel Feinberg, *Harm to Others*, p. 27.

31. H. L A. Hart, *Punishment and Responsibility: Essays in the Philosophy of Law* (New York and Oxford, UK: Oxford University Press, 1968).

> ... it is likely that in our inherited ways of talking or thinking about punishment there is some persistent drive towards an over-simplification of multiple issues which require separate consideration. To counter this drive what is most needed is *not* the simple admission that instead of a single value or aim (Deterrence, Retribution, Reform or any other) a plurality of different values and aims should be given as a conjunctive answer to some *single* question concerning the justification of punishment. What is needed is the realization that different principles ... are relevant at different points in any morally acceptable account of punishment. What we should look for are answers to a number of different questions such as: What justifies the general practice of punishment? To whom may punishment be applied? How severely may we punish?[32]

The distinction between the when and why questions is in the sprit of Hart's analysis. On my view, however, an answer to the when question does not require providing anything as elaborate as a justification of the penal law. It just means delineating some criterion for when punishment is permissible. The answer to the why question, then, is that it is justifiable for the state to punish someone for conduct C because he *deserves* to be punished for having done C, which satisfies the criterion specified by the when question.

Thus, the Argument from Cases is too simplistic. It would have us simply consider various scenarios in which individuals apparently deserve to suffer on the basis of their behavior and straightforwardly conclude that the state would be justified in causing them to suffer for the behavior. What I have suggested is that a desert-based approach should be more complex. One begins by distinguishing different questions pertaining to the justification of punishment. Most important, for our purposes here, is to distinguish between the when and the why questions. The answers to these questions can be combined to yield a subtler, "layered" approach to desert-based based retributivism. Desert still plays a crucial, irreducible role—but it is as part of an answer to the why question, not the when question.

MOTIVATION OF THE LAYERED APPROACH

I have suggested a layered approach to desert-based retributivism, according to which desert plays an ineliminable role at a certain point in the overall theory. On the more nuanced approach I have suggested, a desert-based retributivist theory of moral responsibility need not invoke the simple idea that an individual deserves to suffer insofar as he or she behaves immorally. This may or may

32. Hart, ibid., 2–3.

not be so, but in any case, it is no part of the theory of moral responsibility I am exploring here. Rather, the theory employs the idea that an individual deserves to suffer insofar as he or she violates a just and reasonable law. Further, it does not follow from an individual's deserving to suffer for violating such a law that the state is justified, all things considered, in causing the individual to suffer (for this reason); claims about desert do not entail any members of the family of all-things-considered evaluative judgments.

By introducing a more nuanced theory of this sort, one can avoid certain counterexamples to simpler desert-based approaches to punishment (as I have argued earlier). But how exactly can one motivate the layered approach, apart from the avoidance of the counterexamples? The simpler approach can be motivated more straightforwardly: it seems uncontentious that anyone who behaves immorally (arguably, at least) deserves to suffer for so acting. But exactly why should we suppose that violating a just and reasonable law makes it the case that one deserves to suffer (for so acting)?[33]

On the approach I have commended, the offender deserves to suffer because of law violation, and not simply in virtue of immoral dispositions or behavior. But why should the fact that the offender has violated a law matter in this way? Why should it make it the case that he or she deserves to suffer precisely for violating the law in question?

I can see two potential answers to this question—two separate and, on my view, plausible ways of providing independent motivation for the layered, desert-based retributivism I have been developing. First, I would point to the previous suggestion that it might be in virtue of violating a right specified, for example, by the Harm Principle that one deserves to suffer. Let us stipulate, for simplicity's sake, that the when question is answered by appeal (at least in part) to the Harm Principle. The claim would then be that an offender deserves to be punished because he has violated—or could have violated—someone else's right to be free of certain harms. More carefully, the idea here would be that the offender's deserving to suffer stems from offending against a law that is designed to protect people against certain sorts of rights violations. If one invokes other liberty-limiting principles to answer the when question, then the answer to the question of why an offender deserves to suffer for violating the law will be adjusted accordingly, but the important point is that the answer will stem from the rights and interests at stake—the rights and interests that the law seeks to protect.

I believe that we can go a long way toward providing independent motivation (i.e., motivation apart from the avoidance of counterexamples) for the layered approach in the way just sketched. But perhaps it is unreasonable to suppose

33. I am very grateful to thoughtful comments by David Boonin here.

that all laws can be naturally assimilated to liberty-limiting laws that seek to protect the rights of individuals; maybe it will be difficult to explain why those who violate *any* law deserve to suffer on grounds of offending against a principle designed to protect others from violations of their rights (or, illegitimately, setbacks of their interests). It will then be helpful to consider another promising approach to providing independent motivation for the layered, desert-based approach to the justification of punishment.

I believe that it is at least plausible that individuals have a prima facie (but not necessarily overriding) moral duty to obey the law. (I will assimilate moral duties and obligations here; for our purposes, the distinction is not important. Further, I shall follow a standard usage, according to which a prima facie duty gives rise to or stems from a *pro tanto* moral reason.) If this contention is correct, then it could presumably help to explain why someone who violates a (just and reasonable law) deserves to suffer for so acting; the individual would have failed to fulfill at least a prima facie moral duty, and it is plausible that in virtue of failing to fulfill a moral duty, an individual can deserve to suffer. Of course, the amount of suffering deserved will vary, depending (at least in part) on the nature and significance of the law that has been violated. On this approach, then, the desert claim stems from the putative failure to fulfill a prima facie moral duty to obey the law, rather than the alleged violation of a right or illegitimate setback of an interest (or, perhaps more accurately, the violation of a law designed to protect against such violations of rights and setbacks of interests).

Here it is important to recall that desert claims do not in themselves entail all-things-considered evaluative judgments. So, more specifically, an individual's deserving to suffer for violating a law does not entail that the state should, all things considered, punish him (and thereby seek to cause him to suffer). Let us suppose that the individual in question engaged in what we take to be justified civil disobedience. It could then be the case that, in virtue of violating the law, the individual failed to fulfill a prima facie duty to obey, but that he was not morally required, all things considered, to obey the law. Thus, it could be morally acceptable for the state not to punish him; after all, even though he deserves to suffer for failing to fulfill a prima facie duty, such desert claims do not necessarily correspond to all-things-considered evaluative judgments about what ought to be done. Desert is just one consideration that goes into an all-things-considered evaluative judgment (of the relevant sort). Of course, it might well be morally justified (all things considered) for the state to punish the individual, and it is typically thought that in engaging in civil disobedience, the person ought to anticipate punishment and even perhaps to accept it as appropriate.

Some might insist that the failure to fulfill a prima facie moral duty to obey a law does not generate the claim that the individual in question deserves to suffer, even on the supposition that desert claims do not entail all-things-considered evaluative judgments of the relevant sort. The contention here would be that only the failure to fulfill an *overriding* duty would generate such a claim. I am inclined to think that the failure to fulfill even a prima facie duty to obey a law could generate the desert claim—a desert claim that must go on the scales with other considerations to get to an all-things-considered judgment. Because desert is only a part of an overall evaluation of a situation, I find it plausible that desert can correspond to and arise from prima facie moral reasons. But I do not have a knockdown argument for the view that the failure to fulfill certain prima facie moral duties can give rise to full-fledged claims to the effect that the relevant individual deserves to suffer. If one rejects the view in question, then one would have to fall back on the first approach to providing independent motivation for the layered approach to desert-based retributivism about the justification of punishment.

As I claimed earlier, I think it is plausible that citizens generally do have a prima facie duty to obey the law. Various specific ways of seeking to explain or ground such duties have been suggested, but it is not crucial here to argue for any particular strategy.[34] After all, my point here is not so much that there really is a prima facie moral duty to obey the law; rather, my contention is that a certain sort of retributivism may depend on this contention (a contention that is at least antecedently plausible). And it does seem that the notion that those who violate a law deserve to suffer for so behaving might well depend on the contention that citizens have at least a prima facie duty to obey the law. That is, it seems natural to suppose that there is a connection between desert-based retributivism and the view that citizens have a prima facie moral duty to obey the law. (Of course, if the first way of providing an independent motivation for the layered approach to desert-based retributivism [sketched previously] worked, then it would provide an alternative strategy not dependent on the contention that citizens have a prima facie duty to obey the law.)

34. For a detailed and systematic critical examination of various attempts to ground a prima facie duty to obey the law, see: A. John Simmons, *Moral Principles and Political Obligations* (Princeton, NJ: Princeton University Press, 1979). There is an interesting and attractive development of a "respect-based" strategy for grounding the duty in question in: Philip Soper, *A Theory of Law* (Cambridge, MA: Harvard University Press, 1984).

CONCLUSION

Simple, desert-based retributivist approaches to the justification of punishment face various counterexamples. But one shouldn't throw the baby out with the bathwater. I have argued that a more sophisticated version of desert-based retributivism can avoid the counterexamples. Further, I have sketched some possible motivations for adopting such an approach. Although it can seem that retributivism is less "humane" or attractive than compulsory victim restitution or (alternatively) punishment justified on consequentialist grounds, there are nevertheless deep intuitions that arguably favor desert-based retributivism.

Consider, for example, the link between moral responsibility and punishment. Indeed, it seems that an agent's being morally responsible for his (relevant) behavior is a prerequisite for legitimate punishment for the behavior in question. Thus, it should not be surprising if there were deep connections between the proper account of the concept of moral responsibility and our explanation of the justification of punishment. Of course, there are various proposals for an account of the concept of moral responsibility, and this is not the place to provide a compendium or to explore any of the suggestions in depth. Perhaps it will suffice to sketch just two such accounts here.

Various philosophers have followed Peter Strawson in suggesting that being morally responsible for one's behavior is to be an "apt" or "appropriate" target for a distinctive set of attitudes on the basis of the behavior.[35] Strawson calls these attitudes, which include indignation, resentment, gratitude, and respect, "the reactive attitudes"; earlier I noted that Boonin calls them "reprobative attitudes." An interesting question involves how to interpret the notions of "aptness" and "appropriateness"; one very plausible suggestion is that these notions should be analyzed in terms of desert. Taking this suggestion, one would be morally responsible for an action (roughly speaking) insofar as one *deserved* one of the reactive attitudes on the basis of it. This is perhaps an oversimplification, but the point is that a Strawsonian approach to analyzing the concept of moral responsibility might well invoke the notion of desert in the way indicated (or a related way): moral responsibility is a matter of deserving certain distinctive kinds of responses (involving the reactive attitudes).

Derk Pereboom's account of the concept of moral responsibility explicitly invokes the notion of desert:

35. Strawson, "Freedom and Resentment"; for further discussions, see McKenna and Russell, eds., *Perspectives on P. F. Strawson's "Freedom and Resentment,"* and John Martin Fischer, *The Metaphysics of Free Will: An Essay on Control* (Oxford, UK: Blackwell, 1994), pp. 211–213.

> The term, "moral responsibility," is used in many ways, but there is one sense that has been at issue in the traditional philosophical debate about free will and determinism. My characterization of it is this: for an agent to be morally responsible for an action is for it to belong to her in such a way that she would deserve blame if she understood that it was morally wrong, and she would deserve credit or perhaps praise if she understood that it was morally exemplary. The desert at issue here is basic in the sense that the agent, to be morally responsible, would deserve the blame or credit just because she has performed the action (given that she understands its moral status), and not by virtue of consequentialist considerations.[36]

Again, it is beyond the scope of this chapter to discuss these desert-based accounts of moral responsibility in any detail. Here I simply wish to note the important link between such accounts of moral responsibility and desert-based retributivist approaches to the justification of punishment. As I contended earlier, we can think of punishment as a symbolic expression of certain of the distinctive attitudes identified by Strawson. If one were to interpret the Strawsonian account in terms of desert, it would not be at all surprising—indeed, one would expect—to receive an account of the justification of punishment in terms of desert as well. I reiterate: punishment is appropriate only for those who are morally responsible for the behavior in question. If one is morally responsible, on the Strawsonian approach (interpreted as involving desert), then one deserves certain of the attitudes—precisely the attitudes involved in punishment, insofar as it is the symbolic expression of the relevant attitudes. Of course, the same point applies to Pereboom's account of the concept of moral responsibility, mutatis mutandis.

Punishment involves a "harsh treatment" component as well as the symbolic expression of such attitudes as indignation and resentment. It seems perfectly reasonable that, if a morally responsible agent deserves indignation or resentment on the basis of his behavior, he might also deserve harsh treatment for so behaving. If this were correct, then both elements of punishment would be linked, in just the right way, to the account of moral responsibility. That is, the

36. Derk Pereboom, "Hard Incompatibilism," in John Martin Fischer, Robert Kane, Derk Pereboom, and Manuel Vargas, *Four Views on Free Will* (Oxford, UK: Blackwell, 2007), p. 86. Note that Pereboom's characterization, unlike the rough first approximation to a Strawsonian account in the previous text, leaves room for moral responsibility for morally neutral behavior.

linkage between moral responsibility and the justification of punishment would be tight, given a desert-based retributivism about the justification of punishment. Punishment, then, would involve giving morally responsible people what they deserve for violating the law. Although one might challenge this rather simple idea in various ways, it also has the ring of truth.[37]

37. Some of this chapter was published previously: John Martin Fischer, "Punishment and Desert: A Reply to Dolinko," *Ethics* 117 (2006), pp. 109–118. I have benefited from reading a previous version of this paper at the Kayden Conference at the University of Colorado; on that occasion, I benefited from comments by David Boonin, Stephan Kershnar, and George Sher. Also, I read a previous version to the Philosophy Department at Duke University, where I received helpful comments from Alex Rosenberg, Walter Sinnot-Armstrong, David Wong, and Thomas Nadelhofer. I am also grateful to John Deigh, Gerald Dworkin, Justin Coates, Philip Swenson, and Saul Smilansky for their comments.

2

Brute Retributivism*

SHAUN NICHOLS

> Beside good and evil, or in other words, pain and pleasure, the direct passions frequently arise from a natural impulse or instinct, which is perfectly unaccountable. Of this kind is the desire of punishment to our enemies, and of happiness to our friends; hunger, lust, and a few other bodily appetites
>
> (HUME, *Treatise 2.3.9).*

Our norms of retributive justice are notoriously difficult to justify. This leads many philosophers to reject the legitimacy of those norms. Other philosophers attempt to justify retributivism by relying on moral realism, arguing that retributivism is one of the moral truths. In this chapter, I will assume that moral realism is false and proceed to argue that the retributive norm is part of a set of norms that do not need justification. That is, it is appropriate to retain the norm even if we cannot provide further reasons in favor of the norm. Of course, this does not mean that retributivism should stand, all things considered. To determine whether we should ultimately preserve our retributive norms will depend on a number of other factors, including both the expected utilities and our other core values. Here the aim is simply to keep retributivism on the table.

* I am grateful to Jerry Gaus, John Doris, Michael Gill, Dominic Murphy, Thomas Nadelhoffer, Tamler Sommers, Mark Timmons, and Manuel Vargas for discussion and comments on earlier drafts of this paper. Thanks also to audiences at St. Louis University and the 2010 meeting of the Society for Applied Philosophy.

A BARE RETRIBUTIVIST NORM

Perhaps the most famous proclamation on retributivism comes from Kant's remarks on the last murderer:

> Even if a civil society were to be dissolved by the consent of all its members (e.g., if a people inhabiting an island decided to separate and disperse throughout the world), the last murderer remaining in prison would first have to be executed, so that each has done to him what his deeds deserve and blood guilt does not cling to the people for not having insisted upon this punishment; for otherwise the people can be regarded as collaborators in his public violation of justice. (*Metaphysics of Morals*)

This passage succeeds in illustrating a crucial feature of retributivism—it is a backward-looking, nonconsequentialist view. But Kant's example also includes several elements that are not essential to retributivism. Most obviously, Kant demands *capital* punishment. Retributivists need not accept this. It further suggests that failing to exact retribution renders one complicit (sharing "blood guilt") in the villainy, but this isn't essential to retributivism either. Kant's passage also presumes that the *state* has the authority to deliver punishment, but this assumption is not built into retributivism (Husak 1992; Murphy 1985; Shafer-Landau 1996).

Even setting aside the additional elements in Kant's exhortation, retributivism has been developed and defined in a number of different ways.[1] The kind of retributivism to be defended here is a basic form. Michael Moore offers a representative statement: "Retributivism is a very straightforward theory of punishment: We are justified in punishing because and only because offenders deserve it." (Moore 1987, 181). According to Anthony Duff, despite the diversity in retributive theories, they all attempt to answer the question, "What is the justificatory relationship between crime and punishment that the idea of desert is supposed to capture: why do the guilty 'deserve to suffer'?" (Duff 2008). There are two distinct elements in these characterizations of retributivist theories of punishment:

1. A norm that wrongdoers should be punished because (and only because) of their past wrongdoing
2. A justification for the norm

For reasons that are central to the aim of this chapter, I want to restrict the retributivist theory to the first factor—a retrospective norm prescribing the

1. See Cottingham (1979) for a cranky paper on the diversity of uses of the term "retributivism" in retributive theories of punishment.

punishment of wrongdoers.[2] Call this the *bare retributive norm*.[3] As stated, this is a retrospective, backward-looking norm. This distinguishes the theory from other prominent approaches, all of which are prospective. Most obviously, a consequentialist ethics of punishment looks to future benefits of punishment (e.g., Bentham) (Rawls 1955). But humanitarian approaches (e.g., Menninger 1968) and moral education approaches (e.g., Hampton 1984) are equally forward looking. So, too, are restorative accounts of punishment, which aim to repair relationships (e.g., Braithwaite 1999). By contrast, the bare retributive norm simply says that wrongdoers should be punished for their past actions.[4]

THE BARE RETRIBUTIVE NORM AND THE FOLK

It is widely assumed that ordinary people are retributivists. Indeed, it's often taken for granted that retributivism has its roots in ordinary thought (e.g., Hume 1739/1964 section 2.3.9, Smith 1790/1982, 77-78; 87-91, Mackie 1982). But it is an empirical claim, so it's worth looking to some data. Is there, in folk ethics, a bare retributive norm?

Perhaps the most celebrated empirical work on punishment in recent years comes from experimental economics.[5] Using several different economic games,

2. This is still, of course, quite vague. For instance, it leaves open what makes one a "wrongdoer" in the relevant sense.

3. Etymologically, "retribution" is tied to the notion of repayment. And this accords with many prominent accounts of retributive punishment, including Kant's. But the notion of payback is itself morally thick, for it loads into the norm a *reason* for punishment ("the guilty should be punished because it's payback"). As a result, I want to avoid identifying retributivism with a payback theory of punishment.

4. Desert is often invoked in characterizing retributive theories of punishment (e.g., Duff 2008; Moore 1987, 181). The retributivist typically maintains that wrongdoers *deserve* to be punished for their past wrongs. In some cases, saying "wrongdoers deserve to be punished" might just be a restatement of the bare retributive norm. But often the appeal to desert seems to aspire to provide a substantive *justification* for retributivism—the (alleged) fact that wrongdoers deserve to be punished is supposed to be a value-adding reason for endorsing the bare retributive norm. Again, I want to focus narrowly on the bare retributive norm, not on the justifications for it. As a result, insofar as the appeal to desert is supposed to provide a deeper justification for retributive punishment, I want to set aside the notion of desert.

5. There is a complementary line of research in social psychology on people's judgments about sentencing of criminals. This work indicates that people are largely retributivists about sentencing (see, especially, Carlsmith et al. 2002; Carlsmith 2008). For the purposes of this paper, I want to focus on how people think about punishment in interpersonal interactions rather than how they think about institutionalized forms of criminal punishment. The work in experimental economics is especially apt for this. These experiments involve interaction between individuals in novel scenarios. As a result, there is less chance that subjects are relying on social scripts

researchers have shown that participants will punish—deduct money from—those who are perceived to have acted unfairly.[6] In one study, groups of four participants play public goods games anonymously on computers. Each participant gets an allotment of money and is allowed to use the money to invest in a common fund. For each 1 monetary unit an individual invests, each of the four players (including the investor) gets 4 units. This provides a net benefit for the group, but the investor himself loses on the transaction. Participants play a series of such games, never with any of the same players. After each game, participants are informed about the contributions of each player and are given a chance to pay to have money deducted from any of the other players in the game. For every 1 monetary unit the punisher pays, 3 monetary units are deducted from the punishee's fund. The participants know that they will not play another game with any of these particular players, so punishing apparently has no future benefit for the punisher. Nonetheless, participants often paid to punish those who contributed less than average (Fehr and Gächter 2002, 137).

In a striking extension of this work, Fehr and Fischbacher (2004, 73) explored whether external observers would punish players in an economic game. The third party observed two participants engage in a prisoner's dilemma game. The third party was then given money and asked whether he would use some of this money to pay to deduct funds from either player. Almost half opted to punish a defector in a scenario in which the other player had cooperated.

In both of these studies, the motivation for punishment does not seem to be anything like explicit considerations about utilities—the punisher and punishee both lose money, and the punishers have little reason to think the punishment will materially improve the situation of the other players. As a result, Fehr and colleagues dub it "altruistic" punishment.

De Quervain and colleagues used brain imaging techniques to explore the neural underpinning of this kind of punishment. For their experiment, participants played the trust game (de Quervain et al. 2004). The basic framework of the trust game is explained to all players before the game begins. The trust game is played anonymously by two people. One player, A, is given a sum of money and the option to send the money to B. If A does send the money, the amount will be quadrupled. Then B is given the opportunity to send A half of the money or none of it. In the de Quervain experiment, after playing the trust

about criminal punishment. In the economic experiments, there is no suggestion of criminal behavior, and both the (apparent) wrongdoing and the punishment are fairly minimal. The experiments even avoid explicit mention of "wrongful" action or "punishment."

6. I follow experimental economists in categorizing these actions as punishment. This categorization is perfectly appropriate on various philosophical definitions of punishment that aren't narrowly focused on state-sponsored punishment (see, e.g., Baier 1955; Benn 1967; Gaus 2011).

game, A is given the option to deduct money from B. As expected, when B did not send back any money, A often opted to deduct money from B. And when A did engage in such punishment, there was increased activity in brain regions known to be associated with reward (i.e., caudate nucleus and dorsal striatum). Thus, it seems that punishing, at least in these games, is rewarding.

These are beautiful and justly famous results, but they don't show that people have a retributive norm. There are many activities that I expect myself to do and that no doubt stimulate my reward center but that I don't think that I *should* do. For instance, I expect that I will eat bacon later, and the reward structures in my brain will likely respond enthusiastically. But do I think I *should* eat bacon? Do I think that it is a good thing to eat bacon? Of course not. On neither the moral nor the prudential level do I think I should eat bacon. But that will not prevent my reward structures from firing when I eat bacon. Indeed, as de Quervain and colleagues are happy to note, the structures activated by punishment are also activated by consumption of cocaine and nicotine (Breiter et al. 1997; Stein et al. 1998). So, although the imaging results indicate that punishment is *yummy*, they don't show that punishment is guided by a retributive norm. The results don't speak to whether people normatively endorse the behavior that they find rewarding.

Fortunately, it's pretty easy to investigate whether or not people endorse this kind of punitive behavior. We can just *ask* them.[7] I conducted a small study to investigate the matter.[8] Participants were presented with one of three versions of the trust game. In all cases, participants were told about an instance of the trust game in which A sends his money to B, and B sends no money back. And in all cases, participants were asked whether an agent *should* deduct money from B. In version 1, A has to pay to deduct money from B. In that case, roughly half of the participants said that A should pay to deduct money. This is similar to the proportions found in many of the one-shot pay-to-punish experiments (e.g., Fehr and Fischbacher 2004). In version 2, everything was the same, but A could deduct money from B without A himself having to pay anything.[9] In that case, nearly all of the participants said that A should deduct money from B. In the final version, a third party, C, observes the entire set of transactions between A and B. Then C has an opportunity to deduct money from B without C having

7. Experimental economists tend not to be very interested in people's explanations for their actions. This might be part of the reason that the topic isn't explored in the original studies.

8. Participants were recruited through Amazon's Mechanical Turk (https://requester.mturk.com/mturk/welcome). Users of the site can fill out surveys for modest compensation. Buhrmeister et al. (2011) provide evidence that the data obtained through this site is of comparable quality to that obtained in standard psychology subject pools.

9. De Quervain and colleagues call this version "intentional and free" (1256).

to pay anything. Nearly all of the participants said that C should deduct money from B.[10]

These results indicate that people do indeed endorse the punitive behavior that we see in the experimental economics games, particularly when it isn't costly. So, the case of punishment is importantly different from my bacon eating. Although I don't normatively endorse my bacon consumption, people do normatively endorse punishment. There is a further question, however. Just because there is normative endorsement of the punishment behavior doesn't yet mean that the norm is retributive. To investigate this, we can look at the explanations people gave for their answers. Recall that the critical feature of the bare retributive norm is that it is distinctly backward looking. All of the prominent alternatives, by contrast, are forward looking. When we examine the explanations participants gave for saying that money should be deducted from B, some of the explanations were, in fact, forwarding looking. Here are a couple of examples:

> "B was being selfish and should have some money deducted from him so he will learn not to be so self-centered."
> "I think that A should subtract the money because B should realize that with reward comes responsibility."

Although a few of the explanations included forward-looking considerations, the vast bulk of explanations make no reference at all to the future, focusing instead on *what B did*. Participants were much more likely to invoke only backward looking factors in their explanations.[11] Here are some representative examples:

> "It was a selfish act for B not to send any money back to A."

10. The responses were significantly greater than what would be expected by chance alone in both condition 2 (χ^2 goodness-of-fit $(1, N = 15) = 11.267, p < .001$, two-tailed) and condition 3 (χ^2 goodness-of-fit $(1, N = 15) = 11.267, p < .001$, two-tailed). To provide a contrast, a fourth condition was run in which a different economic game was described, modeled on an egalitarian-motive game (cf. Dawes et al. 2007). In this game, a computer randomly assigned money to two players. Sometimes the assignments were equal, and sometimes they were disproportionate. Participants were asked to judge whether A should deduct money from B if the computer randomly gave B all of the money and A none of it. In this scenario, most people (12 out of 15) said that A *shouldn't* deduct money from B. This was significantly different from chance (χ^2 goodness-of-fit $(1, N = 15) = 5.4, p < .05$) and much different from the parallel trust game (condition 2) (χ^2 goodness-of-fit) $(2, N = 30) = 16.43, p < .0001$, two-tailed).

11. Explanations were categorized by independent coders (agreement was >95%). Participants gave backward-looking explanations significantly more frequently than would be expected by chance (χ^2 goodness-of-fit) $(1, N = 35) = 17.857, p < .0001$).

"B made money off of A's contribution, but A did not get anything in return. B should be punished."

"It is unfair that A gave B $12 and B didn't send anything back to A."

"B is a jerk and didn't give anything back."

These explanations share the idea that money should be deducted from B *because of what B did.*

The fact that most subjects don't mention forward-looking factors doesn't exclude the possibility that consequentialist considerations played a critical causal role in their judgments. Indeed, one natural possibility is that people punish other players because of the communicative effects of such punishment (e.g., for moral education or norm reinforcement). After all, in these experiments, the players expect the punishee to be well aware of having their welfare reduced. To address this limitation of extant work, a recent study explored punishment in an economic game in which it was quite explicit that the punishee would be unaware of any welfare reduction. Even in this case, however, people still preferred to punish players who behaved in ostensibly unfair ways (Nadelhoffer et al. forthcoming). Given that the punishees would not even be aware of the punishment, it is difficult to see how consequentialist reasoning could be driving subjects preferences. Rather, such punishment is plausibly driven by a retributive norm that operates without consulting consequentialist considerations.[12] This nonconsequentialism is not a unique feature of the retributive norm. Many of our ethical norms operate independently of consequentialist reasoning (Gill and Nichols 2008). Consider the norm prohibiting incest. If subjects are presented with a vignette in which a brother and sister have consensual sex, with all the prophylactic caution in the world, many subjects persist in thinking that the action was wrong, even though they can't justify their judgment (Haidt et al. 2000). Presumably what is going on here is that subjects have a norm prohibiting incest, and the behavior is categorized as an instance of the prohibited kind. Critically, however, people embrace this norm without having a deeper justification for it. The incest norm is *inferentially basic*—it is not the product of consciously available inferences from other norms or facts. Inferentially basic norms like the incest norm are at the bottom of the normative pile. The retributive norm is a member of this special class of norms. If the bare retributive norm and its downstream consequences were extirpated from our psychology, the norm would not just regenerate from our

12. Indeed, people tend to agree with a quite explicitly nonconsequentialist justification of punishment: "People who commit crimes deserve to be punished even if punishing them won't produce any positive benefits to either the offender or society—e.g., rehabilitation, deterring other would-be offenders, etc." (Nadelhoffer et al. forthcoming).

other consciously available forward-looking norms and values. The bare retributive norm is a basic, independent part of our moral worldview.

RETRIBUTIVISM AND THE EMOTIONS

It's widely assumed that retributivism itself is a product of rather base emotional reactions like anger or resentment. Anger *is* important to retributivism, but the relation between anger and the retributive norm is indirect. Let's start by looking at evidence on anger and retribution in our comfortable domain of economic games.

In the *ultimatum* game—the most intensively studied economic game—one of two anonymous players is randomly assigned to be the *proposer.* The proposer is given a sum of money and told to offer a division of the money to the other player, the *responder*. If the responder accepts the offer, both players get the money, but if the responder rejects the offer, neither gets any of the money. A large body of evidence indicates that when the proposer makes a highly inequitable offer (80/20 or 90/10), responders often refuse the offer, turning down free money.[13] What precipitates this behavior? Anger, apparently. In an early study on the matter, Pillutla and Murninghan (1996) asked participants in an ultimatum game two open-ended questions: "How did you react when you received your offer?" and "How did you feel?" (215). The responses were coded for reports of anger and perceived unfairness. Subsequent analyses showed that when subjects mentioned anger in their responses, this was an excellent predictor of whether they had rejected the offer, even better than perceived unfairness. The researchers offer a simple explanation: when participants regard the offer as unfair, this often triggers anger, and anger increases the tendency to reject the offer (220; see also Bosman and van Winden 2002, 159; Hopfensitz and Reuben 2009).

Fehr and Gächter offer a similar explanation for why people pay to punish in public goods games. They asked their participants to imagine accidently encountering a fellow player who had invested much less than everyone else in the group. Participants were asked to indicate their feeling toward this person (Fehr and Gächter 2002, 139). As expected, participants indicated that they would feel high levels of anger toward this person. Fehr and Gächter draw on this finding, in conjunction with the pattern of punishment behavior, to argue

13. It's unclear whether we should count these behaviors as instances of punishment (see Gaus 2011). Experimental economists often do presume that rejecting an offer amounts to punishment (e.g., Bolton and Zwick 1995; Sanfey et al. 2003). We don't need to take a stand on this here.

that anger (and perhaps related emotions) plays a critical role in generating punishment in these games.

Anger plausibly plays an on-line role in motivating punishment in economic games. This fits well with a standard picture of the *function* of anger, which dates back at least to Darwin. According to Darwin, anger serves to motivate retaliation. He writes:

> … animals of all kinds, and their progenitors before them, when attacked or threatened by an enemy, have exerted their utmost powers in fighting and in defending themselves. Unless an animal does thus act, or has the intention, or at least the desire, to attack its enemy, it cannot properly be said to be enraged (1872, 74).

Although punishment behavior is plausibly driven by anger, it would be a serious error to conclude that retributive judgment is identical to feeling anger. I can judge that a given wrongdoer should be punished even if I don't feel any anger, perhaps because the description of the incident is too vague to induce emotion. Similarly, I can think that a class of individuals (say, shoplifters) should be punished while on a perfectly even emotional keel. In addition to the emotion, we also have the retributive *norm*. And the retributive norm can be activated even in the absence of emotional reaction. The reverse is also possible. Anger is sometimes triggered when there is no sensible target of punishment, as when a turn in weather destroys your grand plans for a day hike. In this case, the emotion is present, but the norm fails to be activated in any familiar way.

There are thus two elements that are important to retributive punishment—anger and a retributive norm. I've stressed their independence, but there is also, I suspect, an important causal connection between the two. The retributive norm would have inherited cultural strength from its natural links to anger. The idea here draws on epidemiological approaches to cultural evolution (Boyer 2000; Nichols 2002; Sperber 1996). By identifying characteristic features of human psychology, we can get some idea about which kinds of cultural items will be attractive to creatures like us. Many different kinds of emotions—including anger, fear, jealousy, disgust, and sympathy—are characteristic features of human psychology. These emotions make some things naturally attractive and others aversive. As a result, emotions plausibly play an important role in influencing which cultural items are likely to persist. Norms and other cultural items would have increased attractiveness when they resonate with common emotional endowments. For example, etiquette norms prohibiting the display of bodily fluids seem to be preserved once they are introduced into the culture, and a plausible explanation for this is that these prohibitions resonate with our natural proclivity to feel disgust at bodily fluids (Nichols 2004). In the present context, the relation between emotion, motivation, and norms is rather different because the retributive norm is prescriptive rather than proscriptive. But there is obviously a closely related story to tell about the cultural evolution of prescriptive norms:

> *Ceteris paribus,* prescriptive norms that encourage behavior that we are naturally motivated to perform will enjoy an advantage over prescriptive norms that lack any such connection to motivation.[14]

This principle would apply to the case of retributive norms. For the norm that *wrongdoers should be punished* resonates with our natural anger-driven motivation to retaliate against (perceived) wrongdoers. We *want* to retaliate against wrongdoers. This anger-driven motivation would plausibly contribute to the cultural heft of a norm that prescribes inflicting harm on wrongdoers.

Although anger undergirds the retributive norm, anger itself is unruly. In many cultures, including our own recent past, anger-driven retaliation manifested in the practice of blood feuds, which are not characterized by carefully measured responses. In retaliating against an affront, the aim is often to demonstrate one's power, not carefully measure the harm and meet it in proportional kind. Thus, retaliation in blood feud often involves harming uninvolved family members of the enemy (e.g., Miller 1990, 180; 197-198; Sommers 2012).[15] This is *not* the narrow retributive norm that we embrace today. Unlike blood feud, the bare retributive norm directly targets the wrongdoer.

Somehow the unruly retaliatory practices associated with blood feud get displaced by the narrow norm of retribution, tied to the wrongdoer and proportionality. As Biblical scholars have observed for decades (see, e.g., Berlin and Brettler 2004), the injunction to take an *eye for an eye* (Ex. 21:23, 24; Lev. 24:19, 20; Deut. 19:21) was introduced as a more *moderate* approach to retaliation

14. In previous work (Nichols 2002, 2004), I formulate an "affective resonance hypothesis" that is limited to proscriptive norms. Here I am extending the idea to prescriptive norms. There is a complicating feature about prescriptive norms. Insofar as the behavior is motivationally attractive and there are no countervailing considerations, it's not clear that norms play any significant role. Norms become more obviously significant when there are considerations *against* performing the prescribed action. In the interesting cases, there will likely be such considerations. For instance, we have a prescriptive norm of benevolence, and this competes straightforwardly with self-interest. Similarly, the prescriptive norm of punishment often competes with material self-interest in the short term (though perhaps not in the long term [see Frank 1988]).

15. Killing the relatives of wrongdoers is even prescribed in an item in the code of Hammurabi. The son of a carpenter might be executed for his father's shoddy work: If a builder build a house for some one, and does not construct it properly, and the house which he built fall in and kill ... the son of the owner the son of that builder shall be put to death. (*The Code of Hammurabi* 229, 230).

than the dangerously escalating blood feuds (Gen 4: 23-24). We get a similar phenomenon in the history of early English law. As feudalism replaces tribalism in England, compensation takes the place of the feud (Jeffrey 1957, 665; Harding 1966, 21). To pacify the victim or victim's family, the law indicated that the victim needed to be paid. The laws themselves are graphically specific:

> If an ear be struck off, let bot [monetary restitution] be made with 12 shillings.
> If the other ear hear not, let bot be made with 25 shillings.
> If an ear be pierced, let bot be made with 3 shillings.
> If an ear be mutilated, let bot be made with 6 shillings.
> (Laws of Ethelbert)

Eventually, of course, this system of victim compensation gives way to the idea that striking off an ear is a crime against the state, requiring something more from the wrongdoer than payment of damages (cf. Maine 1861, chap. 10). This development in the history of law is a further departure from the anger-driven retaliatory practices of our ancestors.

All of this suggests that our (narrow) retributive norm was not fashioned ex nihilo, spewing forth from rationality. Instead, our retributive norm is a product of cultural pruning. The unfocused retaliatory norms and practices of our ancestors were reshaped and refined, leaving us with the vestige we have today. But *anger* was likely a sustaining factor throughout this cultural evolution of punishment norms. Had our ancestors lacked the propensity for anger at wrongdoers, we would likely not have the retributive norm we do today.

JUSTIFICATION

Thus far, I've argued that (i) judgments about punishment are guided by a bare retributive norm that is inferentially basic and (ii) anger contributed to the cultural success of this norm. If this psychological-historical account of the bare retributive norm is right, it should not be surprising if we can't justify the retributive norm. We inherited our retributive norm from emotion-driven cultural evolution and not through rational discovery.

Retributivism is, as a matter of fact, notoriously difficult to justify. The temptation is to defend retributivism by pointing to its future benefits: If we are retributive, then this will provide a deterrent. Or, if we are retributive, then this will enhance cooperation. Or, if we are retributive, this will forestall the pursuit of vengeance by the victim. These kinds of proposals are philosophically appealing. But they are intuitively unsatisfying because they invoke *prospective* reasons for punishing, whereas the norm is expressly backwards looking (cf. Bedau 1978, 616; Mackie 1982, 4). Insofar as the retributive norm is inferentially basic, it is perhaps unsurprising that these "deeper" justifications are unsatisfying. Consider the inferentially basic norm that parents have special obligations to their children. Attempts to give a "deeper" justification for this norm, e.g., in terms of societal benefits, are bound to seem wrong-headed. So too, the appeal to future benefits is bound to seem intuitively inadequate as a complete justification for the backward-looking retributive norm.

In the face of this, a typical response is to renounce retributivism. Many intellectuals find bare retributivism offensive—it counsels harming someone without getting any offsetting benefit. In this light, people seem to prefer *anything else*—humanitarianism, restorative justice, utilitarianism, etc. Duff makes this point nicely: "Many people, including those who do not take a consequentialist view of other matters, think that any adequate justification of punishment must be basically consequentialist. For we have here a practice which inflicts, indeed seeks to inflict significant hardship or pain: how else could we hope to justify it than by showing that it brings consequential benefits sufficiently large to outweigh, and thus justify, that hardship and pain" (2008).

There is one prominent metaethical view that offers a haven for philosophers trying to defend an uncompromising retributivism: moral realism. According to moral realism, the basic moral truths are "stance independent"; they are not made true because of our (or anyone else's) attitudes, norms, emotions, etc. (see, e.g., Shafer-Landau 2003, 15). A retributivist can draw on this metaethical view to maintain that the retributive norm reflects a moral truth about the rightness of punishment, a truth that is independent of what our norms or emotions or evaluative reactions happen to be. Michael Moore is perhaps the most prominent advocate of this view in the recent literature. He maintains that retributivism is a moral truth, and he argues that the emotions play an important role in getting us to appreciate this truth: "The emotions are ... heuristic guides for us, an extra source of insight into moral truths beyond the knowledge we can gain from sensory and inferential capacities alone" (Moore 1987, 201; also 189). The moral truth of retributivism is independent of the emotions, but the emotions help us tap into moral truths (1987, 186-187). They are "important but not essential in our reaching moral truths" (202). In the case of retributivism, Moore suggests that the emotions of guilt and fellow feeling lead us to appreciate the truth of retributivism (209ff.).

There are reasons to be skeptical of Moore's appeal to emotions as indicators of moral truth, but I want to focus on a broader point. The retributivist realist is true to the cause—no consequentialist in retributive clothing here. But the attempted defense of retributivism is precarious. For should moral realism be false, retributivist realism leave us with no basis for preserving the bare retributive norm. And moral realism is disputed by a great number of philosophers, starting perhaps with Hutcheson and Hume but continuing in a frenzy of late (e.g., Blackburn 1998; Gibbard 1992; Greene 2008; Harman 1996; Joyce 2002; Mackie 1977; Nichols 2004; Prinz 2007; Sinnott-Armstrong 2006; Street 2006; Timmons 1999). Should this wave of dissent to realism be right, the retributivist seems to be left without a hope of sustaining the view.

ETHICAL CONSERVATISM

The tempting defenses of retributivism seem to either fail to be intuitively retributive or rely on highly contentious metaethical assumptions. I am going to assume that moral realism is false—that there is no moral truth that stands independent of our attitudes and feelings. With that (major) assumption in place, I suggest that we don't *need* to have a justification for the retributive norm in order for it to retain its legitimacy for us.[16]

In realist domains, if we show that a belief in the domain is formed by a process that is neither reliable nor rational, this undercuts any basis for sustaining the belief. This kind of debunking argument is nicely illustrated in Freud's views on religion. Freud said that the reason we believe in God is because of wishful thinking. And wishful thinking is an epistemically terrible basis for belief formation. Hence, our belief in God is in bad epistemic repair—we are not warranted in our belief (Freud 1927/1961). Similar kinds of arguments have been suggested for claims in metaphysics of identity (Scholl 2007), metaethics (e.g., Nichols forthcoming), and consciousness (e.g., Fiala et al. forthcoming).

Joshua Greene applies this kind of debunking argument to normative ethics and, in particular, to retributivism (Greene 2008; see also Singer 2005). First, Greene notes that our retributive inclinations are grounded in arational emotions. Attempts at justifying retribution are, Greene suggests, "just rationalizations for our retributivist feelings ... the natural history of our retributivist dispositions makes it unlikely that they reflect any sort of deep moral truth" (2008, 71). Greene uses these considerations about the emotional origins as the basis for debunking retributivism and other deontological principles (Greene 2008; see also Singer 2005, 350).

Discovering that arational emotions generate beliefs in metaphysics, metaethics, or religion might be reason to suspend those beliefs. But in domains in which realism is rejected, it is far from clear that the normal justificatory demands on belief formation apply. The vast bulk of our ordinary ethical worldview likely derives from fundamentally arational emotional processes (Blair 1995; Gill and

16. At least on some readings, similar views are suggested in Strawson (1962) and Mackie (1982).

Nichols 2008; Prinz 2007). For instance, were it not for the fact that we find human suffering aversive, we would likely not have the moral revulsion we do at killing. Nor would we feel the moral obligation for helping strangers. I am assuming here, with irrealism, that there is no ultimate rational justification for these norms. They are the norms we happen to have, given the kinds of emotional propensities we happen to have. But notice how dramatic it would be to cast these norms out of morality. To limit our ethics to norms that have some ultimate rational justification would leave us with an ethics more barren than almost anyone would be willing to accept.[17]

Instead of reverting to such an emaciated ethics, we might adopt an *ethical conservatism,* according to which certain ethical norms do not lose their normative legitimacy even if the norms do not derive from the kinds of processes that confer justification in realist domains (Nichols, Timmons, and Lopez forthcoming). If *none* of our ethical beliefs has an ultimate justification, then, barring a complete upheaval of commonsense ethics, we are bound to grant normative clout to *some* moral norms that lack any ultimate justification.

A full defense of this ethically conservative position is clearly beyond the scope of this paper, but it is important to note that not *all* norms have this privileged status. It accrues, we suggest, to norms that run deep in our psychology—norms that are *entrenched* (Nichols et al. forthcoming). Entrenched norms in this sense have three features. First, they are widespread in the community. Second, entrenched norms are inferentially basic, that is, not inferentially dependent on other norms or facts (see section 2).[18] Finally, entrenched norms are rooted in human emotion—they resonate with our natural emotional

17. Peter Singer presents a Greene-style argument that deontological intuitions are based in arational emotions and hence lack any rational justification (2005, 347ff.). However, he holds out optimism that moral skepticism can be avoided, suggesting that there are some *rational intuitions*, like "it is a bad thing if a person is killed" (Singer 2005, 350–351). Singer doesn't actually provide an argument that this intuition is somehow rationally grounded, and, for my part, I find it hard to see why we should think that this intuition has such an exceptional epistemic status. But in the present context, the more important point is that even if (as moral irrealists would maintain), this intuitive norm lacks a rational ground, that would not be enough to suggest that we should abandon the norm. Indeed, presumably Singer himself, if convinced that there is no rational ground for any of our ethical commitments, would not abandon all of those commitments. (Note that in the lay population, people who claim to reject moral objectivism still retain commitment to familiar moral principles and treat them much the same as people who embrace moral objectivism [Nichols 2004].) None of this is to say that the presence of a rational ground is epistemically irrelevant. If there is a rational ground for some ethical norm, then *that's* the best reason for sustaining the norm. But if the irrealist is right that none of our ethical norms has any ultimate rational ground, that doesn't mean that we are obliged to abandon our norms.

18. Norms that are *not* inferentially basic are undercut if they depend on factual or inferential errors. To take an obvious example, many people who oppose abortion do so on the basis of

endowment. The norm "help suffering children" provides a clear example. That norm is widespread in our culture. And it is plausibly a result of our emotional reactions to suffering and not of a process of rational inference from more basic principles.[19]

Ethical conservatism maintains that the fact that our ethical norms are not ultimately justified does not eradicate their normative legitimacy. This accords well with the classical sentimentalist tradition, which draws a deep analogy between aesthetics and ethics. In both cases, our normative judgments are a function of human nature—it's because of the emotional nature we happen to have that we make the aesthetic and ethical judgments that we do. In addition, classical sentimentalism maintains that the fact that emotions are at the bottom of our ethical and aesthetic lives doesn't undermine the legitimacy of either ethical or aesthetic norms (see Gill 2007).[20]

In sum, ethical conservatism accords a special status for normative commitments that are rooted in human emotion and are not inferentially dependent on other norms or facts. These norms can retain their normative legitimacy even though they might result from patently arational processes. The primary reason for accepting ethical conservatism is that it provides a natural way to preserve commonsense morality in the face of its emotional, arational origins.[21] And the analogy with aesthetics provides a kind of existence argument for how emotion-based norms can retain their normative legitimacy.

factual beliefs (e.g., about whether the fetus has a soul). If the facts that underpin their normative conviction are known to be false, this destroys the warrant for retaining the norm.

19. We have a large body of entrenched norms, including norms against theft, incest, and harming innocents, as well as norms promoting retribution, reparations, and special obligations to family. Some normative ethicists might presume that one of our entrenched norms can be the foundation for all of ethics. These are large issues in philosophical ethics, and I can't do justice to them here. But I see no reason to expect that one of our entrenched norms will serve to fund all of the rest of our cherished ethical commitments. Nor do I see any overwhelming normative reason to impose such a monistic assumption on our ethical theorizing. As a result, I propose to proceed with an ethical conservatism that grants an initial legitimacy to each entrenched norm.

20. I have been maintaining that these entrenched norms don't need justification. Others might prefer to say that such norms are "*self*-justifying." For present purposes, it's not important whether there is a real distinction here. What matters is that the entrenched norms retain their authority.

21. One might maintain that the category of entrenched norms is too broad and that some classes of entrenched norms should not be granted special status of initial normative legitimacy. For example, one might maintain that entrenched norms based on disgust don't merit this status. That is an interesting view, but it would require an argument to motivate it. In the absence of such an argument, I'll proceed with the broad category that grants the special status to all entrenched norms.

COMPETING CONSIDERATIONS

The retributive norm is entrenched—it is widespread, inferentially basic (section 2), and rooted in a basic human emotion (section 3). Because the retributive norms is entrenched, the ethical conservatism sketched above entails that the retributive norm is not undermined by the absence of rational justification. The bare retributive norm thus retains an initial normative legitimacy, even in the face of its arational, emotional basis. But of course the standing of entrenched norms is not unassailable. The view is *conservative*, not *reactionary.* Being an ethical conservative does not entail rigid deference to all entrenched norms. There can be competing moral considerations that lead us to think it right to reject an entrenched norm.

Some entrenched commitments do not face obvious competing moral considerations. For example, "help suffering strangers" seems broadly consistent with the remainder of our moral concerns. Other entrenched norms do face competing moral considerations. Consider first an example quite apart from punishment—organ donation. There continues to be significant resistance to organ donation, with cultural variations in the extent of resistance (see, e.g., Braun and Nichols 1997). There *is* something repellant about the practice of having one's child disemboweled after death. It's likely that there is (or was) an entrenched norm against defiling the body of one's deceased child by extracting her organs. Most Westerners now accept the propriety of organ donation.[22] And we've done so because of a competing ethical consideration—an enormous benefit to another person. In light of the fact that a deceased child's organs can save another person's life, we have overcome our entrenched norm against allowing someone to root around in our dead children's bodies.

Are there competing moral factors when we look to our retributive norm? Of course. Ceteris paribus, it's wrong to harm others. Retributivism involves *intentionally harming* others. This is the core of the familiar complaint against retributivism—retributivism promotes intentionally harming someone without getting any (other) benefit out of it (Duff 2008). This is obviously an important challenge to retributivism. To begin to meet it, I first want to suggest that in Western philosophical ethics, we have come to fetishize harm, as if it trumps any other ethical considerations. But there are plausibly cases in which it can be appropriate to cause harm to someone in the service of other non-harm-based concerns. Say that I promised my grandmother that I would visit her grave every Memorial Day, but that when the time comes, I need to wake my sleeping wife to get the car keys. Waking someone from sleep sets back their welfare, probably more so than a punch on the arm. But we regard waking someone

22. The Gallup Organization, Inc. 2005 National Public Opinion Survey on Organ Donation.

under those circumstances as permissible. Or, to take a pervasive case, most readers will agree that it is okay to tax the successful bachelor farmer even if the government services he gets are not commensurate with the amount of taxes he pays. Many programs that our tax dollars support do not provide any benefit for the successful bachelor farmer: public broadcasting, NEH, NEA, humanitarian aid. The bachelor farmer might well not want to relinquish a penny for any of these programs. At best, they are of no use to him; at worst, he might find them despicable. In any case, taking his money for these services is an unequivocal harm to him. But that doesn't make us think it wrong to tax him. For, at least in some cases, like humanitarian aid, we think that moral considerations outweigh the harm to him.

Of course, the fact that it can be acceptable to cause harm in the service of some competing ethical norms doesn't show that this is okay in the case of retributive punishment. It might be that harming really does globally override the retributive norm. But the nature of the issue is obscured by focusing on the severity of the punishment. Thus, Duff speaks of the worry that our practice of punishment "seeks to inflict significant hardship or pain" (2008). The issue is further obscured by the fact that discussions of retributivism typically revolve around punishing criminals in a large-scale society. But the bare retributive norm doesn't say anything directly about technique or state-sponsored punishment. It just says that wrongdoers should be punished.

I want to argue that there are cases of punishment in which the fact that we are producing a harm isn't, by itself, enough to override the legitimacy of the retributive norm. The fact that we're harming someone isn't enough to undermine the judgment that the wrongdoer should be punished. To soften the ground, though, I want to return to the case of organ donation. In "The Wisdom of Repugnance," Leon Kass maintains that our natural revulsion at various medical procedures is ethically revelatory: "Repugnance … revolts against the excesses of human willfulness, warning us not to transgress what is unspeakably profound" (Kass 1997, 20). This repugnance suggests to us, according to Kass, that there is something wrong with, inter alia, in vitro fertilization, cloning, and organ donation. Kass has been rightly criticized for his faith in repugnance as an ethical indicator (e.g., Harris 1998). Although "wisdom" no doubt inflates the epistemic value of repugnance, there is something to the idea that repugnance is not to be ignored. As noted earlier, there is a natural resistance to the idea that it's okay to have one's child disemboweled after death. In our culture, we have come to accept the propriety of organ donation. But note that the benefits of organ donation are tremendous. Imagine that the benefits were smaller, say, that by organ transplantation, the net gain would be a reduction in the number of sniffles. In that case, it would scarcely be worth suspending the norm against disemboweling dead children. I would not sanction harvesting the organs of my dead child to help relieve someone's runny nose. Kass might be wrong to view repugnance as wise. But it's not like our felt resistance to organ donation counts for *nothing*.

Recall where we are—the claim is that we have an entrenched commitment to the retributive norm and this endows the norm with a legitimacy that isn't eradicated by the fact that the norm has an arational source. Does the fact that retribution involves intentional harm count as sufficient reason to overturn the retributive norm? The point of the organ donation example is that the stakes can make a big difference to how we think about competing ethical considerations. To evaluate the competing considerations in the case of punishment, it will be important to avoid vexed issues about criminality and incarceration. Instead, let's return to our economic games. In these games, people think that those who behave unfairly should have money deducted from their fund. For instance, many people say that one should pay \$.25 to have \$.75 deducted from the unfair player. And virtually everyone says that if it doesn't cost the punisher any money, he should deduct money from the unfair player. Here we have a sharp case of competing factors. The retributive norm says *punish* (by \$.75), and this competes with the fact that we would be setting back B by \$.75 (with no benefit). In this competition, does the loss of \$.75 to B suffice to overturn the norm that wrongdoers should be punished? Does our commitment to retributivism count for so little? 75 cents? It is an affront to commonsense ethics that our commitment to retribution is so cheaply bought off. Of course, as the harms increase in scale, the competition can become more challenging. At some point, no doubt, the retributive norm does get overridden in virtue of the competing considerations. However, if it's right that \$.75 doesn't buy off the retributive norm, then there is no general rejection of retributivism issued by the fact that it involves intentionally harming someone.

Competing considerations about intentional harm might tip the balance against harsh punishments, but that doesn't justify *globally* overturning our entrenched commitment to retribution. When we consider institutionalized forms of punishment, like incarceration or the death penalty, it might be appropriate to oppose those techniques on a variety of grounds. These practices might be excessively severe; the practices might unfairly skew to certain racial groups; the practices might demand a higher standard of evidence of guilt than is typically obtained. There are numerous reasons one might oppose capital punishment or incarceration. But, if the line of argument here is right, the fact that the punishment is retributive is not itself a reason to oppose it.[23]

23. In my defense of brute retributivism, I have avoided appealing to any benefits of retributivism. For to appeal to benefits of retributivism leaves one open to that charge that retributivism is being justified by *nonretributive, consequentialist* considerations (Bedau 1978, 616; Mackie 1982, 208). However, when we turn to the broader question about whether to sustain

CONCLUSION

Despite its ubiquity in ordinary life, the retributive norm has resisted rational justification. This leads many to reject the legitimacy of retributivism. But unless we take on controversial metaethical assumptions like moral realism, we are bound to accept some basic moral norms without justification. For the vast bulk of ordinary moral thought likely emanates from arational, emotional sources. Rather than conclude that this invalidates ordinary moral thought, we can reject the assumption that, in order to carry normative legitimacy, a norm must be justified (or capable of justification). Some norms retain normative legitimacy even if they have no independent justification. I've suggested that the norms that have this special status are those that are widespread, rooted in emotions, and inferentially basic. The bare retributive norm falls in this class. As a result, the fact that we can't justify the norm doesn't defeat the norm. This leaves open a number of issues about punishment—how to punish, what to punish, who should punish. Indeed, it remains an open question whether, all things considered, we should sustain retributivism. But we shouldn't take the lack of independent justification as a reason to abandon our brute retributivism.

REFERENCES

Baier, K. 1955. Is Punishment Retributive? *Analysis*, 16, 25–32.

Bedau, H. 1978. Retribution and the Theory of Punishment, *Journal of Philosophy*, 75, 601–620.

Benn, S. 1967. Punishment. In P. Edwards (ed.), *The Encyclopedia of Philosophy*, vol. 7, 29–36. New York: Macmillan and the Free Press.

Berlin, A., and Brettler, M. 2004. *The Jewish Study Bible*. Oxford: Oxford University Press.

Blackburn, S. 1998. *Ruling Passions*. Oxford: Oxford University Press.

Blair, J. 1995. A Cognitive-Developmental Approach to Psychopathy. *Cognition*, 57, 1–29.

Bolton, G., and Zwick, R. 1995. Anonymity Versus Punishment in Ultimatum Bargaining. *Games and Economic Behavior*, 10, 95–121

Boyer, P. 2000. Evolution of the Modern Mind and the Origins of Culture. In P. Carruthers and A. Chamberlain (eds.), *Evolution and the Human Mind*. Cambridge, UK: Cambridge University Press, 93–113.

Braithwaite, J. 1999. Restorative Justice: Assessing Optimistic and Pessimistic Accounts. In M. Tonry (ed.), *Crime and Justice: A Review of Research*, vol. 23. Chicago: University of Chicago Press, 241–367.

the retributive norm in light of other ethical considerations, we must consider the costs and benefits of the retributive norm. And the benefits appear to be quite significant. In particular, the retributive norm likely plays a crucial role in facilitating cooperation (see Gaus 2011).

Braun, K., and Nichols, R. 1997. Death and Dying in Four Asian American Cultures: A Descriptive Study. *Death Studies*, 21, 327–359.

Breiter H., Gollub R., Weisskoff R., Kennedy D., Makris N., Berke J., Goodman J., Kantor H., Gastfriend D., Riorden J., Mathew R., Rosen B., and Hyman S. 1997. Acute Effects of Cocaine on Human Brain Activity and Emotion. *Neuron*, 19, 591–611.

Carlsmith, K., Darley, J., and Robinson, P. 2002. Why Do We Punish? Deterrence and Just Deserts as Motives for Punishment. *Journal of Personality and Social Psychology*, 83, 284–299.

Carlsmith, K. 2008. On Justifying Punishment: The Discrepancy Between Words and Actions. *Social Justice Research*, 21, 119–137.

The Code of Hammurabi 2007. Translated by L. W. King. Nuvision Publications, LLC.

Cottingham 1979. Varieties of Retributivism. *Philosophical Quarterly*, 29, 238–246.

Darwin, C. 1872. *The Expression of the Emotions in Man and Animals*. London: John Murray.

Dawes, C., Fowler, J., Johnson, T., McElreath, R., and Smirnov, O. 2007. Egalitarian Motives in Humans. *Nature*, 446, 794–796.

De Quervain, D., Fischbacher, U., Treyer, V., Schellhammer, M., Schnyder, U., Buck, A., and Fehr, E. 2004. The Neural Basis of Altruistic Punishment. *Science*, 305(5688), 1254–1258.

Duff, A. 2008. Legal Punishment. *The Stanford Encyclopedia of Philosophy* (Fall 2008 Edition), E. Zalta (ed.), Available at: http://plato.stanford.edu/archives/fall2008/entries/legal-punishment/.

Fehr, E., and Fischbacher, U. 2004. Third Party Punishment and Social Norms. *Evolution and Human Behavior*, 25, 63–87.

Fehr, E., and Gächter, S. 2000. Cooperation and Punishment in Public Goods Experiments. *American Economic Review*, 90, 980–994.

Fehr, E., and Gächter, S. 2002. Altruistic Punishment in Humans. *Nature*, 415, 137–140

Fiala, B., Arico, A., and Nichols, S. (forthcoming). "On the Psychological Origins of Dualism: Dual-Process Cognition and the Explanatory Gap." In E. Slingerland and M. Collard (eds.), *Creating Consilience: Issues and Case Studies in the Integration of the Sciences and Humanities*. New York: Oxford University Press.

Frank, R. 1988. *Passions Within Reason*. New York: W. H. Norton.

Freud, S. 1927/1961. *The Future of an Illusion*. Translated by J. Strachey. New York: Norton & Co.

Gaus, J. 2011. Retributive Justice and Social Cooperation. In M. White (ed.), *Retributivism: Essays on Theory and Practice*. Oxford: Oxford University Press.

Gibbard, A. 1992. *Wise Choices, Apt Feelings*. Cambridge, MA: Harvard University Press.

Gill, M. 2007. Moral Rationalism vs. Moral Sentimentalism: Is Morality More Like Math or Beauty? *Philosophy Compass*, 2, 16–30.

Gill, M., and Nichols, S. 2008. Sentimentalist Pluralism, *Philosophical Perspectives*, 18, 143–163.

Greene, J. 2008. The Secret Joke of Kant's Soul. In W. Sinnott-Armstrong (ed.), *Moral Psychology*, vol. 3. Cambridge, MA: MIT Press.

Haidt, J., Bjorklund, F., and Murphy, S. 2000. Moral Dumbfounding: When Intuition Finds No Reason. Unpublished manuscript. University of Virginia.

Hampton, J. 1984. The Moral Education Theory of Punishment. *Philosophy and Public Affairs*, 13, 208–238.
Harman, G. 1996. Moral Relativism. In G. Harman and J. Thomson (eds.). *Moral Relativism and Moral Objectivity*. Cambridge, MA: Blackwell, 3-64.
Harding, A. 1966. *A Social History of English Law*. Baltimore: Penguin Books.
Harris, J. 1998. *Clones, Genes, and Immortality*. Oxford: Oxford University Press.
Hopfensitz, A., and Reuben, E. 2009. The Importance of Emotions for the Effectiveness of Social Punishment. *Economic Journal*, 119, 1534–1559.
Hume, D. 1739/1964. *A Treatise of Human Nature*. Oxford: Clarendon Press.
Husak, D. 1992. Why Punish the Deserving? *Nous*, 26, 447–464.
Jeffrey, C. 1957. The Development of Crime in Early English Society. *Journal of Criminal Law, Criminology & Police Science*, 47, 647–666.
Joyce, R. 2002. *The Myth of Morality*. Cambridge: Cambridge University Press.
Kass, L. 1997. The Wisdom of Repugnance. *New Republic*, June 2, 17–26.
Mackie, J. 1977. *Ethics: Inventing Right and Wrong*. New York: Penguin.
Mackie, J. 1982. Morality and the Retributive Emotions. *Criminal Justice Research*, 1, 3–10.
Maine, H. 1861. *Ancient Law*. London: John Murray.
Menninger, K. 1968. *The Crime of Punishment*. New York: Viking Press.
Miller, W. 1990. *Bloodtaking and Peacemaking*. Chicago: University of Chicago Press.
Moore, M. 1987. The Moral Worth of Retribution. In F. Schoeman (ed.), *Responsibility, Character, and the Emotions*. Cambridge: Cambridge University Press.
Murphy, J. 1985. Retributivism, Moral Education and the Liberal State. *Criminal Justice Ethics*, 4, 3–11.
Nadelhoffer, T., Heshmati, S., Kaplan, D. and Nichols, S. (forthcoming). Folk Retributivism: In Theory and in Practice. *Economics and Philosophy.*
Nichols, S. 2002. On the Genealogy of Norms. *Philosophy of Science*, 69, 234–255.
Nichols, S. 2004. *Sentimental Rules*. New York: Oxford University Press.
Nichols, S. (forthcoming). Ethics and Debunking.
Nichols, S., Timmons, M., and Lopez, T. (forthcoming). Ethical Conservatism and the Psychology of Moral Luck. In M. Christen et al. (eds.), *Empirically Informed Ethics*. New York: Springer.
Pillutla, M., and Murnighan, J. 1996. Unfairness, Anger and Spite. *Organizational Behavior and Human Decision Processes*, 68, 208–224.
Prinz, J. 2007. *The Emotional Construction of Morals*. Oxford: Oxford University Press.
Rawls, J. 1955. Two Concepts of Rules. *Philosophical Review*, 64, 3–32.
Sanfey, A., Rilling, J., Aronson J., Nystrom L., and Cohen, J. 2003. The Neural Basis of Economic Decision Making in the Ultimatum Game. *Science*, 300, 1755–1758.
Scholl, B. 2007. Object Persistence in Philosophy and Psychology. *Mind & Language*, 22, 563–591.
Shafer-Landau, R. 1996. The Failure of Retributivism. *Philosophical Studies*, 82, 289–316.
Shafer-Landau, R. 2003. *Moral Realism: A Defence*. Oxford: Oxford University Press.
Singer, P. 2005. Ethics and Intuitions. *Journal of Ethics*, 9, 331–352.
Sinnott-Armstrong, W. 2006. *Moral Skepticisms*. Oxford: Oxford University Press.
Smith, A. 1790/1982. *The Theory of Moral Sentiments*. Indianapolis, IN: Liberty Classics, 1982.

Sommers, T. 2012. *Relative Justice*. Princeton, NJ: Princeton University Press.

Sperber, D. 1996. *Explaining Culture*. Cambridge, MA: Blackwell.

Stein, E., Pankiewicz, J., Harsch, H. H., Cho, J. K., Fuller, S. A., Hoffmann, R. G., Hawkins, M., Rao, S. M., Bandettini, P. A., and Bloom, A. S. 1998. Nicotine-Induced Limbic Cortical Activation in the Human Brain: A Functional MRI Study. *American Journal of Psychiatry*, 155, 1009–1015.

Strawson, P., 1962. Freedom and Resentment. *Proceedings of the British Academy*, 48, 1–25.

Street, S., 2006. A Darwinian Dilemma for Realist Theories of Value. *Philosophical Studies*, 127, 109–166.

Timmons, M. 1999. *Morality Without Foundations: A Defence of Ethical Contextualism*. New York: Oxford University Press.

PART TWO

Incompatibilism and Retributivism

3

Free Will Skepticism and Criminal Punishment

DERK PEREBOOM

Perhaps the most frequently and urgently voiced criticism of free will skepticism, the view according to which we lack the sort of free will required for moral responsibility (Pereboom 1995, 2001; cf. Smilansky 2000; Sommers 2012; Spinoza 1677/1985; Strawson 1986; Waller 1990), is that the responses to criminal behavior it would permit as justified are insufficient for acceptable social policy.[1] Indeed, some of the most prominent justifications for punishing criminals, such as retribution theory, are incompatible with free will skepticism. And alternative justifications that are not ruled out by the skeptical view per se face significant independent moral objections. But free will skepticism leaves intact other ways to respond to criminal behavior, in particular preventative detention, rehabilitation, and alteration of relevant social conditions, and I contend that these methods are morally justifiable and sufficient for good social policy.

PRELIMINARIES

We human beings participate in a practice of holding ourselves and each other morally responsible. When an agent behaves in a way that appears to be immoral, we may ask him to explain or excuse the action; when the explanation

1. Thanks to Dana Nelkin, Thomas Nadelhoffer, Brian Leiter, my free will seminar at Cornell University in the Spring of 2011, and an anonymous reviewer for very helpful comments. I also wish to thank William Lee, whose work as a research assistant was highly valuable and much appreciated.

or excuse is unsatisfactory, we may reprimand, ask for apology or restitution, punish, or isolate. Our treatment of suspected criminals is part of this practice, but it is a part that has, throughout the history of civilization, undergone continuous reform in response to challenges based on considerations of fairness, equality, and humanity. Such challenges are fueled by advances in moral reflection and in empirical science, and crucially, they form a core component of the practice of holding responsible itself.

Stephen Morse (2004, 2007) distinguishes between internal and external challenges to this practice, a distinction that stems from Ludwig Wittgenstein (1953) and is famously applied to the practice of holding morally responsible by P. F. Strawson (1962). An external challenge is based on considerations that are not features of the practice, or are at least general enough not to be specific to it. An internal challenge, by contrast, is based on considerations that are specific to the practice. Morse, like Strawson, characterizes the challenge that free will skeptics pose to the practice and to its criminological component in particular, as external, and rejects it for this reason; the skeptical view "generates only an external critique of responsibility that is unrelated to forensic practice and would obliterate the possibility of responsibility altogether" (Morse 2007: 104). I have argued, and will do so again in what follows, that this type of challenge is internal and thus cannot be dismissed for the type of reason Morse proposes (Pereboom 2001: 123). The considerations on the basis of which skepticism about free will challenges the practice of holding responsible are in fact specific to the practice itself. Moreover, contrary to what Morse contends, the changes it aims to justify not only leave the practice intact but also can in fact be recommended on independent moral grounds.

A plausible example of an external challenge is David Hume's argument that our inductive practice is unjustified. Empirical induction, he points out, relies on the assumption that the future resembles the past, or, more broadly, that the unobserved resembles the observed, but we have no a priori or noncircular empirical justification for an assumption of this sort (1739/1978, 1748/2000). This skeptical challenge is external because it is based on highly general standards for adequacy of justification that are not specific to inductive practice. Attempts to respond to Hume have not met with widespread acceptance, and thus the challenge remains in place. To my mind, opponents of external challenges have not made clear what, precisely, is defective about them. But we can add that in this example, no human being has ever opted out of the inductive practice despite the arguably unanswered external challenge, and Hume plausibly contended that it is psychologically impossible for us to do so. Thus, the skeptical challenge to induction is not only external, but also it is merely academic in the sense that it can have no serious effect on how we behave. One might similarly think that the free will skeptic's contention is merely academic in this sense. Strawson has made this, or a closely related, claim (1962). I will argue that this is not so, that the challenge from skepticism about free will can have an effect on our practice of holding responsible and, moreover, that this effect might well be salutary for general moral reasons.

Note first that the free will skeptic does not challenge every element of the practice of holding morally responsible. As a case in point, in everyday life, when we encounter presumptively immoral behavior, we consider it legitimate to ask the agent, "Why did you decide to do that?" or, "Do you think it was the right thing to do?" If the reasons given in response to such questions are morally unsatisfactory, we regard it as justified to invite the agent to evaluate critically what her actions indicate about her intentions and character, to demand apology, or to request reform. Engaging in such interactions is reasonable in light of how they contribute to our understanding of our moral commitments and to our moral improvement. The moral responsibility invoked here has been called the *moral answerability* or the *fittingness of providing a moral explanation* sense, and it is the variety of moral responsibility that is most thoroughly ingrained in our practice and least controversial (Bok 1998; McKenna 2012; Arthur Kuflik, in conversation; Scanlon 1998). It may well characterize human interactions across all cultures. Our capacity to be sensitive to, to act on, and to evaluate behavior on the basis of moral reasons is essential to our being morally responsible in this way. The main thread of the historical free will debate does not pose determinism as a challenge to moral responsibility as answerability, and free will skeptics accept that we are morally responsible in this sense.

Rather, in this debate, skeptics, and incompatibilists more generally, argue that determinism is incompatible with moral responsibility—and the free will required for it—of a distinct kind. The variety of moral responsibility that incompatibilists claim not to be compatible with determinism is set apart by the notion of *basic desert*. For an agent to be morally responsible for an action in this sense is for it to be hers in such a way that she would deserve to be the recipient of an expression of moral resentment or indignation if she understood that it was morally wrong, and she would deserve be the recipient of an expression of gratitude or praise if she understood that it was morally exemplary. The desert at issue here is basic because the agent, to be morally responsible, would deserve to be the recipient of the expression of such an attitude just because she has performed the action, given sensitivity to its moral status, and not, for example, by virtue of consequentialist or contractualist considerations. As I understand it, one might be the recipient of the expression of such an attitude when this expression is either covert or overt. Moral responsibility in this sense is presupposed by our attitudes of resentment, indignation, gratitude, and moral praise because having such an attitude essentially involves the supposition that the agent basically deserves to be the recipient of its expression, and it is thus the variety of moral responsibility that Strawson brings to the fore (1962).[2]

This sense of moral responsibility is backward looking in a distinctive way because it licenses retrospective assignments of basic desert. But moral responsibility in the basic desert sense does not have a monopoly on backward-looking considerations. The answerability sense on its own authorizes retrospective assessments, such as moral disapproval based on failure to act in accord with moral reasons, which do not invoke basic desert. This last notion can appropriately be regarded as a variety of blame, so one need not appeal to basic desert to secure at least one kind of blame.

Thus, it is not the whole practice of holding responsible—not the whole practice of blaming and praising—that is targeted by free will skepticism, but rather a component that relies on the assumption of basic desert. Likewise, it is not the entire practice of holding criminals responsible that is placed under threat by this skeptical view, but only the justification of criminal punishment that depends on basic desert. The retributivist justification of punishment, according to which the punishment of a criminal is justified on the ground that he deserves it just because he has knowingly committed a serious offense, is the one that most intimately invokes the basic desert sense of moral responsibility, together with the freedom it demands. This is evident in Immanuel Kant's retributivist account, and also in those of Morse and Michael Moore (Kant 1797/1963; Moore 1987, 1998; Morse 2004). The connection is simply this: a judgment that an agent is blameworthy in the basic desert sense for a serious offense involves the supposition that he also deserves, in the basic sense, to be punished.[3] As we shall see, however, the main alternatives to retributivism for justifying criminal punishment either rely on retributivism at crucial junctures, and are thus also subject to the free will skeptic's challenge, or else are vulnerable to serious moral objections of other kinds. These other objections are driven by features of the practice of holding morally responsible, and thus elements of the practice itself already threaten to dislodge these attempts to justify punishment.

2. Benjamin Vilhauer (forthcoming) is a free will skeptic who endorses a theory of punishment founded on a contractualist theory of (nonbasic) desert.

3. Thanks to Dana Nelkin for discussion of this point. For minor offenses, perhaps a judgment that an agent is blameworthy in the basic desert sense also involves the supposition that he also deserves, in the basic sense, to be punished because here judging blameworthy involves supposing that the agent deserves, in the basic sense, to be the recipient of the expression of resentment or indignation, and this can count as punishment because targeting someone as a such a recipient involves an intention to inflict psychological pain, which therefore counts as punishment. See Wallace (1994: 51–83) and Nelkin (2011: 31–50) for discussions of related issues.

There is an intuitively legitimate theory for prevention of dangerous crime that is undercut neither by free will skepticism nor by other moral considerations. This theory draws an analogy between treatment of dangerous criminals and treatment of carriers of dangerous diseases (Schoeman 1979). The free will skeptic claims that criminals are not morally responsible for their actions in the basic desert sense. Plainly, many carriers of dangerous diseases are not responsible in this or in any sense for having contracted these diseases. We generally agree that it is sometimes permissible to quarantine them nevertheless. But then, even if a dangerous criminal is not morally responsible for his crimes in the basic desert sense (say, because no one is ever in this way morally responsible), it could be as legitimate to detain him as to quarantine the nonresponsible carrier of a serious communicable disease. Furthermore, just as less dangerous diseases may justify only preventative measures less restrictive than quarantine, so, too, moderately serious criminal tendencies might permit only more moderate restraints. In addition, an account based on this analogy would demand a degree of concern for the rehabilitation and well-being of the criminal that would alter much of current practice. For just as fairness dictates that we must seek to cure the diseased we quarantine, so, too, fairness would require that we attempt to rehabilitate the criminals we detain. And if a criminal cannot be rehabilitated, and our safety requires his indefinite confinement, this account provides no justification for making his life more miserable than needed to guard against the danger he poses. Finally, there are measures for preventing crime more generally, such as providing for adequate education and mental health care, that the free will skeptic can readily endorse.

This is the account I defend (Pereboom 2001, chapter 6). Although it is revisionist relative to widespread and historical punitive practice, similar views have frequently been advocated on independent grounds (e.g., Boonin 2008; Menninger 1968; Montague 1995), and it is sufficiently continuous with traditional and current policies to count as part of our general moral practice of holding morally responsible. Let me add that Morse is right to argue that free will skepticism should not be raised as a relevant issue in specific criminal cases and thus should not serve to alter this component of the practice (Morse 2007). Rather, this position is relevant to which general sorts of treatment of criminals can be justified, and thus for which laws concerning criminal punishment, detention, and rehabilitation are legitimate.

PROBLEMS FOR LIBERTARIANISM

Advocates of the claim that we do have the sort of free will required for moral responsibility in the basic desert sense are either proponents of libertarianism, the incompatibilist conception of this sort of free will, or of a compatibilist view. Recent times have witnessed the explicit differentiation of two widely held versions of libertarianism: the event-causal and the agent-causal types. In event-causal libertarianism, actions are caused solely by way of events, standardly conceived as objects having properties at times, and some type of indeterminacy in the production of actions by appropriate events is held to be a decisive requirement for moral responsibility (Balaguer 2010; Ekstrom 2000; Kane 1996). This position has an ancestor in the Epicurean view according to which a free decision is an uncaused swerve in the otherwise downward path of an atom (Lucretius 50 B.C.E.). According to agent-causal libertarianism, free will of the sort required for moral responsibility is accounted for by the existence of agents who possess a causal power to make choices without being determined to do so (Chisholm 1964, 1976; Clarke 2003; Griffiths 2010; Kant 1797/1963; O'Connor 2000; Taylor 1966, 1974). In this view, it is essential that the causation involved in an agent's making a free choice is not reducible to causation among events involving the agent, but is rather irreducibly an instance of the agent-as-substance causing a choice not by way of events. The agent, fundamentally as a substance, has the causal power to cause choices without being determined to do so.

Robert Kane (1996) has developed a much-discussed version of event-causal libertarianism. In his proposal, the paradigm example of an action for which an agent is responsible is one of moral or prudential struggle, in which there are reasons for and against performing the action in question. The sequence that produces the action begins with the agent's character and motives and proceeds through the agent's making an effort of will to act, which results in the choice for a particular action. The effort of will is a struggle to choose in one way in a situation in which there are countervailing pressures. In the case of a freely willed choice, this effort of will is *indeterminate*, and as a result, the choice produced by the effort is *undetermined*. Kane explains this last specification by drawing an analogy between an effort of will and a quantum event (on one conception; Kane 1996, 128). The effort of will is indeterminate in the sense that its causal potential does not become determinate until the choice occurs. Before this pivotal interaction, there are different ways in which this causal potential can be resolved, and thus when it is resolved, the resulting choice will be undetermined. Significantly, Kane cautions against construing his view in such a way that the indeterminacy occurs after the effort is made: "One must think of the effort and the indeterminism as fused; the effort is indeterminate and the indeterminism is a property of the effort, not something that occurs before or after the effort." If an agent is morally responsible for a choice, it must either be free in this sense or there must be some such free choice that is (or has a key role in) its sufficient ground, cause, or explanation (1996, 232). Kane embellishes his account by endeavoring to show how the particle analogy for free choice might actually work in the functioning of the brain's neural networks (1996, 128-130).

Critics of libertarianism have argued that if actions are undetermined, agents cannot be morally responsible for them. A classical presentation of this objection is found in Hume's *Treatise of Human Nature* (Hume 1739/1978, 411-412; cf. Mele 2006). In Hume's version, the concern highlighted is that if an action is uncaused, it will not have sufficient connection with the agent for her to be morally responsible for it. This idea might profitably be explicated as follows. For an agent to be morally responsible for a decision, she must exercise a certain type and degree of control in making that decision. In an event-causal libertarian picture, the relevant causal conditions antecedent to a decision—agent-involving events—would leave it open whether this decision will occur, and the agent has no further causal role in determining whether it does. With the causal role of these antecedent conditions already given, it remains open whether the decision occurs, and whether it does is not settled by anything about the agent. So whether the decision occurs or not is in this sense a matter of luck, and, intuitively, the agent lacks the control required for taking moral responsibility for the decision.

Libertarians agree that an action's resulting from a deterministic sequence of causes that traces back to factors beyond the agent's control would rule out her moral responsibility for it. The deeper point of this objection is that if this sort of causal determination rules out moral responsibility, then it is no remedy simply to provide slack in the causal net by making the causal history of actions indeterministic. Such a move would yield a requirement for moral responsibility—the absence of causal determinism for decision and action—but it would not supply another—sufficiently enhanced control (Clarke 1997, 2003). In particular, it would not provide the capacity for an agent to be the source of one's decisions and actions that, according to many incompatibilists, is unavailable in a deterministic framework.

The agent-causal libertarian's solution to this problem is to specify a way in which the agent could have this enhanced control, which involves the power to settle which of the antecedently possible decisions actually occurs. The proposed solution is to reintroduce the agent as a cause, this time not merely as involved in events, but rather fundamentally as a substance (for detractors, see Haji 1998; Mele 2006). The agent-causal libertarian maintains that we possess a distinctive causal power—a power for an agent, fundamentally as a substance, to cause a decision without being causally determined to do so. This position might well be incipient in the medieval originators of modern libertarianism, but the Humean objection to indeterministic free will occasioned a more precise formulation. Thomas Reid provides an agent-causal account in direct response to Hume (1788/1983), and arguably, Kant does as well in his account of transcendental freedom (Clarke 2003; Chisholm 1964, 1976; Griffiths 2010; Kant 1797/1963; O'Connor 2000).

One traditional objection to the agent-causal picture is that we have no evidence that we are substances of the requisite sort. Kant expresses two further concerns for the agent-causal view, which in his account calls for our endorsement on practical, but not on evidential, grounds. One is that despite our inability to discern an internal incoherence in our conception of transcendental freedom, our having this power might nonetheless not be really possible. In Kant's view, we can discern something to be really possible only through experience, and we do not experience ourselves as agent causes. The second concern is that agent causation might not be reconcilable with what we would expect given our best empirical theories. Kant himself believed that the physical world, as part of the world of appearance, is governed by deterministic laws, whereas the transcendentally free agent-cause would exist not as an appearance, but as a thing in itself. In this agent-causal picture, when an agent makes a free decision, she causes the decision without being causally determined to do so. On the path to action that results from this undetermined decision, alterations in the physical world, for example, in her brain or some other part of her body, are produced. But it would seem that we would at this point encounter divergences from the deterministic laws. For the alterations in the physical world that result from the undetermined decision would themselves not be causally determined, and they would thus not be governed by deterministic laws. One might object that it is possible that the physical alterations that result from every free decision just happen to dovetail with what could in principle be predicted on the basis of the deterministic laws, so nothing actually occurs that diverges from these laws. However, this proposal would seem to involve coincidences too wild to be credible. For this reason, it seems that agent-causal libertarianism is not reconcilable with the physical world's being governed by deterministic laws. Kant thought that more needed to be said. In one text, he appears to claim that when an agent makes a transcendentally free decision, he, as atemporal noumenal subject, also freely produces everything in the past that causally determines his free actions (1788/1996, Ak 97–98). But this sort of atemporalist line is at best insignificantly more credible than an overt contradiction (Pereboom 2006; Wood 1984).

More recent expositors of the agent-causal view, such as Randolph Clarke (1993, 2003) and Timothy O'Connor (2000, 2009), suggest that quantum indeterminacy can help with the reconciliation project. On one interpretation of quantum mechanics, the physical world is not in fact deterministic, but is rather governed by laws that are fundamentally merely probabilistic or statistical. Suppose, as is controversial, that significant quantum indeterminacy percolates up to the level of human action. Then it might seem that agent-causal libertarianism can be reconciled with the claim that the laws of physics govern at least the physical components of human actions. However, it appears that wild coincidences would also arise on this suggestion (Pereboom 1995, 2001). Consider the class of possible actions, each of which has a physical component whose antecedent probability of occurring is approximately 0.32. It would not violate the statistical laws in the sense of being logically incompatible with them if, for a large number of instances, the physical components in this class were not actually realized close to 32% of the time. Rather, the force of the statistical law is that for a large number of instances, it is correct to *expect* physical components in this class to be realized close to 32% of the time. Are free choices on the agent-causal libertarian model compatible with what the statistical law would lead us to expect about them? If they were, then for a large enough number of instances, the possible actions in our class would almost certainly be freely chosen nearly 32% of the time. But if the occurrence of these physical components were settled by the choices of agent-causes, then their actually being chosen close to 32% of the time would also amount to a wild coincidence. The proposal that agent-caused free choices do not diverge from what the statistical laws predict for the physical components of our actions would be so sharply opposed to what we would expect as to make it incredible.

At this point, the agent-causal libertarian might propose that exercises of agent-causal libertarian freedom do result in divergences from what we would expect given our best assessments of the physical laws. Roderick Chisholm (1964) proposes such a view. Divergences from the probabilities that we would expect absent agent-causes do in fact occur whenever we act freely, and these divergences are located at the interface between the agent-cause and that part of the physical world that it directly affects, likely to be found in the brain. There are different ways in which agent-caused free choices might diverge from what the laws would predict. One way is by not being subject to laws at all. Another is by being subject to different statistical laws, an option on which the agent-cause would be governed by probabilistic laws that are its own because they emerge only in the right sorts of agential contexts, and not to those that generally govern the physical events of the universe (O'Connor 2008). A concern for these kinds of claims is that we currently have no evidence that they are true.

THE FREE WILL SKEPTIC AND COMPATIBILISM

We human beings typically assume that we can be, and often are, morally responsible for our actions in the basic desert sense, and this assumption is manifest in the uncompromised sense of legitimacy that often accompanies the basic desert involving reactive attitudes. But in everyday life, we seldom, if ever, bring to bear on this assumption any theory about the general causal nature of the universe that might threaten its rationality, even if we know that such a theory is likely to be true. For example, in ordinary life, most of us do not question the rationality of this assumption on the basis of the theory that every event, including our choices and actions, results from deterministic causal processes that trace back to a time before we existed; or on the basis of the theory that if this sort of determinism is false, only event-causal indeterminism is likely to be true. Spinoza held that the fact that the complete causal story of our actions is hidden from us accounts for our belief that we are free; "men think themselves free, because they are conscious of their volitions and their appetite, and do not think, even in their dreams, of the causes by which they are disposed to wanting and willing, because they are ignorant of [those causes]" (Spinoza 1677/1985, 440). But he contends that full rationality demands a change in view, the rational integration of the justified claim that all of our actions are deterministically caused requires that we relinquish the belief that we are free in the sense at issue. By contrast, compatibilists, such as Morse, Strawson, and Fischer, hold that the rational response is to retain our everyday assumption that we are free in the sense required for basic desert, together with the attitudes and practices that are founded on this assumption.

How might this disagreement between the free will skeptic (and incompatibilists more generally) and the compatibilist be mediated? I think that the best way for the skeptic to try to do so begins with the intuition that if an agent is causally determined to act by, for example, scientists who manipulate her brain, then she is not morally responsible for that action, even if she meets compatibilist conditions on moral responsibility (Ginet 1990; Kane 1996; Mele 1995, 2006; Pereboom 1995, 2001; Taylor 1974; van Inwagen 1983). The subsequent step is that there are no differences between the manipulated agents and their ordinary deterministic counterparts that can justify the claim that the manipulated agents are not morally responsible while the determined agents are.

My multiple-case version of such an argument first of all develops examples of an action that results from an appropriate sort of manipulation and in which the prominent compatibilist conditions on moral responsibility are satisfied (Pereboom 1995, 2001, 2011). In the setup, in each of the four cases the agent commits a crime, say a homicide, for the sake of some personal advantage. The cases are designed so that the crime conforms to the prominent compatibilist conditions. This action meets certain conditions advocated by Hume: the action is not out of character because for the agent, it is generally true that selfish reasons typically weigh heavily—too heavily when considered from the moral point of view; and in addition, the desire that motivates him to act is nevertheless not irresistible for him, and in this sense he is not constrained to act (Hume 1739/1978). The action fits the condition proposed by Harry Frankfurt (1971), that is, his effective desire (i.e., his will) to commit the crime conforms appropriately to his second-order desires for which effective desires he will have. That is, he wills to kill the victim, and he wants to will to do so, and he wills this act of murder because he wants to will to do so. The action also satisfies the reasons-responsiveness condition advocated by John Fischer and Mark Ravizza (1998): our agent's desires can be modified by, and some of them arise from, his rational consideration of the reasons he has, and if he knew that the bad consequences for himself that would result from the crime would be much more severe than they are actually likely to be, he would have refrained from committing the crime for that reason. This action meets the condition advanced by Jay Wallace (1994): the agent has the general ability to grasp, apply, and regulate his actions by moral reasons. For instance, when egoistic reasons that count against acting morally are weak, he will typically regulate his behavior by moral reasons instead (further advocates of views that privilege reasons and rationality include Bok 1998; Nelkin 2008, 2011; and Wolf 1990). This ability also provides him with the capacity to revise and develop his moral character over time, a condition that Alfred Mele emphasizes (1995, 2006).

These manipulation examples, taken separately, indicate that it is possible for an agent not to be morally responsible in the basic desert sense even if the compatibilist conditions are met and that, as a result, these conditions are insufficient. But the argument has additional force by virtue of setting out three such cases, each of which is progressively more like a fourth, in which the action is causally determined in a natural way. The first case involves manipulation that is local and determining, and hence very likely to elicit the nonresponsibility intuition. The second is like the first, except it restricts manipulation to a remote position at the beginning of the agent's life. The third is similar, except the manipulation results from strict community upbringing; and the fourth, again, is the ordinary deterministic case. The aim is to formulate these examples so that it is not possible to draw a principled line between any two adjacent cases that would explain why the agent would not be morally responsible in the basic desert sense in the first but would be in the second. The conclusion is that the agent is not morally responsible in this sense in all four cases, and the best explanation for this must be that he is causally determined by factors beyond his control in each, and this result conflicts with the compatibilist's central claim.

Strawson contends that features of the practice of holding morally responsible insulate attributions of moral responsibility from scientific or metaphysical challenges such as the one based on causal determinism (1962). And Morse, although he acknowledges that the skeptical view "can produce an internally coherent, forward-looking consequential system that treats human action specially and that might possibly encourage good behavior and discourage bad," claims that it "cannot explain or justify our present blame and punishment practices, which are essentially retrospectively evaluative," and in particular, it "cannot explain or justify the relation between action and desert" (cf. Alexander, Ferzan, and Morse 2009: 13-15; Morse 2004: 433). In the last analysis, these compatibilists want to claim that free will skepticism is to be rejected because it does not cohere with our practice of holding responsible. In my view, the best sort of argument against this position involves what Wallace calls a generalization strategy—arguing from generally accepted excuses or exemptions to the conclusion that causal determinism rules out moral responsibility (Wallace 1994). The excuses and exemptions that form the basis of this sort of argument would have to be generally accepted (but perhaps not uncontested) so that they are plausibly features internal to the practice of holding people morally responsible. The kinds of exemptions that I exploit in the four-case argument are due to deterministic manipulation, and it is a feature of our practice that we exempt agents from moral responsibility in the basic desert sense when they are manipulated in this way, as in the local and remote manipulation examples. It is also a feature of our practice that if no morally relevant difference can be found between agents in two situations, then if one agent is legitimately exempted from moral responsibility in this sense, so is the other. No morally relevant difference can be found between agents in the manipulation examples and agents in ordinary deterministic situations such as the final case. Thus, it is the practice itself—in particular, key rules governing the practice—that renders moral responsibility in the sense at issue vulnerable to causal determinism. Each of these rules is a component of our notion of fairness, and accordingly I dispute Morse's claim that "we currently adhere to no principle of fairness that is related to the truth or falsity of determinism" (2004: 442).

Morse follows Fischer and Wallace in making responsiveness to reasons, and to moral reasons in particular, the core requirement for moral responsibility (Morse 2004). But what it is about reasons-responsive action that justifies the ascription of basic desert and, as Fischer and Wallace maintain, justifies the reactive attitudes that presuppose this notion of responsibility (Fischer 2007; Wallace 1994)? Although it may be natural for us to respond to reasons-responsive actions with reactive attitudes, and for us to refrain from or withdraw such responses when actions fail to meet this standard, it is a further task to show that the reasons responsiveness of an action legitimates the attribution of basic desert moral responsibility and the attitudes that presuppose it. By contrast, the "answerability" or "fittingness of providing an explanation" notion of moral responsibility, which the free will skeptic can endorse, is transparently connected to the notion of reasons responsiveness.

RETRIBUTIVISM

According to the retributivist position, punishment of a wrongdoer is justified for the reason that he deserves something bad to happen to him—pain, deprivation, or death, for example—just because he has done wrong (Kant 1797/1963; Moore 1987, 1998). Hence, a wrongdoer's deserving to be harmed is not reducible to a component of a scheme justified solely on the basis of its consequences. This claim is typically subjected to qualifications such as that the agent had to have committed the wrong knowingly. But what is crucial to the free will skeptic's challenge is that according to the retributivist, it is the basic desert attached to the criminal's immoral action alone that provides the justification for punishment. The retribution theory does not appeal to a good such as the safety of society, or the moral improvement of the criminal in justifying punishment. Rather, the good by means of which retributivism justifies punishment, or the principle of right action that justifies punishment, is that an agent receive what he deserves just because of his having knowingly done wrong.

This position would be undermined if the free will skeptic were right because if agents do not deserve blame just because they have knowingly done wrong, neither do they deserve punishment just because they have knowingly done wrong. Retributivism justifies punishment solely on the grounds of basic desert, and the skeptical position is incompatible with retributivism for the reason that it claims this notion does not apply to us. Free will skepticism thus recommends that the retributivist justification for punishment be abandoned.[4]

Morse argues that libertarianism is not plausible, and of the remaining options, we should reject free will skepticism and accept compatibilism because of these only compatibilism is consonant with our practice. Significantly, he does so without offering replies to the objections that have been raised against this position. Morse is right to assert that given the rejection of libertarianism, only compatibilism would underwrite the uncompromised legitimacy of the reactive attitudes and retributivistically justified punishment. But can retributivism be adequately grounded in compatibilism in this way absent satisfying responses to the objections that compatibilism faces? Consider, for example, the last murderer remaining in prison in Kant's imagined island society that is about to dissolve itself (in the Metaphysical Elements of Justice, a section of Kant's *Metaphysics of Morals*). Kant strenuously advocates that he should be

4. Erin Kelly (2009: 446) expresses a similar idea without endorsing free will skepticism: "Retributivism, as I understand it, is the view that justice requires the punishment of criminal wrongdoers, apart from the (further) social benefits a system of punishment might bring. The case for this notion of justice is built on reactive attitudes that presuppose a wrongdoer's moral capacity to have acted as morality demands. If we drop the assumption that offenders always have this capacity, we must reevaluate the aims of punishment."

executed, just because of the crime he has committed, that is, for reasons of retributive desert alone (1797/1963, Ak VI 331-333). But imagine the offender protesting that he was determined by natural causes to act as he did, and this plausibly undercuts the claim that he is morally responsible in the basic desert sense. Would the following reply count as morally acceptable? "Our practice of punishing criminals for retributivist reasons requires the assumption that we are morally responsible in the basic desert sense, and we need to believe that our being free in the way required for our having this kind of responsibility is compatible with determinism in order to rationally maintain this assumption." It would not. If the retributivist justification of punishment featured by our actual practice requires the rationality of the belief that compatibilism is true, while at the same time there are serious and unanswered objections to this position, we cannot legitimately respond to a challenge to this part of the practice just by saying that it is supported by compatibilism. Punishment inflicts harm, and in general, justification for harm must meet a high epistemic standard. If it is significantly probable that one's justification for harming another is unsound, then prima facie that behavior is seriously wrong, and one must refrain from engaging in it. A strong and credible response to the objections to compatibilism is required to meet this standard.

One might suppose that setting aside the free will skeptic's challenge, retributivism would provide a resilient and powerful justification for punishment. However, there are substantial arguments for the claim that retributivism turns out to be unacceptable even disregarding the skeptic's considerations (e.g., Braithwaite and Pettit, 1990, 156-201; Montague 1995, 11-23, 80-90; Ten 1990, 38-65). Perhaps the deepest problem for this theory derives from the hypothesis that the intuitions that drive the retributivist position are at root fueled by vengeful desires, and that therefore retribution has little more plausibility than vengeance as a morally sound policy for action (Moore 1987). Acting on vengeful desires might be wrong for the following sort of reason. Although acting on such desires can bring about pleasure or satisfaction, no more of a moral case can be made for of acting on them than can be made for acting on sadistic desires, for example. Acting on sadistic desires can bring about pleasure, but in both cases, acting on the desire aims at the harm of the one to whom the action is directed, and in neither case does acting on the desire essentially aim at any good other than the pleasure of its satisfaction. But then, according to the objection, because retributivist intuitions have their source in vengeful desires, acting for the sake of retribution is also morally wrong.

One counterstrategy involves pointing out salient differences between vengeance and retribution. For example, by contrast with vengeance, retribution is in principle limited in its severity, and although vengeance often engenders further vengeance, retribution brings about closure. But one might reply that because what fuels retributivist intuitions are vengeful desires, retributivistically justified punishment would at root amount to a form of controlled vengeance. Another retributivist response is that in central cases, the sentiment of vengeance is an emotional expression of the sense of retributivist justice.[5] In such cases, the sense of retributivist justice is explanatorily before the sentiment of vengeance, and thus if retribution has an independent justification, then it might well not be threatened by the objection from vengeance. But these responses on behalf of the retributivist are not sufficiently convincing for the view to attain the high epistemic standard that a theory of punishment must meet.

In addition, it is not clear that there are strong positive reasons for maintaining that retributivist justification for punishment reflects a genuine moral good, or, on a view in which the right is prior to the good, that it reflects an authentic principle of right. When Kant introduces his retributivist justification of punishment in the Metaphysical Elements of Justice (1797/1963), no apparent link is forged with the comprehensive moral theory expressed in the various formulations of the categorical imperative. Does treating humanity in persons as an end in itself require that we consider each other as subject to punishment retributivistically justified? Will legislation for a kingdom of ends by a community of rational beings invoke retributivist justification? Far from obviously so. Add to this the fact that purely consequentialist or contractualist views will not accommodate this sort of justification and at best can only secure a weaker facsimile.

Lastly, supposing that the requisite capacity for control is in place and that basic desert could be secured as good or right, we can ask whether the state has the right to invoke it in justifying punishment. The legitimate functions of the state are generally held to include protecting its citizens from significant harm and providing a framework for human interaction to proceed without significant impairment. These roles arguably underwrite justification that in the first instance appeals to prevention of crime. But these roles have no immediate connection to the aim of apportioning punishment in accord with basic desert. The concern can be made vivid by considering the proposal that the state set up a well-funded set of institutions designed to comprehensively and fairly distribute rewards on the grounds of basic desert (cf. Husak 2000: 973-974). Political theories that would demand that the state provide such institutions are not widely held. In addition, as Douglas Husak (2000: 974-975) argues against Moore (1998), a state institution designed to give criminals what they deserve is extremely expensive, its benefits do not obviously outweigh its costs, and these resources might be spent on more valuable programs. And as human

5. George Sher once made this suggestion in conversation.

history demonstrates, such an institution is subject to grave and frequent error or abuse, which gives rise to a tremendous amount of unmerited suffering.

If the skeptic's challenge were a good one, then the retributivist justification for punishment would be undermined. But there are independent moral and political grounds for rejecting a retributivist theory of punishment. These other arguments against retributivism adduce moral and political considerations uncontroversially internal to the practice of holding morally responsible. We have already seen that despite initial appearances, close examination indicates that the considerations on which the free will skeptic's case against compatibilism is based are internal to the practice. Now it is also clear that the justification of punishment that the skeptic's challenge targets was already under threat by arguments that are uncontroversially internal. Thus, in taking aim at retributivism, the free will skeptic is not opposing a view that is otherwise free from uncontroversially internal opposition.

MORAL EDUCATION THEORY

There are further ways of justifying criminal punishment that do not appeal to a notion of basic desert, and thus they may not run afoul of free will skepticism specifically. Moral education theories typically draw an analogy to the justification of the punishment of children. Children are not typically punished to exact retribution, but rather to educate them morally. Because moral education is a generally acceptable goal, a justification for criminal punishment based on this analogy is one the free will skeptic can potentially accept.

In developing their views, advocates of the moral education theory have proposed specific ways in which punishment or threat of punishment could serve to educate a child. Herbert Morris argues that punishment educates a child morally by apprising her of the consequences of her wrongdoing for herself and for others. To use his example, if a child cheats, a parent might exclude her from playing the game for a time, thereby making vivid to her the possible game-undermining consequences of cheating for both herself and others (Morris 1981: 160). Similarly, Jean Hampton proposes that a wrongdoer might be "made to endure an unpleasant experience designed, in some sense, to "represent" the pain suffered by her victim(s)" (Hampton 1984: 227). Hampton also contends that punishment can morally educate a child by conveying to him the degree of seriousness of the wrongdoing (1984: 225-226). Different levels of severity can communicate distinct levels of seriousness of wrongdoing and, and partly in consequence of this, they can convey important moral boundaries. A further way, which Morris also points out, is that punishment can indicate the strength of the parents' attachment to the moral rules that have been breached. Finally, one might argue that coercing a child into behaving in accord with morality could serve to acquaint him with the benefits of moral virtue, which he might subsequently come to value for its own sake.

A serious concern for this type of theory is that it is far from evident that punishing adult criminals is likely to result in these sorts of moral improvement. Children and adult criminals differ in several salient respects. Adult criminals, unlike children, typically understand the moral code accepted in their society. Contrary to Hampton's view in particular, one could not justify punishment on the ground that it would convey to these criminals that their actions are morally wrong, and to communicate to them "that there is a barrier of a very special sort against these kinds of actions." There are indeed adult criminals who do not comprehend that their actions are morally wrong, but we are disposed not to punish them for reasons of incompetence. In fact, in many contemporary jurisdictions, it is specifically when a criminal does not know that his actions are morally wrong that he is judged not liable to punishment.

One might instead claim that punishment is nonetheless likely to significantly motivate criminals to improve morally. But relevant differences between children and adult criminals also threaten this proposal. Children are generally more psychologically malleable than adult criminals. For a more contingent difference, punishment that has the best prospect for morally educating children would transpire in a caring environment. Punishment outside of such a context is much more likely to engender resentful attitudes and behavior rather than motivation to moral improvement. Here, the analogy between children and adult criminals is again weak in salient respects, and as a consequence, the claim that punishment can result in such motivation in the case of criminals is insufficiently plausible.

Because criminals differ in significant ways from the sorts of agents for whom the success of punishment in producing moral education might be reasonably thought to have been established, strong empirical evidence that criminals could be similarly educated would be required. Without such evidence, it would be morally wrong to punish criminals for the reason that it can attain such an outcome. In general, if one proposes to harm someone to achieve a salutary result, one must have strong evidence that harming her can have this effect.

Hampton proposes specific ways in which punishment might realize the moral education of a criminal:

> One way the moral education theorist can set punishments for crimes is to think about "fit." Irrespective of how severe a particular crime is, there will sometimes be a punishments that seems naturally suited to it; for example, giving a certain youth charged with burglarizing and stealing money from a neighbor's house the punishment of supervised compulsory service to this neighbor for a period of time, or giving a doctor charged with cheating a

government medical insurance program the punishment of compulsory unremunerated service in a state medical institution. (Hampton 1984: 227-228)

But service requirements of the kind Hampton suggests are not paradigmatic kinds of punishment. One might reasonably question whether they should be classified as punishment at all, and not instead as programs for moral rehabilitation. Hampton might respond that these kinds of service include a punitive aspect—the restriction of a criminal's freedom (1984: 224). And such a program might often involve psychological discomfort or even anguish. Still, compulsory rehabilitative programs also involve restriction of freedom and will often feature psychological pain.

Moreover, what might it be about a service requirement that would plausibly yield moral improvement? Could it be the punitive aspect—the restriction of freedom or the pain of carrying out the service? More likely, what would produce salutary moral change is involvement with the people or the kinds of people the criminal has harmed. The restriction of freedom and the pain of service that such a program involves are best seen as a side effect of the method, and not its goal or its means. This is a further reason for viewing such approaches as programs for moral rehabilitation rather than as cases in which punishment morally educates.

Suppose we had strong evidence that punishment can morally educate criminals. Even then, if there are nonpunitive methods for achieving comparable moral education, they should be preferred, all else being equal. If, for example, a criminal can be effectively morally educated through a humane rehabilitative program, then that method should be favored over a punitive alternative that would realize the same result. By analogy, if a neurophysiological problem such as insufficient serotonin production explains an agent's lack of moral motivation, then effective drug therapy should be preferred to a regimen of punishment that would achieve the same goals. All else being equal, if two methods achieve the same goal for an agent, but one harms an agent whereas the other does not, the one that does not harm the agent should be preferred.

DETERRENCE THEORIES

One objective that societies have in punishing criminals is to prevent them as well as other prospective criminals from committing crimes. On deterrence theories it is the prevention of criminal wrongdoing that serves as the good by means of which punishment is justified. Initially, it would seem that there is no feature of skepticism about free will that makes deterrence theories less acceptable to it than to libertarianism or to compatibilism. As we shall see, however, at least some deterrence theories are not clearly immune to the skeptic's challenge because they presuppose a retributive principle. Furthermore, like retributivism, deterrence justifications of paradigmatic sorts of punishment face difficult objections that are independent of skepticism about free will.

The classic deterrence theory is Jeremy Bentham's. In his conception, the state's policy toward criminal behavior should aim at maximizing utility, and punishment should be administered if and only if it does so. The pain or unhappiness produced by punishment results from the restriction on freedom that ensues from the threat of punishment, the anticipation of punishment by the person who has been sentenced, the pain of actual punishment, and the sympathetic pain felt by others such as the friends and family of the criminal (Bentham 1823/1948). The most significant pleasure or happiness that results from punishment derives from the security of those who benefit from its capacity to deter both the criminal and other potential criminals. No feature of the free will skeptic's position, specifically, challenges this view.

Several more general objections, however, have been raised against the utilitarian deterrence theory (Montague 1995, 6-11; Ten 1987, 7-37). Three of these objections are especially threatening. The first is that this approach will justify punishments that are intuitively too severe. For it would seem that in certain cases, extremely harsh punishments would be more effective deterrents than much milder forms, whereas such punishments are intuitively too severe to be fair. For example, if society is threatened by a crime wave, administering penalties of this sort might well maximize utility. The utilitarian could reply that if we are careful to include the pain of punishment in the calculation, the resulting severity will typically or always be intuitively unacceptable. He might also claim that in certain uncommonly dangerous situations, extremely severe penalties might indeed be justified. But nevertheless, one might reasonably fear that utilitarian recommendations will often fail to conform to our intuitions about fairness.

Second, the theory would seem to justify punishing the innocent (McCloskey 1965). If after a series of horrible crimes, the actual perpetrator is not caught, potential criminals might come to believe that they can get away with serious wrongdoing. Under such circumstances, it might maximize utility to frame and punish an innocent person. Utilitarians might reply that the probability of such a scheme being discovered is always significant and that, as a result, punishing the innocent is unlikely to maximize utility in any situation. However, it is far from obvious that this response is convincing. John Rawls offers a different response on behalf of the utilitarian. There exist good utilitarian reasons for a punishment policy to be general, stable, and public, in short, to be institutionalized. Consequently, there will be solid utilitarian reasons against deceptively punishing the innocent (Rawls 1955).[6] As a matter of practical fact, it is doubtful that a general, stable, and public scheme that would allow deceptively punishing the innocent could achieve the envisioned maximization of utility. Rather, an institution of this sort could easily engender massive disutility in society. A worry about Rawls's reply is that this practice would seem to be more deeply wrong than can be accounted for by the utilitarian reasons he presents.

A further serious misgiving raised against utilitarian deterrence theory is the "use" objection. A general problem for utilitarianism is that it allows people to be harmed severely, without their consent, in order to benefit others, and this is often intuitively wrong. Punishing criminals for the security of society would appear to be just such a practice. Even if this problem fails to undermine utilitarian deterrence theory decisively, it should challenge one's confidence in this approach. Again, in assessing justifications for punishment, it is crucial that for a theory to be legitimately applicable in practice, we must be reasonably confident that it can withstand the objections that have been raised against it. Criminal punishment involves treating people severely—often it has very harmful short- and long-term consequences for the person being punished. If we were only mildly confident about the justification for such punishment, it would be morally wrong to administer it. Thus, we have solid reasons not to employ the classic utilitarian deterrence theory in justifying actual punishment policy—whether or not the free will skeptic is right.

At this point, one might combine retributivism and utilitarianism and argue that there is a retributivist justification for the legitimacy of using criminals for the good of society more generally. I suspect that many who think that the main point of punishment is deterrence are relying on a retributivist assumption of this sort. But if the skeptic is right, such a view is unavailable, and, as we have seen, there are other moral and political reasons to question retributivism.

PUNISHMENT JUSTIFIED BY THE RIGHT TO HARM IN SELF-DEFENSE

In my view, the free will skeptic should invoke the right to self defense and defense of others in justifying its policy for treatment of criminals. I don't think

6. Rawls writes about an institution, "telishment," that would allow for punishing the innocent. Once one realizes that one is involved in setting up an *institution*, one sees that the hazards are very great. For example, what check is there on the officials? How is one to tell whether their actions are authorized? How is one to limit the risks involved in allowing such systematic deception? How is one to avoid giving anything short of complete discretion to the authorities to telish anyone they like? In addition to these considerations, it is obvious that people will come to have a very different attitude toward their penal system when telishment is adjoined to it. They will be uncertain as to whether a convicted man has been punished or telished. They

that the skeptic should aim to justify punishment by appealing to this right, but rather, for the most dangerous criminals, should aim for a policy of detention modeled on quarantine. Several theorists, however, have argued that it is indeed punishment that might be justified on such grounds. Daniel Farrell offers one of the finest developments of a theory of this sort (Farrell 1985; Kelly 2009; cf. Quinn 1985). Farrell's theory is impressive if only because it justifies punishment on grounds that are widely accepted.[7] Because the free will skeptic can also endorse the right to harm in self-defense and defense of others, even she may aspire to accepting a justification of punishment of the kind that Farrell develops. But as we shall see, again, there are reasons independent of the skeptic's position to doubt the soundness of this type of view.

Farrell's account highlights the distinction between special deterrence—punishment aimed at preventing the criminal from engaging in criminal behavior, and general deterrence—punishment aimed at preventing agents other than the targeted criminal from doing so. In his view, special deterrence is significantly easier to ground in the right to harm in self-defense or defense of others than is general deterrence. Farrell also distinguishes between the right of *direct* self-defense, your right to harm an unjust aggressor to prevent him from harming you or someone else, and the right of *indirect* self-defense, your right to threaten an unjust aggressor with a reasonable amount of harm to prevent him from harming you or someone else.

In broad outline, Farrell's justification of punishment as special deterrence is this. Each of us has the right of direct self-defense, and each of us also has the right of indirect self-defense. Because we have the right of direct self-defense, we have the right to inflict a reasonable amount of harm on a potential unjust aggressor to prevent him from harming us. Because we have the right of indirect self-defense, we also have the right to threaten to inflict this amount of harm. Our right of direct self-defense permits us carry out this threat against him once the condition has been violated. But also, because we have these rights, the state, acting as proxy for us, may issue appropriate general threats to harm

will wonder whether or not they should feel sorry for him. They will wonder whether the same fate won't at any time fall on them. If one pictures how such an institution would actually work, and the enormous risks involved in it, it seems clear that it would serve no useful purpose. A utilitarian justification for this institution is most unlikely (Rawls 1955, 3–32).

7. Warren Quinn's theory is similar, but differs from Farrell's in the following way (Quinn 1985). Although Farrell contends that it is legitimate to threaten to harm an aggressor in certain circumstances because one may harm him in those circumstances, Quinn argues that one may harm him just because one may threaten to harm him. Accordingly, Quinn aims to establish that punishing criminals is legitimate because threatening to punish them is legitimate. Kelly (2009: 447–448) endorses Farrell's justification.

unjust aggressors, and may also carry out such threats once their conditions have been violated. In this way, the right to self-defense can ground a legitimate state institution of punishment as special deterrence.

This special deterrence theory avoids some of the key objections to its utilitarian counterpart. On the concern for justifying punishment that is intuitively too severe, one may not, on grounds of indirect self-defense, issue a threat to inflict harm more severe than the minimum required to effectively deter the target crime. So, if a threat of 1 year in prison would be sufficient to deter auto theft, the state may not issue a threat of a 10-year term. On the concern for punishing the innocent, the right to self-defense justifies harming only unjust aggressors themselves. For instance, the right does not justify harming an unjust aggressor's innocent children even if this would deter him.

At the same time, harming an unjust aggressor in self-defense or defense of others does involve harming him, without his consent, for the benefit of persons other than himself, and this arguably would count as an instance of using him as a means to the benefit of others. Perhaps this is a legitimate kind of use because its target brings it upon himself by his unjust aggression. But this suggestion might seem to invoke the notion of basic desert. Significantly, Farrell argues that the right of self-defense assumes a type of retributivism, albeit a weak form. In his view, underlying the right to direct and indirect self-defense, and thus also special deterrence on his account, is a "weakly retributive" principle of distributive justice:

> If an aggressor forces one to make a choice between harming the aggressor or allowing him/herself or others to be harmed, then one may harm the aggressor to the degree that preventing the harm to oneself or others requires (Farrell 1985).

(Farrell plausibly contends that this principle applies only within bounds—if the harm threatened is minor, but killing the aggressor would be required to prevent it, then killing the aggressor is wrong.) If this principle is in fact retributive, and thereby presupposes basic desert, and it does indeed underlie the right to self-defense, it would appear that the arguments for the skeptical position imperil this right and a theory of punishment on which it is based. However, it is not correct, I think, to call this principle "retributive" if in doing so basic desert is invoked. For this principle and the right to harm in self-defense more generally very plausibly apply to aggressors who are not morally responsible in the basic desert sense, such as people who have been brainwashed, those who are significantly mentally impaired, and animals.

Now the "use" problem arises again—isn't the aggressor who threatens to seriously injure me whom I then harm in self-defense being used merely as a means to secure my own safety? I think the answer is affirmative, but that in such cases, if the harm inflicted is the minimal amount reasonably required to prevent the serious injury, the force of the "use" objection is outweighed by the right to harm in self-defense. Farrell contends that the type of theory he proposes will not extend to full-fledged general deterrence, for this would involve harming someone to prevent not just his aggression but also the potential aggression of others, and this gives rise to a convincing "use" objection. Yet he argues that some general deterrence can be justified on the basis of his principle of distributive justice. When an agent wrongs you in such a way as to make you more vulnerable than you would otherwise be to the aggression of others, then you are justified in countering just this degree of added vulnerability by harming him. My sense is that, in such cases, the force of the "use" concern is plausibly outweighed by the right to harm in self-defense, by contrast with a practice of full-fledged general deterrence.

Thus, so far it seems that Farrell has proposed a justification for criminal punishment that the free will skeptic can endorse. And I do accept it in its essentials. The concern I have is whether for dangerous violent criminals, Farrell's line of reasoning can justify punishment, by contrast with preventative detention. What makes it appear as if punishment can be justified in this way is, I think, the model of an unjust aggressor in a situation in which state law enforcement and criminal justice agencies have no role—let's call it a "state of nature" situation. A state of nature situation in which an aggressor poses an immediate danger is very different from the circumstances of criminals in our society when state punishment is carried out. They are then in the custody of the law. And the kinds of harms that the right of self-defense justifies in the case of aggressors in the state of nature differ in kind from those that this right would justify for those in the custody of the law.

An analogy will help show why it is wrong to carry out a threat against a criminal in custody that would legitimately be carried out in circumstances in which he poses an immediate danger. Threats that can legitimately be carried out against an immediately dangerous potential aggressor specify what one would reasonably believe to be the minimum harm required to prevent his aggression. Suppose that someone clearly aims to kill you, and that to prevent his doing so you may knock him out with a baseball bat. It would then be permissible for you to threaten him with this amount of harm. Suppose he does attempt to kill you, but in the process he trips over the toys on the floor, and this allows you to pin him to the ground and tie him up. At this point is it still legitimate for you to knock him out with the bat? To do so would clearly be wrong, and not justified by the right to harm in self-defense. For this right justifies only what one would reasonably believe to be the minimum harm required to prevent what the aggressor threatens to inflict. Or suppose the aggressor clearly aims to kill your companion, and that to protect her it is legitimate for you to knock him out with the bat and threaten to do so. Suppose that despite your efforts, he kills her, but that subsequently he trips and you tie him up. Is it then legitimate for you to knock him out with the bat? Not on the basis of the right to harm in self-defense and defense of others because he no longer poses an immediate threat. You retain the right to protect yourself and others against him, but not by carrying out the threat designed to prevent a harm that has already occurred.

So, then, a threat that one could justifiably make and carry out to protect against an aggressor in a state-of-nature situation cannot legitimately be carried out in a situation in which the aggressor is in custody. The reason for this is clear. The minimum harm required to protect ourselves from someone who is immediately dangerous in a state-of-nature situation is typically much more severe than the minimum harm required for protection against a criminal in custody. If our justification is the right to harm in self-defense, what we can legitimately do to a criminal in custody to protect ourselves against him is determined by the minimum required to protect ourselves against him in his actual situation. If one proposed to harm him more severely, for instance, to provide credibility for a system of threats, the right to harm in self-defense would not supply the requisite justification, and one would again be in danger of endorsing a position subject to the "use" objection.

What is the minimum harm required to protect ourselves from a violent and dangerous criminal in custody? It seems evident that nothing more severe would be required than isolating him from those to whom he poses a threat. Thus, it would appear that Farrell's reasoning cannot justify *punishment* of criminals, exactly, supposing that punishment involves the intentional infliction of significant harm, such as death or severe physical or psychological suffering. Rather in the case of violent and dangerous criminals, this reasoning would at best justify only preventative detention.

AN INCAPACITATION ACCOUNT

A more resilient proposal for treatment of dangerous criminals than either the moral education or deterrence theories, and one that is compatible with free will skepticism, invokes our right to defend ourselves and to secure our safety, but employs the analogy to quarantine. Ferdinand Schoeman has argued that if protection of society justifies quarantining carriers of severe communicable diseases, then it also justifies isolation of the criminally dangerous (Schoeman 1979). Suppose an agent poses a danger to society by a demonstrably strong tendency to commit murder. Even if he is not in general a morally responsible agent in the basic desert sense, the state would nevertheless seem to have as much right to isolate him as it does to quarantine a carrier of a deadly communicable disease who is not responsible in this sense for being a carrier. The concern about using people merely as means has force in this context, and this together with the weight of the general right to liberty should restrict preventative detention to especially dangerous cases. Crucially, these countervailing factors count more heavily against punishment policy justified on consequentialist grounds than it does against preventative detention based on the quarantine analogy. For on the quarantine view, just as it is morally wrong to treat carriers of a disease more severely than is necessary to keep them from being dangerous to society, it will be wrong to treat those with violent criminal tendencies more harshly than is required to keep them from being a danger to society. Furthermore, the less dangerous the disease, the less invasive the legitimate prevention methods would be; and similarly, the less dangerous the criminal, the less invasive the legitimate methods of incapacitation would be. For certain minor crimes, perhaps only some degree of monitoring could be defended.

Schoeman explores the acceptability of preventative detention for those who have not yet committed crimes, reflection on which occasions the following concern for this incapacitation account. If justification of detention by this analogy is tenable, must it not then be legitimate to detain those who have not committed a violent crime, if by some means it has been ascertained that they are likely to do so? Schoeman contends, and I agree, that the right to liberty must carry weight in this context, as should the concern about using people merely as means. In addition, the risk posed by a state policy that allows for preventative detention of nonoffenders needs to be taken into serious consideration. In a broad range of societies, allowing the state this option stands to result in much more harm than good because misuse would be likely. Schoeman also argues that although the kinds of testing required to determine whether someone is a carrier of a communicable disease may often not be unacceptably invasive, the type of screening necessary for determining whether an agent has violent criminal tendencies might well be invasive in ways that raise serious moral difficulties. Moreover, available psychiatric methods for discerning whether an agent is likely to be a violent criminal are not especially reliable, and as Morse points out, detaining someone on the basis of a screening method that frequently yields false positives is seriously objectionable (Morse 1999; Nadelhoffer et al., 2012).

However, there is reason to think that impressive neural methods of testing for violent tendencies are being developed (Nadelhoffer et al., 2012). The time may come soon when we are able to determine with reasonable accuracy on the basis of neural factors that an agent is likely to commit violent crimes in his normal environment. Wouldn't an account based on the quarantine analogy endorse preventative detention even if the agent had not yet manifested such violence, supposing the violence would be very serious and highly likely in his normal environment, and less invasive measures such as effective monitoring or drug therapy were unavailable? Perhaps it would. But this should not count as a strong objection to this incapacitation account because virtually everyone should agree that preventative detention of nonoffenders would be legitimate under some possible conditions. Imagine that an agent has involuntarily been given a drug that makes it virtually certain he will brutally murder at least one person while he is under its influence, which is for a period of 1 week. There is no known antidote, and because he is especially strong, mere monitoring would be ineffective. I daresay almost everyone would affirm that it would be at least prima facie permissible to preventatively detain him for the week. If you agree, then in principle you accept that preventatively detaining nonoffenders is legitimate under some possible circumstances. Now suppose that reliable neural screening reveals that an agent, if left in his normal environment, is virtually certain to murder at least one person within the next 5 years. There is no known viable drug therapy, and mere monitoring would be ineffective. Whether detaining this agent is also prima facie legitimate might be judged by how similar his case is to that of the drug victim. And it might well be similar enough. Here, it is important to understand that the advocate of the incapacitation account will specify that the circumstances of such detention should not be harsh, and that allowing the agent to be reasonably comfortable and to pursue fulfilling projects must be given high priority. But at the same time, in many societies, the danger of a state policy that allows for preventative detention of even highly dangerous nonoffenders is a grave concern that stands to outweigh the value of the safety provided by such a policy.[8]

When a person with cholera is quarantined, she is typically made to experience deprivation she does not deserve. Society benefits by this deprivation. It is plausibly a matter of fairness that society should do what it can, within reasonable bounds, to make the victim safe for release as quickly as possible. If we quarantined cholera victims but were unwilling to provide medical care for them because it would require a modest increase in taxation, then we would be acting unfairly. Similarly, when a dangerous agent, whether or not he has already committed crimes, is preventatively detained, then supposing that the free will skeptic is right, he is also made to experience a deprivation he does not fundamentally deserve, and from which society benefits. By analogy with the cholera case, here also it is a matter of fairness for us to do what we can, within reasonable bounds, to make him safe for release. For a society or state to oppose

8. For additional discussion of objections to the quarantine analogy, see Pereboom 2001: 174–177.

programs for rehabilitation because it is unwilling to fund them would involve serious unfairness.

Policies for making an agent safe for release would address conditions that underlie actual or potential criminal behavior. These conditions include psychological illness, but also problems that are not plausibly classified as illness, such as insufficient sympathy for other people, or a strong tendency to assign blame to others for whatever goes wrong. What binds these policies together is not that they treat the agent as mentally ill and therefore in need of psychiatric treatment. Rather, they are policies that attempt to bring about moral change by non-punitively addressing conditions that underlie actual or potential criminal behavior.

It is often argued that rehabilitative views are objectionable because they treat an offender as suffering from an illness and not as a morally responsible agent. Morris contends that the problem for typical forms of therapy proposed for altering criminal dispositions is that they circumvent rather than address the qualities in human beings that confer dignity, in particular our abilities to regulate actions autonomously and rationally (Morris 1968). However, an offender may be in need of therapy and may correctly be regarded as morally responsible in the sense of answerability or of the fittingness of providing a moral explanation, and this sense of moral responsibility is grounded precisely in these capacities for autonomy and rationality in action. Moreover, in the case of many criminals, these capacities are impaired, but then regard for their humanity would recommend therapeutic measures to restore them. All of this the free will skeptic can unequivocally endorse.[9]

FINAL WORDS

Thus, if the free will skeptic is right, criminal punishment for retributive reasons is ruled out. We would then need to relinquish one of the most prominent ways for justifying criminal punishment, although there are independent objections to this position. Moreover, deterrence theories of punishment, although typically not overtly retributivist, are objectionable on independent grounds, and some may need to avail themselves of retributivist justifications at crucial junctures. But a theory of crime prevention that would be acceptable whether or not the skeptic is right can be developed by analogy with our rationale for quarantining carriers of dangerous diseases. Such a theory would not justify the sort of criminal punishment whose legitimacy is most dubious, such as death or confinement in the most common kinds of prisons in our society.

9. For further discussion of objections to rehabilitation programs, see Pereboom 2001: 178–185.

More than this, it demands a certain level of care and attention to the well-being of criminals, which would change much of current procedure. The free will skeptic would also endorse measures for reducing crime that aim at altering social conditions, such as improving education, increasing opportunities for fulfilling employment, and enhancing care for the mentally ill (Kleiman 2009, 117-163; Slobogin 2006). These proposals would not extinguish our practice of holding morally responsible, not even its criminological component. Rather, they amount to revisions to the practice that its own rules would recommend. Thus, the challenge that the free will skeptic proposes is not external, but rather thoroughly internal to our practice of holding morally responsible.

REFERENCES

Alexander, Larry, and Kimberly Kessler Ferzan, with Stephen Morse (2009). *Crime and Culpability*, Cambridge, UK: Cambridge University Press.

Balaguer, Mark (2010). *Free Will as an Open Scientific Problem*, Cambridge, MA: MIT Press.

Bentham, Jeremy (1823/1948). *Introduction to the Principles of Morals and Legislation*, New York: Macmillan.

Bok, Hilary (1998). *Freedom and Responsibility*, Princeton NJ: Princeton University Press.

Boonin, Daniel (2008). The Problem of Punishment, Cambridge, UK: Cambridge University Press.

Braithwaite, John, and Philip Pettit (1990). *Not Just Deserts*, Oxford: Oxford University Press.

Chisholm, Roderick (1964). "Human Freedom and the Self," The Lindley Lecture, Department of Philosophy, University of Kansas. Reprinted in *Free Will*, ed. Derk Pereboom, Indianapolis: Hackett, 2009.

Chisholm, Roderick (1976). *Person and Object*, La Salle IL: Open Court.

Clarke, Randolph (2003). *Libertarian Theories of Free Will*, New York: Oxford University Press.

Ekstrom, Laura W. (2000). *Free Will, A Philosophical Study*, Boulder CO: Westview.

Farrell, Daniel M. (1985). "The Justification of General Deterrence," *Philosophical Review* 104, 367–394.

Fischer, John Martin, and Mark Ravizza (1998). *Responsibility and Control, A Theory of Moral Responsibility*, New York: Cambridge University Press.

Fischer, John Martin (2007). "Compatibilism," in Fischer, John Martin, Robert Kane, Derk Pereboom, and Manuel Vargas. *Four Views on Free Will*, Oxford: Blackwell Publishers.

Frankfurt, Harry G. (1971). "Freedom of the Will and the Concept of a Person," *Journal of Philosophy* 68, 5–20.

Ginet, Carl (1990). *On Action*, Cambridge, UK: Cambridge University Press.

Griffiths, Meghan (2010). "Why Agent-Caused Actions Are Not Lucky," *American Philosophical Quarterly* 47, 43–56.

Hampton, Jean (1984). "The Moral Education Theory of Punishment," *Philosophy and Public Affairs* 13, 208–238.

Haji, Ishtiyaque (1998). *Moral Accountability*, New York: Oxford University Press.

Hume, David. (1739/1978). *A Treatise of Human Nature*, Oxford: Oxford University Press.

Husak, Douglas (2000). "Retribution in Criminal Theory," *San Diego Law Review* 37, 959–986.

Kane, Robert (1996). *The Significance of Free Will*, New York: Oxford University Press.

Kant, Immanuel (1797/1963). *The Metaphysical Elements of Justice*, New York: Bobbs-Merrill, tr. John Ladd, 99–107.

Kelly, Erin (2009). "Criminal Justice without Retribution," *Journal of Philosophy* 106, 440–462.

Kleiman, Mark (2009). *When Brute Force Fails: How to Have Less Crime and Less Punishment*, Princeton, NJ: Princeton University Press.

McCloskey, H. J. (1965). "A Non-utilitarian Approach to Punishment," *Inquiry* 8, 239–255.

McKenna, M. (2012). *Conversation and Responsibility*, New York: Oxford University Press.

Mele, Alfred (1995). *Autonomous Agents*, New York: Oxford University Press.

Mele, Alfred (2006). *Free Will and Luck*, New York: Oxford University Press.

Menninger, Karl (1968). *The Crime of Punishment*, New York: Penguin.

Montague, Philip (1995). *Punishment as Societal Defense*, Lanham, MD: Rowman and Littlefield.

Moore, Michael (1987). "The Moral Worth of Retribution," in *Responsibility, Character, and the Emotions*, Ferdinand Schoeman, ed., Cambridge, UK: Cambridge University Press, pp. 179–219. Reprinted in Punishment and Rehabilitation, 3rd edition, Jeffrie G. Murphy, ed., Belmont, CA, Wadsworth Publishing Company, 1995, pp. 94–130.

Moore, Michael (1998). *Placing Blame*. Oxford: Oxford University Press.

Morris, Herbert (1968)."Persons and Punishment," *The Monist* 52, 475–501

Morris, Herbert (1981). "A Paternalistic Theory of Punishment," *American Philosophical Quarterly* 18. Reprinted in *Punishment and Rehabilitation*, 3rd edition, Jeffrie G. Murphy, ed., Belmont, CA: Wadsworth Publishing Company, 1995, page numbers are from the latter edition.

Morse, Stephen (1999). "Neither Desert nor Disease," *Legal Theory* 5, 265–309.

Morse, Stephen (2004). "Reasons, Results, and Criminal Responsibility," *University of Illinois Law Review* (2004), 363–444.

Morse, Stephen (2007). "The Non-Problem of Free Will in Forensic Psychiatry and Psychology," Scholarship at Penn Law, paper 157. Available at: http,//lsr.nellco.org/upenn_wps/157.

Nadelhoffer, Thomas, Stephanos Bibas, Scott Grafton, Kent A. Kiehl, Andrew Mansfield, Walter Sinnott-Armstrong, and Michael Gazzaniga (2012). "Neuroprediction, Violence, and the Law: Setting the Stage," *Neuroethics*. 5, 67–99.

Nelkin, Dana (2008). "Responsibility and Rational Abilities, Defending an Asymmetrical View," *Pacific Philosophical Quarterly* 89, 497–515.

Nelkin, Dana (2011). *Making Sense of Freedom and Responsibility*, Oxford: Oxford University Press.

O'Connor, Timothy (2000). *Persons and Causes*, New York: Oxford University Press.
O'Connor, Timothy (2008). "Agent-Causal Power," in *Dispositions and Causes*, Toby Handfield, ed., Oxford: Clarendon Press, pp. 189–214.
Pereboom, Derk (1995). "Determinism Al Dente," *Noûs* 29, 21–45.
Pereboom, Derk (2001). *Living Without Free Will*, Cambridge, UK: Cambridge University Press.
Pereboom, Derk (2004). "Is Our Conception of Agent Causation Incoherent?" *Philosophical Topics*. 32, 275–286.
Pereboom, Derk (2005). "Defending Hard Incompatibilism," *Midwest Studies in Philosophy* 29, 228–247.
Pereboom, Derk (2006). "Kant on Transcendental Freedom," *Philosophy and Phenomenological Research* 73, 537–567.
Pereboom, Derk (2007). "Hard Incompatibilism," and "Response to Kane, Fischer, and Vargas," in *Four Views on Free Will*, Robert Kane, John Martin Fischer, Derk Pereboom, and Manuel Vargas, eds., Oxford UK: Blackwell, pp. 85–125, 191–203.
Quinn, Warren (1985)."The Right to Threaten and the Right to Punish," *Philosophy and Public Affairs* 14, 327–373.
Rawls, John (1955). "Two Concepts of Rules," *The Philosophical Review* 64, 3–32.
Scanlon, Thomas (1998). *What We Owe to Each Other*, Cambridge, UK: Harvard University Press.
Schoeman, Ferdinand D. (1979). "On Incapacitating the Dangerous," *American Philosophical Quarterly* 16, 27–35.
Slobogin, Christopher (2006). *Minding Justice*, Cambridge, MA: Harvard University Press.
Smilansky, Saul (2000). *Free Will and Illusion*, Oxford: Oxford University Press.
Sommers, Tamler (2012). *Relative Justice: Cultural Diversity, Free Will, and Moral Responsibility*, Princeton, NJ: Princeton University Press.
Spinoza, Baruch (1677/1985). Ethics, *in The Collected Works of Spinoza*, Edwin Curley, ed. and tr., Vol. 1, Princeton, NJ: Princeton University Press.
Strawson, Galen (1986). *Freedom and Belief*, Oxford: Oxford University Press.
Strawson, Peter F. (1962). "Freedom and Resentment," *Proceedings of the British Academy* 48 (1962), 1–25.
Taylor, Richard (1966). *Action and Purpose*, Englewood Cliffs, NJ: Prentice-Hall.
Taylor, Richard (1974). *Metaphysics*, 4th ed., Englewood Cliffs, NJ: Prentice-Hall.
Ten, C. L. (1987). *Crime, Guilt, and Punishment*, Oxford: Oxford University Press.
van Inwagen, Peter (1983). *An Essay on Free Will*, Oxford: Oxford University Press.
Vilhauer, Benjamin (forthcoming). "Persons, Punishment, and Free Will Skepticism," *Philosophical Studies*, Online First, DOI 10.1007/s11098-011-9752-z.
Wallace, R. Jay (1994). *Responsibility and the Moral Sentiments*, Cambridge MA: Harvard University Press.
Waller, Bruce (1990). *Freedom Without Responsibility*, Philadelphia, Temple University Press.
Wittgenstein, Ludwig (1953). *Philosophical Investigations*, tr. G. E. M. Anscombe, Oxford: Basil Blackwell.
Wolf, Susan (1990). *Freedom Within Reason*, Oxford: Oxford University Press.
Wood, Allen (1984). "Kant's Compatibilism," in *Self and Nature in Kant's Philosophy*, Ithaca NY: Cornell University Press, pp. 73–101.

4

Why Do We Resist Hard Incompatibilism? Thoughts on Freedom and Punishment

MICHAEL LOUIS CORRADO

> Laws imposed on men should always be in keeping with their condition, for, as Isidore says, law should be "possible both according to nature and according to the customs of the country."[1]

WHAT ARE WE AFRAID OF?

The Incompatibilist Vision

In *Living Without Free Will*,[2] Derk Pereboom defends a worldview[3] to which he gives the new name Hard Incompatibilism.[4] According to this view of the

1. Thomas Aquinas, Summa Theologica I-II, Q. 96, Art. 2, in *Saint Thomas Aquinas, On Law, Morality and Politics* 67, (ed. William Baumgarth 1988).

2. Derk Pereboom, *Living Without Free Will* (2001).

3. Under the title "hard determinism" a closely related idea may be found in Paul Edwards, "Hard and Soft Determinism," in Sidney Hook, ed., *Determinism and Freedom* 117 (1961); in John Hospers, "What Means This Freedom," in *id.* at 126. Along with Pereboom, more recent contributors to this line of thought are Galen Strawson, "The Impossibility of Moral Responsibility," in Gary Watson, ed., *Free Will* 212 (2d ed. 2003); Saul Smilansky, *Free Will and Illusion* (2000); and Ted Honderich, *How Free Are You?* (1993). On the difference between hard determinism and hard incompatibilism, see below. Although the view was not clearly formulated by the Greeks, it was, for example, the view that Stoic compatibilism was formulated to avoid. See, for example, Seymour Feldman, "Debate Concerning Determinism in Late Medieval Jewish Philosophy," 51 *Proceedings of the American Academy for Jewish Research* 15 (1984).

4. *Living Without Free Will* at xix.

way things are, human beings lack what might be called "ultimate freedom to choose" their actions, since their behavior is caused by events beyond their control, and so they are not morally responsible for what they do.

In chapter 6, "Hard Incompatibilism and Criminal Behavior," Pereboom draws out what he sees as the consequences of this view for criminal justice. The most important consequence is that punishment as we understand it must be ruled out, for punishment entails responsibility. Recognizing that crime must be controlled nevertheless, he examines various alternatives to punishment to see whether any are consistent with his incompatibilist vision and finds two main answers: rehabilitative therapy and quarantine.

> A theory of crime prevention that would be acceptable whether or not hard incompatibilism is true can be developed by analogy with our rationale for quarantining carriers of dangerous diseases. Such a theory would not justify the sort of criminal punishment whose legitimacy is most dubious, such as death or confinement in the most common kinds of prison in our society. More than this, it demands a certain level of care and attention to the well-being of criminals that would radically change our current practice. *Just as society has a duty to attempt to cure those who are quarantined for its protection, so it has a duty to attempt to morally educate or cure the criminals it detains for its protection. When this is not possible, and a criminal must be confined indefinitely, his life should not be made unnecessarily unpleasant.*[5]

The answer, in other words, is preventive detention with the possibility of therapy. Those who have proved themselves dangerous to society should be detained for an indefinite period, until therapy can render them safe to reintroduce into the community; and if therapy does not work, the only alternative is continued detention.

Pereboom's position will meet resistance from those many who have, with good reason, opposed the "therapeutic" approach to crime control. By appearing to breach the border between madness and malice it would threaten to treat all criminals alike, subjecting all to forced treatment and indefinite confinement until cured. In particular it would treat all as sick, and deny to those who are competent the special respect we believe they are due as autonomous agents. The length of detention and the amount of treatment would be determined entirely by the persistence of the offender's dangerousness and not at all by the seriousness of the crime—or (at least at the level of theory) by whether or not a crime had been committed. Those who commit a serious crime but do not remain dangerous can be released immediately;[6] the only reason for *not*

5. *Living Without Free Will* at 186.

6. Id. at 176.

detaining those who are dangerous but have not yet committed a crime is the present poverty of our methods of detecting dangerousness.[7]

Indeed, these apparent consequences of Hard Incompatibilism will make many uncomfortable who are otherwise sympathetic with the position. The system he proposes does seem like a criminal justice system designed for a brave new world, the world, for example, of *A Clockwork Orange*. Those who are competent to guide their own behavior—and whom we would more traditionally have described as responsible for their behavior—are not to be treated differently from those who are incompetent because of mental illness, or because of severe addiction; indeed, they will not be treated differently from misbehaving children. All who present a danger will be subjected to therapy until they are no longer dangerous, or, if therapy is ineffective, they will remain in detention. If this outcome—which I will call the Awful Outcome—is what Hard Incompatibilism entails then, I believe, the criticisms are justified. And if none of the alternatives to Hard Incompatibilism are plausible—and I think that none are—then we are in a very difficult situation indeed.

The task I have set myself in this paper, therefore, is to determine whether Hard Incompatibilism deserves these criticisms—whether Hard Incompatibilism really means that the line between malice and madness must fall, and consequently whether it entails the Awful Outcome. My approach will be to explore whether certain distinctions, commonly assumed to be essential to a system of criminal justice that treats competent human beings with dignity and respect, might be maintained under the propositions that constitute Hard Incompatibilism. Traditionally the law has distinguished the treatment of the insane and of juveniles from the treatment of those who are considered autonomous persons[8]; to the insane and juveniles I would add the category of those who are severely addicted.[9] Some line of this sort between those who act autonomously and those who do not is essential to maintaining a humane system of justice and to avoiding the Awful Outcome. I believe that it may be possible to reconstitute such a line within Hard Incompatibilism, and my aim is to propose a theory that does just that.

7. Id. at 176–177.

8. For the traditional view, see Frederick Woodbridge, "Physical and Mental Infancy in the Criminal Law," 87 U. Penn. L. Rev. 426 (1939) ("[F]or present purposes there have been two streams of evolution respecting incapacity to commit crimes. The first stream is independent of the second and deals with the criminal responsibility of infants. The second stream is part of the general current of tests of irresponsibility of adults.")

9. See my "Addiction and the Theory of Action," 25 *Quinnipiac Law Review* 117 (2006), available at SSRN: <http://ssrn.com/abstract=896104>; "Responsibility and Control," 34 *Hofstra Law Review* 59 (2005), available at SSRN: <http://ssrn.com/abstract=735224>, reprinted in *Crime and Mens Rea: Emerging Scenarios*, edited by G. V. Mahesh Nath (2009); "Addiction and Causation," 37 *San Diego Law Review* 913 (2000); "Addiction and Responsibility: An Introduction," 18 *Law and Philosophy* 579 (1999).

The Argument

The argument for the inference from Hard Incompatibilism to the Awful Outcome is this: If the scientific view of man is correct, then human beings have no ultimate control over their actions.[10] That is, they do not have the freedom to choose between alternative actions: Every choice is caused by some prior event, which is itself caused by a prior event; and every chain of such events either extends back indefinitely in time, or ends with an event that has no cause—a merely random event. Either way, every action is ultimately caused by events beyond the actor's control. But if ultimate control does not rest with the actor, then there is no responsibility for the actions that are chosen; and if there is no responsibility, then punishment is not justified. For the justification of punishment requires that those punished deserve their punishment.[11] And if punishment is not justified, then all that is left for crime control is incapacitation and therapy.

A more traditional version of this argument involves the view known as "hard determinism." Hard determinism holds (1) that all events are fully determined causally by prior events, (2) that human actions are events like any other in the universe, and (3) that determination of human choices by prior events is inconsistent with moral responsibility for actions. The first two theses are the principles of universal determinism; the last thesis is the principle of incompatibilism. Together the three premises entail that no one is responsible for what he does.[12] Put that conclusion together with the proposition that where there is no responsibility there can be no punishment, and (as with the argument from Hard Incompatibilism) you reach the conclusion that there can be no punishment.

The problem with hard determinism is that for all we know the first thesis may not be true. It is in fact consistent with the scientific view of the world that some events have sufficient causal conditions and others do not.

10. "Ultimate control" is defined in Robert Kane, *A Contemporary Introduction to Free Will* (2005) at pages 120–131: "The basic idea is this: to be *ultimately responsible* for an action, an agent must be responsible for anything that is a sufficient reason, cause, or motive for the action's occurring." I recommend this book highly as an introduction to the field.

11. The proposition that punishment presupposes desert is supported by the historically long and unsuccessful utilitarian effort to replace retribution as a necessary condition for punishment, or to reconstruct "desert" as a utilitarian notion. See, e.g., John Rawls, "Two Concepts of Rules," 64 *Philosophical Review* 3 (1955). See also Michael Louis Corrado, "The Abolition of Punishment," 35 *Suffolk Law Review* 257 (2001).

12. See the discussion above. For an elegant but slightly different formulation of the argument, see Roderick M. Chisholm, "Responsibility and Avoidability," in Sidney Hook, ed., *Determinism and Freedom in the Age of Modern Science* (1961), at page 157. Chisholm was himself an incompatibilist but not a determinist.

But even accepting that possibility a similar argument may be made by anyone who accepts the second thesis. For if human actions are events like any other in the universe, then each human action has a causal history that either extends back indefinitely in time, or else ends in an event that is not fully determined—that is partially determined and partly up to chance. But no one is responsible for an event that is not fully determined, that happens at least in part by chance, any more than anyone is responsible for an event that is fully determined.[13] And if each of our actions is the result of a causal chain that we are not in control of, because every event in the chain is either fully determined by prior events or partly due to chance, then we are not responsible for our actions.

Taking "the scientific view of man" to be the view that all human actions are the outcome of causal chains that either extend backward indefinitely or else end in an event that is to some extent determined and to some extent due to chance, we may return to the argument for Hard Incompatibilism. It proceeds like this: (1) the "scientific view of man" is true (or at least is the most plausible of all views of human action); (2) the scientific view of man is inconsistent with moral responsibility[14]; and (3) therefore no one is responsible for what she does. There is no need to rehearse the arguments behind the two premises here. My task is not to demonstrate that they are true and that Hard Incompatibilism is therefore true, but rather to examine the consequences of this view, the conclusion of the argument, for the criminal law. I will say, however, that something like Hard Incompatibilism is beginning to encroach upon the traditional dominance that compatibilism enjoys among philosophers and legal theorists.[15]

13. See the discussion of the "libertarian dilemma" in Kane's *Contemporary Introduction to Free Will* at 33–34.

14. Someone who accepts the second premise, the thesis of incompatibility, need not accept the first premise, the scientific view of man. One important group of *libertarians*, the agent-causation libertarians, believe that the scientific view of man is incompatible with moral responsibility, and reject the scientific view. Roderick Chisholm and Richard Taylor are two well -known advocates of agent-causation. A contemporary overview of all these positions is found in *Four Views on Free Will* (2007), by John Martin Fischer, Robert Kane, Derk Pereboom, and Mauel Vargas. A more comprehensive and demanding survey of contemporary views, containing work by many of the best known contributors to the field, may be found in *Freedom and Determinism* (2004), edited by Joseph Keim Campbell, Michael O'Rourke, and David Shier; see my review at 10 *Essays in Philosophy* # 1 (2009), available at SSRN: <http://ssrn.com/abstract=1491318>.

15. The list of contemporary compatibilists is too long and too well known to repeat here. Perhaps the most sophisticated work defending the compatibility of the scientific view with moral responsibility is that of John Martin Fischer in a series of essays and books beginning with *The Metaphysics of Free Will: An Essay on Control* (1994).

The Problem

In popular culture there are two different ways of reacting to this world without responsibility, both of them focusing on the implications for punishment. One way of reacting is to welcome it. We find this in Samuel Butler's *Erewhon*, for example, and we find it advocated by philosophers and psychologists as well as by novelists. The criminal is not bad, he is sick or defective, and realizing that he is permits us to do something about it, something involving therapy for those who can be fixed; indefinite detention for those who cannot. The positivist school in Italy promoted a theory of this sort[16]; Wooton·urged something of the sort on British law.[17] The other way of reacting is with horror. This is the reaction evoked by *A Clockwork Orange*, where a method known as the Ludovico Method consisted in aversively conditioning criminals to avoid crime. This reaction too has had its popular writers and its academic support and in fact is one of the main reasons, I would argue, for the deep repugnance toward and resistance to Hard Incompatibilism. It is to this line of thinking that I want to turn now.

According to this way of looking at things, to deprive human beings of responsibility is to deprive them of the respect due to persons. In treating criminals as sick rather than as bad we do them no service. We treat them much as we would treat animals, and we deprive them of any rights that might give them the least protection from the state's control. They may be subjected to treatment without their consent; they may be detained indefinitely if they cannot be cured of their illness. When C. S. Lewis wrote "The Humanitarian Theory of Punishment,"[18] he was reacting against theories from the turn of the 20th century, theories that he derisively called "humanitarian," that proposed to treat the criminal not as bad but as sick. What such theories mainly leave out is the concept of desert, and "desert is the only connecting link between punishment and justice."

The theories he is talking about are the theories of Ferri and Wooton and others—not theories of punishment but proposals to abolish punishment and to

16. See, for example, Enrico Ferri, *The Positive School of Criminology: Three Lectures* (trans. 1968); *Criminal Sociology* (trans. 1917). In the Italian "double-track" system of criminal policy, inspired in part by the positivist school of Ferri and others, preventive detention and treatment are taken for granted as a complement to punishment, even for those who are considered "responsible" for what they do. The double track makes preventive detention available not only for habitual and professional criminals but also for children between the ages of 14 and 18 years, and for addicts. See Articles 109, 221–222, 225 of the Italian Penal Code. It also makes preventive detention a possibility for "responsible" adults who have committed no actual crime.

17. For example, in Barbara Wootton, *Crime and the Criminal Law* (second edition, 1981); *Crime and Penal Policy* (1978).

18. 6 *Res Judicatae* 224 (1953).

replace it with something else. The "humanitarian" theory that Lewis opposed was a theory of treatment and deterrence, not of punishment. The crux of his argument is that if what the state is doing to criminals is not punishment, then there is no limit to the inhumanity the state may engage in: it may detain the criminal indefinitely, until he is cured, and it may treat him to free him of anti-social ambitions, without his consent. The state may even inflict pain on him to deter crime; but without the limitations found in the notion of retribution there was no reason to suppose that it had to be inflicted only on the guilty, or that it had to be proportional to the crime. On the other hand, if the state were limited to punishment, then none of those things would be possible. Punishment would have to be limited to the guilty and would have to be proportional to the crime.

The law moves from theory to practice only very slowly, and so the effect of these theories on American law before they were discredited midcentury was limited. Still, it is possible to find traces of it. We find in the criminal code adopted in Washington State in 1909, for example, the following provision eliminating the insanity defense:

> It shall be no defense to a person charged with the commission of a crime that at the time of its commission he was unable, by reason of his insanity, idiocy or imbecility, to comprehend the nature and quality of the act committed, or to understand that it was wrong; or that he was afflicted with a morbid propensity to commit prohibited acts; nor shall any testimony or other proof thereof be admitted in evidence.[19]

Although at first glance this provision would seem to require treating the insane as responsible agents, in fact it did just the reverse. It treated both the mentally ill and the mentally competent the same it is true, but the way it treated both was as nonresponsible. In support of the constitutionality of the law, in the case of *State v. Strasburg*, counsel for the state argued that the whole intent of the law was humanitarian, and that it was no longer the intent of the criminal law to punish:

> The central idea upon which the whole fabric of criminal jurisprudence was formerly built was the idea that every criminal act was the product of a free will possessing a full understanding of the difference between right and wrong and full capacity to choose a right or wrong course of action, and, as one error naturally and logically follows another, it was only natural and

19. Washington Criminal Code, section 2259, Rem. & Bal. Code; Laws 1909, p. 891, § 7, cited in State v. Strasburg, 60 Wash. 106, 111–112, 110 P. 1020, 1021 (1910).

> logical that society should have prescribed punishments as a central feature of its scheme for correction. *A better understanding of crime and the science of criminology now convinces us that this theory is wholly wrong* ... An understanding of this fact has made readily apparent the folly of expecting that punishment could relieve the condition, and accordingly stocks, whipping posts, and chain gangs are giving way to workhouses, reformatories, and asylums, the purpose of which is to instruct, educate, and reform rather than further to debase the individual, and the modern systems of criminal classification and segregation are themselves a recognition of the fact that every criminal is a concrete problem."[20]

The purpose of the law, counsel said, "is to put in operation in this state a scheme of criminal jurisprudence that gives recognition to these ideas."[21] Naturally there was no longer a need for a special plea of insanity, since all were to be subject for treatment to cure their "mental or moral degeneration," or their addiction to intoxicating liquors. There could not be any better example of the vision that made Lewis shudder. Though the whole effort seems to have collapsed midcentury, a collapse that was mirrored in ethical theory by the return to retributivism, the very principle of these early efforts was to remove the line between malice and madness.[22]

Lewis wrote for the popular press, but a similar argument has been heard in academic quarters. Perhaps the best known is found in Herbert Morris's "Persons and Punishment."[23] Morris described a system of crime control that would follow from refusing to see human beings as responsible for their behavior. He contrasted the institution of punishment with an institution very much like the one that Pereboom argues for, a system of therapy and detention:

> In this world we are now to imagine when an individual harms another his conduct is to be regarded as a symptom of some pathological condition in the way a running nose is a symptom of a cold.... This distinction between

20. State v. Strasburg, 60 Wash. at 122, 110 P. at 1025 (1910). The law was struck down as unconstitutional.

21. 60 Wash. At 123, 110 P. at 1025.

22. For a more recent assessment of the implications of the scientific view for the criminal law, see Joshua Greene and Jonathan Cohen, "For the Law, Neuroscience Changes Nothing and Everything," 359 *Philosophical Transactions: Biological Sciences* 1775 (2004). Greene and Cohen argue that the law as it stands is consistent with the scientific view, but as the scientific view becomes more entrenched the notion of responsibility will disappear from the law. I take issue with the first part of that claim in this paper.

23. Herbert Morris, "Persons and Punishment," 52 The Monist 475 (1968).

> mere events or happenings and human actions is erased in our imagined system.[24]

Crime is assimilated to disease; in both,

> The abnormality is looked upon as a happening with a causal explanation rather than an action for which there were reasons.[25]

There are five points at which the therapeutic approach and punishment may be distinguished, according to Morris: (1) Punishment is a response to past fault; therapy is aimed at a present condition and at the future. (2) Punishment inflicts a burden, therapy confers a benefit.[26] (3) Punishment involves paying a debt; there is no such thing in therapy. (4) Punishment requires proportionality between crime and burden; therapy does not. (5) Punishment must be for an actual crime; therapy need not be. It could be for thoughts or tendencies.[27] Procedural safeguards have no role in therapy.[28]

The main objection to the therapy system is that it fails to respect human beings as persons. Morris attempts to give this claim some content:

> I want now to turn attention to … what is meant by 'treating an individual as a person' … [W]hat we imply by our words is a contrast between the manner in which one acceptably responds to human beings and the manner in which one acceptably responds to animals and inanimate objects. When we treat a human being merely as an animal or some inanimate object our responses to

24. Id. at 480.

25. Id. at 482.

26. But punishment can do both, Morris says in his later response to David Dolinko. See Herbert Morris, "Some Further Reflections on Guilt and Punishment," 18 *Law and Philosophy* 363 (1999).

27. Although it is generally assumed that no existing system of preventive detention would detain merely for thoughts, without a conviction for the commission of a crime, I would note that in Italy's fully developed double-track system "responsible" (or imputable) actors can be detained who have committed no known crime. See Article 115 of the Italian Penal Code, subjecting those who have agreed to commit a crime, where no crime was actually committed, and those who have solicited a crime, where no crime was actually committed, to "measures of security," including preventive detention—but *not to punishment*. In Italian law the agreement to commit a crime is not by itself a crime; nor is the solicitation to commit a crime, where no crime has been committed. In connection with *tendencies*, the commission of a crime by someone who has "criminal tendencies" raises the possibility of preventive detention in conjunction with punishment. See Articles 108 and 109 of the Italian Penal Code.

28. "Persons and Punishment" at 483–484.

> the human being are determined, not by his choices, but ours in disregard of or with indifference to his. And when we 'look upon' a person as less than a person or not a person, we consider the person as incapable of rational choice[29] . . . We treat a human being as a person provided: first, we permit the person to make the choices that will determine what happens to him and second, when our responses to the person are responses respecting the person's choices.[30]

That is what we do when we punish, he would want to say. But it is not true, for example, when we treat a person as incompetent or when we subject him to quarantine for an illness.

To save us from the Awful Outcome, he concludes, we must stick by the system of punishment. We are obligated to improve it, of course. The laws that punishment enforces must be just. The way we deal with those convicted of crimes must respect their rights and must not degrade them. But at all costs we should avoid the mechanistic world of therapy and detention. We must have punishment, and accordingly we must accept the human being as a responsible agent. This point of view therefore collides with the presuppositions of Hard Incompatibilism, according to which human beings cannot be held responsible for what they do.

The Project

I think there is a great deal to be said for the system of therapy and detention. As things are now, people are often punished for things they cannot help, and sometimes people are punished for actions that are rational responses to their situations. Nevertheless, it is hard not to be impressed by the disastrous consequences predicted for an all-out adoption of a system of detention and therapy. The question is this: If Hard Incompatibilism is true, is there any way to avoid the therapeutic approach to crime control?

I think there may be, and in the sections that follow I will try to sketch out one way to do it. I want to be clear about this: I am not proposing to justify punishment. I don't think it can be done, certainly not by anyone who accepts Hard Incompatibilism. For given the most plausible view of the place of man in the universe, the distinction between the *concept* of punishment and the *concept* of therapy, involving as it does responsibility, retribution, and desert on one side but not on the other, cannot be maintained. If the Hard Indeterminist is right, the notions of responsibility, retribution, and desert simply have no denotation.[31]

29. Id. at 490.

30. Id. at 492.

31. And in any case, that distinction is not useful in a humane state, as I have argued in another paper. See my "Abolition of Punishment," above.

Instead I propose to try to maintain a distinction that appears to be essential to a humane and democratic state, a distinction found in the difference between the *treatment* accorded to those who are competent to conform their behavior to the law and the *treatment* of those who are not, and to show that the allocation of what Joel Feinberg called "hard treatment"[32] to those who are competent, along with the avoidance of indefinite preventive detention and compulsory therapy, can be justified without appeal to the notion of responsibility. Whether or not my particular effort succeeds, some such effort will have to succeed if the Awful Outcome that is entailed by Hard Incompatibilism is to be avoided.

A DECENT SYSTEM OF CRIME CONTROL

Lewis appropriated the term "humanitarian" to describe (ironically) the therapeutic approach to crime control. Clearly he believed, and certainly Morris believed, that a truly humanitarian system would be one that preserved the line between those who were competent to conform their behavior to the law and those who were not and that treated the two groups differently. To avoid confusion I will eschew the use of the words "humanitarian" and "humane" and instead refer to a system that maintains that distinction as a *decent* system of criminal justice, one that avoids obliterating the distinction between madness and malice. The question then becomes whether someone who accepts the scientific view of man can justify such a decent system. The plausibility of the scientific view combined with repugnance toward the therapeutic vision accounts, as I have suggested, for the prolonged popularity of compatibilism in action theory and the sustained effort to make that analysis of action and responsibility work. But the result of all that effort has been to make clear, at least to a growing body of theorists, that there is no alternative to incompatibilism and, therefore, among those who accept the scientific view, to Hard Incompatibilism.

The Institution of Correction

If we give up the notion of responsibility, to what extent can (and should) we try to duplicate the line that now exists between the treatment of those who are said to be responsible for what they do and those who are said not to be responsible for what they do? I would like to propose an analogue for punishment, which I will call "correction." Correction, I think, can be limited in ways to avoid the horrors of the therapeutic vision of Lewis and Morris and of *A Clockwork Orange*, while at the same time not making any assumptions about responsibility.

32. Joel Feinberg, "The Expressive Function of Punishment," 49 *Monist* 397 (1965).

Punishment and Preventive Detention

In American law the difference between punishment and preventive detention is, or until very recently has been, relatively clear:[33] Those who have the capacity to conform their behavior to the law may be punished for their crimes, but may not be preventively detained. Those who do not have the capacity to conform their behavior to the law may be preventively detained if dangerous, but may not be punished. This distinction between punishment and preventive detention is currently justified by appeal to the notions of responsibility and desert. My thesis is that any theory of criminal justice that proposes both to eliminate those notions and to qualify for the label "decent" must find some way to reconstruct the line that those notions are supposed to represent.

The two main instances of nonresponsibility that the law takes into account are insanity and infancy.[34] A person who was not responsible because of mental illness at the time of the crime cannot be punished, but may be detained (for as long as he remains mentally ill and dangerous). Children of a certain age are considered not to be responsible in the sense required by the law and may not be punished; but they can be subjected to a form of juvenile justice that may include temporary detention. Older children—the line depends on the jurisdiction—may be punished under certain conditions but not under others. To some small extent the law also recognizes the inability of the addict to control his behavior and provides, in some cases, for detention with or without treatment instead of punishment for addicts who break the law by possessing and using drugs.[35]

This theoretically founded line between punishment and preventive detention is under heavy attack, but it has so far managed to survive, if just barely. The most direct assault has been through the line of American cases reaching from *Salerno*,[36] in which the argument that preventive detention was regulation and not punishment (and therefore not subject to constitutional limits on punishment) was accepted, through *Crane*,[37] in which the Supreme Court held that

33. But see my "Sex Offenders, Unlawful Combatants, and Preventive Detention," 84 North Carolina Law Review 77 (2005); "Responsibility and Control," 34 *Hofstra Law Review* 59 (2005), available at SSRN: <http://ssrn.com/abstract=735224>.

34. See, for example, Frederick Woodbridge, "Physical and Mental Infancy in the Criminal Law," 87 *University of Pennsylvania Law Review* 426, 427 (1939).

35. See Elizabeth Patterson and Arlene Bowers, "Civil Commitment for Pregnant Substance Abusers," 15 *Politics and the Life Sciences* 64 (1996); Sandra Anderson Garcia and Ingo Keilitz, "Involuntary Civil Commitment of Drug Dependent Persons with Special Reference to Pregnant Women," 15 *Mental and Physical Disability Law Reporter* 418 (1991).

36. United States v. Salerno, 481 U.S. 739 (1987).

37. Kansas v. Crane, 534 U.S. 407 (2002).

sexual offenders could be subject to both punishment and subsequent indefinite detention. Nevertheless the tradition is deep, and the line has managed to stand in one form or another. Sexual predators may be confined after serving their penal sentences, but only if it can be shown that they lack "control."[38] Those found guilty but mentally ill will, in some states, be committed indefinitely in addition to serving a prison term, but only if they suffer from serious mental illness just short of legal insanity. In some jurisdictions that level of illness corresponds to a lack of "control."

The greatest breach in the line consists in allowing both punishment and preventive detention in certain cases. But that breach is self-evidently wrong, under the traditional notions of responsibility and desert. Anyone who considers the matter directly—these are, logically speaking, cases in which persons not in control of their behavior are being punished for what they did, or else persons in control of their behavior are being detained indefinitely, just as a person found legally insane would be—will see that to impose punishment as well as preventive detention is wrong under the traditional theory of responsibility and the traditional justifications for punishment and preventive detention. If some sexual predators really are not in control of what they do (which is now a requirement for the imposition of preventive detention upon them), they are not responsible and should not be punished. If a child of 13 is not capable of conforming his behavior to the law when he commits a minor crime, he does not magically become capable when he commits a more serious crime.

A firm line between those who are competent and those who are not competent is what the traditional notions of responsibility and desert promised to provide and a corresponding line between methods of treatment of offenders, represented in the tradition as the line between punishment and preventive detention, are a requirement for a decent system of law.

Correction as Intentional Harsh Treatment

The fundamental point is this: As Morris and Lewis and others have shown, we cannot preserve a decent system of law by treating all offenders the same under a system of therapy and detention. The undesirability of such a system has nothing to do with the question of responsibility and has everything to do with the quality of life. Under that system, those who are in control of their behavior and are caught in the web of criminal justice are treated just like those who are not in control. Those who are not yet caught in that web must be preoccupied by the fact that at any time they might be found to be dangerous, and that there is nothing that they can do to avoid that finding. Those who might have committed a minor offense cannot know that they will be subjected to the

38. 534 U.S. at 412–413.

limited sanctions of a prison term; they might be detained indefinitely. Civil disobedience would become too costly to consider.

The system we are looking for must therefore distinguish between those who have the capacity to conform their behavior to the law (whether they exercise that capacity or not) and those who do not. And we cannot preserve a decent incompatibilist system that treats those who are competent in a way that is different from those who are incompetent without providing for a system of harsh treatment that makes use of the *machinery* of punishment without the assumptions that underlie the *institution* of punishment. As a way of talking about the machinery of punishment without presupposing responsibility, desert, or retribution, I will talk about harsh treatment inflicted not as an unavoidable consequence of achieving other aims (as the harshness of detention is an unavoidable consequence of satisfying the aim of incapacitation), but as something desirable as a means to achieving aims that depend precisely upon it being harsh treatment. A surgeon's invasive procedures might involve harsh treatment, including the cutting of flesh; but it is not ordinarily part of the surgeon's aim that the treatment be harsh. If she could accomplish what she wanted without the harsh treatment, she would do so. Medicine always looks for less invasive ways of doing things. On the other hand, boxing involves harsh treatment, and to eliminate the harsh treatment would destroy the sport of boxing. Like boxing, correction requires harsh treatment: it is treatment *intended* to be harsh. Like medicine, preventive detention involves harsh treatment, but only as a means to other ends and as something to be avoided if possible.

Think now of the harsh treatment involved in crime control without the window dressing of retribution and desert, but aiming at deterring crime. If you like, you may think of what I am after here as what would be left of punishment if bathed in Holmes' "cynical acid" or looked at as a bad man would look at it[39]: harsh treatment intended to change behavior. "Correction," as I mean to use the term here, refers to that employment of harsh treatment, whether it is caning or imprisonment or the death penalty. When detention is preventive merely, any harshness is incidental to the aim of taking the offender out of circulation. The offender who is to be only incapacitated and nothing else need not be treated harshly; conceivably he could be made better off than he is, with

39. Holmes, "The Path of the Law." 10 *Harvard Law Review* 457 (1897) ("Take … a notion which as popularly understood is the widest conception which the law contains—the notion of legal duty, to which already I have referred. We fill the word with all the content which we draw from morals. But what does it mean to a bad man? Mainly, and in the first place, a prophecy that if he does certain things he will be subjected to disagreeable consequences by way of imprisonment or compulsory payment of money … You see how the vague circumference of the notion of duty shrinks and at the same time grows more precise when we wash it with cynical acid and expel everything except the object of our study, the operations of the law.")

benefits that would outweigh his loss of certain of his freedoms. With correction, the very point is that the offender should be made to feel the harshness of his treatment.

The question now is whether it is possible for us to justify and limit correction in ways that will preserve some of the boundaries that we consider most important and that are now enshrined in the responsible—nonresponsible divide, while at the same time avoiding the assumption that the offender *deserves* what he gets.

The Benefits of Correction

We begin, then, with the observation that it is unlikely that the state will soon be able to operate without some form of intentional harsh treatment toward offenders, or what I am calling correction. But how are we to justify such treatment if we do not have responsibility, retribution, and desert to work with? The justification of correction, I am going to propose, will lie in the benefit it offers to the one corrected. This can be true only for those who have the capability of converting the harsh treatment they receive into benefit, and that fact will suggest a natural line approximating the line between responsibility and nonresponsibility. It will also suggest the limits of permissible correction, here approximating the role that responsibility and desert were supposed to play in limiting the *amount* of punishment.

How are we to justify correction? There are at least three questions to be answered here: What social consequences justify the great social expense the institution of correction will entail? What entitles us to use the offender to bring about those social consequences? And what are the limits, if any, upon the state's power to correct? In fact we may borrow the answer to the first question from the justification of punishment: Correction is justified only if it reduces the social cost of crime and disorder. Of course it does that by making an example of the offender, and that leads to the much harder second question: What entitles us so to use the offender? It is easy for traditional responsibility theory to answer that question: The responsibility theorist can say that what entitles us to use the offender so is that he deserves it. He did a bad thing that he could have avoided doing, and in that way brought the machinery of punishment down upon himself.[40] If we give up responsibility and all that goes with it, we have a much harder time explaining why we have the right to inflict the suffering that

40. You may be tempted to think here of the quip attributed to H. L. Mencken: "For every difficult problem there is a solution that is simple and elegant, and usually wrong." Traditional religions, when they became self-conscious, were forced to this sort of justification for the actions of a good God in consigning sinners to a tortured after-life. It makes no more sense in that context than it does here.

harsh treatment entails. I propose the following outline as the beginning of one possible source of the entitlement.

The consequence in terms of which we may be entitled to use the offender to achieve our social ends is the correction of the offender himself, sometimes called "specific deterrence." The argument in outline is this: First, it is a benefit to individuals to learn how to live within the rules of their society. It is a benefit in itself and, given the community's need to protect its members from crime, it is a benefit to the individual to be subjected to harsh treatment for a limited period rather than to be subjected to therapy and indefinite detention. Second, harsh treatment is a way, certainly not the only way, but a way nevertheless, to teach the significance of rules. The conclusion to be drawn is that if there is not a better way to teach the significance of rules (whatever "better" may mean in this context), then if the benefit to the offender is great enough, correction is justified in terms of that benefit.

There are, of course, qualifications to each of the premises of the argument that should be acknowledged. For one thing, the benefit that accrues will accrue whether or not the offender ever chooses to make use of his knowledge and ability to avoid violating the law. It is not a benefit to be deprived of the choice whether or not to obey the law. Furthermore it is not true that it is a benefit to learn how to live within the rules of an *unjust* society. And finally, as we have learned in the case of children,[41] harsh treatment may be counterproductive in trying to teach the significance of rules. Nevertheless, given a relatively just society and the proper use of corrective measures, I maintain that each of these assumptions is true. Beyond saying a bit about what they mean, I will not attempt to defend them further here. My larger point in this paper, that there is a way to mirror the line between responsibility and nonresponsibility, does not depend upon accepting this particular justification.[42]

I recognize the prima facie implausibility of arguing that correction benefits the offender. It is as clear as can be that nearly everyone who is subjected to correction (or to punishment) would prefer not to be subjected to it. The notion of benefit, therefore, cannot depend on the subjective state of the person so treated; it must be an objective notion, and it is difficult to make out just what that objective benefit may be. I take encouragement, nevertheless, from two sources. First, I side with those who believe that a large part of the justification for a theory lies in the consequences that the theory entails, much like the confirmation of a

41. Valerie F. Reyna and Frank Farley, "Risk and Rationality in Adolescent Decision Making: Implications for Theory, Practice, and Public Policy," 7 *Psychological Science in the Public Interest* 1 (2006) (excessive sentences inuring children to punishment).

42. I do believe, however, that it does depend upon finding a nonutilitarian consequentialist justification.

scientific hypothesis lies in the predictions that hypothesis supports.[43] Part of the justification for the idea of a benefit in harsh treatment lies in the fact that it leads to the desired end: It enables the incompatibilist who believes that libertarianism is untenable to support a decent criminal justice system. The plausibility and desirability of maintaining the line between correction and preventive detention lends itself, then, in support of the assumption of the benefit that I am trying to characterize here: if a line there must be, then a benefit there must be.[44]

In the second place, much of the benefit to the offender and the potential offender lies in plain view. The competent but dangerous man (whatever the criterion for dangerousness) may avoid harsh treatment by avoiding crime; the man who has committed a crime may enjoy the limits on correction imposed by a rule of proportionality. All of the limits historically associated with punishment add up to a benefit when compared with the possibility of therapy and detention, and have traditionally been viewed as such. We will see that such an arrangement, when properly instituted, allows the greatest possible freedom consistent with a desirable level of security.

The Good Life and the Capacity to Conform to the Law

The first premise is this: It is a benefit to individuals to learn how to live within the rules of their society. To see that that is so requires a discussion of what we may call "the good life." The good life, for our purposes, is one that can be lived without running afoul of the machinery of the criminal justice system.[45] In an unjust society, like Nazi Germany or apartheid South Africa, it may be impossible for some members of the society to avoid the law no matter what they do. Jews, gypsies, and homosexuals in Germany were hounded by the law. Blacks in South Africa could avoid the law only by remaining docile in their appointed places. Part of the very point of a just society is that a person may so plan a productive and fruitful life in such a society to avoid conflict with the law.[46]

43. Joseph Keim Campbell points out that this view is not uncontroversial and cites the debate in philosophy of science between "predictionism" and "explanationism." He concedes, however, that in every theory predictions provide at least some evidence. Private correspondence, June 3, 2011.

44. See "Persons and Punishment" at 485–486; David Dolinko, "Morris on Paternalism and Punishment," 18 *Law and Philosophy* 345, 345 (1999). I am encouraged in principle by Herbert Morris's analysis of benefit in "A Paternalistic Theory of Punishment" and of rights in "Persons and Punishment," though I do not follow it in detail, and the errors I will make cannot be attributed to Morris. The main contribution that Morris made, I believe, was to show that one of the great benefits of punishment for the offender was precisely that it was *not* therapy and detention.

45. Compare Morris, "Paternalistic Theory of Punishment," at 265.

46. This avoids the question of the place of the impoverished in a just society; the very poor do not have the same relative freedom to adopt the life plan of their choosing.

Attempting to control crime by incapacitating all those who might present a danger to society would be unthinkable. It would preserve the security of some at the cost of the freedom of many; it would be devastatingly expensive to those whose security was assured; and of course to the extent that no one could be certain of not being labeled dangerous to society, there would be a psychological cost as well to those whose security was being assured. On the other hand, controlling crime through the threat of correction allows the greatest possible freedom consistent with some reasonable level of security. For this reason, it is important that the guidelines set down by the threat of correction be able to be processed by the citizen, and that correction itself be capable of having an effect on the citizen. The good life (as I understand it here) requires understanding, the ability to reason counterfactually from what we understand, and the ability to control behavior in conformity with our reasoned conclusions.[47] We may refer to these capacities, taken together, as the capability of converting one's better judgment into action. This capability enables the citizen to grasp the threat of correction, to foresee the consequences of compliance and noncompliance, and to conform her behavior to the law.

Moreover, given society's obligation to secure some sort of order and safety, the offender will be subject either to some sort of limited correction or to indefinite confinement or treatment. It is a benefit to the offender to be dealt with in the first way rather than the second, provided that corrective treatment maintains the respect for the offender that is appropriate—an assumption that has not always been true of the treatment of prisoners in our prisons. Some of the reasons that it is preferable have already been canvassed in the early sections of this paper.[48] The offender subjected to correction remains, in a limited way, in charge of his life and is not subject to manipulation for an indefinite period of time. Again, we should concede that the offender himself might not acknowledge the preferability of correction over preventive detention, and in that sense benefit is an objective notion, not dependent upon personal preferences or beliefs.

The Educative Function of the Law

The second premise—that correction is a way of teaching the meaning and importance of the rules—presents a different sort of problem. It is an empirical

47. These requirements are more or less equivalent to the requirements for "reasons-responsiveness." See John Martin Fischer and Mark Ravizza, *Responsibility and Control, passim* (1998). The difference between my view and theirs is that in their view satisfaction of these requirements is sufficient for responsibility, and on my view it is not. I owe the comparison between the views to Thomas Nadelhoffer.

48. And of course corrective measures may be so degrading, as has happened in American prisons in the past, that preventive detention would be the preferable option.

question. Though a great deal of ink has been expended defending the idea of the educative nature of the criminal law, it remains a defeasible claim that may be refuted by facts. I accept it tentatively here. The notion of benefit that I am advancing depends upon it, and if it turns out to be false the question would be whether some other notion of individual benefit would be supportable.[49]

The Line

This justification of correction, skeletal though it may be, suggests a natural line between those who may benefit from correction and those who cannot. We must distinguish between (a) those who are capable of converting their better judgment into action and (b) those who are not.[50] Among those who lack the requisite capacity to adapt, we must distinguish:

(ai) those who are unlikely to ever be able to acquire it

from

(aii) those who (with or without help) are likely to be able to acquire it.

Again, among those who have the capacity, we must distinguish:

(bi) those who will use it to avoid getting into trouble

49. Benefit to the offender must also be distinguished from benefit to the community because of the danger of collapsing this proposal into general utilitarianism. We may notice this striking difference between benefit to the offender and benefit to the community: Imagine a society in which it is possible to tailor persons so that they would not commit crimes. Individuals, in other words, would not be autonomous; their behavior would be programmed to the extent necessary to prevent them from violating the law. If such a thing were possible, and at a reasonable cost, the utilitarian might well be required to opt for it. You might reject that conclusion, of course: such a world would not be a world of maximum happiness and so not utilitarian, you might argue (though on what grounds I am not sure). But the point is this: What if it *were* a world of the greatest possible happiness? We would still prefer a world of autonomous human beings; human beings, we think, are better off making their own decisions. Each individual life is fuller, even if by any measurement the sum of happiness is less. Maintaining a world of autonomous human beings controlled only by the threat of punishment is a very different thing from merely seeking a world with the minimum of crime and a maximum of happiness, and it may well cost considerably more.

50. Although all of this is a matter of more or less, and that must be considered in a fully developed system of correction, for the sake of simplicity I will ignore the point here and assume that everyone can be fit neatly into (a) or (b).

from

(bii) those who refuse to.

A different sort of justification is required for the use of force by the state in each of these cases.

Consider first those who are incapable of adapting to the circumstances. There are three different reasons why this might be so: (1) a deficit in the capacity to understand the circumstances; (2) a deficit in the ability to reason counterfactually from the circumstances; or (3) a deficit in the ability to control behavior. Someone who is unable to understand the circumstances will for obvious reasons not be able to adapt to the circumstances; and the circumstances we are in, including the circumstance of the law's prohibitions, dictate the likelihood that our actions will yield the consequences we are aiming for. Very much the same thing is true of someone who is unable to reason counterfactually, though for a different reason. And someone who is unable to control her behavior may not be able to bring about the consequences she wishes, even though she understands her circumstances and can reason perfectly well to the consequences of her actions.

None of the three capacities requires metaphysical freedom; all are consistent with determinism, as they are with a world in which causation and chance are intermingled. All three would be necessary for responsible action, but not sufficient; all three are possible in a world in which there is no responsible action. The class of individuals I am circumscribing here and the line I hope to draw between them and those who can convert their judgment into action does not depend upon responsibility.[51]

The question, then, is whether correction has any role to play in these cases. We begin a search for the answer by noting that the effectiveness of the threat of correction is weakened in these cases by the fact that a threat depends for its effectiveness upon the object of the threat acting to avoid the dire consequences promised. Threats are not always effective, even with those capable of converting their best judgment into action; in such cases an individual's best judgment may be that the negative consequences the threat promises are better than the alternative. Even so, where the individual is capable of converting information into action that benefits her, the threat of correction will often be effective.

It is a different matter when the individual who is the object of the threat has difficulty comprehending the circumstances created by the threat, or in working out which of his actions will enable him to avoid the negative consequences,

51. See my "Case for a Purely Volitional Insanity Defense," 42 *Texas Tech Law Review* 481 (2009), section II.B.

or in bringing the information he has to bear in order to bring about the action that accords with his best judgment. (It is all, I repeat, a matter of more or less; I mean here to be dealing with those who are most handicapped in these respects.) In these cases we cannot trust to corrective threats to control crime, and correction will be more or less ineffective.

H. L. A. Hart argues, against Bentham, that the utilitarian cannot make this argument because punishing those who cannot control their behavior may be effective in deterring others who *can* control their behavior and who are considering the criminal path. But the only concern of the utilitarian is with overall or average happiness or utility; there is no specific concern for the individual punished, except as one among the many whose utility is to be counted. The difference in what I am proposing is that the individual corrected must derive some benefit (other than his share of the overall social benefit) from the correction administered. If there is no possibility of such a benefit, then correction is without foundation.[52]

Is the state entitled to take other action in such cases? Is the state entitled to detain an individual who falls into this category? Is it entitled to treat him without his consent? In the case of those who are not able to conform to the law, there is reason for caution. Since the state cannot, at any given time, be distinguished from the particular government in control of it, this interest in security is an interest best hedged with precautions; it should only be used when clearly called for, when the possible harm is very serious, when the likelihood of it is great, and when less restrictive alternatives have proved futile. Nevertheless, there will be times when treatment or detention is called for.

Among those who cannot conform their behavior to the law, we must distinguish between (ai) above and (aii). There is a great difference in the treatment to be accorded to those who are unlikely ever to gain or regain the capacity to convert their best judgment into action (ai), and those who are likely (with or

52. Perhaps this is the best place to deal with a question that confronts theories like the one I am advocating: Why not grant the benefits of harsh treatment to individuals who are considered dangerous but have not yet offended? The question is a difficult one, and not only for incompatibilist theories. As I have argued elsewhere the requirement of desert is no protection for the innocent in our current system of law. For if we give a label like "regulation" to detention and treatment, there is nothing either in the law or in ethical theory to prevent us from imposing detention and treatment on those who are dangerous but have not yet broken the law. Desert would preclude *punishment*, but regulation for the good of the community is not punishment since it is not intended to inflict suffering, and it is not given out on the basis of any prior crimes. Desert, I have argued, is nothing more than a label that makes us feel better about what we are doing. It is no insulation against detention and therapy for the innocent. "The Abolition of Punishment," *supra*. The question is therefore a question for all theories concerning the state use of force to prevent crimes and does not raise a special problem for this incompatibilist theory.

without help) to do so (aii). The psychopath (if anyone fitting that personality type really exists) is a paradigm of the first classification. The child is a paradigm of the second classification, as is the person whose incapacity will respond to therapy. A full discussion would be necessary to illuminate each of these cases. For now it is sufficient that a ground exists to separate both these sorts of individuals from those who may be subjected to correction, and that the ground is independent of the notions of responsibility.

The Limits of Correction

What about the other side of the question? Are there any limits on the imposition of correction, limits roughly corresponding to the limits that we believe mark the perimeters of punishment? There are three sorts of limits to be accounted for here. The first would correspond to the limitation of punishment to those who are responsible for what they do, which in the past has excluded young children and the mentally ill. Such a limit is implicit in the line between those who have the capability to convert their best judgment into action and those who do not. The second would be a limitation of correction to those who have actually committed a crime. Not correcting those who have not yet committed crimes is part of the trade-off, as I see it. The continued freedom of the person who has not yet committed a crime is what he gains in return for giving up, when he does commit a crime—his right not to be harshly treated. It is in virtue of giving up that right that the offender is not corrected *until* he has offended.

The third limitation is a limitation upon the length of sentences for those subjected to correction. This limitation on punishment—we once imagined—was imposed by the elusive thing called desert. One guilty of a serious crime deserves a longer sentence; one guilty of a lesser crime deserves a lesser sentence. Our resistance to hard incompatibilism has in part been motivated by the concern that this limitation would fall away, and there would be nothing to prevent the state from imposing the most serious sentences for the most minor crimes. The fear was not that if no one is responsible then no one may be punished, but rather that if no one is responsible then there is no limit to the severity of the measures the state might adopt.

If there is an equivalent limitation on correction, it must derive from the limits of the benefit that the person corrected may derive. The benefit to be derived comes in large part from the role of correction in impressing upon the offender the meaning of the prohibition and the seriousness of the consequences. This consideration entails that initial sentences be as short as possible, for several very different reasons. The first is that there is a process of acclimatization that, after a period, is counterproductive. The person who learns to live his life in prison will be less threatened by it in the future. The second reason is that the offender who reoffends must be offered a supplemented sentence the second time around, on the ground that (given our rationale for correction) the first sentence was insufficient to make the point. But if the first sentence is long, there will be little room to expand the second sentence. Third, the length of sentences is a way of conveying the seriousness of crimes, and so serious crimes must be attended by longer sentences. And finally the economy of controlling crime through threats is lost if every offender ends up serving the longest possible sentence. We can add here the rationale of Bentham: When we punish each crime as severely as possible, we lose the opportunity to create an incentive for the offender to limit his crimes. For these reasons, then, prison sentences should be relatively short, at least initially; should be of determinate length; and should correspond in length roughly to the seriousness of the crime.

The Hard Case

In his paper "A Jurisprudence of Dangerousness,"[53] Christopher Slobogin has undertaken to deal with an especially troublesome case, the case of the individual who, though capable of conforming his behavior to the requirements of the law, refuses to do so. This is not, I think, simply a question of the recidivist or the "hardened criminal," both of whom are likely to respond to the threat of imminent reprisal for their bad behavior, but of someone who for some reason, perhaps as a matter of principle, cannot be moved by any threat to avoid breaking the law. I will confine my category (bii)—those who have the capacity to adapt their behavior to the law but refuse to use it—to such individuals, assuming that recidivists or hardened criminals may be dealt with by repeated and increasingly lengthy prison terms, justified as attempts to get the message through to them. We cannot assume, however, that the terrorist and the person committed to civil disobedience, just to take two examples, will be so easily dealt with.

This problem suggests an approach that is consistent with the general outlook of the hard incompatibilist, and that is this: The trial of those competent to guide their own behavior should include a "personality" component, much as the French trial does.[54] Once the offender has passed the initial psychological screening and is entered into the criminal correction system—that is, once the offender is adjudged capable of conforming his behavior to the law—a second psychological investigation should be undertaken, if called for[55]; and

53. 98 *Northwestern Law Review* 1 (2003). See my "Sex Offenders, Unlawful Combatants, and Preventive Detention," 84 *North Carolina Law Review* 77 (2005), available at SSRN: <http://ssrn.com/abstract=735266>.

54. Richard Posner, *Law and Literature* 62 (3rd ed. 2009)

55. My feeling is that only in exceptional categories of cases will it be called for.

if the offender is determined to put himself into category (bii), the sentences that face him will be increased to include a period of incapacitation. Indeed, these should be the only cases in which very long periods of imprisonment are countenanced. The details of this proposal of course need to be worked out. The important point, however, is that this sort of recalcitrance is not sufficient reason to redraw the line. Those who are competent to convert their own best judgment into action should be subject to determinate correction and not to indefinite detention or forced treatment.

In German law, as in Italian law, a period of preventive detention may be added, in the case of those judged to be especially dangerous, to the sentence required by the criminal law. But the outer limits of that period must be decided upon at the original sentencing for his crime.[56] In terms of correction, that would mean that the first part of his corrective sentence would be punitive and the second part incapacitative. The European Court of Human Rights has given its sanction to that way of doing things, with the understanding that the subsequent period of detention is *penal*, or, in our terms, aimed at correction.[57] The wisdom of this course is this: Since it is and probably always will be impossible to distinguish between the competent offender who does not obey the law and the competent offender who will not under any circumstances obey the law, the fact that the period of incapacitation imposed may be dispensed with if the offender proves to be less recalcitrant than originally imagined is both an incentive for the offender to prove the original judgment wrong and an opportunity to reassess the character of the offender after his punitive sentence is complete.

CONCLUSION

The question we began with was whether the incompatibilist could account for certain important distinctions in treatment of offenders, distinctions that exist in a criminal law premised upon responsibility, retribution, and desert and that seem to be essential to a decent system of law. I have proposed what seems to me an incompatibilist system that would preserve as much of this list of distinctions as deserves to be preserved. The proposal includes corrective harsh treatment for those capable of benefiting from such treatment, but only insofar as could be justified by the benefit; for others I have proposed detention and treatment. There is no need to assume responsibility for behavior, at least insofar as responsibility entails desert and retribution. All of this depends crucially on the notion of "benefit" involved, and I readily concede that no ordinary notion of benefit will do the trick. The benefit required by the theory is in large part defined by the theory.

56. See Articles 61 to 66 of the German Criminal Code.

57. M. v. Germany, ECtHR, application #19359/04, 10/05/2010.

Whatever knowledge or information the offender acquires that inclines him to adapt to the demands of a just criminal law will help to fill out the notion.

There is one more obvious objection to be addressed, and it is an objection that must be met by any theory that proposes to do what I have undertaken in this paper: If you succeed in finding some feature that distinguishes the sort of case that calls for correction from the sort of case that does not, why not simply call it "responsibility"? Why not see what you have done as a kind of compatibilism—or semi-compatibilism—and admit that responsibility is just as consistent with a scientific view of the world as are the ability to understand, the ability to reason counterfactually, and the ability to control. Joseph Keim Campbell, for example, espouses such a view.[58] I feel no obligation to answer this point here, since my point is not to show that there is no such thing as responsibility, but rather to see if those who reject the notion of responsibility (as I in fact do) can make sense of a two-track system of crime control, with correction (or some other substitute for punishment) on one side and therapy and detention on the other.

Nevertheless, I believe that there is an answer. It lies in the difference between a system that justifies harsh treatment for the offender by appealing to the fact that he deserves it and a system that justifies such treatment by appealing to the benefit it brings to the offender, as an alternative to indefinite detention. The hard incompatibilist rejects the view that sees the criminal offender under the ancient rubric of "sinner," but sees him rather as someone who is at a disadvantage because of his inadequate appreciation of society's norms. Although it is of course possible to *label* the ability to convert harsh treatment into benefit as responsibility, the question is whether the sense of the word is retained—the sense that justifies us in seeing harsh treatment inflicted without any feeling of regret. It is a sense that depends upon a notion of desert, the mark of Cain that distinguishes the good people from the bad—those who, in Western tradition, were said to be headed by their own choice for everlasting damnation.[59]

58. See his "Compatibilist Theory of Alternative Possibilities." 88 *Philosophical Studies* 319 (1997).

59. The compatibilist agrees with the hard incompatibilist about the nature of the world. The difference between them is that the compatibilist applies the word "responsible" where the incompatibilist refuses to apply it, gaining thereby the advantage of a shortcut to the justification of harsh treatment: If you are responsible for wrongdoing then you deserve punishment, and though the compatibilist may have to spend time working out when and whether it would, in the particular case, be appropriate to give you the punishment you deserve, he will have no problem justifying giving it to you. He thereby saves himself all the hard work that goes into trying to explain why we may punish people who have no true freedom of choice. Indeed, if you read the literature with a critical eye you will discover that this is one of the selling points for compatibilist theories. The incompatibilist, on the other hand, cannot hide from himself the difficulty of the task that faces us, of justifying the brutal but apparently indispensible institution of harsh treatment for criminal offenders.

The cash value of the difference can be found in the shorter sentences and the milder treatment: If the harsh treatment is administered not because the offender has lost his right to be treated with respect, but rather out of respect and for his own benefit, a very different approach to criminal justice will be called for. At the same time, the hard incompatibilist may reject the view that all crime must be a result of neurological *defect* of some sort, and admit the possibility that neurologically sound individuals may yield to temptation and commit crimes.

PART THREE

Compatibilism and Retributivism

5

Compatibilist Criminal Law*

STEPHEN J. MORSE

INTRODUCTION

The criminal common law is a beautiful, albeit sometimes ramshackle, institution devoted to blaming and punishing culpable agents that has been developing for well over half a millennium. In this chapter, I shall use the term, "common law," more broadly than its usual definition as judge-made law, to include penal legislation and the interaction between the legislature (influenced by politics of course) and judges to develop the penal law.[1] Although all United States jurisdictions have a statutory penal code, the criminal law can be fully comprehended only if the accretion of interpretations by the courts is considered. Indeed, most penal codes are based on preexisting common law. Many legislative changes are responses to common law innovations, changes that will then be interpreted by the courts. So it goes. The common law is the product of

* This chapter, in revised form, is reprinted by permission of Oxford University Press from Nicole Vincent (ed.) NEUROSCIENCE AND LEGAL RESPONSIBILITY (2013).

1. A classic example is the federal law of legal insanity. Before 1984, the federal criminal code did not contain an insanity defense. Instead, each of the circuit courts of appeal had made the law of legal insanity by adopting one test or another. By 1984, all but the First Circuit had adopted the Model Penal Code test, which excuses a defendant if, at the time of the crime, as a result of mental disorder the defendant lacked substantial capacity either to appreciate the wrongfulness of his action or to conform his conduct to the requirements of the law. American Law Institute, MODEL PENAL CODE, §4.01(1) (1962). In response to the unpopular Hinckley verdict, which was based on the MPC test in the US Court of Appeals for the District of Columbia, in 1984 Congress passed the Insanity Defense Reform Act, which imposed a uniform and much more limited "cognitive" test for legal insanity that would apply in all federal trials nationwide. 18 USC17(a). Since then, the federal courts have been interpreting the federal test.

an immense number of penal statutes and judicial decisions over the years, and it has stood the test of time as the product of human trial and error. We common lawyers like to think that it is impossible to produce an ex ante watertight criminal code and that the bottom-up, "organic" methodology of the common law process will ultimately produce reasonably coherent and just, but not perfect, criminal law.

The thesis of this chapter is simple and straightforward. The criminal law is a thoroughly folk psychological enterprise that is completely consistent with the truth of determinism or universal causation. It does not claim that judges and legislators throughout the centuries of development of modern criminal law explicitly adopted the compatibilist position in the metaphysical debate about determinism, free will, and responsibility. Far from it. Most criminal justice actors are probably implicitly libertarian and believe that we somehow have contra-causal free will. Criminal law doctrine and practice are also fully consistent with metaphysical libertarianism, but I consider this position extremely implausible in the modern, scientific age.[2] Human beings, as complex as they are, are still part of the physical universe and subject to the same laws that govern all phenomena. In short, I believe that libertarianism does not furnish a justifiable foundation for an institution that is essentially about blaming and punishing culpable agents. If determinism or something quite like it is true, as I assume it is, then only compatibilism provides a secure basis for criminal responsibility.

I do not aim to argue for the truth of compatibilism. It is sufficient that it is one of the two plausible positions in the metaphysical debate—the other being hard determinist incompatibilism, of course—and, in one form or another, it is probably the position held by the vast majority of professional philosophers.[3] Thus, I will simply assume that compatibilism is a thoroughly acceptable, albeit contestable, metaphysics. I am not suggesting that compatibilism is monolithic; there are many compatilisms that differ widely in details. But all have in common the possibility of genuine responsibility in a deterministic or universally caused universe, and this is an entirely plausible, defensible position. Based on it, I will try to demonstrate that it provides an accurate positive account of criminal law and that compatibilist criminal law is normatively desirable.

I begin with a brief account of desert–disease jurisprudence that explains under what conditions the state may constrain a person's liberty. The purpose

2. For a particularly trenchant critique, *see*, Hilary Bok, Freedom and Responsibility (1998).

3. *See*, http://philpapers.org/surveys/results.pl (reporting the results of a 2009 survey of professional philosophers that showed that a majority are either compatibilists or tend toward compatibilism).

is to situate in legal context the place of criminal justice as a means of social control. Next, the chapter offers an introduction to the criminal law's implicit psychology and view of the person that underpins desert–disease jurisprudence. Following that, the chapter offers a nutshell summary of foundational assumptions of criminal law and of criminal law doctrine. The next section demonstrates that the doctrines and practices we have are fully consistent with the truth of determinism. Then, the chapter turns to the external challenges to compatibilist criminal law and demonstrates why they do not succeed and would lead to normatively undesirable doctrines and practices. The final section addresses the normative desirability of compatibilist criminal law.

DESERT–DISEASE JURISPRUDENCE

At present, the state's ability to deprive people of their liberty is constrained by desert–disease jurisprudence. The state may imprison people in the criminal justice system if they deserve punishment for crimes they have committed,[4] and it may civilly commit dangerous people if they are not responsible agents—usually because they have a mental abnormality, such as a major mental disorder.[5] Otherwise, with rare, limited exceptions, such as rejecting bail for dangerous agents,[6] the state must leave people at liberty no matter how potentially dangerous they may be. The concern with justifying and protecting liberty that produces the desert–disease constraints is deeply rooted in the conception of rational personhood. Only human beings self-consciously and intentionally decide how they should live; only human beings have projects that are essential to living a good life. Only human beings have expectations of each other and require justification for interference in each other's lives that will prevent seeking the good. If liberty is unjustifiably deprived, a good life is impossible. In sum, both the criminal and the medical-psychological systems of behavior control require a justification in addition to public safety—desert for wrongdoing or nonresponsibility (based on disease)—to justify the extraordinary liberty infringements that these systems impose.

4. The notion of desert I am employing is simply the traditional retributive conclusion that if an offender's behavior satisfies the elements of a charged offense and no justification or excuse obtains, then the offender is culpable and deserves the ensuing blame and punishment. All these concepts are discussed in more detail below.

5. I have explored the civil-criminal distinction as a basis for confinement elsewhere and will therefore provide only the briefest sketch here. *See generally*, Stephen J. Morse, *Uncontrollable Urges and Irrational People*, 88 Virginia L. Rev. 1025 (2002) [hereinafter Morse, *Irrational People*]; Stephen J. Morse, *Blame and Danger: An Essay on Preventive Detention*, 76 B.U. L. Rev. 113, 116–122 (1996) [hereinafter Morse, *Blame and Danger*].

6. United States v. Salerno, 481 U.S. 739, 741, 755 (1987).

Virtually all criminals are rational, responsible agents, and according to the dominant story, the deprivation imposed on them—punishment—is premised on considerations of desert. No agent should be punished without desert for wrongdoing, which exists only if the agent culpably caused or attempted prohibited harm. The threat of punishment for a culpable violation of the criminal law is itself arguably a form of preventive infringement on liberty, but it is an ordinary, "base-rate" infringement that requires no special justification. After all, no one has a right to harm other people unjustifiably. In our society the punishment for virtually all serious crimes, and thus for dangerous criminals, is incapacitation, which is preventive during the term of imprisonment. But criminals must actually have culpably caused or attempted harm to warrant the intervention of punishment. We cannot detain them unless they deserve it, and desert requires culpable wrongdoing. In the interest of liberty, we leave potentially dangerous people free to pursue their projects until they actually offend, even if their future wrongdoing is quite certain. We are willing to take great risks in the name of liberty.

For people who are dangerous because they are disordered or because they are too young to "know better," the usual presumption in favor of maximum liberty yields. Because the agent is not rational or not fully rational, the person's choice about how to live demands less respect, and the person is not morally responsible for his or her dangerousness. The person can therefore be treated more "objectively," like the rest of the world's dangerous but nonresponsible instrumentalities, ranging from hurricanes to microbes to wild beasts.[7] In brief, agents incapable of rationality do not actually have to cause or attempt harm to justify nonpunitive intervention. We can take preemptive precautions, including broad preventive detention, with nonresponsible agents based on an estimate of the risk they present. Justified on consequential grounds, such deprivation will be acceptable if the conditions of deprivation are both humane and no more stringent than is necessary to reduce the risk for harm. Such deprivations are forms of greater or lesser quarantine and may include "treatment," but in theory they are not punishment, and they should never have a punitive justification or effect.[8]

In sum, the normative basis of desert–disease jurisprudence is that it enhances liberty and autonomy by leaving people free to pursue their projects

7. Such people, of course, continue to deserve enhanced concern and respect in virtue of their being human, and they can never be completely objectified.

8. The civil and nonpunitive characterization of such interventions often justifies lesser procedural protections for the potential subject. *See, e.g.*, Allen v. Illinois. 478 U.S. 364, 374–375 (1986) (holding that the Fifth Amendment guarantee against compelled self-incrimination does not apply in a proceeding to determine whether a person is a "sexually dangerous person" because the proceeding is not "criminal").

unless they responsibly commit a crime or unless they are nonresponsibly dangerous through no fault of their own. This scheme maximizes respect for liberty, dignity, and autonomy. Responsible agents are left free to pursue their projects on the theory that a rational agent may always recognize the wrongness and danger to oneself of criminally infringing the legitimate interests of others. Therefore, the state may not intervene unless the agent has attempted or committed a crime. If agents are not responsible for their danger, then the usual presumptions in favor of liberty and autonomy yield because they are based on rational agency.

This is a satisfyingly neat account, but desert–disease jurisprudence leaves a "gap." It provides no mechanism to restrain dangerous people who may not be punished because they have committed no crime or have completed their sentence and who may not be civilly committed because they are responsible agents. The state tries to fill the gap by expanding desert and disease jurisprudence. For example, desert jurisprudence is widened by lengthening sentences or by recidivist sentencing laws. Disease jurisprudence is expanded by widening the definition of nonresponsibility, most egregiously in sex offender civil commitment statutes. Both types of expansion are open to substantial normative and practical problems, however, so the gap inevitably remains. There is no seamless set of alternative means to preventively detain dangerous agents. Nonetheless, legislatures continue to try, and the Courts usually approve.[9]

THE IMPLICIT PSYCHOLOGY AND CONCEPT OF THE PERSON IN CRIMINAL LAW

What is the law's implicit psychology and concept of the person that underpins desert–disease jurisprudence and criminal justice more generally? Lawyers take the law's implicit psychology for granted because there is seldom any need to identify or to question it. It is crucial to recognize it consciously, however, in order to understand the doctrines and practices of criminal law.

The law presupposes the "folk psychological" view of the person and behavior. "Folk psychology" is the term used to identify any psychological theory that causally explains behavior *in part* by mental states such as desires, beliefs, intentions, and plans. Biological, psychological, and sociological variables also play a role, but folk psychology considers mental states fundamental to a full explanation of human action. Human behavior cannot be adequately understood if mental state causation is completely eliminated. Lawyers, philosophers, and scientists do, of course, argue about the definitions of mental states and

9. Ewing v. California, 538 U.S. 11, 14–15, 30 (2003) (upholding enhanced sentences under California's three strikes law).

about theories of the nature of human action, but that does not undermine the general claim that mental states are fundamental. Indeed, the arguments and evidence disputants use to convince others presuppose the folk psychological view of the person. Brains don't convince each other; people do.

Folk psychology does not presuppose the truth of free will, it is perfectly consistent with the truth of determinism, it does not hold that we have minds that are independent of our bodies (although it, and ordinary speech, sound that way), and it presupposes no particular moral or political view. It does not claim that all mental states are necessarily conscious or that people go through a conscious decision-making process each time that they act. It allows for "thoughtless," automatic, and habitual actions and for nonconscious intentions. Folk psychology does presuppose that human action can at least be explained by mental state explanations or that it will be responsive to reasons, including incentives, under the right conditions. The definition of folk psychology being used here does not depend on any particular bit of folk wisdom about how people are motivated, feel, or act. Any of these bits, for example, that people intend the natural and probable consequences of their actions, may be wrong. The definition insists only that human action is in part causally explained by mental states.

Brief reflection should indicate that the law's psychology must be a folk psychological theory, a view of the person as a conscious (and potentially self-conscious) creature who forms and acts on intentions that are the product of the person's other mental states such as desires, beliefs, and plans. We are practical reasoners, the sort of creatures that can act for and respond to reasons. The law does not treat persons generally as nonintentional creatures or mechanical forces of nature. As a system of rules that guides and governs human interaction, law tells citizens what they may and may not do, what they must or must not do, what abilities are required competently to perform certain tasks, and what consequences will follow from their conduct. Law is primarily action guiding[10] and could not guide people ex ante and ex post unless people could use rules as premises in their reasoning about how they should behave. Otherwise, law as an action-guiding normative system of rules would be useless, and perhaps incoherent.[11] Law can directly and indirectly affect the world we inhabit only by its influence on human beings who can potentially use legal rules to guide conduct. Unless people were capable of understanding and then

10. See, George Sher, In Praise of Blame 123 (2006) (stating that although philosophers disagree about the requirements and justifications of what morality requires, there is widespread agreement that "the primary task of morality is to guide action"); John R. Searle, *End of the Revolution*, 43 N.Y. Rev. of Books, at 33, 35 (2002).

11. Scott J. Shapiro, *Law, Morality, and the Guidance of Conduct*, 6 Legal Theory 127, 131–132 (2000).

using legal rules to guide their conduct, law would be powerless to affect human behavior.[12]

The legal view of the person does not hold that people must always reason or consistently behave rationally according to some preordained notion of what rationality entails. Rather, the law's view is that people are capable of acting for reasons and are capable of minimal rationality according to predominantly conventional, socially constructed standards. What the law requires is the ordinary person's commonsense view of rationality, not the technical notion that might be acceptable within the disciplines of economics, philosophy, psychology, computer science, and the like. Virtually everything for which people deserve to be praised, blamed, rewarded, or punished is the product of mental causation[13] and, in principle, responsive to reason. People are intentional agents with the potential to act, to violate expectations of what they owe each other, and to do wrong.

Many scientists and some philosophers of mind and action consider folk psychology to be a primitive or prescientific view of human behavior. For the foreseeable future, however, the law will be based on the folk psychological model of the person and behavior described. Until and unless scientific discoveries convince us that our view of ourselves is radically wrong, a claim discussed in the penultimate section of this chapter, the basic explanatory apparatus of folk psychology will remain central. It is vital that we not lose sight of this model lest we fall into confusion when various claims about criminal responsibility are made. Any evidence allegedly relevant to criminal responsibility must be translated into the folk psychological framework.

CRIMINAL LAW ASSUMPTIONS

The predominant view is that criminal law is generated by the harm and fault principles. The harm principle guides which actions and omissions the criminal

12. *Id.* at 131–132. This view assumes that law is sufficiently knowable to guide conduct, but a contrary assumption is largely incoherent. As Shapiro writes:

> "Legal skepticism is an absurd doctrine. It is absurd because the law cannot be the sort of thing that is unknowable. If a system of norms were unknowable, then that system would not be a legal system. One important reason why the law must be knowable is that its function is to guide conduct." *Id.*

I do not assume that legal rules are always clear and thus capable of precise action guidance. If most rules in a legal system were not sufficiently clear most of the time, however, the system could not function. Further, the principle of legality dictates that criminal law rules should be especially clear.

13. I do not mean to imply dualism here. I am simply accepting the folk-psychological view that mental states—which are fully produced by and realizable in the brain—play a genuinely causal role in explaining human behavior.

law should prohibit. There is great controversy, of course, about what types of harms should be criminalized, but virtually all criminal law theorists believe that decision to criminalize behavior should be based on the harm that behavior causes or risks.[14] The fault principle guides judgments about which agents may fairly be blamed and punished and how much they should be punished. As we shall see, indicia of fault are part of the definition of virtually all crimes.

Criminal blame and punishment entail the intentional infliction of pain by the state, and they therefore require substantial justification. Although the Supreme Court of the United States has never held that the Constitution requires a jurisdiction to adopt any particular justification of punishment, there is widespread agreement that retributivism and consequentialism (especially deterrence and incapacitation) are the leading justifications. Retributivism is a form of deontological justice that holds that offenders should receive their just deserts. No one should be punished unless the agent deserves such treatment, and no one should be punished more than they proportionately deserve for their criminal conduct. Retribution is not revenge, of course, and contrary to what many people think, retribution is silent about how much punishment is deserved in an ultimate sense. Unless one is a moral realist who thinks that there is in principle a right answer to how much punishment of what type each offender deserves, one can be either a tough or tender retributivist. Retributivism is not committed to harsh punishments. Finally, a retributivist can be either obligatory or permissive. The former argues that the state is obliged to give offenders their just deserts. The latter thinks that the state has permission to impose just deserts, but need not do so if it has good reason not to. This is an important distinction, but for the purposes of this chapter, it is not relevant.

Consequentialists think that the major goal of punishment is to prevent crime by general and specific deterrence and by incapacitating offenders. A purely consequential theory would not punish even a blameworthy offender if no social good would be achieved by punishment, and it would apportion punishment to maximize crime prevention. In its pure form, the offender's desert would be neither a necessary nor a limiting principle because desert bears no necessary relation to the goal of crime prevention. Notions of fault would simply be epistemic guides for deciding when prevention is maximized by punishing an offender.

Most criminal law theorists are not pure consequentialists, but a substantial number are pure retributivists. The majority are probably mixed theorists who

14. *See generally,* Joel Feinberg, The Moral Limits of the Criminal Law: Harm to Others (Vol. 1,1987); Offense to Others (Vol. 2, 1988); Harm to Self (Vol. 3, 1986); Harmless Wrongdoing (Vol. 4, 1990) (providing a complete account of the limits of criminalization based on the harm principle).

believe that desert is a necessary condition for just punishment and that desert should set a proportionality limit on how much punishment an offender receives. Within the range of justifiable punishment that desert sets, the punishment imposed may be adjusted to achieve consequential goals. Thus, among criminal law theorists, desert plays a crucial role because it is both a necessary and limiting condition on punishment.

If one examines the penal codes and appellate court decisions that explicitly address the justifications for punishment, the picture is less clear. Many penal codes contain a provision setting forth the jurisdiction's justifications, but these are usually just vague lists of retributive and consequential concerns and give no guidance for how they should be weighed, balanced, and applied. Nonetheless, there has been an apparent and major shift in penal policy in the United States beginning in the 1960s. For much of the 20th century, American sentencing schemes strongly favored indeterminate sentencing with very wide ranges for most serious crimes. Although in theory and to some degree in practice, desert set a cap to the permissible ranges, the justification for this practice was largely a rehabilitation model. Deciding when to release the prisoner would depend on the professional judgment of the parole officers concerning the prisoner's rehabilitation progress. At the maximum term, the prisoner would of course have to be released even if he had not been rehabilitated and was still dangerous, but the maximum was typically quite long. Thus, lengthy incapacitation was possible, and many otherwise unrehabilitated prisoners would simply "age out" of future violent conduct.

Although the indeterminate sentencing model was conceptually coherent, in practice it was subject to severe problems that led to its demise in many jurisdictions. First, it led to unprincipled and arbitrary discretion. Parole officials had virtually unreviewable authority to make release decisions, but they had neither a coherent conceptual approach to such problems nor accurate predictive validity about who would be dangerous if released. The alleged rehabilitative programs available in the prisons were either paltry or unvalidated. In a word, the officials were "flying blind," and this produced differential treatment that could not possibly be justified and was widely believed to be racially biased. In addition, many believed that the sentences actually served and the maximum terms bore insufficient relation to the punishment that offenders deserved.

In the late 1960s and early 1970s, the critiques of indeterminate sentencing reached an unusually bipartisan crescendo. Critics and politicians from across the political spectrum called for a new regime that would tie offenders' punishments to their just deserts, and the legislatures responded.[15] Simultaneously, and

15. *See* American Friends Service Committee, Struggle for Justice: A Report on Crime and Punishment in America (1971); Marvin Frankel, Criminal Sentences: Law Without

in response to concerns about arbitrary discretion and unjustifiably unequal treatment, legislatures also began to adopt determinate sentences with relatively limited ranges for most crimes and sentencing guidelines that limited judicial sentencing discretion to various degrees. Although the new regime also faces substantial criticisms, it has been adopted in a considerable number of jurisdictions, including federal criminal jurisdiction, and it exerts influence on those jurisdictions that still retain more indeterminate sentencing. Most recently, the influential American Law Institute's revision of the general *Model Penal Code* provisions on the purposes of sentencing replaced the previously consequential aims with a balance of just deserts proportionality and consequential goals.[16]

In sum, among criminal law theorists and in the positive law, desert plays a central role in the justification for criminal blame and punishment. The final assumption, addressed previously when considering desert–disease jurisprudence, is that only offenders who are genuinely culpable, who are genuinely at fault, deserve punishment. Let us therefore turn to the criminal law's criteria for blame and punishment.

CRIMINAL LAW DOCTRINE

Crimes are defined by what lawyers call their "elements," the criteria the prosecution must establish beyond a reasonable doubt to prove prima facie guilt. If the prosecution cannot prove any requisite element, the defendant must be acquitted (but may be convicted of another similar crime that does not require the missing element). Even if a defendant is prima facie guilty, the defendant may still avoid criminal liability by establishing what is known as an affirmative defense.[17] Let us consider the meaning of all these terms and their relation to culpability.

ORDER (1972); Twentieth Century Fund Task Force on Criminal Sentencing, FAIR AND CERTAIN PUNISHMENT (1976); Ernest van den Haag, PUNISHING CRIMINALS: CONCERNING A VERY OLD AND PAINFUL QUESTION (1975). There were also proposals to use selective incapacitation more effectively. *See* James Q. Wilson, THINKING ABOUT CRIME, ch. 8 (1975). This was not coupled, however, with calls for extensive lengthening of sentences. *See, e.g.*, Uniform Determinate Sentencing Act, ch. 1139, 1976 Cal. Stat. 5062.

16. American Law Institute, MODEL PENAL CODE: SENTENCING §1.02(2) (*Tentative Draft No. 1* 2007).

17. I use the locution, "establish an affirmative defense," because the US Supreme Court has made it clear that a jurisdiction may shift the burden of persuasion to the defendant for affirmative defenses. *See*, Leland v. Oregon, 343 U.S. 790 (1952) (permitting shifting the persuasion burden for legal insanity to the defendant); Rivera v. Delaware, 429 U.S. 877 (1976) (same); Dixon v. United States, 126 U.S. 2437 (2006) (permitting shifting the persuasion burden for duress to the defendant). Many jurisdictions have taken advantage. For example, in federal insanity defense cases, the defendant must prove that he or she was legally insane by clear and

There are five types of elements that define crimes: acts (sometimes referred to as "conduct" elements), an accompanying mental state (termed "mens rea"), attendant circumstances, results, and causation (in cases in which there is a result element). Here is an example of a crime that involves all five: "the intentional killing of a police officer knowing that the victim is a police officer." The act element is any type of intentional killing conduct, such as shooting, stabbing, bludgeoning, and the like. The accompanying mens rea is the intent to kill. If the agent shoots with the intent only to wound or to scare the victim, the defendant lacks the intent to kill (but may be guilty of a different type of homicide crime). The attendant circumstance is that the victim is a police officer, and this element has its own mens rea: the defendant must know the victim is an officer. If the victim is not a police officer or the defendant does not know that the victim is an officer, the defendant cannot be convicted of this particular homicide crime. The result element in this crime is the victim's death. If the victim does not die, at most the defendant can be convicted of an attempt to commit this crime. Finally, the defendant's action must be the legal cause of the death. This is a very complicated requirement, but, in brief, it means that how death occurred should not be a remote or unforeseeable consequence of the defendant's action. For example, suppose the defendant inflicts what would be a mortal wound, but the emergency room doctor commits gross malpractice, and the victim dies immediately as a result of the doctor's error. In such a case, the "causal chain" between the defendant's conduct and the victim's death might be "cut," and once again the defendant could be convicted only of attempting to kill the police officer.

All criminal statutes require an act element.[18] Although the meaning of this element is often not clear in statutes and the cases that interpret them, here is a rough approximation of the meaning. An act is an intentional bodily movement (or omission) performed by an agent whose consciousness is reasonably intact. Thus, a reflex or convulsive movement of the body would not satisfy the act requirement even if it caused harm to another because it is not an action at all. In most US jurisdictions, an act performed in a substantially dissociated state of consciousness, such as sleepwalking, is also not considered an action, although it may appear responsive to the environment and goal directed. The

convincing evidence. Of course, a jurisdiction can also place the burden of persuasion on the prosecution. In practice, wherever the burden of persuasion is placed for affirmative defenses, the defendant will have the burden of producing sufficient evidence to warrant submitting the defense to the finder of fact.

18. This element is sometimes referred to as the "voluntary act" requirement, but this is simply a legal label affixed after the criteria for it have been established. If the criteria are met, the movement is referred to as a "voluntary act"; if they are not, the movement is not an action. The term voluntary does not have its ordinary-language meaning in this case.

rationale for an act requirement for criminal guilt should be apparent. If the defendant's movements were not his actions, they cannot be imputed to him as an agent and be the foundation for culpability. The harm caused is simply not the defendant's fault, and it would be unjust to blame and punish the agent.

Mens rea terms, such as intention, purpose, knowledge, recklessness (conscious awareness of a substantial risk that another element is satisfied and disregard of the risk), and negligence (the failure to be aware of a substantial risk that a reasonable person should have been aware of) have their ordinary-language, commonsense meanings. No degree of commitment or rationality is included in the definitions of mens rea. An act committed ambivalently for irrational reasons is considered intentional if it was done on purpose.

An agent who does not act is acquitted outright. Similarly, if the agent lacks a requisite mental state, the agent is also not prima facie criminally responsible and must be acquitted outright of the crime requiring that mental state. Return to the example concerning the intentional killing of a police officer. In Clark v. Arizona,[19] defendant Eric Clark shot and killed a police officer who was in full uniform and made a traffic stop of Clark's vehicle using the officer's marked police vehicle. Clark indisputably suffered from paranoid schizophrenia and was delusional. He claimed that he delusionally believed that the officer was a space alien impersonating a police officer. If Clark's testimony was believed, the shooting was intentional action, but he did not intend to kill a human being knowing the victim was a police officer. He intended to kill a space alien. Thus, he could not be guilty of intentional homicide of any sort, but he might have been guilty of a lesser offense such as negligent homicide because his belief that the officer was a space alien was unreasonable. A reasonable person would have recognized that he was creating a substantial and unjustifiable risk of death to a human being.

Even if the agent is fully prima facie responsible, however, the agent ultimately may still not be criminally responsible if an affirmative defense can be established. A defendant raising an affirmative defense is claiming that although his behavior satisfied the definitional elements of the crime, there is some further reason that the defendant should not be held responsible. Affirmative defenses can be either justifications or excuses. In the case of justifications, the defendant was a responsible agent, but his behavior in the specific circumstances was the permissible or perhaps right thing to do. Self-defense, in which an agent intentionally uses otherwise unlawful force proportionately to prevent a wrongful attack on the agent, is the classic example. In cases of excuse, the defendant has done the wrong thing, but for some reason should not be held to be responsible. The two primary examples in US and English criminal law are legal insanity

19. 548 U.S. 735 (2006).

(essentially a rationality defect) and duress (a compelling "hard choice" situation, such as a "do-it-or-else" threat at gunpoint).

Like the definitions of crimes, affirmative defenses also have specific criteria. Consider first the insanity defense, using the Model Penal Code test as an example.[20] To be found legally insane, at the time of the crime the defendant must have been suffering from a mental disorder and, as a result, lacked substantial capacity to appreciate the criminality of his action or to conform his action to the requirement of the law. Thus, if the defendant is not sufficiently disordered to meet the law's definition of mental disorder, or did not lack the requisite substantial capacity, a legal insanity defense will fail. The justification for the excuse is that a defendant who does wrong but is sufficiently irrational at the time is not a rational agent who deserves blame and punishment. Now consider the Model Penal Code standard for the affirmative defense of duress.[21] Duress is established if the defendant is threatened with wrongful force unless he harms another and a person of reasonable firmness would have yielded in this situation. The common law standard was even stricter, granting the defense only if the threat was death or grievously bodily harm, and it did not apply to homicide crimes. The justification for the excuse is that demanding agents to accept harm to themselves rather than to harm another asks too much of agents in some circumstances. The choice is simply too hard. The defense will fail if the threat was not of sufficient magnitude, say, a threat to destroy only the defendant's valued property, or if a person of reasonable firmness would not have yielded, say, killing five people to save one's own life. In cases of excuse, the defendant will be acquitted if the defense is established, but defendants who have been acquitted by reason of legal insanity may be committed to a secure hospital if they are still mentally disordered and dangerous. The Supreme Court has affirmed that such commitments are not punishment[22]—the defendant cannot be punished because he has been acquitted—and that the commitments must end if either criterion for the commitment, disorder or dangerousness, is no longer present.[23]

Criminal law has many wrinkles that have not been addressed,[24] and the details vary from jurisdiction to jurisdiction, but the foregoing is an accurate account of the essential conditions for criminal culpability. The defendant will

20. Model Penal Code, §4.01(1).

21. *Id.*, §2.09(1).

22. Jones v. United States, 563 U.S. 354 (1983).

23. Foucha v. Louisiana, 504 U.S. 71 (1992).

24. For example, there are affirmative defenses such as the statute of limitations or jurisdictional limits that are irrelevant to culpability but that may lead to acquittal if they are established.

be culpable for the crime charged if all the elements are proved and no affirmative defense is established. In contrast, the defendant will be found not guilty of the crime charged if either the elements cannot be proved beyond a reasonable doubt or an affirmative defense is established.

For the purpose of this paper, it is crucial to recognize that libertarian free will is not an element of any crime or of any affirmative defense. To establish prima facie guilt, the prosecution never needs to prove that the defendant had free will. To establish an affirmative defense, the party with the burden of persuasion never needs to prove the presence of absence of free will. To defeat the prosecution's prima facie case, the defendant must negate the elements of conscious, intentional action and mens rea; to establish an affirmative defense, the defense must introduce sufficient evidence of the criteria for the defense. People will often say that a defendant who acted under duress or who was legally insane lacked free will. In such cases, however, free will is simply a confusing and conclusory way of saying that the legal criteria for excuse were met. Lack of free will independent of the behavioral legal criteria for excuse does no work whatsoever in explaining why such a defendant is excused.

For a final confirmation of the thesis that free will plays no role in the positive criteria for criminal responsibility, consider the Supreme Court's recent decision, *Clark v. Arizona*, in which the Court had one of its rare opportunities to clarify the relation between mens rea and insanity.[25] The questions presented were whether Arizona's unusually narrow insanity defense test, which asked only if the defendant could distinguish between right and wrong, violated substantive due process and whether an Arizona rule that excluded virtually all expert evidence concerning mental disorder offered for the purpose of negating mens rea violated procedural due process. Although legal insanity and the presence of mens rea are probably the criminal law issues to which free will is allegedly most relevant, and although there was extensive discussion of the history of legal insanity and of the role of mens rea, the Court did not so much as mention free will to decide the issues. There were many problems with the Court's analysis, especially of the mens rea issue,[26] but failure to discuss free will was not among them. In short, free will or lack of it is not a criterion for criminal responsibility or nonresponsibility. Once again, it is irrelevant to the actual practice of criminal law.

It is true that many lawyers, including Supreme Court justices and lower court judges, practicing lawyers and some law professors, talk as if free will were important in criminal law, but this is clearly wrong as a matter of positive

25. *Clark*, *supra* note 19.

26. See Stephen J. Morse & Morris B. Hoffman, *The Uneasy Entente Between Insanity and Mens Rea: Clark v. Arizona*, 97 J. Crim. L. & Criminol. 1071 (2008).

law. As noted, when they use the locution it is simply a confused proxy for the conclusion that some culpability doctrine was or was not present. They sometimes mean, however, that free will is a necessary foundational justification for responsibility, even if it is not a criterion in any legal doctrine. The next section, which discusses the metaphysical free will problem, demonstrates that this assumption is not necessary to justify responsibility doctrines and practices under a compatibilist account of the relation of determinism, free will, and responsibility.

THE COMPATIBILITY OF CRIMINAL LAW AND COMPATIBILISM

Readers of this chapter will be familiar with the metaphysical determinism/free will/responsibility debate, so I will not rehearse the various views. It is true that many people think that libertarian free will is necessary for criminal responsibility. As I noted earlier in the chapter, I do not consider libertarianism a plausible metaphysics; with P. F. Strawson, I believe it is "panicky."[27] If those who think that libertarianism is true are incorrect, then many legal doctrines and practices, especially those relating to responsibility, may be entirely incoherent. But, as we shall see, on the most natural reading of what ordinary people mean by claiming that free will is foundational, it is not necessary even for them, and determinism is not inconsistent with current responsibility doctrines and practices.

Based on my reading of the cases and legal commentary that mention free will and from talking with numerous judges and lawyers about this question, I believe that most criminal justice system participants and commentators have not even thought about and certainly do not have genuine understanding of the metaphysical debate and do not situate their views in that debate. I believe that most confuse libertarian free will with freedom of action, the ability to do what one wants. I recognize that one interpretation of hard determinism is that agents cannot do what they want because there is no alternative possibility other than the action that was performed. But this position is contested, and it is entirely consistent with determinism that people can act freely in the sense of doing what they choose to do based on their reasons for action and doing so without compulsion. Determinism is not fatalism.[28] As I have already mentioned, when adherents of foundational free will say a defendant should be excused because the defendant lacked free will, this is usually just shorthand for a conclusion based on the usual criteria for folk psychological irrationality, such as legal insanity, or for folk psychological compulsion, such as duress. If

27. P. F. Strawson, *Freedom and Resentment*, in G. Watson, Ed., Free Will 59, 80 (1982).

28. Daniel Dennet, Elbow Room: The Varieties of Free Will Worth Wanting (1984).

pressed, some will say things like the defendant could not help himself, but, again, they are not referring to the principle of alternative possibilities or the like. They are speaking loosely of standard folk psychological excusing conditions. If pressed further, they will recognize that all people have or do not have free will, and they really cannot coherently distinguish those they wish to excuse on the ground that those people lack libertarian freedom. In short, most nonphilosopher adherents of foundational free will as a necessary component of just blame and punishment are not committed to this view in any principled fashion, and it has no practical consequences in the practice of criminal law.

Now let us turn to some facts about the criteria for criminal responsibility—the prima facie elements of crime, justifications and excuses—that cannot reasonably be denied, even if determinism is true. Most bodily movements that appear to satisfy the act element of criminal prohibitions are intentional, but some, like reflexes or movements performed while sleepwalking, are not. Most criminal defendants had some mens rea, but some did not because they made a mistake, were not paying attention, or had other perfectly ordinary reasons. The otherwise criminal behavior defendants commit may in fact be justified, but most often it is not. Some defendants commit crimes while legally insane or acting under duress, but most do not. Again, these are true facts about the world that no one who accepts the importance of agency and the partial explanatory power of folk psychology could reasonably deny.[29]

There are two striking things to notice about these facts. First, they are entirely consistent with the truth of determinism or universal causation. Indeed, the partial explanatory power of folk psychology, the psychology that is foundational for criminal responsibility, is perfectly consistent with the truth of determinism. It may not be true that folk psychology is genuinely partially causally explanatory of behavior, but if it is false, it is not because determinism is true. If it is false, it is false because we will have discovered that mental states do not play a causal role. Determinism is consistent with both folk psychology and epiphenomenalism about mental states even if they are not consistent with each other. And to be more specific about doctrine, most bodily movements may be determined to be intentional, and some will be determined not to be. Most defendants will be determined to form mens rea, and some will be determined

29. Even those theorists who believe that genuine agency is impossible and that folk psychological explanations are primitive and wrong, such as epiphenomenalists about mental states, act as if they are agents and primarily use folk psychological concepts to explain the behavior of others and themselves and to understand and shape their interpersonal interactions. Skeptics about agency and folk psychology may believe that they have no real alternative at present—a situation future science and conceptual work might alter—but they live their daily lives as folk psychologists. At present, even they would have to concede as a practical matter that the facts adduced above are indeed facts about the world.

not to form it. Determinism will also account for the presence and absence of justifications and excuses. The distinctions the criminal law draws are perfectly consistent with the truth of determinism per se.

The second striking aspect of these facts is that the distinctions drawn matter morally and legally and are consistent with principles of justice that virtually all adopt. All of them are consistent with retributive, consequential, and mixed theories of the justification of punishment. For example, defendants who caused harm in the absence of action do not deserve punishment, and they cannot be deterred. Defendants who lack mens rea do not demonstrate the types of attitude and lack of concern for others that are crucial to fault and desert. For similar reasons, they do not present a danger to the community and do not need to be restrained. Of course, in some cases, retributive and consequential aims may be at odds. Consider a defendant with mental abnormalities that may compromise desert but that may also render the defendant particularly dangerous. The pure retributivist or consequentialist is not bothered by such a case, but even a mixed theorist who is bothered by this example is working with a set of considerations—culpability and danger—that everyone agrees are normatively crucial for deciding what to do. Criminal law assuredly operates imperfectly, but it is driven by conceptions of justice that are at the heart of Western morality.

In short, libertarian freedom is not even foundational for criminal responsibility. The criminal law holds most defendants responsible and excuses some. This is fully consistent with the compatibilist view of the relation between determinism and responsibility if one stays internal to the positive criminal law we have.[30] Compatibilism is the only metaphysical position that is consistent with both the criminal law's robust conception of responsibility *and* with the contemporary scientific worldview. If one is not a compatibilist criminal lawyer, one is forced to adopt the panicky metaphysics of libertarians or to abandon the concept of responsibility altogether. Neither prospect is inviting, and neither is necessary. As this section has shown, the criminal law is consistent with the truth of determinism or something like it, and as the next section indicates, no external challenge to the very coherence of criminal responsibility is successful.

30. An external critique of the concept of criminal responsibility is of course possible, but then one is no longer trying to explain and to normatively justify criminal law. Instead, one is seeking to abolish all notions of responsibility. This chapter turns to such challenges in the next section.

EXTERNAL CHALLENGES TO CRIMINAL RESPONSIBILITY

The two external challenges to criminal responsibility are hard determinism (hard incompatibilism)[31] and the even more radical claim and hope (of some) that neuroscience or other sciences will cause a paradigm shift in criminal responsibility by demonstrating that we are "merely victims of neuronal circumstances"[32] or of our genes, or some similar claim that denies human agency altogether. Both simply deny that human beings can be genuinely responsible. Many proponents claim further that these challenges, if successful, would lead to a pure prediction–prevention system of social control unmoored from considerations of responsibility, desert, and punishment that would be far kinder, gentler, and more rational than current criminal justice. In this section, I first address each challenge separately and then consider criticisms common to both.

The hard determinist challenge is completely familiar. The intuition that fuels it—roughly, that if all events in the universe were causally determined by prior events subject to the universe's causal laws, then no one could ever do otherwise; there never are genuine alternative possibilities—is profound. After all, how could anyone be praised or blamed, punished or rewarded, if what they did was in some ultimate sense not "up to them"? Therefore, if determinism or something like it is true, how can anyone rationally be held responsible? Many compatibilists claim that they do not feel the force of this intuition, but I feel its tug. On the other hand, most professional philosophers are compatibilists,[33] suggesting at the least that there are many good arguments in favor of compatibilism, and there is no resolution of the metaphysical dispute in sight. Moreover, the technical progress made in the professional free will literature often depends on intuitive reactions to complicated, unrealistic hypotheticals, intuitions that are not well-grounded in ordinary experience and that are not remotely related to the intuitions that ground criminal doctrine and practice.[34]

The criminal law cannot wait for the doctors of metaphysics to arrive and to cure the philosophical ailments that bedevil the responsibility literature. Moreover, as argued previously, criminal justice agents really do not care about

31. *See*, generally, Derk Pereboom, Living Without Free Will (2001) (explaining hard compatibilism, contrasting it with compatibilism and libertarianism, and suggesting that human welfare would be improved by the whole-hearted embrace of hard compatibilism).

32. *E.g.*, Joshua Greene & Jonathan Cohen, *For the Law, Neuroscience Changes Nothing and Everything*, *in* Law & the Brain 207, 217–218 (Semir Zeki & Oliver Goodenough eds., 2006), at 218.

33. *See*, survey results, *supra* note 1.

34. I thank Gideon Yaffe for a brief, helpful discussion of this point.

the genuine metaphysical dispute. Indeed, there is empirical evidence, admittedly nondispositive, that ordinary people are intuitive compatibilists, and my hunch is that even most committed hard incompatibilists actually live as if they were compatibilists. Finally, despite claims to the contrary,[35] it seems clear that interpersonal life would be exceptionally impoverished if concepts of responsibility, including genuinely deserved praise and blame, were extirpated from our lives, even assuming that this is possible. If people came to be treated as objects to be manipulated rather than full agents, much that we most treasure would be lost.[36] What reactive attitudes would still be justified, if any would be, would be pallid compared with those that enrich our lives now. Needless to say, such losses may be the price one pays for living in truth, but it is inconceivable that a practical institution such as the criminal law would transform itself in apparently negative ways as the result of an insoluble theoretical, metaphysical debate. I am not claiming that reactive attitudes that fuel retributive desert, such as indignation and anger, cannot have negative consequences. They can and do. The issue is whether a more pallid world is preferable. I think not, and as this section argues, we need not seek to attain it.

It appears that most hard determinists do not necessarily deny that human beings have mental states and that those mental states may play a partial causal role in explaining behavior. What distinguishes them from compatibilists is whether such causal determination is consistent with responsibility. The hard determinist need not deny, however, that human behavior presents at least a simulacrum of genuine agency. What if we are not agents at all, however? What if our mental states are simply epiphenomenal or the like?

At present, the law's "official" position—that conscious, intentional, rational, and uncompelled agents may properly be held responsible—is justified unless and until neuroscience, genetics, or any other discipline demonstrates convincingly that humans are not the type of creatures that we think we are. The law's implicit theory of action presupposes that its subject is an agent who acts based on his or her mental states, such as desires, beliefs, and intentions.[37] Agents are praised and blamed, rewarded and punished. Because it is an agent who acts, it makes sense to ask that person to give an account of his or her behavior and to be held accountable. Asking another animal without practical reason or a mechanistic force that does not act to answer to charges does not make

35. *E.g.*, Pereboom, *supra* note 27, at 199–213.

36. *See*, C. S. Lewis, *The Humanitarian Theory of Punishment*, 6 Res Judicatae 224 (1953).

37. Stephen J. Morse, *Lost in Translation? An Essay on Neuroscience and Law*, *in* Law and Neuroscience 529, 540 (Michael Freeman ed., 2011), at 529–533. *See, generally*, Robert Audi, Action, Intention and Reason 109–178 (1993) (providing an account of practical reason); Katrina L. Sifferd, *In Defense of the Use of Commonsense Psychology in the Criminal Law*, 25

sense. If humans are not intentional creatures who act for reasons and whose mental states play a causal role in their behavior, then the foundational facts for responsibility ascriptions are mistaken. If it is true that we are all automata, then no one is an agent and no one can be responsible. If the concept of mental causation that underlies folk psychology and current conceptions of responsibility were false, our responsibility practices, and many others, would appear unjustifiable. Why not move, then, to a system of pure preventive detention for dangerous agents and perhaps to mandated early detection and intervention for those who will become dangerous later?

This claim is not a straw man. Here is a lengthy quote from a widely noticed article by neuroscientists Joshua Greene and Jonathan Cohen that expresses the mechanistic conception:

> [A]s more and more scientific facts come in, providing increasingly vivid illustrations of what the human mind is really like, more and more people will develop moral intuitions that are at odds with our current social practices... Neuroscience has a special role to play in this process for the following reason. As long as the mind remains a black box, there will always be a donkey on which to pin dualist and libertarian intuitions... What neuroscience does, and will continue to do at an accelerated pace, is elucidate the "when," "where" and "how' of the mechanical processes that cause behaviour. It is one thing to deny that human decision-making is purely mechanical when your opponent offers only a general, philosophical argument. It is quite another to hold your ground when your opponent can make detailed predictions about how these mechanical processes work, complete with images of the brain structures involved and equations that describe their function... At some further point... [p]eople may grow up completely used to the idea that every decision is a thoroughly mechanical process, the outcome of which is completely determined by the results of prior mechanical processes. What will such people think as they sit in their jury boxes?... Will jurors of the future wonder whether the defendant... *could have done otherwise*? Whether he really *deserves* to be punished...? We submit that these questions, which seem so important today, will lose their grip in an age when the mechanical nature of human decision-making is fully appreciated. The law will continue to punish misdeeds, as it must for practical reasons, but the idea of distinguishing the truly, deeply guilty from those who are merely victims of neuronal circumstances will, we submit, seem pointless.[38]

LAW & PHIL. 571 (2006) (providing an extensive defense of the use of folk psychology that underpins criminal law and claiming that criminal law does not need a substitute).

38. Greene & Cohen, *supra* note 32, at 217–218 (internal citation omitted).

Greene and Cohen are not alone among thoughtful people in making such claims. The seriousness of science's potential challenge to the traditional foundations of law and morality is best summed up in the title of an eminent psychologist's recent book, *The Illusion of Conscious Will.*[39]

If our mental states play no role in our behavior and are simply epiphenomenal, then traditional notions of responsibility based on mental states and on actions guided by mental states would be imperiled. But is the rich explanatory apparatus of intentionality simply a post hoc rationalization that the brains of hapless *Homo sapiens* construct to explain what their brains have already done? Will the criminal justice system as we know it wither away as an outmoded relic of a prescientific and cruel age? If so, not only criminal law is in peril. What will be the fate of contracts, for example, when a biological machine that was formerly called a person claims that it should not be bound because it did not make a contract? The contract is also simply the outcome of various "neuronal circumstances." Compatibilism will not save us from this challenge because compatibilism presupposes that we are agents, a view the radical challenge denies.[40]

Given how little we know about the brain–mind–action connections,[41] to claim based on neuroscience that we should radically change our picture of ourselves and our legal doctrines and practices is a form of neuroarrogance. Although I predict that we will see far more numerous attempts to use neuroscience in the future as evidence in criminal cases and to affect criminal justice policy, I have elsewhere argued that for conceptual and scientific reasons, there is no reason at present to believe that we are not agents and that our mental states do not matter.[42] It is possible that we are not agents and that mental states

39. Daniel M. Wegner, The Illusion of Conscious Will (2002); *see also* Daniel M. Wegner, *Précis of the Illusion of Conscious Will*, 27 Behav. & Brain Sci. 649 (2004). The *précis* is followed by open peer commentaries and a response from Professor Wegner. *Id.* at 679. In more recent work, Professor Wegner appears to have softened the radical interpretation of his claim, which is that we, as agents, are not really "controllers" whose mental processes cause action. Daniel M. Wegner, *Who Is the Controller of Controlled Processes?*, *in* The New Unconscious 19, 32 (Ran R. Hassin et al. eds., 2005) ("This theory is mute on whether thought does cause action"). On the other hand, Professor Wegner seems ambivalent and unwilling to give up the radical interpretation. *See id.*at 27 (arguing that the "experience of conscious will is normally a construction" and referring to mental causation as "apparent"). This apparent ambivalence is present in the work of others.

40. *See* Stephen J. Morse, *The Non-Problem of Free Will in Forensic Psychiatry and Psychology*, 25 Behav. Sci. & L. 203, 214–216 (2007) (discussing the meaning of compatibilism and its relation to criminal law).

41. For example, we have no idea how the brain enables the mind. Paul R. McHugh & Phillip R. Slavney, The Perspectives of Psychiatry 11–12 (2d ed. 1998).

42. *See* Stephen J. Morse, *Determinism and the Death of Folk Psychology: Two Challenges to Responsibility from Neuroscience*, 9 Minn. J.L. Sci. & Tech. 1, 19–34 (2008); Morse, *supra*

are epiphenomenal, but the current science does not remotely demonstrate that this is true. The burden of persuasion is firmly on the proponents of the radical view. There is simply no present justification for concluding that the foundational folk psychological view of agency upon which criminal law is based is incorrect.

Now let us turn to two considerations that apply to both external challenges. First, neither view, and especially not the radical position, entails any normative agenda, despite the claim sometimes made that each entails consequentialism. If it is unjustified according to hard determinism to say to a harm-doer, "you should not have done that," because no alternative is possible, what is the justification for saying to anyone, "you should/should not do that in the future," because there are no alternative possibilities in the future either.[43] Moreover, when the hard determinist allegedly engages in normative reasoning, is it really reasoning, or is it simply a simulacrum of deliberation? And, if we cannot genuinely be guided by reason, if what we come to believe was simply the product of causal variables, what reason do we have as agents for adopting any normative view? And if we can be guided by reason, as compatibilists claim, then why does the hard determinist deny the possibility of responsibility?

This problem is even more dire for the radical challenge. Suppose we were convinced by the mechanistic view that we are not intentional, rational agents after all. (Of course, the notion of being "convinced" would be an illusion, too. Being convinced means that we are persuaded by evidence or argument, but a mechanism is not persuaded by anything. It is simply neurophysically transformed.) What should we do now? We "know" (another mental state, but never mind) that it is an illusion to think that our deliberations and intentions have any causal efficacy in the world. We also know, however, that we experience sensations such as pleasure and pain and that we care about what happens to us and to the world. We cannot just sit quietly and wait for our brains to activate further, for determinism to happen. We must and will deliberate and act.

If we still thought that the radical view was correct and that standard notions of genuine moral responsibility and desert were therefore impossible, we might nevertheless continue to believe that the law would not necessarily have to give up the concept of incentives. Indeed, Greene and Cohen concede that we would have to keep punishing people for practical purposes.[44] Such an account would be consistent with "black-box" accounts of economic incentives that simply

note 37, at 543–554; *see also*, Mario Beauregard, *Mind Does Really Matter: Evidence from Neuroimaging Studies of Emotional Self-Regulation, Psychotherapy, and Placebo Effect*, 81 Progress in Neurobiology 218 (2007).

43. Mitchell Berman, *Punishment and Justification*, 118 Ethics 258, 271 n. 34 (2008).

44. Greene & Cohen, *supra* note 32, at 218.

depend on the relation between inputs and outputs without considering the mind as a mediator between the two. For those who believe that a thoroughly naturalized account of human behavior entails complete consequentialism, such a conclusion might not be unwelcome.[45]

On the other hand, coming to conclusions and making decisions about whether or not to maintain a practice of punishment (and why should it be punishment as opposed to some other nonpunitive form of social control?) are mental acts that presuppose folk psychology. Moreover, the radical's concession seems to entail the same internal contradiction just explored. What is the nature of the "agent" that is discovering the laws governing how incentives shape behavior? Could understanding and providing incentives via social norms and legal rules simply be epiphenomenal interpretations of what the brain has already done? How do "we" "decide" which behaviors to reward or punish? What role does "reason"—a property of thoughts and agents, not a property of brains—play in this "decision"?

If the truth of pure mechanism is a premise in deciding what to do, this premise yields no particular moral, legal, or political conclusions. It will provide no guide as to how one should live or how one should respond to the truth of reductive mechanism.[46] Normativity depends on reason, and thus the radical view is normatively inert. Neurons and neural networks do not have reasons. Only people do. If reasons do not matter, then we have no genuine, nonillusory reason to adopt any morals or politics, any legal rule, or to do anything at all. Thus, this view does not entail consequentialism or a pure preventive scheme of social control.

The second major criticism of the external challenges concerns the assumption that a social control system that abandon notions of agency, desert, and punishment will be kinder and gentler than current practice. This is an open,

45. A clear implication of the disappearing-person argument is that it would not be fair to punish dangerous people because no one deserves punishment (or anything else). We might need to deprive dangerous people of their liberty to ensure social safety, but then we would be morally bound to compensate for the unfairness of restraining liberty by making the conditions of confinement (or other restraints) sufficiently positive. In other words, a regime of "funishment" would be morally required. Saul Smilansky, *Hard Determinism and Punishment: A Practical Reductio*, 30 LAW & PHIL. 353, 355 (2011). I leave the perverse incentives this would create to the reader's imagination, but defenders of the disappearing-person view would be required to institute funishment and somehow to avoid the perverse incentives. Smilansky's argument is directed at hard determinists, but it is a fortiori directed at those who make the disappearing-person claim, as long as the latter can make any moral claims at all. See *infra* note 46 and accompanying text.

46. I was first prompted to this line of thought by a suggestion Mitch Berman made in the context of a discussion of determinism and normativity. Mitchell Berman, *Punishment and Justification*, 118 ETHICS 258, 271 n.34 (2008).

empirical prediction, but the current situation suggests that the opposite will be true. I agree with critics of current American criminal justice that many of our doctrines and practices are too harsh. They lock up too many people for too long. But although retribution has played an increasingly large role since the 1960s in theory in justifying criminal punishment, most of the most draconian aspects of punishment have been motivated by consequential concerns. Striking examples are recidivist sentencing enhancements, the approval of strict liability crimes, the "war on drugs," the vast proliferation of regulatory crimes, mandatory minimum sentences, and truth in sentencing. None of these can be retributively justified, and all punish disproportionately to desert. They are mainly justified by considerations of general deterrence, specific deterrence, and incapacitation, all of which are consequential justifications.

Now, it is open to consequentialists to argue that the legislatures have misunderstood the costs and benefits of what they have done and that they are unnecessarily creating welfare losses, which are a consequential form of "disproportion." But if we cannot be sure of the net social effects of our consequential policies, why does it matter if we get it wrong if people are not agents and do not have rights. After all, it was Bentham who claimed that rights were nonsense on stilts. Moreover, why wait for criminal conduct to occur to intervene in the kinder, gentler world? Why not have a regime of "screen and intervene" if we are convinced that we could increase social safety? In fact, it is the compatibilist view of agency, coupled with notions of desert and retribution, that is the foundation of proportionality and the protection of human rights within our desert–disease system of social control.

It is also not clear that a social control system without agency and responsibility would be more rational than a system that took desert seriously. A prediction–prevention, screen–intervene system would be rational if social control were our main goal and we had the technology to achieve it, but it would not be kinder and gentler. More important, if we took desert seriously, including being willing to take the risks in the name of liberty to respect desert, that system, too, would be rational. The question would then be which type of rational world one wished to live in: the brave new world or the messy current world that takes people seriously as agents capable of being and taking responsibility.

CONCLUSION: CRIMINAL COMMON LAW COMPATIBILISM REDUX

There is simply no question that the criminal law we have is completely consistent with the truth of determinism, avoids a panicky metaphysics, and employs moral and political concepts that we have reason to endorse. Like all human institutions, it is messy and imperfect, but in principle, it takes people seriously and attempts to maximize liberty, autonomy, and dignity.

There are external challenges possible, of course, and hard determinists will not be persuaded that genuine responsibility and desert are possible. The criminal law is the product of centuries of development, however, and has the attractive features this chapter has described. The burden of persuasion is surely on the external challengers. They must not only mount a theoretical argument but also provide a practical, concrete proposal of what their social control system would look like, including how it would be administered by imperfect creatures like ourselves who will virtually always have inadequate information to make fully informed decisions. The critics must also provide an account of why, in concrete terms, human welfare would be enhanced in the brave new world. The record of social engineering in history is unappealing, to say the least, which simply enhances the externalist's burden of persuasion.

Ultimately, I believe that the vision of the person, of interpersonal relations, and of society the externalist endorses bleaches the soul. I have no incontrovertible argument to prove that the externalist view is incorrect or would lead to dire consequences, but neither does the externalist have an incontrovertible argument against the internalist. In the concrete and practical world we live in, however, we must be guided by our values and a vision of the good life. I do not want to live in the externalist's world that is stripped of genuine agency, desert, autonomy, and dignity. For all its imperfections, common criminal law compatibilism is more respectful and humane.

6

Neuroscience, Normativity, and Retributivism

MICHAEL S. PARDO AND DENNIS PATTERSON

Theories of criminal punishment provide accounts that purport to legitimate and justify criminal punishment. The theoretical project takes as its impetus that criminal punishment is a form of state-sponsored violence; under the auspices of criminal punishment, states inflict pain and suffering on citizens—depriving them of life, liberty, or property to which they would otherwise be entitled—for their transgressions of the criminal law. What would make such coercive actions by the state legitimate? When is the exercise of this power justified? Finally, how much punishment is justified in particular circumstances? Much ink has been spilled trying to answer these difficult questions. Although a variety of different theories and approaches have been proposed throughout the ages, modern criminal law theory centers around two groups of punishment theories.[1] Broadly construed, theories in the first group purport to justify punishment on "consequentialist" grounds. Despite important differences among them, theories in this group rely on the beneficial social consequences that are claimed to flow from criminal punishment (primarily, reduced future crime) because of its deterrent, incapacitating, or rehabilitating effects.[2] Broadly construed, theories

1. In an insightful and clarifying recent article, Mitchell Berman observes that despite the "rich diversity of justificatory theories, including deterrence (Bentham and Beccaria), reform (Plato), retribution (Kant), annulment (Hegel), and denunciation (Durkheim), a striking feature of twentieth century punishment theory... has been the steady and generally successful pressure to fold this seeming multiplicity of justifications into a simple dichotomy of justifications that at least appears to mirror the fundamental organizing distinction in moral theory between consequentialism and deontology." Mitchell N. Berman, "Two Kinds of Retributivism," in *Philosophical Foundations of Criminal Law* 433 (Duff & Green, eds., 2011).

2. The classic deterrence-based accounts are Cesare Baccaria, *On Crimes and Punishments* (1764) and Jeremy Bentham, *An Introduction to the Principles of Morals and Legislation*

in the second group purport to justify punishment on "retributivist" grounds. Theories in this group, despite important differences among them, rely on the notion that criminal offenders somehow *deserve* punishment proportionate to their transgressions of the criminal law.[3]

Although debates rage on within each side and across the consequentialist-retributivist divide, most theorists acknowledge some role for both types of considerations. The US Supreme Court has also explained that, as a matter of constitutional law, the federal and state governments may as a general matter rely on multiple justifications for punishment.[4] Empirical work suggests that subjects support both rationales for punishment (although particular punishment decisions may be more consistent with retributivist rationales).[5] We do not wish to take sides or offer new arguments in favor of retributivist or consequentialist theories of criminal punishment. Rather, we examine the relationship between neuroscience and this theoretical project, focusing in particular on arguments and inferences regarding criminal punishment drawn from current neuroscientific data.

In an influential article, Joshua Greene and Jonathan Cohen challenge retributivism by arguing that neuroscientific data will undermine retributivist intuitions *indirectly* by undermining *directly* the "free will" intuitions on which, they claim, retributivist theories depend.[6] This argument requires some unpacking before we can evaluate its underlying assumptions. Before we explore the details

(1789). For an overview of more recent consequentialist rationales, see Anthony Duff, "Legal Punishment," *Stanford Encyclopedia of Philosophy* (2008), available at: http://plato.stanford.edu/entries/legal-punishment/.

3. The classic retributive account is Kant's. See Immanuel Kant, *The Metaphysics of Morals* 1797 (Gregor trans. 1996). See also Berman, supra note 1, at 6 (referring to the "desert claim" as the "core retributivist contention" that "punishment is justified by the offender's ill-desert.") For overviews, see Duff, supra note 2; David Wood, "Punishment: Nonconsequentialism," 5/6 *Philosophy Compass* (2010), available at http://ssrn.com/abstract=1659453.

4. See Harmelin v. Michigan, 501 U.S. 957, 1001 (1991) (Kennedy, J., concurring) ("the Eight Amendment does not mandate adoption of any one penological theory... The federal and state criminal systems have accorded different weights at different times to penological goals of retribution, deterrence, incapacitation, and rehabilitation".) See also Ewing v. California, 538 U.S. 11 (2003).

5. See, e.g., Kevin M. Carlsmith, John M. Darley & Paul H. Robinson, "Why Do We Punish? Deterrence and Just Desserts as Motives for Punishment," 83 *Journal of Personality and Social Psychology* 284, 294 (2002) (noting that "[w]hen asked about just deserts and deterrence, participants generally supported both perspectives" and "[p]eople seemed to support these two philosophies and generally to have a positive attitude toward both").

6. Joshua Greene & Jonathan Cohen, "For Law, Neuroscience Changes Nothing and Everything," in *Law and the Brain* (Zeki & Goodenough eds., 2006).

of this argument, however, it is important to understand more generally how the argument relates to current criminal law doctrine. The criminal law presupposes "folk psychological" explanations of human action, and neuroscientific data may provide inductive empirical evidence that is relevant for deciding issues within that conceptual framework.[7] A variety of proposals have suggested ways in which neuroscience may provide evidence for deciding issues within this current conceptual framework, including issues regarding mens rea, insanity, competence, voluntariness, and lie detection. Importantly, however, the inferences and conclusions drawn from the neuroscientific data must not run afoul of the conceptual contours of that framework in order to contribute meaningfully to these doctrinal issues.[8]

At the theoretical level of criminal punishment, however, neuroscience may offer a deeper and more radical challenge to the entire doctrinal framework of the criminal law by undermining the assumptions on which it is based and, with it, theories of punishment that depend on such assumptions. This is the nature of Greene and Cohen's challenge. It concedes that the current doctrinal edifice of the criminal law remains largely unshaken by neuroscience. Instead, they argue that important aspects of the doctrinal edifice depend upon a retributivist foundation—which in turns rests upon a nondeterministic, free will foundation—and thus, so the argument goes, if neuroscience can bring down the nondeterministic, free will foundation, it will also bring down retributivism and the legal doctrine built upon it. We discuss several problems with this argument, and we argue that if neuroscience has the potential to cause the changes Greene and Cohen predict, it will do so by fostering a number of unwarranted and problematic inferences and ought to be resisted.

A BRIEF TAXONOMY OF THEORIES OF CRIMINAL PUNISHMENT

Theories of criminal punishment are primarily normative accounts that purport to answer the question of when the state is justified in subjecting citizens (and noncitizens) to criminal punishment, and derivatively, how much punishment is justified when punishment in general is warranted.[9] In addition to this

7. See Stephen J. Morse, "Criminal Responsibility and the Disappearing Person," 28 *Cardozo Law Review* 2545, 2253–2254 (2007) ("The law's view of the person is thus the so-called 'folk psychological' model: a conscious (and potentially self-conscious) creature capable of practical reason, an agent who forms and acts on intentions that are the product of the person's desires and beliefs. We are the sort of creatures that can act for and respond to reasons.").

8. For a discussion, see Michael S. Pardo & Dennis Patterson, "Philosophical Foundations of Law and Neuroscience," 2010 *U. Illinois L. Rev.* 1211 (2010).

9. See Duff, supra note 2; Berman, supra note 1.

normative project, theories of punishment may also be directed at answering explanatory questions as to why the state would engage in acts of criminal punishment—whether it is justified or not—and why it would choose particular forms and amounts of punishment.[10] There is also a distinct conceptual project of delineating the scope of what constitutes punishment.[11]

One dominant strategy for answering such questions focuses on the future consequences of punishment. According to this "forward-looking" strategy, the perceived beneficial consequences include deterring others not punished from committing similar acts in the future, and preventing (or reducing the likelihood) that those punished will commit future crimes by rehabilitating, incapacitating, or deterring them specifically.[12] Under this consequentialist strategy, punishment is not an end in itself but rather serves an instrumental value in bringing about the social good of reducing future crime; punishment may be justified to the extent the positive social benefits it brings about exceed the harms it causes.[13] Moreover, specifics about whom should be punished, how, and how much may be justified under this strategy based on whatever would bring about the socially optimal or desirable level of benefits to costs. In addition to these normative issues, a consequentialist account may also explain why the state would choose to exercise its right to punish (assuming it is justified in doing so) and would undergo the expense of doing so (including expenses to those punished and citizens generally).[14]

The second dominant strategy for answering such questions focuses on the acts (together with the mental states and surrounding circumstances) of those subjected to criminal punishment. Under this backward-looking strategy, actions by those who violate the dictates of the criminal law are such that the actor may deserve punishment and ought to punished (and conversely those who do not violate the criminal law do not deserve punishment and should not be punished), regardless of whether any future beneficial consequences will follow.[15] For this strategy, it is the fact that the guilty defendant deserves criminal

10. See John Bronsteen, "Retribution's Role," 84 *Indiana L.J.* 1129 (2009).

11. See H. L. A. Hart, *Punishment and Responsibility* (1968).

12. Although the criteria for justifying punishment under this strategy are "forward looking" (i.e., consequences), the strategy also employs a number of "backward-looking" considerations in assessing likely consequences. These include, most important, the details of the particular criminal act and its surrounding circumstances, as well as other criminal acts committed by the defendant in the past.

13. See Berman, supra note 1.

14. See Bronsteen, supra note 10.

15. See Berman, supra note 1.

punishment that justifies the state's actions.[16] Retributivists may cash out exactly how desert justifies punishment in a variety of ways. For instance, punishment of those who deserve it may have some innate, intrinsic worth.[17] The desert aspect may also serve a particular type of instrumental value that justifies punishment—for example, it may serve to "cancel out," denounce the criminal acts, or express the community's disapproval of the various acts.[18] Or, under a more "pure" form of retributivism, the desert aspect may justify punishment regardless of whether punishment itself has any intrinsic worth or serves any other intrinsic value.[19] Turning to the specifics of punishment, the retributivist strategy purports to justify whom should be punished, how, and how much by appealing to whether the person is in fact guilty and, if so, the amount of punishment that is proportional to her culpability or ill desert.[20] In addition to these normative issues, a retributivist account may also explain why the state chooses to punish and chooses to do so in the ways that it does. Under this explanatory account, such punishment tracks the intuitions of citizens about what is just and may also reduce acts of vengeance and reciprocal violence.[21]

The initial distinction between these two strategies raises a number of additional issues. First, the considerations at issue under each strategy may play a variety of theoretical roles. They may each be taken to provide one consideration in whether punishment is justified in a particular context.[22] Under such a view, the criteria of any particular strategy may be neither necessary nor sufficient to justify punishment. Or, each strategy may be taken to provide a *necessary* condition for justifying punishment.[23] Or, each may be taken to provide a *sufficient* condition for justifying punishment.[24] Second, the strategies may also combine and interact in various ways. For example, each may provide a "constraint" on

16. Id.

17. See Michael Moore, *Placing Blame* (2007).

18. Berman, supra note 1, at 9.

19. Id. at 16–19.

20. Under retributivist theories, "proportionality" may be cashed out in various ways. See Alice Ristroph, "Proportionality as a Principle of Limited Government," 55 *Duke L.J.* 263, 279–284 (2005).

21. See Paul H. Robinson & John M. Darley, "Intuitions of Justice: Implication for Criminal Law and Justice Policy," 81 *S. Cal. L. Rev.* (2007).

22. Under this view, the strategies are consistent with each other.

23. For example, satisfying the criterion of desert may be required to justify punishment, but it alone may not be sufficient.

24. For example, deterrence may provide a sufficient condition for punishment under some conceptions, but it may not be necessary.

the other that would defeat otherwise legitimate punishment. Punishment that would produce good consequences, all things considered, may be illegitimate if it punishes someone more than he deserves. Punishing someone as much as he deserves may be illegitimate if it would otherwise lead to terrible social consequences.[25] Finally, although the two strategies lend themselves to the familiar distinction in moral theory between utilitarian and deontological theories, they are conceptually distinct.[26] One may believe that deontological considerations ground moral theory or make particular moral judgments right or wrong (true or false)[27] and also think (consistently) that the state is not justified in punishing for retributivist reasons.[28] Similarly, one may believe that utilitarian considerations ground moral theory or particular moral judgments and also think (consistently) that the state is justified is engaging in criminal punishment for retributivist reasons.[29]

As our language is meant to suggest, we do not intend to take sides in these debates or to argue that any particular theories in these categories succeed or fail on their own terms. Our aim in this brief section has been simply to explicate the theoretical issues sufficiently in order to properly assess the challenge to retributivism advanced by Greene and Cohen. We now turn to that challenge.

25. Under such conceptions, each strategy may provide "defeasible" conditions for justifying punishment. For example, desert might be taken to justify punishment unless it can be shown that the punishment will lead to more crime. For further details on different possible ways to conceptualize retributivism, see Berman, supra note 1; Larry Alexander & Kimberly Kessler Ferzan, with Stephen Morse, *Crime and Culpability: A Theory of Criminal Law* (2009) (distinguishing "mild," "moderate," and "strong retributivism"); Kenneth W. Simons, "Retributivism Refined—or Run Amok?," 77 *U. Chi. L. Rev.* (2010) (book review essay); Michael T. Cahill, "Punishment Pluralism," in *Retributivism: Essays on Theory and Policy* (White ed., forthcoming), available at http://papers.ssrn.com/sol3/abstract=1705682.

26. Larry Alexander & Michael Moore, "Deontological Ethics," *Stanford Encyclopedia of Philosophy* (2007), available at http://plato.stanford.edu/entries/ethics-deontological/; Berman, supra note 1, at 4–5.

27. This point holds regardless of whether moral truths are understood in realist or anti-realist terms.

28. See Alexander & Moore, supra note 26 ("Retributivism has two aspects: [1] it requires that the innocent not be punished, and [2] it requires that the guilty be punished. One could be a deontologist generally and yet deny that morality has either of these requirements.").

29. This may be one normative implication of Paul Robinson's work on "empirical desert." See Paul H. Robinson, "Empirical Desert," in *Criminal Law Conversations* 29 (Robinson, Garvey & Ferzan eds., 2009). See also Alexander & Moore, supra note 26 ("a retributivist might alternatively cast these two states of affairs (the guilty getting punished and the innocent not getting punished) as two intrinsic goods, to be traded off both against each other (as in burden of proof allocation) and against other values. Some retributivists urge the latter as a kind of explicitly 'consequentialist retributivism'").

NEUROSCIENCE AND INTUITIONS ABOUT PUNISHMENT

Greene and Cohen focus on the neural activity of criminals while committing criminal acts, and, indeed, the neural activity underlying all human action. Through such focus, Greene and Cohen argue, "[n]euroscience will challenge and ultimately reshape our intuitive sense(s) of justice" and with it retributivism.[30]

Before turning to the details of their argument, Greene and Cohen outline familiar[31] philosophical positions regarding free will (or freedom of action) and physical determinism, on which their argument will rely. "Determinism" is the position that the world in its current state is "completely determined by (1) the laws of physics and (2) past states of the world," and that future states will be likewise so determined.[32] "Free will," as they define it, "requires the ability to do otherwise."[33] "Compatibilism" is the position that determinism, if true, is compatible with human free will.[34] "Incompatibilism" is the position that determinism and free will are incompatible and thus both cannot be true. Within incompatibilism, "hard determinism" recognizes the incompatibility and denies free will; by contrast, "libertarianism" recognizes the incompatibility but denies determinism and accepts free will.[35]

30. Greene & Cohen, supra note 6, at 208.

31. Although familiar, these notions and their implications are not always clear.

32. Id. at 210 ("Given a set of prior conditions in the universe and a set of physical laws that completely govern the way the universe evolves, there is only one way that things can actually proceed.") Greene and Cohen acknowledge the existence of a certain amount of indeterminacy or randomness in the universe based on quantum effects, but they point out that this amendment adds little to the debate about how free will can emerge within the physical universe. Id. at 211. See also Peter van Inwagen, "How to Think About the Problem of Free Will," 12 *Ethics* 327, 330 (2008) ("Determinism is the thesis that the past and the laws of nature together determine, at every moment, a unique future."); David Lewis, "Are We Free to Break the Laws?," 47 *Theoria* 112 (1981).

33. Id. at 210. See also van Inwagen, supra note 32, at 329 ("The free-will thesis is that we are sometimes in the following position with respect to a contemplated future act: we simultaneously have both the following abilities: the ability to perform the act and the ability to refrain from performing the act. (This entails that we *have been* in the following position: for something we did do, we were at some point prior to our doing it able to refrain from doing it, able not to do it)").

34. Greene & Cohen, supra note 6, at 211. See also van Inwagen, supra note 32, at 330 ("Compatibilism is the thesis that determinism and the free-will thesis could both be true.") Note that the compatibilist need not take a stand on the empirical question of whether determinism is actually true. Rather, assuming the truth of determinism, the compatibilist is committed to the possibility that some human actions will be consistent with free will. Likewise, an incompatibilist also need not take a stand on the truth of determinism but may instead endorse the conditional position that, if determinism is true, then free will does not exist.

35. Greene & Cohen, supra note 6, at 211–212. Note also that one may reject free will for reasons independent of the issue of determinism. In other words, one could reject hard determinism and also reject free will.

Turning now to the details of their argument, the first step is to link the legitimacy of law with whether it "adequately reflect[s] the moral intuitions and commitments of society."[36] They note that although "current legal doctrine" (including criminal law and sentencing) may be "officially compatibilist," the intuitions on which the doctrine is based are "incompatibilist" and "libertarian."[37] Indeed, they contend that within "modern criminal law" there has been a "long, tense marriage" between "compatibilist legal principles" and "libertarian moral intuitions."[38] Neuroscience will "probably render the marriage unworkable" by undermining the moral intuitions: "if neuroscience can change those intuitions, then neuroscience can change the law."[39]

The tension between legal doctrine and underlying moral intuitions is particularly acute with criminal punishment based upon retributivist principles. Retributivism and the doctrine it supports depend on notions of moral responsibility and "the intuitive idea that we legitimately punish to give people what they deserve based on their past actions."[40] Both "retributivism" and "moral responsibility," they contend, are incompatibilist, libertarian notions that rely on some kind of "magical mental causation"[41] within a "folk psychological system" of explaining human action.[42] The "folk psychological system deals with

36. Id. at 213.

37. Id. at 208. Given their preference for empirical data over philosophical arguments, it is curious how little empirical support Greene and Cohen provide for the claim that criminal law doctrine is based on libertarian intuitions. They rely on two sources that, for different reasons, raise the possibility that brain damage (one source) or brain development in juveniles (the other source) may be relevant to criminal responsibility. See id. at 213–217. As an empirical matter, however, nonlegal actors appear to be "compatibilist" in their moral intuitions about particular cases. See Eddy Nahmias, Stephen Morris, Thomas Nadelhoffer & Jason Turner, "Surveying Freedom: Folk Intuitions and Free Will and Moral Responsibility," 18 *Philosophical Psychology* 561 (2005). Moreover, legal doctrine in this area does not appear to depend on explicit or tacit libertarian assumptions. See Stephen J. Morse, "The Non-Problem of Free Will in Forensic Psychiatry and Psychology," 25 *Behavioral Science & the Law* 203 (2007); Peter Westen, "Getting the Fly Out of the Bottle: The False Problem of Free Will and Determinism," 8 *Buffalo Criminal L. Rev.* 599 (2005). If Greene and Cohen are intent on debunking libertarian presuppositions in law, then perhaps a better target would be the doctrine in criminal procedure regarding the voluntariness of confessions and *Miranda* warnings, not criminal responsibility writ large. See Ronald J. Allen, "*Miranda*'s Hollow Core," 100 *Northwestern U. L. Rev.* 71 (2006).

38. Greene & Cohen, supra note 6, at 215.

39. Id. at 215, 213.

40. Id. at 210.

41. Id. at 217.

42. They contrast the "folk psychological system" with the "folk physics system," which "deals with chunks of matter that move around without purposes of their own according to the laws

unseen features of minds: beliefs, desires, intentions, etc."[43] A "crucial, if not the defining feature" of a "mind" and its mental states ("beliefs, desires, intentions, etc.") is "that it is an uncaused causer."[44] They contend that retributivism depends on moral blameworthiness[45] and that moral blameworthiness depends on the "folk psychological system" and its "crucial . . . defining feature" of minds and mental states as uncaused causers. As Greene and Cohen put it, "folk psychology is the gateway to moral evaluation"[46] and "[s]eeing something as an uncaused causer is a necessary but not sufficient condition for seeing something as a moral agent."[47]

The problem, as they see it, is that "hard determinism is mostly correct," and the "folk psychological system" based on "uncaused causation" is "an illusion."[48] The notions of free will, moral responsibility, blameworthiness, and retributive punishment that depend on the folk psychological system are therefore without a legitimate foundation. Neuroscience will help us to see the light by undermining "people's common sense, libertarian conception of free will and the retributivist thinking that depends on it, both of which have been shielded by the inaccessibility of sophisticated thinking about the mind and its neural basis."[49] Once the folk psychological illusion has been revealed, we can "structure our society accordingly by rejecting retributivist legal principles that derive their intuitive force from this illusion."[50]

How exactly will neuroscience do this? It will do so, they predict, by revealing the "mechanical nature of human action," along with the "when," "where," and "how," of the "mechanical processes that cause behavior." [51] As they acknowledge, this is not a new conclusion: "[s]cientifically minded philosophers have been saying this ad nauseam."[52] But the neuroscience will reveal this mechanical

of intuitive physics." Id. at 220. The two systems are different "cognitive systems" for "making sense of the behavior of objects in the world." Id.

43. Id.

44. Id.

45. Id. at 210.

46. Id. at 220. They add: "To see something as morally blameworthy or praiseworthy . . . one has to first see it as 'someone,' that is, as having a mind." Id.

47. Id. at 221.

48. Id. at 221, 209.

49. Id. at 208.

50. Id. at 209.

51. Id. at 217.

52. Id. at 214.

nature in a way that "bypasses complicated [philosophical] arguments," for it is one thing to hold your ground in the face of a "general, philosophical argument" but "quite another to hold your ground when your opponent can make detailed predictions about how these mechanical processes work, complete with images of the brain structures involved and equations that describe their functions."[53]

To illustrate how this might work, they present the following hypothetical. Imagine a group of scientists who create an individual ("Mr. Puppet") who engages in criminal activity. At Mr. Puppet's trial, the lead scientist explains his relationship to Mr. Puppet as follows:

> I designed him. I carefully selected every gene in his body and carefully scripted every significant event is his life so that he would become precisely what he is today. I selected his mother knowing that she would let him cry for hours and hours before picking him up. I carefully selected each of his relatives, teachers, friends, enemies, etc. and told them exactly what to say to him and how to treat him.[54]

According to Greene and Cohen, Mr. Puppet is guilty according to the law if he was rational at the time of his actions, which, they assume, he was. However, they conclude that given the circumstances of his creation "intuitively, this is not fair."[55] It is not fair, they contend, because "his beliefs and desires were rigged by external forces, and that is why, intuitively he deserves our pity more than our moral condemnation."[56] What neuroscience will reveal—without the need for recourse to philosophical argument—is that all criminal defendants (and indeed all humans) are like Mr. Puppet in the relevant respects. Although not designed by scientists, our beliefs, desires, and "rational" actions are all "rigged by external forces" beyond our control (some combination of genes, history, culture, and perhaps randomness). If Mr. Puppet is not morally responsible, then no one else is either.

Neuroscience will reveal the mechanical nature of our actions with examples like the following:

> Imagine, for example, watching a film of your brain choosing between soup and salad. The analysis software highlights the neurons pushing for soup

53. Id. at 217.

54. Id. at 216.

55. Id. at 216.

56. Id. at 216.

> in red and the neurons pushing for salad in blue. You zoom in and slow down the film, allowing yourself to trace the cause-and-effect relationships between individual neurons—the mind's clockwork revealed in arbitrary detail. You find the tipping-point moment at which the blue neurons in your prefrontal cortex out-fire the red neurons, seizing control of your pre-motor cortex and causing you to say, "I will have the salad, please."[57]

What goes for the soup-or-salad choice, also goes for the choice of whether to murder, rape, assault, or steal.

Greene and Cohen do not see these neurorevelations as the end of criminal punishment, however. They note that the "law will continue to punish misdeeds, as it must for practical reasons,"[58] and that "if we are lucky" our retributivist reasons for punishment will give way to consequentialists reasons,[59] because "consequentialist approaches to punishment remain viable in the absence of common-sense free will."[60] Under a consequentialist punishment regime, legal doctrine may, for deterrence purposes, make many of the same distinctions it does today (e.g., regarding infancy and insanity), "but the idea of distinguishing the truly, deeply guilty from those who are merely victims of neuronal circumstances will, we submit, seem pointless."[61] With rhetorical flourish, they conclude: "the law deals firmly but mercifully with individuals whose behavior is obviously beyond their control. Some day, the law may treat all convicted criminals this way. That is, humanely."[62]

There are a number of problems with this argument. Carefully examining each of these distinct problems will reveal how little the neuroscience of human action *tout court* bears on the normative project of justifying criminal punishment on the basis of moral blameworthiness or desert. Each problem by itself is sufficient to raise doubts about the conclusions Greene and Cohen draw

57. Id. at 218.

58. Id. at 218. Although Greene and Cohen conclude that retributivism will be undermined, they also conclude that we will still invoke folk psychological concepts for other practical purposes (including, e.g., deciding who has committed a criminal act in the first place). It is only for the special case of determining criminal punishment that we will rely on the conclusion that retributive punishment is unjustified because no one is *really* responsible. But if folk psychology is founded on an illusion and is thus an illegitimate basis on which to ground and justify criminal punishment, it is not clear why Greene and Cohen think it would be an appropriate basis for singling out people to punish in the first place.

59. Id. at 224.

60. Id. at 209.

61. Id. at 218.

62. Id. at 224.

regarding retributivism; collectively, they illustrate why their conclusions ought to be rejected.

The first problem with the argument is the assumption that the intuitions of most people necessarily answer the normative questions of whether criminal punishment is justified or how it ought to be distributed. Although lay intuitions may be relevant to reform, and some agreement between punishment and lay intuitions may be *necessary* for the legitimacy of punishment, accord with the intuitions of most people is not *sufficient* to justify punishment decisions. It is possible for widely shared intuitions about what is just punishment to be mistaken. Thus, even if neuroscience were to cause a significant shift away from retributive intuitions (as they predict),[63] it simply begs the question to assume that this shift would lead to more just (or more unjust) punishment decisions. The key issue is whether neuroscience will contribute evidence that provides epistemic support for arguments concerning determinism, compatibilism, moral blameworthiness, and just punishment.

The second problem with their argument is that the neuroscientific evidence that they envision would not provide this epistemic support. As Greene and Cohen appear to concede with their dismissal of "complicated [philosophical] arguments,"[64] neuroscience adds nothing new to extant conceptual arguments for or against compatibilism, incompatibilism, or hard determinism.[65] If this is so, and the presence of neuroscientific information causes people to form and hold new beliefs about these positions, then the neuroscience is persuading people for psychological reasons other than the epistemic support it provides. As may be the case in other contexts, the presence of neuroscientific information may cause people systematically to draw faulty or unsupported inferences rather than true or justified ones.[66] In other words, the very effects that Greene

63. Although exposure to the basics of determinism may reduce punishment in certain circumstances, in other circumstances accepting deterministic thinking may cause more, not less, punishment. For example, consider current practices of indefinite "civil commitment" of convicted sex offenders after they have completed their prison sentences because of fears of recidivism. The assumption that getting rid of retributivism will reduce punishment neglects the constraining or limiting effects retributivist thinking may provide. Moreover, exposure to determinism may cause other negative effects. See Kathleen D. Vohs & Jonathan W. Schooler, "The Value of Believing in Free Will: Encouraging a Belief in Determinism Increases Cheating," 19 *Psychological Science* 49 (2008).

64. See Greene & Cohen, supra note 6, at 217.

65. Indeed, both the "Mr. Puppet" and "soup/ salad" examples are consistent with a variety of different positions on these issues.

66. The causal role played by neuroscientific evidence in drawing inferential conclusions may not be a justificatory role. See Jessica R. Gurley & David K. Marcus, "The Effects of Neuroimaging and Brian Injury on Insanity Defenses," 26 *Behavioral Sciences & the Law* 85

and Cohen predict may prove to be widespread cognitive mistakes. The neuroscientific information may cause people to draw problematic (or philosophically dubious) inferences regarding issues relating to free will, determinism, and criminal responsibility.[67] Perhaps Greene and Cohen would respond that this causal effect is at least pushing people toward the correct positions, albeit for the wrong reasons. But this presupposes that retributivism depends necessarily on libertarianism (for reasons unrelated to neuroscience). This takes us to a third problem with their argument.

The third problem is that their presupposition is mistaken. It is not the case that retributivism depends necessarily on a metaphysically problematic version of libertarian incompatibilism. Greene and Cohen assume that retributivism—and indeed all moral blame and praise—must be built on a foundation of "uncaused causation." But a retributivist can coherently reject the notion of uncaused causation and still allow for moral judgments. Even in a world of physical determinism, moral desert may be grounded in the control people have over their actions through the exercise of their practical rationality.[68] If people act for reasons—more generally, if they act on the basis of their beliefs, desires, and other mental states—then we can blame or praise their actions (in light of their mental states).[69] Indeed, in their appeal to consequentialist justifications for punishment based on deterrence, Greene and Cohen appear to concede this type of responsiveness to reason[70]: deterrence works precisely by affecting the practical rationality of potential offenders, by giving them a reason to refrain from criminal activity that (ideally) outweighs their reasons for

(2008); David P. McCabe & Alan D. Castel, "Seeing is Believing: The Effect of Brain Images on Judgments of Scientific Reasoning," 107 *Cognition* 343 (2008); Deena Skolnick Weisberg et al., "The Seductive Allure of Neuroscience Explanations" 20 J. *Cognitive Neuroscience* 470 (2008). Whether the inferences are justified or not will depend on other criteria (including philosophical and conceptual arguments) beyond what caused them.

67. For a recent argument exposing some of these problematic inferences, see Saul Smilansky, "Hard Determinism and Punishment: A Practical *Reductio*," 30 *Law & Philosophy* 353 (2011).

68. See John Martin Fischer & Mark Ravizza, *Responsibility and Control: A Theory of Moral Responsibility* (1999). Rational control does not imply "uncaused causation." It implies that people have the ability and the opportunity to act in accord with their mental states. For a discussion that develops these points, see Anthony Kenny, *Freewill and Responsibility* 32 (1978).

69. This does not assume that actors are always conscious of their mental states or that mental states necessarily precede actions. In some cases, there may be no unique mental state that may be distinguished from the action that manifests the mental state (e.g., a want, knowledge, or an intention).

70. Other aspects of their argument, however, may imply that this sort of reason-responsiveness is an illusion because mental states may not exist or may be epiphenomenal. We explore this tension in their argument below.

criminal activity. Sufficient control over one's actions in light of one's practical rationality is sufficient to ground moral desert, regardless of whether the same actions may be explained in purely physical (i.e., nonmental) terms. In other words, one can coherently be a compatibilist and a retributivist, a combination that is consistent with current law.[71]

We first explicate this position in general terms and then illustrate it with Greene and Cohen's example of Mr. Puppet. Greene and Cohen assume that retributivism depends on "uncaused causation" because, if determinism is true, then agents could not have done otherwise and are thus not subject to moral evaluation.[72] Confusion arises because in discussions of whether an agent could have done otherwise, can act or refrain from acting, or has the power to act or not, the terms "could," "can," and "power" are ambiguous. As Anthony Kenny explains, these terms may be referring to one of four different notions: (1) *natural powers* (e.g., the ability of water to freeze) in which physical conditions may be sufficient for their instantiation; (2) *abilities* that depend for their exercise on an agent's wanting to exercise them; (3) *opportunities* to exercise one's abilities (e.g., one cannot ride a bicycle if there are no bicycles around); and (4) the presence of both an *ability* and an *opportunity* to exercise it. The fourth sense is the one that is relevant to moral blame and praise: agents who have the ability and the opportunity to act differently, but do not, are properly the subject of moral evaluation.[73] A key issue is thus whether this conception is consistent with determinism. Greene and Cohen assume it is not and that neuroscience will illustrate this inconsistency. We disagree with both points.

The idea that people possess the ability and the opportunity to do otherwise is consistent with determinism.[74] How can ability and opportunity be consistent with determinism? Consider first, ability. Possessing an ability (e.g., to ride a bicycle) depends on whether one satisfies the criteria for possessing the ability. These criteria include successfully exercising this ability when one wants to

71. To suppose otherwise would be a mistake, regardless of how many people think so, and regardless of what neuroscience shows. Rather than causing people to abandon retributivism and a libertarian conception of free will, perhaps increased neuroscientific knowledge will instead cause people to abandon confused views about free will and its relationship with responsibility. An important role for philosophy in this endeavor will be to aid in integrating increased knowledge of the brain coherently into the conceptual schemes we use to explain human behavior and the world.

72. They could not have done otherwise because their actions are all "rigged by external forces" beyond their control. Id. at 216.

73. See note 68 supra.

74. See Kenny, supra note 68, at 34 ("it does not follow from determinism that agents always lack the opportunity and ability to do otherwise than they do. Consequently it does not follow from determinism that it is unfair to hold people responsible for their actions.")

(and has the opportunity to) and refraining when one does not want to (and has the opportunity to refrain). Such criteria can be fulfilled even if one does not exercise the ability on the particular occasion in question. Second, consider opportunity. One has an opportunity to act (or not to act) if conditions external to the person are not forcing or preventing the exercise of the ability on a particular occasion. But, are an agent's brain states forcing him to act one way and preventing him from acting another (are they an "external force rigging his behavior") and, thus, depriving him of the opportunity to do otherwise? Not necessarily. We presume that if an agent had wanted to do something different (e.g., to ride a bicycle or not), then his brain states also would have been different. It would be a different story if his brain states caused him to ride a bicycle (or not) when he wanted to do the contrary. In such circumstances, there would be a breakdown of the type of rational control on which criminal responsibility depends.

The example of Mr. Puppet will help to illustrate these general points. Suppose Mr. Puppet has robbed a bank. Let's assume determinism is true and that we must decide whether to hold Mr. Puppet responsible for his actions. Assume further that Mr. Puppet is responsible only if he acted freely in robbing the bank, in the sense that he had the ability and the opportunity to not rob the bank. We ask him why he did so, and he says, "I wanted the money." We might say the money (or his wanting the money) caused him to rob the bank, but surely this would not negate moral blame.[75] Presumably, Mr. Puppet had the ability to refrain from robbing the bank, in the sense that his mental states (his beliefs and desires) played some causal role in his conduct and he was responsive to reasons for and against his conduct at the time of his actions.[76] His ability to act or not in robbing the bank was thus distinct from someone sleepwalking or insane at the time. If, for example, Mr. Puppet were to learn that the police were waiting inside the bank, we presume that he would respond to this information and (given his beliefs and desires to have the money and

75. Causation, even abnormal causation, does not necessarily equal excuse. See Morse, supra note 7. Moreover, the wanting need not be a distinct event that precedes robbing the bank; it may be manifested in the robbing itself.

76. This is based on the assumptions by Greene and Cohen that Mr. Puppet: "is as rational as other criminals and, yes, it was his desires and beliefs that produced his actions." Id. at 216. They also raise the possibility of defining "rationality" in neurocognitive rather than behavioral terms. Id. at 224 n. 3. But this would either be changing the subject (i.e., we would no longer be talking about what we currently mean by rationality) or incoherent as an explanation of rationality as currently conceived. People, not brains, behave rationally (or not). It is an instance of the "mereological fallacy" (i.e., mistakenly ascribing attributes to parts that make sense only when ascribed to the whole) to assume rationality may refer to states of the brain. See M. R. Bennett & P. M. S. Hacker, *Philosophical Foundations of Neuroscience* (2003).

not go to jail) abandon his plan to rob the bank—thus exercising this ability. By contrast, a sleepwalker or an insane person may not have the ability to respond to this information in a similar manner. Possessing an ability does not require exercising it whenever possible, so even though Mr. Puppet did not exercise it in the deterministic world in which he robs the bank, this does not mean that he lacked the ability to do otherwise.[77]

But did Mr. Puppet have an opportunity to do otherwise? In an important sense—yes. No external forces were coercing Mr. Puppet when he acted.[78] We can also assume that if Mr. Puppet did not want the money, his brain states would be different from his brain states when he wanted the money and robbed the bank and, thus, he would have acted differently.[79] Therefore, whatever Mr. Puppet's neurological and other physical states are, it is not case that if Mr. Puppet did not want to rob the bank, these physical states would cause him to do so anyway or deprive him of the opportunity to adhere to the law. Once again, compare Mr. Puppet with a person who cannot exercise this control. Suppose a person cannot bring her actions to conform to her desires, goals, plans, and intentions, or, for a variety of reasons, cannot control her bodily movements.[80] It is precisely in such cases that we withhold judgments of moral

77. Mr. Puppet had the ability to refrain from robbing the bank if he could exercise that ability when he wanted to (and when there is an opportunity to do so).

78. Although, under some formulations of the hypothetical, we might have grounds for inferring that the scientists who designed Mr. Puppet coerced his behavior. Some type of coercion by third parties is typically what people mean by the claim that one's action was not free. See Nahmias et al., supra note 37; van Inwagen, supra note 32, at 329 ("['Free will's'] non-philosophical uses are pretty much confined to the phrase 'of his/her own free will' which means 'uncoerced.'")

79. Similarly, if one had wanted soup rather than salad in Greene and Cohen's previous example, we assume that one's neurons would have been different. To suppose otherwise, Greene and Cohen would have to defend much stronger claims than they do: namely, that (1) there is a one-to-one correspondence between brain states and particular mental states, and (2) the relationships between various mental states and between mental states and actions are governed by the same physical laws that govern brain states (or are reducible to those laws). They do not defend either claim, cf. Greene & Cohen, supra note 6, at 225 ("we do not wish to imply that neuroscience will inevitably put us in a position to predict any given action based on a neurological examination"), and neither claim necessarily follows from determinism. Plausible positions that reject either claim are consistent with physical determinism. See Donald Davidson, "Mental Events," in *Essays on Actions and Events* 207 (2001); Richard Rorty, "The Brain as Hardware, Culture as Software," 47 *Inquiry* 219, 231 (2004). Stronger claims may be implied by their claim that folk psychology is founded on an illusion, but these claims deny rather explain the causal role of mental states. We turn to this aspect of the argument below.

80. Examples of the latter might include some cases of "alien hand" syndrome or "utilization behavior." See Iftah Biran et al., "The Alien Hand Syndrome: What Makes the Alien Hand Alien?" 23 *Cognitive Neuropsychology* 563 (2006).

blame—and indeed often do not even consider such movements to be "actions" at all—and the criminal law withholds punishment.

The consistency between moral judgment and determinism becomes even clearer when focusing on acts of moral praise. Suppose that, instead of a criminal act, Mr. Puppet commits an act of heroic bravery or kindness—for example, sacrificing himself in some way to save a stranger. Does his heroic or kind act cease to be morally praiseworthy if it takes place in a deterministic physical world and he is the product of his genes and upbringing? We think not. As with moral blame, what matters is whether Mr. Puppet can act for reasons and can exercise control over his actions on the basis of those reasons. Did he have the ability and opportunity to do otherwise and act voluntarily in performing this praiseworthy act? Contrast this with someone whose bodily movements were not within that person's rational control. For example, if someone in a state of epileptic seizure or while fainting engages in bodily movements that turn out to somehow save a third party, has the person acted heroically or bravely? Do they deserve moral praise? Have they acted at all? As with moral blame, we think the distinction here is plain as well.[81] Mr. Puppet deserves praise for his morally good acts, along with any other praiseworthy accomplishments, and blame for morally bad acts, when he had the ability and opportunity to do otherwise.

To suppose moral praise or blame require uncaused causation is to miss (or misconstrue) the normativity in human action. Our normative judgments about human actions are not inconsistent with explanations that involve physical action; they require, at a minimum, that our bodily movements be *human actions* and not mere bodily movements—that is, that they are explainable based on the actor's mental states[82]—and that these actions meet or fail to meet various moral standards or criteria, not that they be the product "uncaused causation." Greene and Cohen deny normativity at this level, however, along with the distinctions we have been drawing with Mr. Puppet, by arguing that they are based on the "illusion" of the folk psychological system.

This leads to a fourth problem with their argument: it implies untenable claims about folk psychology. Neither determinism in general nor neuroscience in particular undermines folk psychology in the ways they presuppose. Recall that, for Greene and Cohen, (1) moral evaluation depends on folk psychological

81. We also doubt that most people would be persuaded by neuroscience to think otherwise, but this is an empirical question, perhaps one for "experimental philosophy." Similar to the "Knobe effect" with regard to ascriptions of intentions, subjects might distinguish between good acts and bad acts for reasons other than the relationship between determinism and free will. See Joshua Knobe, "Intentional Actions and Side Effects in Ordinary Language," 63 *Analysis* 190 (2003).

82. See G.E.M. Anscombe, *Intention* (1957).

explanations of human behavior, (2) folk psychological explanations depend on the notions of mind and mental states (i.e., beliefs, desires, and intentions), and (3) mind and mental states depend on "uncaused causation." But the latter is an illusion. This implies that the notions of mind and mental states under this system are likewise illusory, which, for purposes of their argument, is what consequently leaves moral evaluation without a legitimate foundation. Although Greene and Cohen do not explicitly endorse the claim that mental states are nonexistent (or, alternatively, are epiphenomenal),[83] this implication appears to follow from their claim that the "crucial, if not the defining feature" of mind and mental states is "uncaused causation." Moreover, this implication is necessary to undermine moral evaluation. If moral evaluation depends on folk psychological explanations generally, and mental states exist and do causal work, then folk psychology is not illusory and provides a legitimate foundation for moral evaluation. In other words, to undermine moral evaluation in the ways they suppose, neuroscience would need to undermine the folk psychological system more generally.

If the argument by Greene and Cohen depends on this stronger implication about mental states, then it faces additional difficulties.[84] It is important to be clear about the aspect of their argument linking moral evaluation to folk psychology more generally. We can reconstruct this thread as follows: (1) retributivist punishment depends on moral evaluation; (2) moral evaluation requires that people punished had some control over their actions; (3) to have such control, they must have been able to act or refrain from acting; (4) the ability to act or refrain from acting requires that their mental states played a causal role in regulating their behavior; (5) but mental states do not exist, or they do no causal work[85]; (6) thus, people have no control over their actions; and (7) thus, retributive punishment is unjustified. Neuroscience enters the picture in support of premise (5) by illustrating that behavior is causally determined by physical states (including brain states). But this does not follow. Mental states may exist and play a causal role while also having underlying neurological

83. Indeed, they sometimes appear to endorse the causal power of mental states. See, e.g., note 76.

84. We note that the other four problems that we explicate in our critique do not depend on this implication. Thus, readers who disagree that this implication follows are free to accept our other arguments.

85. This aspect of the argument does not necessarily depend on a notion of "uncaused causation." Rather, we contend that premise (5) is implied by the fact that mind, mental states, and folk psychology (as conceived by Greene and Cohen) all depend on uncaused causation. If the latter does not exist, then neither do the former (as least as they conceive of them). Notice also that if Greene and Cohen are not committed to premise (5), then, for the reasons given above, agents would have the requisite control over their actions, and moral evaluation would follow.

correlates. Thus, the simple fact that mental states have accompanying brain states that are part of the physical universe and subject to its law does not render the former illusory or epiphenomenal. Moreover, as an empirical matter, some mental states (e.g., intentions) do appear to play a causal role in a manner that would be impossible if folk psychology generally were an "illusion."[86]

Moreover, reflect for a moment on what it would mean for folk psychology generally to be an illusion (i.e., that there are no such things as beliefs, desires, wants, fears, knowledge, intentions, or plans). One obvious implication is that there is no difference between us (and Mr. Puppet) and someone engaged in bodily movements caused by a seizure or conditions beyond their "rational" control. A second implication is that psychological explanations would be false, and there would be nothing real (or nothing that affects behavior) for psychology to explain. A third implication is that human action would indeed cease to be "human" or "action," at least as we currently conceive of these notions. Thus, if the argument by Greene and Cohen depends implicitly on these more radical claims about folk psychology, then this provides a *reductio ad absurdum* for their argument.[87]

Finally, there is a fifth problem with their argument. Even if they are right in their predictions, even if people are persuaded based on neuroscience to believe in hard determinism, even if they therefore conclude that their folk psychological system for explaining human behavior is based on an illusion, and even if they therefore abandon retributivism as a basis for justifying punishment, Greene and Cohen are wrong to suppose that we would be "lucky" and punishment would necessarily be more "humane." Although Greene

86. For an overview of some of the relevant literature, see Peter M. Gollwitzer & Paschal Sheeran, "Implementation Intentions and Goal Achievement: A Meta-Analysis of Effects and Processes," 38 *Advances in Experimental Social Psychology* 69 (2006). For a discussion of the relevance of these studies to debates about free will, see Alfred R. Mele, *Effective Intentions: the Power of Conscious Will* (2009). See also Mario Beauregard, "Mind Really Does Matter: Evidence from Neuroimaging Studies of Emotional Self-Regulation, Psychotherapy, and Placebo Effect," 81 *Progress in Neurobiology* 218 (2007).

87. Notice also how self-defeating this is as a challenge to *retributivism* and as a defense of *consequentialist* criminal punishment. Recall, they argue that we will still punish for practical reasons, for example, to deter future crime. Well, why? Do we *want* to deter crime? Do we *believe* or *know* punishment will deter crime? Will we therefore *choose* certain forms of punishment over others? Notice also that consequentialist justifications for punishment also involve folk psychological concepts; deterrence works by affecting the practical reasoning of potential criminals. Do potential criminals *believe* punishment will follow if they commit crime, do they not *want* to be punished, and therefore will they *choose* to not commit crimes? This aspect of their argument presupposes the existence of these entities. We concur with Anthony Kenny that "[a] legal system which took no account of states of mind would be as chimeric as it would be abhorrent." Kenny, supra note 68, at 93.

and Cohen predict that abandoning retributivist reasons for punishment will reduce punishment,[88] a brief history of actual criminal-sentencing practices in the United States during the past 30 years suggests the converse to be true. Indeed, when the US Supreme Court upheld prison sentences of "25 years to life" and "50 years to life" for stealing golf clubs and shoplifting videotapes, respectively (both "three strikes" cases), it did not justify its decision based on notions of desert but rather on other penological purposes such as deterrence and incapacitation.[89] In addition to "three strikes" laws, abandoning retributivist rationales for punishment in favor of deterrence, incapacitation, and general crime control has paved the way for harsh sentences for drug crimes, prosecuting juveniles as adults, strict liability crimes, proposals to abolish the insanity defense, and the felony-murder rule.[90] The absence of retributivist constraints also allows for the indefinite "civil commitment" of criminals after the completion of their prison sentences.[91] Indeed, more widespread acceptance of the idea that criminal offenders cannot stop and are "determined" to continue their criminal behavior does not appear to us to be a recipe for more compassionate and humane punishment. Moreover, psychologically persuasive but epistemically dubious neuroscience may only exacerbate rather than alleviate this problem.[92] We share what we believe to be the sentiment of Greene and Cohen that criminal punishment ought to be more humane, but we do not believe that the way to get there is by denying our shared humanity. A crucial part of that shared humanity is that our behavior may be explained and evaluated in the language of folk psychology.

* * *

We close with a final point. Imagine a group of open-minded policymakers faced with the task of constructing a justified system of legal punishment; they decide to listen to and take seriously the arguments of Greene and Cohen regarding retributivism, hard determinism, and neuroscience. At the end of the day, they could evaluate the various claims and the reasons for them; deliberate about the various avenues open to them and the benefits and costs of each; and

88. See Greene & Cohen, supra note 6, at 224.

89. Ewing v. California, 538 U.S. 11 (2003); Lockyer v. Andrade, 538 U.S. 63 (2003).

90. See Paul H. Robinson, Owen D. Jones & Robert Kurzban, "Realism, Punishment, and Reform," 77 *U. Chi. L. Rev.* 1611, 1630 (2010).

91. See Kansas v. Hendricks, 521 U.S. 346 (1997).

92. This prediction was made recently by Richard Sherwin. See Richard K. Sherwin, "Law's Screen Life: Criminal Predators and What to Do About Them," in *Imaging Legality: Where Law Meets Popular Culture* (Sarat ed., 2011).

then choose a course of action that they think is justified or more justified than the alternatives. Or they could simply sit back and wait for their neurons to make the decision for them. Or they could flip a coin. For the normative project of justifying criminal punishment, these distinctions matter a great deal to the issue of whether the criminal punishment that followed would be justified and legitimate.[93] From the perspective of Greene and Cohen, however, these differences ultimately do not matter (just as they do not matter at the level of criminal responsibility). If no one is *really* blameworthy or praiseworthy, justified or unjustified, then the same goes for lawmakers who decide how and when to distribute punishment. If it is just causally determined neuronal activity all the way down, and if the folk psychological explanations of punishment behavior are founded on an illusion, then for purposes of moral evaluation, it does not matter *why* anyone chooses to engage in criminal punishment or *how* they go about doing so.[94] The same goes for theorists engaged in the normative project of critiquing and defending possible policies regarding the distribution of criminal punishment. If so, then one wonders why they bothered to make the argument.

93. And it appears to matter for Greene and Cohen, who apparently think that punishment should proceed for consequentialist reasons and not for retributivist reasons.

94. See also Joshua D. Greene, "The Secret Joke of Kant's Soul," in *Moral Psychology, Vol. 3: Emotion, Disease, and Development* (Sinnott-Armstrong ed., 2007), in which Greene argues against retributivist punishment decisions and in favor of consequentialist punishment decisions on the ground that the former involve more "emotional" cognitive processes and the latter more "rational" ones.

7

Cognitive Neuroscience, Moral Responsibility, and Punishment

NANCEY MURPHY

1. INTRODUCTION

Although there are interesting justifications for (sometimes) punishing people whom we do not believe to be responsible for the act in question (Hodgson 2009), in most cases we tend to assume that punishment is deserved only by responsible parties. The focus of this chapter, then, is on the question of what constitutes responsibility.

I shall be writing against the background of claims to the effect that current developments in science, particularly in the cognitive neurosciences, tend to call into question our justifications for believing in moral (and therefore legal) responsibility. To address this worry I shall, in a sense, begin from the opposite direction; I shall first focus on the question of whether and how science helps *explain*, and thereby justify, belief in responsibility. Here I use Alasdair MacIntyre's account of morally responsible action (1999). In condensed form, it may be expressed as follows: one is capable of moral responsibility if one has the capacity to evaluate that which moves one to act in light of some concept of the good. I shall not repeat here MacIntyre's rationale for this account. I believe it has prima facie plausibility and that its usefulness in approaching the topics with which this volume is concerned will provide adequate justification for adopting it as a starting point for my investigation. The central focus of the chapter, then, is a cognitive-science analysis of the intellectual and affective capacities that *enable* morally responsible action, with brief mention along the way of neural systems and structures that are taken to subserve these capacities.

On the basis of this analysis, I shall address briefly some of the arguments from neuroscience that are taken to call free will into question, research first by Benjamin Libet and then followed up with more dramatic results by John-Dylan Haynes.

Finally, I consider the implications of my own work here for the role of punishment, arguing that a restorative rather than retributive justice system, particularly for juvenile offenders, has great potential for enhancing moral (and therefore legal) responsibility.

2. PREREQUISITES FOR MORAL RESPONSIBILITY

Dennis Patterson and Michael Prado claim correctly (see chapter 6) that one cannot derive theories of criminal punishment from the brain. Nor can one, I argue, derive an account of moral responsibility from neuroscience. Instead one needs to work the other way around. One needs to begin (1) with an account of the high-level cognitive capacities that are needed for morally responsible action (a philosophical task), and then (2) ask what elementary cognitive abilities go into each of these (a cognitive-science task), and finally (3) consider what we know about the neural substrates that enable each of these more basic cognitive capacities. In this section, I draw upon the work of Alasdair MacIntyre for the philosophical analysis and then summarize some of my work with Warren Brown (Murphy and Brown 2007) on the second and third sorts of analysis.

2.1. What Counts as Morally Responsible Action?

Alasdair MacIntyre is justly famous for his contributions to virtue theory (1981/1984). He published *Dependent Rational Animals: Why Human Beings Need the Virtues* (1999) in part to remedy what he came to perceive as an inadequacy in his earlier accounts of morality, namely the assumption that one could do ethics independently of biology. He says that "no account of the goods, rules and virtues that are definitive of our moral life can be adequate that does not explain—or point us to an explanation—how that form of life is possible for beings who are biologically constituted as we are..." (1999, *x*). His contribution to this explanation begins with what we share with the higher social animals. He then works out an account of what needs to be added to our animal capacities in order to allow us to become moral reasoners.

MacIntyre understands actions, both human and in higher animals, to originate in the biological needs and drives of the species—the goods at which such a form of life must aim if it is to flourish. Humans have the capacity to expand their range of goals, but the whole system of valuation could not get off the ground if we were not innately goal directed and if our goal-directed behavior at its simplest were not already subject to evaluation. MacIntyre says that denial of reasons for action shared with dolphins and chimpanzees "would render the transition to specifically human rationality unintelligible" (1999, 56).

What constitutes the difference, then, between animal and human rationality? MacIntyre argues that the ability to act voluntarily and for a reason depends on the capacity to evaluate one's own reasons. The capacity to evaluate one's reasons depends in turn upon language, and not only on possession of abstract concepts but also on a high level of syntactical competence. This sort of meta-level judgment requires language with the resources necessary for constructing sentences that contain as constituents a representation of the first-order judgment (1999, 53f.). That is, mature human rationality develops when children attain the ability to consider why they are doing what they are doing, and then to raise the question of whether there might be better reasons for acting differently.

Children become independent *moral* reasoners when they can change from acting to please parents or peers to acting on the basis of some abstract concept of the good; not just what seems good to them at the time, but what is good *per se* (1999, 71f., 84). MacIntyre says: "In so evaluating my desires I stand back from them. I put some distance between them and myself *qua* practical reasoner, just because I invite the question both from myself and from others, of whether it is in fact good for me to act on this particular desire here and now" (1999, 69).

Note that MacIntyre's concern here is not to present a criterion by which particular actions can be judged as morally responsible, but rather to ask the philosophical question of what are the essential requirements for anyone's attaining the capacity to act in a fully mature, rational, responsible, and moral manner. (For practical purposes weaker criteria apply. For example, much behavior is based on previous reflections of our own or of others.) Here is how MacIntyre ties together the capacities that comprise practical reasoning:

> ...as a practical reasoner I have to be able to imagine different possible futures *for me*, to imagine myself moving forward from the starting point of the present in different directions. For different or alternative futures present me with different and alternative sets of goods to be achieved, with different possible modes of flourishing. And it is important that I should be able to envisage both nearer and more distant futures and to attach probabilities, even if only in a rough and ready way, to the future results of acting in one way rather than another. For this both knowledge and imagination are necessary. (1999, 74f.)

2.2. A Cognitive-Science Analysis of Responsibility

I summarized MacIntyre's account of moral responsibility in section 1 as being able to "evaluate that which *moves* one to act." This is a somewhat inadequate characterization in that it fails to reflect the fact that humans (as well as other animals) are always already active. Brown and I argue that motivations and reasoning can best be understood in the context of action-feedback-evaluation -action loops (2007). Thus, it would be better to speak of evaluation that leads to the *redirection* of one's activity. This is as often inhibition of possible actions as it is initiation, and also often reshapes earlier patterns of action.

Brown and I have analyzed MacIntyre's account of moral responsibility into component cognitive capacities ("cognitive" here including the affective as well as the intellectual), as follows:

1. A symbolic sense of self (as MacIntyre says, "different possible futures *for me*")
2. A sense of the narrative unity of life ("to imagine myself moving forward from... the present"; "nearer and more distant futures")
3. The ability to run behavioral scenarios ("imagination") and predict the outcome ("knowledge"; "attach probabilities... to the future results")
4. The ability to evaluate predicted outcomes in light of goals
5. The ability to evaluate the goals themselves ("alternative sets of goods... different possible modes of flourishing") in light of abstract concepts of the good (Murphy and Brown 2007, 244)

Although MacIntyre is, of course, aware of the problem of *akrasia*, the inability to act as one believes one should, he does not devote attention to it in *Dependent Rational Animals*. Thus, Brown and I added an additional capacity:

6. The ability to act in accordance with 1 to 5

Each of these six capacities involves a complex set of more basic abilities, some of which I shall describe below and note, as well, a small sampling of their neural prerequisites.

2.2.1. A Sense of Self

What is at issue in a sense of self is not the (confused) idea of *being* a self, but rather having a self-*concept*. Such a concept arises early in life but becomes much more complex through maturation. Child development specialist Michael Lewis distinguishes two stages of development: The first is implicit self-awareness, which he calls the "biological machinery of self." The second is explicit self-awareness, "the idea of me." We share the machinery of self with other animals—the distinction of self from non-self (Lewis, 2003). Some of the brain systems involved relate to awareness of bodily states such as hunger, posture, and location in space. A part of the brain, the temporal-parietal juncture, is known to play a role in the experience of embodiment—that is, a sense of being spatially situated in one's body (Arzy 2006).

Explicit self-consciousness depends on the development of a "theory of mind." This allows for recognition of others in the environment who have bodies of their own as well as thoughts and feelings and, thus, for being able to recognize oneself as a member of the class of persons. Leslie Brothers has shown that we come well equipped neurobiologically to develop and use what she calls the "person concept." We have remarkable abilities to recognize faces, and we have neurons that specialize in detecting bodily motions that indicate other actors' intentions (Brothers 1997, chap. 3).

Terrence Deacon emphasizes the essential role of language in the development of a *symbolic* self-concept:

> Consciousness of self in this way implicitly includes consciousness of other selves, and other consciousnesses can only be represented through the virtual reference created by symbols. The self that is the source of one's experience of intentionality, the self that is judged by itself as well as by others for its moral choices, the self that worries about its impending departure from the world, this self is a symbolic self. (Deacon 1997, 452)

Thus, it is no accident that use of personal pronouns serves as a *measure* of the possession of a self-concept and that the appearance of personal pronoun use correlates with development of a theory of mind. M. R. Bennett and P. M. S. Hacker point out that to have concepts is to know how to use words. "The idea of me" is thus dependent on the ability to use the words "I" and "me." These words cannot be used correctly without acquisition of a *system* of words, including second- and third-person pronouns, which depends on the ability to distinguish other people from inanimate objects (Bennett and Hacker, 2003, 348).

Brothers argues that mature self-consciousness emerges from participation in a network of persons, a network that is intrinsically moral, being made up of "shoulds and oughts, triumph and shame, villains and heroes" (1997, 4). This relationship between individuals and the social order develops in narrative form; it is created and maintained by telling and reworking our stories in conversation with others (1997, 80f.).

2.2.2. Narrative Unity

Another prerequisite for moral responsibility is a narrative understanding of the history of one's life, and recognition that the narrative will continue into the future with alternative possibilities for the nature of that continuance. This capacity depends on the existence of a long-term, conscious memory for events from our past, called *episodic memory* (memory for previous life episodes) or *autobiographical memory* (memory of one's own autobiography). Episodic memory is recall of the events that are marked by specifics of time and place. It develops during early childhood, not being fully developed until after the third year of life (Ornstein et al. 1992). That other forms of memory are fully functional before this is attested by the vast amount of procedural and semantic learning that takes place during these early childhood years.

An important ingredient in human episodic memory (it is not clear whether higher animals share it) is the capacity of language to preserve historical detail. To be able not only to preserve an experience as a specific, historical sensory memory but also to add to it a memory of verbally encoded labels (such as "at my 50th birthday party") adds important dimensions of autobiographical coding.

The frontal lobes are important for the temporal organization of behavior, that is, of behaviors that are complex and require sequences of purposive behavior extending over long periods of time. Based in part on the remarkable development of frontal neocortex, humans have the capacity to remember the previous steps in, and current status of, very complex plans that have extended over considerable periods of time; that is, we have episodic memories for the events that constitute progress thus far in carrying forward a complex plan.

2.2.3. "Off-line" Imagination and Prediction

As symbolic language enhances mature humans' episodic memory, it also creates the capacity to imagine behavioral scenarios and predict their likely outcome. This involves imagining stretches of time beyond the present moment and placing oneself in that future. It is likely that higher animals have the capacity to run off-line emulations of potential behaviors. A famous experiment involved the chimpanzee Sultan, who solved the problem of how to reach bananas outside his cage by attaching two sticks end to end without trial and error. He was apparently able to manipulate representations of the sticks imaginatively and thus to imagine the outcome of such potential actions (Köhler 1956).

Thomas Metzinger is one of several authors who have developed neurobiologically plausible accounts of consciousness (2003). His theory of consciousness is based on the idea that complex organisms operate out of models of the external world in which consciousness is constituted by the currently activated world model. The most complex form of consciousness is *cognitive subjective consciousness*. What is important about this highest form of consciousness is the ability to elicit and process various world models off-line. Such off-line processing means for Metzinger that the organism (largely, humans) can "engage in the activation of globally available representational structures *independently of current external input*" (2003, 205). That is, cognitive subjective consciousness allows the individual to model potentialities for action in the world off-line. In this manner, one can "engage in future planning, enjoy explicit, episodic memories, or start genuinely cognitive processes like the mental formation of concepts" (2003, 5).

Andy Clark has developed a concept of "external scaffolding"—external devices we can manipulate in order to increase our capacity to predict consequences of action. Symbolic language is one of the most important sorts of external scaffolding for mental operations. The limitless possibilities for combining linguistic elements in new ways enhances humans' abilities to construct scenarios for possible future actions (Clark 1997). Terrence Deacon notes that the increasingly indirect linkages between symbolic mental representations and their grounds of reference free our imaginations to roam over possibilities of which we have had no previous experience.

> Symbolic analysis is the basis for a remarkable new level of self-determination that human beings alone have stumbled upon. The ability to use virtual reference to build up elaborate internal models of possible futures, and to hold these complex visions in mind with the force of the mnemonic glue of symbolic inference and descriptive shorthands, gives us unprecedented capacity to generate independent adaptive behaviors. Remarkable abstraction from indexically bound experiences is further enhanced by the ability of symbolic reference to pick out tiny fragments of real world processes and arrange them as buoys to chart an inferential course that predicts physical and social outcomes. (1997, 434)

These symbolically mediated models "exhibit complicated nonlinearity and recursive structures as well as nearly infinite flexibility and capacity for novelty due to their combinatorial nature" (Deacon 1997, 434). Therefore, the typical adult is capable of imagining an immense number of possible actions and is often able to predict their consequences.

MacIntyre notes, however, that this ability is not likely to develop in children if they are provided by their caretakers and teachers with too impoverished a view of future possibilities. Children need to be "educated in imagining alternative possibilities" (1999, 75). Educational failure in this regard can be of three types. One is the result of inculcating false beliefs about how far our lives are determined by uncontrollable circumstances. The second is by encouraging children to indulge in fantasies that blur the difference between realistic expectations and wishful thinking. The third sort is failure to question children's reasons for acting as they do and thus failure to alert them to the range of objects of desire and range of goals that constitute possible alternative reasons for action (1999, 76).

2.2.4. Goals and Evaluation

The fourth capacity that Brown and I have emphasized is the ability to evaluate predicted outcomes of behavior in light of goals. Much of this prediction and evaluation is done at the emotional level. Antonio Damasio has developed a thesis regarding "somatic markers" (1994). His work shows that no matter what capacities one has for predicting, at an intellectual level, the outcomes of anticipated behavior, without these "gut reactions," behavior is capricious and not appropriately linked to the attainment of goals. Thus, the experience of the emotional responses of our bodies is important in translating moral reasoning into adequate practical behavior. Loss of these somatic markers is associated with damage to the orbital frontal cortex, largely on the left side (H. Damasio 1994).

Although the pursuit of goals would never get off the ground without both built-in and conditioned emotional motivators, the capacity for symbolic language clearly enhances human ability to predict and evaluate the probable outcomes of behavior. Antonio Damasio (1994) reports on an illuminating series of experiments with chimpanzees. A chimpanzee is given the opportunity to choose between two unequal piles of candy; it always chooses the bigger one. Then the situation is made more complicated: the chimpanzee chooses, but the experimenter gives the chosen pile to a second chimpanzee, and the first ends up with the smaller one. Children older than 2 catch on quickly and choose the smaller pile. But chimpanzees have a very hard time catching on; they watch in agitated dismay, over and over, as the larger pile of candy is given away. Deacon says that the task poses a difficulty for the chimpanzees because the presence of such a salient reward undermines their ability to stand back from the situation and subjugate their desire to the pragmatic context, which requires them to do the opposite of what they would normally do to achieve the same end.

Now the experiment is further complicated. The chimpanzees are taught to associate numbers with the piles of candy. When given the chance to select numbers rather than the piles themselves, they quickly learn to choose the number associated with the smaller pile. Deacon argues that the symbolic representation helps reduce the power of the stimulus to drive behavior. Thus, he argues that increasing ability to create symbols progressively frees responses from stimulus-driven immediacy (1994, 413–415).

Sophisticated language allows not only for understanding a variety of abstract possibilities but also for second-order evaluations of one's own evaluative processes. For example, suppose one has read about empirical research on the tendency to make irrational judgments in favor of immediate versus later rewards. If given a choice between $100 today and $120 in 3 days, most people choose $100 today, despite the fact that there is no way to make $20 in profit on the money in 3 days. Robert H. Frank notes that an awareness of this tendency allows us to devise "commitment devices" that set up ways to avoid such temptations (1988, 86–88).

2.2.5. Self-Transcendence and Moral Evaluation

Recall that my primary concern here is with MacIntyre's account of *morally* responsible action, but there is another sense in which we speak of responsibility—for example, some children are responsible about getting their homework done, and others are not. Children become responsible in this sense when they attain the ability to evaluate that which shapes and reshapes their action. Such evaluation is what Daniel Dennett calls "going meta" (1984, 29). Humans, like all other organisms, are intrinsically active, and their actions are directed by biological drives and emotions, by immediate desires and longer-term goals, and by social expectations. The forms their action take are shaped by learning, by imagination, by judgments about what will be effective. *Responsible* action, as here understood, is that which is consequent upon the ability to represent to oneself what one is doing and why one is doing it. This level of responsibility is relevant for some legal purposes, but other cases require the additional ability to distinguish right from wrong.

Bennett and Hacker emphasize, here as well, the role of language. One who has developed the sophisticated linguistic powers

> ...to use proper names and pronouns, as well as psychological predicates and predicates of action, in both the first- and third-person cases and in the various tenses....is a self-conscious creature, who has the ability to be transitively conscious of its own mental states and conditions, who can think and reflect on how things are with it, who can not only act but also become and be conscious of itself as so acting. And it will also have the ability to reflect on its own past, on its character traits and dispositions, on its preferences, motives and reasons for action. (2003, 334)

One can act for a motive without having the concept for denoting such a motive, but one cannot know that one is acting for such a motive (Bennett and Hacker 2003, 350). *Moral* responsibility, then, depends on the capacity to use moral *concepts* to describe (and *in so doing* to evaluate) one's own actions, character traits, dispositions, and so on.

The capacity for symbolic language has occurred again and again in my account here of the prerequisites for moral responsibility. Needless to say, a great deal is known at this point about the vast number of regions and neural systems that go into human linguistic abilities. Just to give sense of the complexities here, consider this quotation from Peter Hagoort, summarizing data from 50 brain-imaging studies that mapped the regions involved in the simple task of producing a single word.

> All core steps in the speaking process are subserved by areas in the left hemisphere, which is the language dominant hemisphere in the large majority of people. Selecting the appropriate concept for speaking...seems to involve the left medial temporal gyrus. From there the activation spreads to Wernicke's area, which is pivotal in retrieving the phonological code of a word stored in memory. Wernicke's area plays a crucial role in the whole network of language processing by linking the lexical aspects of a word form to the widely distributed associations that define its meaning. This role is played by Wernicke's area in both language production and language comprehension. The lexical word form information is relayed to Broca's area in the left frontal cortex and/or the middle part of the superior temporal lobe in the left hemisphere. These areas play a role in the conversion of the phonological codes in memory into phonological words from which the abstract articulatory program is derived. In the final phase of preparing for articulation and execution of articulation sensorimotor areas become activated, with the possible additional contribution of the supplementary motor area and the cerebellum. (Hagoort 1999, 45–56 *passim*)

So, in the briefest possible summary, the most basic prerequisites for morally responsible action are sophisticated symbolic language; the capacity for self-transcendence, in the sense of being able to evaluate one's own cognitive processes; and the ability to imagine alternative sorts of behavior and motivation.

2.3. Putting Moral Reasoning into Action

I have already mentioned Hanna and Antonio Damasio's research on the consequences of damage to the orbital frontal cortex—the loss of the somatic markers that initiate and inhibit actions that are judged to be either beneficial or harmful. In addition, a great deal of work has been done on the brain regions that, in the normal case, enable one to act upon one's judgments. Much of this research, in fact, has been stimulated by the questioning of voluntary action in light of Benjamin Libet's research, described below.

One example is that of Mark Hallett, who has developed a model to represent the normal relations among volition, action, and perception of agency, along with suggested neural correlates. Movement begins with motivation, and this leads to planning of a movement. He reinforces a point made in this chapter: that it would be misleading to look for *an* initial event of willing because the brain is always working and providing for possible actions; thus, the relevant question is why the particular action that occurred was selected. When selected, the action can be executed. The perceptual component is alerted to upcoming movement from both planning and execution modules by feed-forward signals.

Motivation is associated with limbic and prefrontal regions of the brain. Studies show that selection of the action to perform depends on different regions, depending on whether the choice is which action to choose (supplementary motor area) or when to move (dorsolateral prefrontal cortex). It is likely that movement is initiated in mesial motor areas and premotor cortex. The movement command then goes to primary motor cortex. Corollary discharges appear to come from the supplementary motor area and dorsal premotor cortex to parietal areas. Parietal and frontal areas maintain a relatively constant bidirectional communication. It is likely that this network of structures includes the insula. The sense of agency that comes from the appropriate match of volition and movement feedback is likely also centered in the parietal area (Hallett 2009).

3. NEUROSCIENCE: FOR OR AGAINST RESPONSIBILITY?

In the preceding section, I began with a philosophical account of the cognitive abilities that go into the development of mature moral reasoning, and then sketched some of what is known so far about the complexities and neural bases of these cognitive capacities. This is just a small sampling of a vast body of scientific literature that not only is consistent with our traditional concept of human responsibility but also begins to explain how it is possible. My argument for the possibility of morally responsible action, in brief, is as follows: If humans are to be morally responsible, they need (something like) the six cognitive capacities listed in section 2.2. We know from observation that humans (sometimes or usually) have these capacities. For example, developmental psychologists are able to chart and date the acquisition of a sense of self. The neuroscientific findings presented here do not provide any significant reason to *doubt* these (apparent) facts of normal human functioning. If anything, they add to our confidence regarding the possibility of responsible action by explaining, as MacIntyre says we must, how this "form of moral life is possible for beings who are biologically constituted as we are" (1999, *x*).

Scientific studies showing correlates between brain damage and lack of behavioral control are immensely important for a variety of reasons, not the least of which is their relevance to the criminal justice system.

I have already reported on Hanna and Antonio Damasio's conclusions regarding the role of damage to the orbital frontal cortex: loss of the emotional impulses and restraints that normally assist us in acting prudently. In addition, studies show that 25% of defendants are medically or legally incompetent to stand trial. Clinical diagnosis of antisocial personality disorder (APD), defined as lack of regard for others' feelings and failure to abide by societal rules, has been found to be 10 times higher in the prison population than the rate in the general population. Furthermore, people with APD often have a history of childhood trauma and maltreatment (see Mobbs et al. 2009 for references). Dean Mobbs and his colleagues argue that the primary role of neuroscience in the legal system will be to improve the court's ability to identify those cases that fall within the category of "not guilty by reason of insanity" (Mobbs et al. 2009). However, as important as these findings are for understanding the behavior of people with abnormal brain function, it would be wrong to conclude directly from them that they call moral or legal responsibility into question for those *without* neural deficits.

There is, however, a different sort of neuroscientific research that has been taken to call free, conscious agency into question, even for those with intact neural systems. I shall consider one type of such research here and indicate why I take it to have minimal significance for the issues addressed in this volume.

Benjamin Libet's research (1999; 2004; see also chapter 12 of this volume) has shown that the performance of "self-paced voluntary actions" is preceded by a slow electrical change, recorded on the scalp, called the readiness potential (RP), or *Bereitschftpotential*. He devised a method for measuring the relations among the RP, subjective feelings of volition, and action. Subjects in his studies were told to flick their wrists "at any time they felt the urge or wish to do so." These acts were to be performed "capriciously, free of any external limitations or restrictions" (Libet 1999, 49). He used an electroencephalogram to measure the RP and an electromyogram to record muscle movements. He asked the subjects to report when they were first aware of the wish or urge to act.

Averaging across numerous trials, Libet found that the RP preceded the action by approximately 550 milliseconds, whereas the wish or urge to act occurred approximately 200 milliseconds before the muscle movement. The significance, according to Libet, is that the volitional process is initiated unconsciously, whereas in the traditional view of conscious will, "one would expect the conscious intention to appear before, or at the onset of, the RP, and thus command the brain to perform the intended act" (Libet 1999, 49). Many scholars have followed Libet in concluding that his research has negative implications regarding free will. (For a contrasting set of arguments, see Murphy, Ellis, and O'Connor 2009.)

In addition, more recent research by John-Dylan Haynes has used brain scans to record activity in the frontopolar cortex and has found that this activity can be used to predict which hand the subjects would use in an experiment similar to Libet's. He and his colleagues found a gap of up to 7 seconds between the measurable brain activity and the subjects' experience of having made a decision (see Soon et al. 2008; see also chapter 12). Although Haynes himself is careful not to overinterpret his research, it has been touted as an indication that human decisions are not made freely, but rather, as Brandon Keim concludes, that "your brain made the decision long before you knew about it" (Keim, 2008).

First, a note about two thorny philosophical issues raised by claims to the effect that Libet's and Haynes's research studies call free will into question. The first is what or whom is the subject of actions; the second, of course, is the nature of free will.

There is a tendency, illustrated by Keim's remark, to distinguish between the brain and a conscious event, and to propose that if the brain event preceded the conscious event, then the subject was not acting freely. However, I suggest that the identification of the person with her or his conscious awareness is a holdover from dualist accounts of human nature. Warren Brown and I (2007) use Daniel Dennett's term "Cartesian materialism" to refer to any conception of persons that identifies them with something "inner" such as a brain event.[1]

In contrast to the view that *I* am my consciousness, Brown and I argue that all brain events, including whatever turns out to be the source of conscious awareness, need to be understood within the context of the operation of the whole brain, within the whole body, and acting in the environment, particularly the social environment. Humans, as noted above (see section 2.2) are always already acting, and their acts form part of an action-feedback-evaluation-action cycle (Murphy and Brown 2007). Thus, the subject of an action is the whole human organism, including both brain events and conscious states, and questions of moral responsibility and free will rightly pertain to the whole person and to this larger picture of human action.

The second philosophical quagmire in which interpreters of Libet's and Haynes's research may find themselves is the question of what it *means* to have free will. The philosophical community is sharply (and perhaps interminably) divided over this issue (for a sampling of the discussion, see other chapters in

1. Dennett uses the term more narrowly to refer to the belief, on the part of brain scientists, that there must be some location in the brain (the Cartesian theater) where all neural/mental activity comes together (1991, 107).

this volume). Because I do not believe it is possible to settle debates about the meaning of free will here, I have concentrated instead on moral responsibility. Free will is often taken as one of the prerequisites for morally responsible action, and if by "free will" we mean merely the ability to act without constraint or coercion, this is unproblematically true. However, if space permitted, I would argue that something like the capacities considered above for moral responsibility are in fact the capacities needed for free will (for the beginning of such an argument, see Murphy and Brown 2007; Murphy, Ellis, and O'Connor 2009). If I could make this argument successfully, it would follow that trivial acts such as flicking a finger are not even candidates for considerations of free will. In fact, we never attribute free will to animals, and they make such "voluntary" movements constantly.

In like manner, the sort of spontaneous responses involved in Haynes's research are not cases in which questions of responsibility should be thought to arise—and this is a good thing. Most of our day-to-day action needs to happen too quickly to involve the degree of self-reflection required to count as responsible, let alone morally responsible. It has been estimated that we have only enough cognitive capacity to consciously direct 5% of our daily behavior (Baumeister and Sommer 1997). Some of the other 95% of activity is prereflective, such as the finger-lifting exercise in the laboratory. However, a much greater and more important component of human life is made up of habitual behaviors that once were established by learning and shaped by reflection but now have become automatic. An important factor here is the role of the somatic markers described above (see section 2.2.4). These instantaneous gut reactions register a vast amount of previous experience and stimulate the behavioral responses that are most appropriate in light of that experience.

One of the major virtues of MacIntyre's account of moral responsibility is that it allows us to recognize the extent to which our behavior *is* determined, at least initially, by neurobiologically instantiated dispositions, but to recognize, as well, that conscious reflection on these drivers of behavior gives us a chance either to own them or to change them. Sean Spence proposes that our moral accountability lies in whether we exercise "meta-responsibility" for our own future behavior, given that we know we cannot always take control of immediate responses. We live in long-term relations with our behaviors and propensities, and we become ourselves as we take charge of planning for them. There are simple cases, such as deciding not to drink to excess because of knowledge of what one is likely to do when under the influence. In addition, agents may choose over long time scales to rehearse certain behaviors in preference to others, in light of a cultivated understanding of and concern about the consequences of their actions for others (Spence 2009).

4. PUNISHMENT AND THE ENHANCEMENT OF MORAL RESPONSIBILITY

I leave it to other authors in this volume to discuss implications for the legal system of identifiable brain abnormalities. My focus will be on what changes might be called for in the legal system by my work here. In particular, I shall argue that a change from retributive to restorative justice, particularly for juvenile offenders, can be expected to bear immense fruit for offenders, victims, and society at large.

In an earlier book, coauthored with George Ellis, I argued in favor of restorative, as opposed to retributive, justice systems (1996). Our purpose there was the development of a social ethic based on Christian conceptions of nonviolence and self-renunciation for the sake of the other. I want to extend that argument here, focusing particularly on juvenile justice, in light of the account of the development of moral responsibility developed in the present chapter. Ellis and I drew heavily on the works of Jim Consedine (1995) and Howard Zehr (1989). Zehr claims that throughout most of Western history, crime has been understood as an offence of one person against another, and it was assumed that the central response must be to somehow make things right; restitution and compensation were very common, perhaps normative. Both victim and offender had a responsibility in this process, as did the community. The state had a role as well, but it was limited and was by necessity responsive to the wishes of victims.

To some extent, our history has been a dialectic between two modes of justice: state justice and community justice. State justice was imposed, punitive, hierarchical justice. In English law in the time of Henry I (ca. 1116), the king became the primary victim in offences such as robbery and murder, taking the place of the victim before the law. Actual victims lost their position in the process, and the state and the offender were left as the sole concerned parties. As a result, the system, rather than being concerned to make the victim whole, now focused on upholding the authority of the state. Criminal justice became future oriented, concerned rather to make the offender and potential offenders law abiding than to make them atone for their past offence. Restitution, being past oriented and concerned with the victim, was gradually abandoned (Zehr 1989, quoted in Consedine 1995, 54). Consedine, a prison chaplain in New Zealand, points out that when the victims of crimes hand over to the state the right to seek retaliation, they also lose the right to forgive and seek healing between themselves and offenders (see chapter 11, this volume).

Zehr has been called the grandfather of restorative justice. He began his work in the United States in the 1970s, and since then a variety of programs and approaches, for both juveniles and adults, have been developed in thousands of communities and countries (Zehr 2002 4–5). Although restorative justice programs usually operate alongside or within the standard criminal justice system, it became the primary approach to juvenile justice in New Zealand in 1989. A typical approach brings together the offender and the victim as well as the families or support groups of both parties. A judge or other official of the state is usually present to facilitate a process that includes an opportunity for the victim to describe in personal terms the suffering and loss that has been occasioned. The families of both victim and offender may be present to speak of their grief. The offender is given a chance to express regret. In cases in which restitution is possible, a plan is set up that is agreeable to the victim, but that does not make unrealistic demands on the offender. Consedine reports that in 90% of cases in the New Zealand children's court, offenders express regret, and the victims often forgive the offender.

I now want to examine some of the virtues of a restorative justice system such as this in light of Brown's and my MacIntyrean analysis of the prerequisites for moral responsibility.

1. *The development (and maturation) of a symbolic self-concept.* David Hodgson, in an argument for retributive justice, makes a point that applies even more directly to the value of a restorative system. He says that it is important that offenders be treated not as objects to be manipulated but as people who are capable of acting rationally and as capable of taking responsibility for their conduct (2009, 233). As noted above, Leslie Brothers describes the development of a mature sense of self as a consequence of being able to locate oneself within social networks, telling and revising narratives regarding ourselves and others, in terms of shoulds and oughts, triumphs and shame, villains and heroes (1997, 4). The conversations conducted in the process of restorative justice conferences are ideally designed to contribute to the maturation of the offenders' sense of social location. Consider, in contrast, the destabilizing effect of being incarcerated, and thus removed from one's community of origin and placed into one with strikingly different norms.
2. *A sense of the narrative unity of life.* Restorative justice conferences involve placing the offender's action into a narrative. The victim and any other concerned parties are asked to describe the effects of the crime in order for the offender to appreciate the impact of her action. Zehr says that an important element in healing or transcending the experience of a crime is an opportunity to tell the story of what happened (2002, 14). Victims also need to hear narratives from offenders: Why did this happen, and why did it happen to me?

> The offender's narrative must involve taking responsibility for the action and its effects.

Zehr speaks of the possibility for victims to transcend the trauma of a crime by "re-storying" one's life and receiving acknowledgement of the harm received (2002, 15). James McClendon provides insight into the process of re-storying. In contrast to those who claim that forgiving requires forgetting, he argues that forgiveness is rather a special kind of remembrance. "One who forgives knows the other's offense to be offense" but "the forgiving one takes that offense up into his or her life... makes the other's story part of his or her own story, and by owning it destroys forever its power to divide forgiver and forgiven." To forgive is "to learn a new and truer story about myself and by discovering how fully my life is bound up with those whose sins are also sins against myself" (McClendon 2002, 228). And in the happy case, that act is two sided, with the one forgiven, in a sense, saying, "I accept forgiveness" (2002, 229).

Consedine notes that in some cases in the New Zealand system, the reconciliation between offender and victim goes far beyond merely setting things right for the victim:

> ...sometimes moving gestures of healing come from the victim side. They waive their right to compensation from an unemployed young offender who cannot afford it. They invite them to their home for dinner a week after the conference. They help to find an unemployed young offender a job, a homeless young person a home. In one amazing case, a female victim who had been robbed by a young offender at the point of a gun had the offender live in her home as part of the agreed plan of action. (Consedine 1995, 102)

3. *Increased ability to run behavioral scenarios and predict the outcome.* I have already reported (in section 2.2) MacIntyre's account of factors that inhibit the development of mature moral reasoning; these pertain particularly to failure to inculcate a realistic range of ideas about possible future actions and the goods to be achieved thereby. The stories told by victims and their families are likely to increase offenders' capacities to imagine the outcome of their future behavior in terms of effects on future potential victims. Zehr says that, in contrast, little in the process of the criminal justice system encourages offenders to understand the consequences of their actions and to empathize with the victims. In fact, offenders are often "discouraged from acknowledging their responsibility and are given little opportunity to act on this responsibility in concrete ways" (2002, 16). However, in a

restorative system, suggestions are provided for future actions to make things right.

4. *The ability to evaluate behavioral scenarios in light of goals.* The three prerequisites described above put the offender in the position to carry out the sort of self-evaluation that MacIntyre puts at the heart of responsible action: the ability to identify and evaluate the factors that have moved one to action in the past, and to make appropriate changes on the basis of that self-examination—to ask oneself whether one might have better reasons for acting differently in order to pursue one's goals more effectively. Zehr claims that crimes often result from the offender's feeling victimized and thus from an attempt to even the score. Thus, he says, we cannot expect offending to stop without acknowledging and addressing the sense of victimization. In a retributive system, however, the punishment often leads to an increased sense of victimization (2002, 31). In a restorative system, there is opportunity to acknowledge and address other sources of antisocial behavior such as addiction and make arrangements for appropriate treatment.
5. *The ability to evaluate goals in light of a concept of the good.* Bernard Williams has argued that complete amoralism is impossible except in rare cases such as sociopathy (1972). Thus, all criminal behavior is aiming at something the perpetrator perceives as good. So, the restorative system can be seen as an opportunity to open the offenders' imaginations to higher forms of goodness—particularly as a result of being treated with respect and having their needs acknowledged. This is the point at which offenders are encouraged, in MacIntyre's terms, to ask whether what they took to be good reasons for their actions really were sufficiently good reasons, and they are enabled "to imagine realistically alternative possible futures" (1999, 83).

In short, the implementation of restorative justice systems recognizes that offenders' moral formation is at least incomplete, if not badly deficient, and the kinds of processes recommended provide an ideal opportunity for society to assist in the remediation and further development of the capacity for morally responsible action. The assumption that such remediation is possible, even for adults, is based on recognition of neural plasticity, the ability for development of new sorts of brain processes. The processes involved here, as described above, are a more sophisticated self-concept, one based on a better appreciation for where one stands in the community; an improved sense of the narrative of one's own life and of the role of others (such as victims) in those stories; an increased store of imaginable behavioral scenarios, along with the ability to better predict their outcome; and a better grasp of moral concepts.[2]

REFERENCES

Arzy, Shahar, et al. (2006). Neural Basis of Embodiment: Distinct Contributions of Temporoparietal Junction and Extrastriate Body Area. *Journal of Neuroscience* 26, no. 31: 269–270.

Baumeister, R. F. and K. L Sommer. (1997). Consciousness, Free Choice, and Automaticity. In R. S. Weyer, Jr. (ed.), *Advances in Social Cognition*, vol. X. Mahwah, NJ: Erlbaum. Pp. 75–82.

Bennett, M. R. and P. M. S. Hacker. (2003). *Philosophical Foundations of Neuroscience.* Oxford: Blackwell.

Brothers, Leslie. (1997). *Friday's Footprint: How Society Shapes the Human Mind.* New York: Oxford.

Clark, Andy. (1997). *Being There: Putting Brain, Body, and World Together Again.* Cambridge, MA: MIT Press.

Consedine, Jim. (1995). *Restorative Justice: Healing the Effects of Crime.* Lyttleton, NZ: Ploughshares Publications.

Damasio, Antonio R. (1994). *Descartes' Error: Emotion, Reason, and the Human Brain.* New York: G. P. Putnam's Sons.

Damasio, Hanna, et al. (1994). The Return of Phineas Gage: The Skull of a Famous Patient Yields Clues about the Brain. *Science* 264: 1102–1105.

Deacon, Terrence W. (1997). *The Symbolic Species: The Co-evolution of Language and the Brain.* New York: Norton.

Dennett, Daniel C. (1984). *Elbow Room: The Varieties of Free Will Worth Wanting.* Cambridge, MA: MIT Press.

Dennett, Daniel C. (1991). *Consciousness Explained.* Boston: Little, Brown.

Hagoort, Peter. (1999). The Uniquely Human Capacity for Language Communication: From POPE to [po:p] in Half a Second. In Robert J. Russell et al., eds., *Neuroscience and the Person: Scientific Perspectives on Divine Action.* Vatican City State: Vatican Observatory Press. Pp. 45–56.

Hallett, Mark. (2009). Physiology of Volition. In Nancey Murphy, George F. R. Ellis, and Timothy O'Connor, eds. (2009). *Downward Causation and the Neurobiology of Free Will.* Berlin and Heidelberg: Springer Verlag. Pp. 127–143.

Hodgson, David. (2009). Criminal Responsibility, Free Will, and Neuroscience. In Nancey Murphy, George F. R. Ellis, and Timothy O'Connor, eds. (2009). *Downward Causation and the Neurobiology of Free Will.* Berlin and Heidelberg: Springer Verlag. Pp. 227–241.

Keim, Brandon. (2008). Brain Scanners Can See Your Decisions Before You Make Them. http://www.wired.com/science/discoveries/news/2008/04/mind_decision. Accessed Oct. 24, 2012.

2. I thank Thomas Nadelhoffer and an anonymous reviewer for suggestions that have strengthened this chapter.

Köhler, Wolfgang. (1956). *The Mentality of Apes.* London: Routledge & Kegan Paul.

Lewis, Michael. (2003). The Emergence of Consciousness and Its Role in Human Development. In Joseph LeDoux, Jacek Debiec, and Henry Moss, eds. *The Self: From Soul to Brain, Annals of the New York Academy of Sciences*, vol. 1001. New York: New York Academy of Sciences. Pp. 104–133.

Libet, Benjamin. (1999). Do We Have Free Will? In Benjamin Libet, Anthony Freeman, and Keith Sutherland, eds. *The Volitional Brain: Towards a Neuroscience of Free Will.* UK and USA: Imprint Academic. Pp. 47–57.

Libet, Benjamin. (2004). *Mind Time: The Temporal Factor in Consciousness.* Cambridge, MA: Harvard University Press.

MacIntyre, Alasdair. (1981/1984). *After Virtue: A Study in Moral Theory.* 2nd ed. Notre Dame, IN: University of Notre Dame Press.

MacIntyre, Alasdair. (1999). *Dependent Rational Animals: Why Human Beings Need the Virtues.* Chicago: Open Court.

McClendon, James W., Jr. (2002). *Ethics: Systematic Theology*, Volume 2, 2nd rev. ed. Nashville, TN: Abingdon Press.

Metzinger, Thomas. (2003). *Being No One: The Self-Model Theory of Subjectivity.* Cambridge, MA: MIT Press.

Mobbs, Dean, et al. (2009). Law, Responsibility, and the Brain. In Nancey Murphy, George F. R. Ellis, and Timothy O'Connor, eds. (2009). *Downward Causation and the Neurobiology of Free Will.* Berlin and Heidelberg: Springer Verlag. Pp. 243–269.

Murphy, Nancey and Ellis, George, F. R. (1996). *On the Moral Nature of the Universe: Theology, Cosmology, and Ethics.* Minneapolis, MN: Fortress Press.

Murphy, Nancey, and Brown, Warren S. (2007). *Did My Neurons Make Me Do It? Philosophical and Neurobiological Perspectives on Moral Responsibility and Free Will.* Oxford: Oxford University Press.

Murphy, Nancey, Ellis, George F. R., and O'Connor, Timothy, eds. (2009). *Downward Causation and the Neurobiology of Free Will.* Berlin and Heidelberg: Springer Verlag.

Ornstein, P. A., Gordon, B. N., and Baker-Ward, L. E. (1992). Children's Memory for Salient Events: Implications for Testimony. In M. L. Howe, C. J. Brainerd, and V. F Reyna, eds. *Development of Long Term Retention.* New York: Springer Verlag. Pp. 135–158.

Soon, Chun Siong, et al. (2008). Unconscious Determinants of Free Decisions in the Human Brain. *Nature Neuroscience* 11: 543–545.

Spence, Sean. (2009). Thinking Beyond the *Bereitschafts Potential*: Consciousness of Self and Others as a Necessary Condition for Change. In Nancey Murphy, George F. R. Ellis, and Timothy O'Connor, eds. (2009). *Downward Causation and the Neurobiology of Free Will.* Berlin and Heidelberg: Springer Verlag. Pp. 211–223.

Williams, Bernard. (1972). *Morality.* Cambridge, UK: Cambridge University Press.

Zehr, Howard. (1989). *The Restorative Vision.* Akron, PA: The Mennonite Central Committee. Pp. 1–15.

Zehr, Howard. (2002). *The Little Book of Restorative Justice.* Intercourse, PA: Good Books.

PART FOUR

Punishment and Folk Intuitions

8

Free Will, Science, and Punishment

ALFRED R. MELE

In a fascinating article, Joshua Greene and Jonathan Cohen argue that "New neuroscience will change the law...by transforming people's intuitions about free will and moral responsibility" (2004, p. 1775). In their opinion, "Most people's view of the mind is implicitly *dualist* and *libertarian*" (p. 1779), and they contend that new neuroscience will undermine this view of the mind, "people's common sense, libertarian conception of free will and the retributivist thinking that depends on it" (p. 1776).

Elsewhere, I have argued that scientific studies that have been claimed to show that free will is an illusion fail to do so (Mele 2009). My arguments do not depend on any particular conception of free will. The scientific arguments at issue use data to support empirical propositions that are then conjoined with a proposition about the meaning of "free will" to yield the conclusion that free will is an illusion. These empirical propositions include, for example, Benjamin Libet's contention that, in studies he conducted, the brain produces unconscious decisions to act about one third of 1 second before the person becomes aware of them (1985, 2004) and Daniel Wegner's claim that conscious intentions are never among the causes of corresponding actions (2002, 2004, 2008). I have argued that these propositions are not warranted by the evidence offered to support them. If I am right, the debate ends before there is any need to examine the meaning of "free will."

It may be claimed that I am missing the real point of the scientific arguments at issue. The real point, it may be said, is that substance dualism is false, and that the falsity of substance dualism is sufficient for the nonexistence of free will.

Such dualism includes, as Dean Zimmerman reports, a commitment to the idea that "associated with each human person, there is a thinking thing... not composed of the same kinds of stuff as... nonmental things" (2006, p. 115). He describes the "thinking thing" as a soul, but some dualists prefer to use the word "mind."

I myself believe that we sometimes act freely (exercise free will), and I am not a substance dualist. Greene and Cohen recognize that people who are like me in this respect exist. But, in their opinion, our view is out of line with "most people's view of the mind" (2004, p. 1779).

Just as we can use empirical methods to study how the brain works, we can also use empirical methods to study how people conceive of the mind, free will, moral responsibility, and the like. However, Greene and Cohen offer no hard evidence for their claim that "Most people's view of the mind is implicitly *dualist* and *libertarian*" (2004, p. 1779), and this claim is important for their project in the article at issue. If most people's view of the mind is not dualist, then a persuasive neuroscientific argument against dualism might leave most people exactly where they were. Greene and Cohen contend that "neuroscience has a special role to play" in the development of "moral intuitions that are at odds with our current social practices" because "as long as the mind remains a black box, there will always be a donkey on which to pin dualist and libertarian intuitions" (p. 1781). But do "most people" in fact have such intuitions?

The question I just raised is one of this article's main topics. Before I get down to business, I want to cancel a possible misimpression. Greene and Cohen advocate a consequentialist, nonretributivistic system of legal punishment, and they believe that "new neuroscience" will help pave the way for such a system by showing that free will, as most people conceive of it, is an illusion. I myself—as a private citizen; I have not written about the issue—favor, in Greene and Cohen's words, "a consequentialist approach to the criminal law" (2004, p. 1775). My disagreements with them are not about this important social issue.

SOME PHILOSOPHICAL BACKGROUND

Some philosophical background will prove useful. I start with libertarianism, a philosophical position on free will mentioned in some passages quoted in my introduction. Libertarianism is the conjunction of two propositions: (1) free will is incompatible with determinism; (2) free will exists. Determinism, as most philosophers who work on free will understand it, is the thesis that a complete statement of the laws of nature, together with a complete description of the entire universe at any point in time, logically entails a complete description of the entire universe at any other point in time. (Human beings are parts of the universe, and a description of what we were doing 10 minutes ago is part of a complete description of the universe at that point in time.)

Compatibilism is the thesis that free will is compatible with the truth of determinism. Owing to their acquaintance with contemporary physics, the great majority of contemporary compatibilists do not believe that determinism is true; but they do believe that even if it were true, that would not preclude our having free will. (Compatibilism can sound very strange to nonspecialists. In Mele 2009, pp. 153–155, I try to explain why the strange sound might be misleading and why compatibilism should be taken seriously. I will not do so again here.) Obviously (given 1, above), libertarians reject compatibilism. According to a standard philosophical definition of "libertarianism" (about free will, not politics), *what it is* to be a libertarian is to be an incompatibilist believer in free will.

Greene and Cohen understand libertarianism more narrowly. For example, they write: "It is hard to imagine a belief in free will that is materialist but not compatibilist, given that ordinary matter does not seem capable of supplying the nonphysical processes that libertarianism requires" (2004, p. 1779). Seemingly, as they understand libertarianism, it entails substance dualism. Now, I do not find it "hard to imagine a belief in free will that is materialist but not compatibilist." All I have to do is to call to mind Robert Kane's belief in free will (Kane 1996). Kane is a leading incompatibilist believer in free will who does not appeal to substance dualism. He is a nondualistic libertarian, given the standard philosophical definition of libertarianism. I have developed two different (but overlapping) sets of alleged conceptually sufficient conditions for free will—one for compatibilist believers in free will and the other for libertarians (Mele 1995, 2006). Dualism does not enter into either set of conditions.

I make these points about libertarianism simply for the purposes of clarification. Henceforth, I focus on the *dualistic* libertarianism that concerns Greene and Cohen.

ARE MOST PEOPLE DUALISTIC LIBERTARIANS?

Consider the following two propositions:

1. Having free will requires having (or being) an immaterial soul or mind.
2. As most people conceive of free will, having free will requires having (or being) an immaterial soul or mind.

The first proposition is a statement of an alleged conceptual truth, and it is not a candidate for direct empirical investigation. The second proposition is an empirical one. Some data that bear on it are discussed shortly. Brief attention to the first proposition will prove useful as background.

As I understand free will, proposition 1 is false (Mele 2006, 2009). But my understanding of free will definitely is out of line with that of some scientists. Consider, for example, the following from P. Read Montague:

> Free will is the idea that we make choices and have thoughts independent of anything remotely resembling a physical process. Free will is the close cousin to the idea of the soul—the concept that "you," your thoughts and feelings, derive from an entity that is separate and distinct from the physical mechanisms that make up your body. From this perspective, your choices are not caused by physical events, but instead emerge wholly formed from somewhere indescribable and outside the purview of physical descriptions. This implies that free will cannot have evolved by natural selection, as that would place it directly in a stream of causally connected events. (2008, p. 584)

Here Montague represents free will as something that depends for its existence on the truth of substance dualism.

Montague offers no arguments for his assertions about what "free will" means. However, Anthony Cashmore does produce an argument of sorts for believing that free will depends on substance dualism. He asserts that "if we no longer entertain the luxury of a belief in the 'magic of the soul,' then there is little else to offer in support of the concept of free will" (2010, p. 4499). And he makes the following claim:

> In the absence of any molecular model accommodating the concept of free will, I have to conclude that the dualism of Descartes is alive and well. That is, just like Descartes, we still believe (much as we pretend otherwise) that there is a magic component to human behavior. Here I argue that the way we use the concept of free will is nonsensical. (p. 4503)

Cashmore seems to suggest here that if there were a molecular model that accommodates "the concept of free will," people who believe that free will exists would not be committed thereby to a belief in substance dualism. And he may be thinking both that there *cannot* be such a model and that, because that is so, having free will depends on having (or being) an immaterial soul or mind.

A simple observation is in order: our current lack of a molecular model that accommodates free will does not entail that there will never be a model of this kind nor that such a model is impossible. Obviously, Cashmore believes that substance dualism is false. And if the claim I quoted about the absence of a molecular model is to be taken seriously, part of his reason for holding that belief in free will implies belief in substance dualism is that we now lack a molecular model of free will. It is noteworthy in this connection that although Cashmore grants that we now lack a molecular model of consciousness (2010, p. 4502), he does not conclude that belief in consciousness depends on belief in substance dualism. Nor does he contend that consciousness is an illusion. Indeed, he holds that "consciousness acts on behavior" (p. 4502). So Cashmore cannot consistently believe that the simple fact that we currently lack a molecular model that accommodates free will entails that free will depends on substance dualism (and therefore is an illusion).

Why is Cashmore a substance dualist about free will but not about consciousness even though he believes that we lack molecular models of both? He describes a belief in free will as "a belief that there is a component to biological behavior that is something more than the unavoidable consequences of the genetic and environmental history of the individual and the possible stochastic laws of nature" (2010, p. 4500). And he contends that although stochasticity "may remove the bugbear of determinism, it would do little to support the notion of free will: I cannot be held responsible for my genes and my environment; similarly, I can hardly be held responsible for any stochastic process that may influence my behavior!" (p. 4500). Now, Cashmore evidently is open to the possibility of a nondualistic solution to the mind–body problem that is consistent with the truth of his assertion that "consciousness acts on behavior" (p. 4502). An attractive nondualistic solution would presumably allow for conscious deliberation about what to do, conscious decisions about what to do, and the like. Suppose that some episodes of practical deliberation and some decision-producing processes are stochastic processes. Why should it be thought that we cannot have any responsibility for them? Cashmore might claim that we cannot have any responsibility for them because what they result in is "unavoidable." But given that the processes at issue are, by hypothesis, stochastic, this claim about results would be very puzzling. Other things being equal, a stochastic process that results in *x* might not have—precisely because it is stochastic.

It may be claimed that all causation occurs at too low an ontological level for deliberation about what to do to have an effect on what one does. But this is not Cashmore's view: again, he asserts that "consciousness acts on behavior" (p. 4502). On his view, "there must be a mechanism by which consciousness does influence behavior. There must be a flow of information from consciousness to neural activity." So, for Cashmore, some relatively high-level events do have effects.

Cashmore apparently understands free will in such a way that, necessarily, we exercise it only if our "will" is uncaused (2010, p. 4501). That is, he seems to understand free will in such a way that, necessarily, any free decision is an uncaused decision. But what puts him in a position to be confident that this theoretical proposition is true? It is not as though research in biology—Cashmore's field—tells us what "free will" means.

Biologists know that the simple fact that they are biologists does not give them any special insight into what the expression "free will" means. (A biologist might believe that philosophers do not have any special insight into the meaning of "free will" either, and he or she might offer as evidence the great amount of disagreement among philosophers about what "free will" means.) They can be led to entertain the thought that their understanding of that expression might just be an artifact of their own personal upbringing and to consider the hypothesis that they are out of touch with ordinary use of "free will." In experiments with human participants ("subjects," in slightly older terminology), scientists definitely prefer to have a sample size larger than one person; and any scientist can see that if the way she goes about determining what "free will" means is simply to consult her own feeling or intuition about the meaning, then—to the extent to which it is important not to be mistaken about the meaning of "free will"—she should seek a better method.

Even if there is no way to gain widespread agreement about the meaning of "free will," it may be that attention to common use of the expression would motivate Cashmore and others to take seriously the idea that free decisions do not have to be uncaused and that free will does not depend on substance dualism. Possibly, such attention would even motivate them to take seriously the idea that free decisions can be deterministically caused. As I said, Cashmore and I disagree about the meaning of free will. He may claim that my understanding of the expression is idiosyncratic and that I am definitely out of touch with ordinary use; and I may claim that his magical use of "free will" is out of line with mainstream use. Once we get to this point, we should look for relevant data.

Greene and Cohen claim that most people are dualistic libertarians (2004, p. 1779), and Cashmore seems to agree. Are they right about most people? As I mentioned, libertarianism entails incompatibilism. So one question to ask in this connection is whether most people are incompatibilists. I discuss some data that bear on this question and then move on to *dualistic* libertarianism in particular.

Eddy Nahmias, Stephen Morris, Thomas Nadelhoffer, and Jason Turner conducted survey studies about free will that bear directly on this question about incompatibilism (2005, 2006). One of the studies—conducted with undergraduates who had not studied free will—featured the following story:

> Imagine there is a universe that is re-created over and over again, starting from the exact same initial conditions and with all the same laws of nature. In this universe the same conditions and the same laws of nature produce the exact same outcomes, so that every single time the universe is re-created,

> everything must happen the exact same way. For instance, in this universe a person named Jill decides to steal a necklace at a particular time, and every time the universe is re-created, Jill decides to steal the necklace at that time. (2006, p. 38)

The universe described here is a deterministic one. Even so, in response to the question of whether Jill decided to steal the necklace of her own free will, 66% of the participants answered yes (p. 38). Very similar results (ranging from 68% to 79%) were obtained for other stories designed to portray actions in deterministic universes—whether those actions were bad, good, or neutral (p. 39). In each of these studies, the majority response is consistent with a compatibilist conception of free will.[1]

Eddy Nahmias, Justin Coates, and Trevor Kvaran conducted a study designed to test, among other things, how the kind of causation featured in a probe affects judgments about free will (Nahmias et al. 2007). In some of the probes decisions are "completely caused by the specific chemical reactions and neural processes" occurring in a person's "brain," whereas in other, parallel probes, decisions are "completely caused by the... thoughts desires, and plans" occurring in the person's "mind" (p. 223). The expression "completely caused" is suggestive of determinism; the difference at issue is, as it were, the *style* of deterministic causation. This difference had the biggest effect when the probe was "abstract" (i.e., did not mention specific actions) and featured scientific hypotheses about the actual universe.

Bracketed material in the text below appeared in a parallel probe:

> Many respected neuroscientists [psychologists] are convinced that eventually we will figure out exactly how all of our decisions and actions are entirely caused... If these neuroscientists [psychologists] are right, then once specific earlier events have occurred in a person's life, these events will definitely cause specific later events to occur. For instance, once specific chemical reactions and neural processes [thoughts, desires, and plans] occur in the person's brain [mind], they will definitely cause the person to make the specific decision he or she makes. (Nahmias et al. 2007, p. 224)

1. Nahmias and his coauthors also asked participants about moral responsibility. In response to the question of whether "it would be fair to hold [Jill] morally responsible (that is, blame her) for her decision to steal the necklace" (in the re-run scenario quoted above), 77% of the participants answered yes (2006, p. 38). Very similar results (ranging from 60% to 88%) were obtained for other stories designed to portray actions in deterministic universes—whether those actions were bad or good (p. 39).

Participants were asked to indicate their degree of agreement or disagreement with the following statement: "If the neuroscientists [psychologists] are right, then people make decisions of their own free will" (p. 225). When the probe featured causation by "thoughts, desires, and plans," 82.9% agreed with the statement; and when it featured causation by "chemical reactions and neural processes," 38.3% agreed (p. 227). This is, of course, a huge difference. But it is interesting that 38% of the participants count even decisions that are "entirely caused [by] specific chemical reactions and neural processes" as being made of the person's own free will. Such participants would seem to see no need for a nonphysical mind or soul to be at work in the production of free decisions.

It also is interesting that when the setting is switched from the actual universe to a possible universe and the probes involve an agent who performs a good or a bad action, most participants regard the decisions as being made of the person's own free will. The results were as follows (*N* indicates causation by "chemical reactions and neural processes" and *P* indicates causation by "thoughts, desires, and plans")[2]:

Of One's Own Free Will: Agree

	Bad	*Good*
N	59.8	57.4
P	66.1	61.1

Apparently, when they entertain these *N* probes, a *majority* of people see no need for a nonphysical soul or mind to play a role in the production of decisions made of the person's own free will. That is, they see no need for substance dualism in this connection.

I conducted a three-part survey study that bears on the connection between substance dualism and free will in lay thinking. Participants in part 1 ($N = 69$) were students in a basic philosophy class at Florida State University. Free will and moral responsibility were not on their syllabus. About half (33) were presented with the following text:

> First answer the question on page # 1. Then turn the sheet over and answer the question on page # 2.
>
> We're interested in how you understand free will. Please read the following sentences and answer the question by circling your answer.

2. See Nahmias et al. 2007, p. 227.

> In 2019, scientists finally show exactly where decisions and intentions are found in the brain. Our decisions are brain processes, and our intentions are brain states.
>
> In 2009, John Jones saw a 20 dollar bill fall from the pocket of the person walking in front of him. He considered returning it to the person, who did not notice the bill fall; but he decided to keep it. Of course, given what scientists later discovered, John's decision was a brain process.
>
> Question: Did John have free will when he made his decision?

On page 2, the participants read an expression of interest in how they understand "deserved moral blame," the same vignette as on page 1, and the following question: "Does John deserve to be blamed for what he does?" The other participants (36) were presented with the same material in the opposite order. (Order did not have a significant effect.)

The results were as follows. About 90% (89.85%) of the participants answered yes to the question about free will, and about 87% (86.95%) answered yes to the question about deserved blame. Apparently, for the overwhelming majority of participants, viewing a person's decisions as brain processes did not preclude deeming the person to have free will when he made the decision (nor as deserving blame).

Another group of students in basic philosophy courses at Florida State University participated in part 2 of the study. Again, free will and moral responsibility were not on the course agendas. This time, I asked only about free will, using a version of the initial story that was augmented to include the idea that "our decisions and intentions are caused by other brain processes" (see note 3). Of the 86 participants, 74 (86%) said that John had free will when he made his decision. For the overwhelming majority, viewing a person's decision as "a brain process that was caused by other brain processes" was compatible with regarding the person as having free will.[3]

3. This probe read as follows:

In 2019, scientists finally show exactly where decisions and intentions are found in the brain and how they are caused. Our decisions are brain processes, and our intentions are brain states. Also, our decisions and intentions are caused by other brain processes.

In 2009, John Jones saw a 20 dollar bill fall from the pocket of the person walking in front of him. He considered returning it to the person, who did not notice the bill fall; but he decided to keep it. Of course, given what scientists later discovered, John's decision was a brain process, and it was caused by other brain processes.

The survey also asked whether students were taking their first philosophy class after high school. The breakdown was 58 yes and 28 no. This difference did not have a statistically significant effect on their answers about free will. About 88% of the first group and 82% of the second group answered yes to the question about free will.

Some readers may worry that my participant pool has unusually permissive standards for ascriptions of free will when it comes to human beings who are making decisions. Readers may also worry that many participants assume that nonphysical minds or souls are at work somewhere in the causal chain that issues in John's decision. Part 3 of the study was designed with these two worries in mind. Participants were another group of Florida State University undergraduates (*N* = 90) taking a basic philosophy course that did not deal with free will. I presented them with two stories. One is a version of the story used in part 2 in which the physicalist aspect is strengthened by adding (at the beginning of the story) that in 2019, "scientists finally prove that everything in the universe is physical and that what we refer to as 'minds' are actually brains at work." (The remainder of the story is the same as the story in part 2.) The other story features a "compliance drug"; it reads as follows:

> In 2019, scientists who work for a secret military organization finally develop a fool-proof compliance drug. The drug is used to make people decide to do various things. Whenever they give a person the drug and then suggest a course of action, that person is irresistibly caused to decide to take that course of action. They make their suggestions through a tiny computer chip that they implant in a person's brain.
>
> These chemists gave the compliance drug to John Jones, a very honest man. When John saw a 20 dollar bill fall from the pocket of the person walking in front of him, they suggested keeping it. John considered returning it to the person, who did not notice the bill fall; but, of course, he decided to keep it. After all, the combination of the compliance drug and the suggestion forced John to decide to keep it.

The order of presentation was counterbalanced. Participants answered the question on the front of the sheet, turned the sheet over, and answered the question on the back. They were instructed not to change their answer to the first question in light of their answer to the second.

Only 21.11% of the participants said that John had free will when he made his decision in the compliance drug story, and 73.33% said this in the physicalist scenario.[4] The low "free will" response to the compliance drug story indicates that the great majority of participants do not have a free-will-no-matter-what

4. Of the participants who saw the physicalist story first (*N* = 43), 79.07% answered yes to the question about that story, and 25.58% answered yes to the question about the compliance drug story. The figures for those who saw the story in the reverse order were 68.09% vs. 17.02%. Students who were taking their first philosophy course (*N* = 53) and those who were not (*N* = 37) gave very similar responses: grand averages for yes answers were 71.70% vs. 22.64% for the first-time students and 75.68% vs. 18.92% for the others.

attitude toward human decision making. And the scenario in which physicalism is very salient elicits a high "free will" response. That scenario leaves no room for nonphysical minds or souls to be at work, unless they are doing their work from beyond the confines of the universe.[5]

Andrew Monroe and Bertram Malle conducted a study in which participants responded to the following request: "Please explain in a few lines what you think it means to have free will" (2010, p. 214). The 180 participants were undergraduates at the University of Oregon. Monroe and Malle report that "no assumptions of substance dualism... were expressed" (p. 216). Nahmias reports related findings:

> ...a surprisingly low proportion of respondents: (1) *agreed* with the statement "Humans have free will only because they have nonphysical souls" (15–25%); (2) *agreed* with the statement "Our power of free will is something that is not part of our brain" (18%); or *disagreed* with the statement "It is because our minds are the products of our brains that we have free will" (only 13% when the statement followed a description of our brains as complex and unique, and still only 25% when the statement followed a description of the brain as mechanistic, governed by physical laws, and soon to be understood scientifically). (2011, p. 20, n. 5)[6]

There is substantial evidence that most nonspecialists are not committed to a conception of free will according to which nonphysical souls or minds need to be at work in the production of free decisions.

FREE WILL, LEGAL REFORM, AND THE HUMAN CONDITION

If a significant minority of people conceive of free will in such a way that it depends for its existence on the truth of substance dualism, might the probability of legal reform of the sort Greene and Cohen advocate be significantly increased by persuading these people that substance dualism is false? This question merits attention. The same is true of the following question: Would widespread disbelief in free will improve the human condition? Both questions are discussed in the present section.

Some dualistic libertarians might come to believe that free will is an illusion as a consequence of being convinced that substance dualism is false. But others

5. Some philosophers have thought that we have souls that exist outside of space and time. It is possible that some lay folk do as well. It is also possible that some lay folk who do believe this do not believe that only beings with such souls can have free will.

6. Also see Stillman, Baumeister, and Mele 2011.

might revise their view about what free will is. At the end of a book in which he argues in great detail for incompatibilism, Peter van Inwagen suggests that he would become a compatibilist if science were to "present us with compelling reasons for believing in determinism" (1983, p. 223). Perhaps many lay dualistic libertarians would become nondualistic libertarians if science were to present them with compelling reasons for believing that substance dualism is false. People with a dualistic view of reality may be expected to have a conception of free will that coheres with their general outlook on reality. If they come to be convinced that this outlook is mistaken, they might modify their conception of free will accordingly. Nondualistic libertarianism may be a real option for them. The same might even be true of compatibilism.

Greene and Cohen contend that "Many people, particularly those who are religious, are explicitly dualist libertarians" (2004, p. 1779). Two points should be made. First, even religious people who believe in life after death do not have to believe in immaterial souls or minds. One option is that the life at issue is another physical one (see van Inwagen 1978). Second, someone who is both a dualist and a libertarian may believe that free will is not *necessarily* dualistic. Such a person might believe, for example, that although actual human beings have immaterial minds or souls and free will, God could have created purely physical human beings with free will. (Purely physical beings with minds or souls have physical minds or souls.) People who believe in an omnipotent God might be very confident that creating such beings is within God's power.

Greene and Cohen have a grassroots movement in mind. They write: "The legitimacy of the law itself depends on its adequately reflecting the moral intuitions and commitments of society. If neuroscience can change those intuitions, then neuroscience can change the law" (2004, p. 1778). If dualistic libertarians are in the minority, converting some of them to the view that free will is an illusion might not result in much of a movement.

I turn to the second question raised in the introduction to this section. Would widespread disbelief in free will improve the human condition? Evidently, different people understand free will differently. My question is this: If the great majority of people were to believe that we all lack free will, as they themselves understand free will, would that improve the human condition?

There is evidence that lowering the subjective probability people give to the proposition that free will exists increases bad behavior. In a study reported by Kathleen Vohs and Jonathan Schooler (2008), people who read passages in which scientists deny that free will exists cheat significantly more often on a subsequent task than others do; and when they are paid for their correct answers, these people steal, in effect, more often than the others. (People who read pro–free will passages do about the same as those who read neutral passages.) In a study reported by Roy Baumeister, E. J. Masicampo, and C. Nathan

DeWall (2009), people who read anti–free will passages behave more aggressively than a control group that reads neutral passages: they serve significantly larger amounts of spicy salsa to people who say they dislike spicy food, despite being told that these people have to eat everything on their plates. Possibly, any improvements in the criminal law that are promoted by spreading the "news" that free will is an illusion would be counterbalanced by another effect of that news—a significant increase in the number of criminals!

I do not know how seriously people take reports in the popular press that scientists have shown that free will is a myth. But I do think this issue is worth studying. Here is a sentence from an article for the general public: "'Free will' is not the defining feature of humanness, modern neuroscience implies, but is rather an illusion that endures only because biochemical complexity conceals the mechanisms of decision making" (Siegfried, 2008). Perhaps most people who read this sentence take it to be about free will as they themselves conceive of it. If so, and if what is really being claimed is simply that modern neuroscience implies that we do not have immaterial minds or souls, then many people will be misled. And the misleading news might have a detrimental effect on their behavior.

I have as much concern for truth as most people, I hope; and I do not advocate censorship about free will. But if, despite the evidence that there is no free will as, for example, Montague and Cashmore conceive of it (and as Greene and Cohen believe most people conceive of it), we lack good evidence that there is no free will on a much more common conception of it, persuading scientists who share Montague's and Cashmore's understanding of free will that they are out of touch with mainstream use of "free will" may prove useful. It may reduce the amount of misleading and potentially harmful news about free will; and a better understanding of what "free will" means may foster experiments that have more to do with free will than with substance dualism.

CONCLUSION

I would like to see retributivistic systems of legal punishment move toward consequentialism, but I do not believe that claiming that science has shown that free will is an illusion is a good means to this end. We lack weighty scientific evidence that free will is an illusion (Mele 2009), and, as I have explained, we have some evidence that lowering the subjective probability people give to the proposition that free will exists increases bad behavior.

Scientific arguments for the nonexistence of free will, as I mentioned, use data to support empirical propositions that are then conjoined with a proposition about the meaning of "free will" to yield the conclusion that free will is an illusion. Elsewhere, I have argued that various empirical propositions put forward for this purpose are not warranted by the evidence offered to support them (Mele 2009). It might be replied that the only empirical proposition needed in this connection is that substance dualism is false, because free will depends on the existence of immaterial minds or souls. This theoretical proposition about free will seems to have more adherents among present-day neuroscientists and biologists than among present-day philosophers. But, as I have observed, the fact that one is a neuroscientist or biologist (or both) does not give one any special insight into what the expression "free will" means, and there is evidence that mainstream use of "free will" does not make the truth of substance dualism a necessary condition for the existence of free will. Those who advocate a move toward consequentialism in retributivistic systems of legal punishment would do well to seek an alternative route to that goal.[7]

REFERENCES

Baumeister, R., E. J. Masicampo, and C. N. DeWall. 2009. Prosocial Benefits of Feeling Free: Disbelief in Free Will Increases Aggression and Reduces Helpfulness. *Personality and Social Psychology Bulletin* 35: 260–268.

Cashmore, A. 2010. The Lucretian Swerve: The Biological Basis of Human Behavior and the Criminal Justice System. *Proceedings of the National Academy of Sciences of the United States of America* 107: 4499–4504.

Greene, J., and J. Cohen. 2004. For the Law Neuroscience Changes Nothing and Everything. *Philosophical Transactions of the Royal Society B: Biological Sciences* 359: 1775–1785.

Kane, R. 1996. *The Significance of Free Will*. New York: Oxford University Press.

Libet, B. 1985. Unconscious Cerebral Initiative and the Role of Conscious Will in Voluntary Action. *Behavioral and Brain Sciences* 8: 529–566.

Libet, B. 2004. *Mind Time*. Cambridge, MA: Harvard University Press.

Mele, A. 1995. *Autonomous Agents: From Self-Control to Autonomy*. Oxford: Oxford University Press.

Mele, A. 2006. *Free Will and Luck*. New York: Oxford University Press.

Mele, A. 2009. *Effective Intentions*. New York: Oxford University Press.

Monroe, A., and B. Malle. 2010. From Uncaused Will to Conscious Choice: The Need to Study, Not Speculate About People's Folk Concept of Free Will. *Review of Philosophy and Psychology* 1: 211–224.

Montague, P. R. 2008. Free Will. *Current Biology* 18: R584–585.

Nahmias, E. 2011. Why "Willusionism" Leads to "Bad Results": Comments on Baumeister, Crescioni, and Alquist. *Neuroethics* 4: 17–24.

7. Some of the material in this article was presented at Peking University and Brown University. I am grateful to my audiences for their input. This article was made possible through the support of a grant from the John Templeton Foundation. The opinions expressed in this publication are those of the author and do not necessarily reflect the views of the John Templeton Foundation.

Nahmias, E., S. Morris, T. Nadelhoffer, and J. Turner. 2006. Is Incompatibilism Intuitive? *Philosophy and Phenomenological Research* 73: 28–53.

Nahmias, E., S. Morris, T. Nadelhoffer, and J. Turner. 2005. Surveying Freedom: Folk Intuitions About Free Will and Moral Responsibility. *Philosophical Psychology* 18: 561–584.

Nahmias, E., J. Coates, and T. Kvaran. 2007. Free Will, Moral Responsibility, and Mechanism: Experiments on Folk Intuitions. *Midwest Studies in Philosophy* 31: 214–242.

Siegfried, T. 2008. The Decider. *Science News* 174: 28–30.

Stillman, T., R. Baumeister, and A. Mele. 2011. Free Will in Everyday Life: Autobiographical Accounts of Free and Unfree Actions. *Philosophical Psychology* 24: 381–394.

van Inwagen, P. 1978. The Possibility of Resurrection. *International Journal for Philosophy of Religion* 9: 114–121.

van Inwagen, P. 1983. *An Essay on Free Will*. Oxford: Clarendon Press.

Vohs, K., and J. Schooler. 2008. The Value of Believing in Free Will: Encouraging a Belief in Determinism Increases Cheating. *Psychological Science* 19: 49–54.

Wegner, D. 2002. *The Illusion of Conscious Will*. Cambridge, MA: MIT Press.

Wegner, D. 2004. Précis of The Illusion of Conscious Will. *Behavioral and Brain Sciences* 27: 649–659.

Wegner, D. 2008. Self Is Magic. In J. Baer, J. Kaufman, and R. Baumeister, eds. *Are We Free? Psychology and Free Will*. New York: Oxford University Press.

Zimmerman, D. 2006. Dualism in the Philosophy of Mind. In D. Borchert, ed. *Encyclopedia of Philosophy*, 2nd ed. Detroit: Thomson Gale, vol. 3, 113–122.

9

The Mind, the Brain, and the Law

THOMAS NADELHOFFER, DENA GROMET, GEOFFREY GOODWIN, EDDY NAHMIAS, CHANDRA SRIPADA, AND WALTER SINNOTT-ARMSTRONG

SETTING THE STAGE

Although there is a long-standing debate among philosophers and legal scholars concerning the nature, limits, and legal relevance of free will,[1] judges, journalists, and the public more generally view free will as important to the concept of legal responsibility. For instance, in *Morissette v. United States*, Justice Jackson claimed that "a belief in freedom of the human will" is "universal and persistent in mature systems of law."[2] Similarly, in *United States v. Grayson*, Chief Justice Burger suggested that the adoption of "a deterministic view of human conduct" would be "inconsistent with the underlying precepts of our criminal justice system."[3]

One area of the criminal law in which free will seems especially relevant is mental health law. After all, one explanation for why mental illnesses are sometimes mitigating or even exculpating is that they undermine offenders' free will and hence minimize their responsibility. As one federal judge observed in this

1. Indeed, one legal commentator goes so far as to suggest that "enough has been written from a philosophical perspective on the relationship between free will and the law that it is not easy to justify yet another such undertaking" (Green 1995, 1915).

2. *Morissette v. United States*, 342 U.S. 246, 250 (1952).

3. *United States v. Grayson*, 438 U.S. 41, 52 (1978).

context, "the concept of lack of 'free will' is both the root origin of the insanity defense and the line of its growth."[4] On this view, it is precisely because the mentally ill are sometimes viewed as having less free will that we do not hold them as responsible for their behavior.

Because free will is sometimes assumed to have this foundational role in criminal law, it is unsurprising that recent developments in neuroscience that purportedly challenge free will have generated such interest and controversy. According to some researchers, as neuroscientists uncover the neural mechanisms that undergird both normal and abnormal human behavior, we will see a radical shift in how we think about agency and responsibility (e.g., Greene & Cohen 2004). According to others, although neuroscience will continue to shed new light on how the human mind works, it will likely leave our traditional views and practices largely intact (e.g., Morse 2008).

When exploring this debate, it is crucial to make a distinction between the *descriptive* question of whether advances in the modern mind sciences will in fact change people's views and attitudes about agency and responsibility and the *normative* question of whether these discoveries *should* have a transformative effect. For present purposes, we limit our attention primarily to the descriptive question. More specifically, our goal in this chapter is to explore the potential influence that advances in neuroscience may have on legal decision makers by describing recent studies that probe folk intuitions concerning the relationship between neuroscience, agency, responsibility, and mental illness. Addressing whether recent and future advances in neuroscience *should* influence our moral and legal beliefs and practices is a task for another day.

In examining the descriptive question, we will first familiarize the reader with some of the early research in experimental philosophy on people's intuitions about agency and responsibility (section 1). We will then focus on a more specific issue—namely, whether people respond to explanations of human behavior framed in neuroscientific terms differently than they respond to explanations framed in more traditional folk psychological terms. Some parties to this debate have provided evidence that people's intuitions about agency and responsibility are differentially influenced by neural explanations than mental explanations (see Nahmias et al. 2007), whereas others have provided evidence to the contrary (see De Brigard et al. 2009). We will present the results of some new studies, which provide evidence for the former view (section 2). As we will see, explanations of criminal behavior that are couched in neural terms appear to make people less punitive than explanations couched in mental terms, especially in the context of mental illness. We will then offer what we take to be the best explanation of these differences in people's intuitions: when people are

4. *United States v. Brawner*, 471 F.2d 969, 986 (D.C. Cir. 1972) (en banc) (footnote omitted).

presented with neural explanations of human behavior, they tend to think that the agents' "deep self" (the values and beliefs they identify with) is somehow left out of the causal loop or bypassed, which in turn mitigates the agent's responsibility (section 3). In short, it is bypassing of the deep self, and not determinism per se, that seems to be motivating people's concerns when it comes to the relationships between neuroscience, agency, and responsibility. Although we provide some preliminary empirical and philosophical support for this position, more research is required to improve our understanding of people's complex and sometimes puzzling beliefs about the mind, the brain, and the law.

1. EXPERIMENTAL PHILOSOPHY, FREE WILL, AND MORAL RESPONSIBILITY

Experimental philosophy is a recent movement whose participants use the methods of psychology to probe the way people make judgments that bear on debates in philosophy. Although the movement has a name, it includes a variety of projects driven by different interests, assumptions, and goals.[5] Just in the past few years, philosophers have carried out experimental work in areas as diverse as epistemology, action theory, the philosophy of language, ethics, the philosophy of law, the philosophy of mind, and the philosophy of science. All of this work shares a two-fold commitment to using controlled and systematic studies to explore people's intuitions and to examining how the results of such experiments bear on traditional philosophical debates. In this paper, we are going to limit our attention to work in experimental philosophy on agency and responsibility. But first we set the stage with a brief discussion of the free will debate more generally.

The dominant issue in the traditional philosophical debates about free will has been whether free will and moral responsibility are compatible with determinism—that is, the metaphysical thesis that given the actual past and the laws of nature, there is only one possible future (see Van Inwagen 1983).[6] Incompatibilists, who claim that free will and determinism cannot coexist, run the gamut from pro-free will libertarians who deny the truth of determinism and suggest that we are unmoved movers (Chisholm 2003) to free will skeptics who claim that we can't be free and responsible regardless of the truth of determinism (Strawson 1986). A number of incompatibilists lie on a continuum

5. For an overview of the field of experimental philosophy, see Nadelhoffer & Nahmias 2007.

6. For helpful introductions to the major views in the free will debate, see Fischer et al. 2007; Kane 2011; and Watson 2003.

between these two extremes. The two main categories of pro–free will incompatibilist views are event-causal libertarianism (Ekstrom 2000; Kane 1996) and agent-causal libertarianism (Clarke 2003; O'Connor 2000)—each of which maintains that determinism is false and that human beings are (sometimes) free and morally responsible. Skepticism about free will and moral responsibility comes in several varieties as well (see Double 1991; Honderich 1998; Pereboom 2001; Smilansky 2000)—some of which are driven by worries about determinism and some of which are not.

There are just as many varieties of views that take free will and determinism to be compatible. Most of the original compatibilists, such as Hobbes and Hume, were known as soft determinists, and claimed that free will and responsibility actually *require* determinism (Ayer 2003; Stace 1960). Most contemporary compatibilists, however, are merely committed to the conditional view that we could be free and responsible even if the universe were deterministic. These compatibilists offer various analyses of what is required to be free and responsible agents, emphasizing, for instance, our identification with some of our desires over others (Frankfurt 1971), our ability to understand what is true and good (Wolf 1990), our sometimes being appropriate targets of reactive attitudes such as indignation or approbation (Strawson 2003), or our capacity to be appropriately responsive to reasons (Fischer 1994; Fischer & Ravizza 1998). In general, compatibilists argue that free will and moral responsibility do not require the unconditional ability to do otherwise, holding fixed the actual past and laws. Instead, compatibilists argue that free and responsible agency requires the capacities involved in self-reflection, practical deliberation, and self-control (see also Mele 1996).

Traditionally, both compatibilists and incompatibilists have assumed that their own respective views enjoy wide-scale intuitive support among nonphilosophers. Robert Kane, for instance, writes, "most ordinary people start out as natural incompatibilists...Ordinary persons have to be talked out of this natural incompatibilism by the clever arguments of philosophers" (1999, 218). Similarly, Galen Strawson argues that the incompatibilist's libertarian conception of free will, though impossible to satisfy, is precisely "the kind of freedom that most people ordinarily and unreflectively suppose themselves to possess" (1986, 30). Compatibilists also frequently appeal to commonsense intuitions, suggesting that the folk do *not* demand the libertarian requirements for free will, such as an unconditional ability to do otherwise. For instance, Daniel Dennett claims that when ordinary people assign moral responsibility, "it simply does not matter at all...whether the agent in question could have done otherwise in the circumstances" (1984, 558). William Lycan similarly argues that compatibilism is "the default position...not only true, but the only position rationally available to impartial observers" (2003, 107).

Motivated by the dearth of empirical data on what people actually think about the relationships between free will, responsibility, and determinism, Eddy Nahmias, Stephen Morris, Thomas Nadelhoffer, and Jason Turner (2005; 2006) developed some of the first studies in experimental philosophy to explore the relevant folk intuitions. Using three different descriptions of determinism, they found that a significant majority of participants (typically 65% to 85%) judged that agents in a deterministic scenario act of their own free will and are morally responsible. These early findings suggested that contrary to what incompatibilists have traditionally assumed, most people do not have intuitions that support incompatibilism. However, as is often the case when it comes to the free will debate, it soon became clear that things were more complicated than they initially appeared.

For instance, Shaun Nichols and Joshua Knobe (2007) designed and ran some follow-up studies to explore the psychological mechanisms that generate intuitions about moral responsibility. Participants were randomly assigned to either an "abstract" condition that describes a deterministic universe (A) and indeterministic universe (B) or a "concrete" condition that describes these universes but also describes a person in universe A, Bill, who murders his wife and family to be with his secretary. Whereas 72% of subjects gave the *compatibilist* response that Bill *is* "fully morally responsible for killing his wife and family" in the concrete condition, in the abstract condition 84% gave the purportedly *incompatibilist* response that it is *not* possible in universe A "for a person to be fully morally responsible for her actions."

On the surface, at least, these findings appear to put pressure on the claim that people's intuitions are robustly compatibilist. Instead, whether people are inclined to give compatibilist answers may depend less on the presence (or absence) of determinism and more on the moral features of the vignettes and questions. Whereas people tend to display compatibilist leanings when asked to make judgments concerning the responsibility of specific agents, when they are asked instead to think about responsibility in the abstract, their intuitions trend toward incompatibilism. There is an ongoing debate about how best to explain these findings (see Feltz et al. 2009; Nahmias 2011; Nahmias & Murray 2011; Sinnott-Armstrong 2008), but Nichols and Knobe take these results as evidence that people have an incompatibilist theory of free will but apply this theory mistakenly when they consider a concrete, emotionally charged, situation.

In addition to the conflicting intuitions identified by Nichols and Knobe, Nahmias, Coates, and Kvaran (2007) found another interesting asymmetry in people's intuitions about free will and responsibility that is especially germane for present purposes. According to this research, people treat explanations of human behavior that are couched in neuroscientific terms differently than they treat explanations couched in folk psychological terms. In order to explore this issue, Nahmias and colleagues (2007) systematically varied merely the level at which determinism was described and found that it made a significant difference in people's responses. In one study, participants read the following scenario, either in the "neuro case" or the "psych case," which varied only the bracketed words:

> Most respected [neuroscientists / psychologists] are convinced that eventually we will figure out exactly how all of our decisions and actions are entirely caused. For instance, they think that whenever we are trying to decide what to do, the decision we end up making is completely caused by the specific [chemical reactions and neural processes / thoughts, desires, and plans] occurring in our [brains / minds]. The [neuroscientists / psychologists] are also convinced that these [chemical reactions and neural processes / thoughts, desires, and plans] are completely caused by our current situation and the earlier events in our lives, and that these earlier events were also completely caused by even earlier events, eventually going all the way back to events that occurred before we were born.
>
> So, if these [neuroscientists / psychologists] are right, then once specific earlier events have occurred in a person's life, these events will definitely cause specific later events to occur. For instance, once specific [chemical reactions and neural processes / thoughts, desires, and plans] occur in the person's [brain / mind], they will definitely cause the person to make the specific decision he or she makes. (Nahmias et al. 2007, 224)

Although a *minority* of participants said that people would have free will (38%), be morally responsible (41%), or deserve praise and blame if the *neuroscientists* were right, a substantial *majority* said that people would have free will (83%), be responsible (89%), and deserve praise and blame if the *psychologists* were right.

A plausible explanation for these results is that most people see no conflict between determinism and free will or responsibility when the folk psychological framework remains in place, as it does in the "psych case." But when the causes of our decisions are described in the reductionistic and mechanistic language of neuroscience, many people interpret that to mean that our conscious beliefs, desires, and plans are not playing a causal role in our decisions. That is, many people likely interpret neuroscientific descriptions of our decision making in terms of *bypassing*.[7] If our decisions and actions are produced by our psychological makeup, then people think we are responsible for them, even if

7. It is worth pointing out that there are at least two possible kinds of bypassing: (a) weak bypassing, whereby our *conscious* mental states play no etiological role, but maybe our *unconscious* mental states still do play a role; and (b) strong bypassing, whereby *neither* our conscious *nor* our unconscious mental states play an etiological role. The reductionistic and mechanistic

our psychological makeup itself is completely caused by prior events. But if our decisions and actions are produced by chemical and neural processes in our brains, then many people interpret that as an explanation that competes with a folk psychological explanation. It is not determinism per se that is threatening their beliefs in free will and responsibility, but rather there appears to be something unique about the kind of reductionistic and mechanistic explanations one finds in neuroscience that influences people's intuitions about free will and responsibility.

Two other research projects lend further support to these descriptive claims about the impact of neuroscience on these intuitions. First, recent studies by Nahmias and Dylan Murray suggest that when people take determinism to threaten free will and moral responsibility, most do so because they misinterpret determinism to involve bypassing (Nahmias & Murray 2011). In these studies, participants read a variety of different descriptions of determinism, and across these cases, most of those who interpreted these descriptions to threaten free will and responsibility also interpreted them to mean that people's beliefs, desires, and decisions have no effect on what they end up doing. Indeed, people's responses to the questions about bypassing statistically mediated their responses to questions about free will, responsibility, and blameworthiness, providing evidence that bypassing, and not determinism per se, is doing the causal work of mitigating judgments of freedom and responsibility. So, although determinism, properly understood, does not entail that our mental states have no effect on what we do, certain descriptions of determinism or causation seem to prime people to mistakenly assume that it does. One way to prime the bypassing mistake is with neuroscientific or reductionistic explanations that are taken to compete with folk psychological explanations. If neural processes completely explain our actions, then what causal work is left for our beliefs and desires to do? This "competition" between levels of explanation will be especially salient to people who think that the mind and brain are distinct substances or that mental processes cannot be understood in terms of neural processes.

Another research project that supports the descriptive claim that neuroscience may pose problems for the law comes from recent work showing that diminishing people's belief in free will can change their behavior. For instance, when people read a passage by the neuroscientist Francis Crick that tells them "you are nothing but a pack of neurons," or a series of statements, such as "Every action that a person takes is caused by a specific pattern of neural

language of neuroscience sometimes seems to suggest strong and not just weak bypassing. Figuring out whether people take advances in neuroscience to entail strong rather than merely weak bypassing is an issue that calls for more systematic testing.

firings in the brain," then they are more likely than controls to cheat and to lie (Vohs & Schooler 2008), and they are less likely to help others and more likely to be aggressive toward others (Baumeister et al. 2009). After reading such primes, participants are less likely to agree with statements that affirm free will and responsibility. There are various explanations for these effects. But the relevant point for present purposes is that the primes used in these studies present the threat to free will using scientific, reductionistic, often specifically neuroscientific, explanations of human behavior. And these primes have effects on people's responses to statements about free will, on their social behavior, and on whether they hold others responsible. Again, it appears that regardless of whether people *should* interpret neuroscience as a potential threat to free will and responsibility, they *do*.

As we discussed earlier, one area in which these issues are especially germane is mental health law. Researchers are making great strides in uncovering and understanding neurobiological causes of abnormal thought and behavior, and their findings are increasingly making their way into both the popular press and the courtroom. Given that the law already correctly views mental illness as something that sometimes bypasses normal human cognition and behavior, explanations of mental illness that are couched in the language of neuroscience might be especially likely to influence the intuitions and judgments of legal decision makers, including judges and juries, regarding responsibility and punishment. In the following section, we will look at the findings from new studies that probe folk intuitions about the relationships between the mind, the brain, and the law.

2. THE MIND, THE BRAIN, AND THE LAW: SOME NEW STUDIES

As neuroscience continues to advance, it may be possible to use brain imaging to identify, diagnose, and explain some psychiatric illnesses (e.g., Caspi & Moffitt 2006; Farah 2002). This prospect, though not yet fully realized, is likely to be accompanied by a host of challenging legal and psychological issues. One in particular is that neuroscientific explanations of mental illnesses may conflict with the way that people ordinarily think about behavior and its causes. This possibility is particularly pertinent in the legal domain, in which judgments of wrongdoing hinge on everyday mental concepts (folk psychology). Whereas ordinary psychological explanations of wrongdoing tend to focus on the causal role of mental states such as intentions, beliefs, and desires, neuroscientific explanations instead focus attention on the causal role of physiological states within the brain. Although these explanations may be seen as compatible, emphasizing the role of brain states (as opposed to mental states) may nonetheless differentially affect the way individuals judge wrongdoers. In particular, because brain-based explanations emphasize the causal power of mechanistic, physiological events instead of people's inner mental life (their beliefs, desires, and intentions) that are informative of their true characters (see Pizarro & Tannenbaum 2011; Sripada 2010), brain-based explanations may diminish the perceived culpability of criminal wrongdoers, in turn lessening the punishment that is deemed appropriate for them. It's unclear at this stage whether these brain-based explanations diminish perceived culpability because they are thought to bypass all mental states, because they are thought to bypass character (i.e., long-lasting dispositions to act), or because they are thought to bypass the deep self (even if not all mental states). Some of our recent research has further explored these possibilities, with a particular emphasis on how judgments of culpability and punishment are affected by the inferences people make about the connection between a wrongdoer's bad actions and his character (Gromet et al. 2011).

In these studies, participants evaluated wrongdoers who committed intentional actions that caused another person's death. In each case, the wrongdoer's actions were caused by an emotional dysfunction that was described either as a product of the mind (mental/psychological) or as a product of the brain (neural/neurological). These descriptions were identical except for the framing of the dysfunction in neurological or psychological terms. For example, in one study, following a description of a killing carried out by a man named Gary, participants read that he suffered from an emotional dysfunction that impaired his ability to regulate his anger. We presented the following expert testimony that varied whether mental or neural terms were used to describe the wrongdoer's dysfunction, with the information in square parentheses varied between subjects:

> This [psychological/neurological] dysfunction impairs a person's ability to regulate his anger and control his violent impulses. The expert also testified that as a result of this [psychological/neurological] dysfunction, Gary tends to overreact in social situations. Furthermore, his [psychological/neurological] dysfunction makes it very difficult for Gary to control his behavior in these situations, which can lead to violent outbursts.

Framing an offender's action as caused by a dysfunction, described in either psychological or neurological terms, reduced his perceived culpability compared with control conditions, in which no dysfunction was mentioned. But framing a wrongdoer's dysfunction and behavior in neurological terms had a mitigating effect on people's assessments of his culpability (as well as blameworthiness and responsibility) and their judgments about appropriate punishment for him, compared with framing his dysfunction in psychological terms. We found that this effect holds regardless of whether the dysfunction is described as due to an environmental cause (i.e., childhood abuse) or a genetic cause (a genetic predisposition). Moreover, this mind-versus-brain difference appears to arise because brain-based framings decouple the wrongdoer's actions from his true character. In the study described above, for instance, when the neurological framing was used, participants rated Gary's actions as being less reflective of whom he is as a person and of his true character than when the psychological framing was used. Essentially, neurological information about a wrongdoer's dysfunction is seen as less diagnostic of the wrongdoer's character than the same information framed in psychological terms. We have examined alternative accounts for this mitigating effect of brain-based explanations, including whether the different framings produce differences in the offender's perceived control over his actions, in the plausibility of the dysfunction causing behavior, or in the credibility of expert testimony. However, none of these alternative accounts have received strong support.

To further corroborate the role of character in underlying the extra mitigating power of brain-based explanations, an additional study showed that the mitigating effect of neuroscientific information was eliminated when there was already a strong connection between a wrongdoer's actions and his moral character. Independent of the mind-versus-brain difference, this study experimentally manipulated how diagnostic the wrongdoer's criminal behavior was of his overall character, by varying whether the wrongdoer had a strong preexisting reason to desire his eventual victim's death. When no such preexisting desire existed, consistent with the previous studies, participants viewed the wrongdoer whose dysfunction was framed as neurological to be less culpable and less worthy of punishment than the wrongdoer who had the identical dysfunction framed in psychological terms. However, when the wrongdoer did have a strong preexisting desire for his victim's eventual death, participants viewed the wrongdoer's actions as highly reflective of his character, regardless of whether his conduct was framed in psychological or neurological terms. And, based on this judgment, participants then no longer viewed brain-based explanations as more mitigating than mind-based explanations.[8]

In sum, these findings illustrate that people make different inferences based on whether criminal behavior is explained in terms of mental states or brain states, and these inferences influence people's judgments of responsibility and punishment. When people are presented with behavior that is described as a product of the brain, this information serves to reduce the connection that people see between how an offender acted and who he is as a person, thus leading to reductions in perceived responsibility and punishment. If future research

8. This conclusion also seems supported by Woolfolk et al. 2006.

yields similar results, we may need to rethink the role that neuroscience will play in determinations of criminal responsibility during legal trials. But before we talk about some of the potential implications of our research on people's views concerning neuroscience and responsibility, we will first offer what we take to be the best explanation of the gathering data.

3. NEUROSCIENCE AND THE DEEP SELF

In social psychology, one of the most influential approaches to understanding judgments of moral responsibility derives from the work of Franz Heider, in his 1958 classic, *The Psychology of Interpersonal Relations*. Heider conceived of judgments of moral responsibility as consisting of an ordered sequence of progressive stages. Early stages draw a *physical* link between the agent and outcome (Did the agent cause the outcome?), whereas later stages draw a *volitional* link (Did the agent foresee that the outcome would occur? Did the agent desire the outcome? Did the agent intend the outcome?). Progression through each stage marks a "tighter" link between the agent and the outcome, and the degree of assessed moral responsibility commensurately rises. Subsequent theorists in social psychology have elaborated on Heider's stage theory in various ways but have largely kept the overall structure (see Shaver 1985; Schlenker et al. 1994). For our purposes, the most import feature of these Heiderian-inspired models is the central role accorded to the latter stages comprising the volitional link, and in particular the role of action-directed mental states such foresight, desire, and intent. According to what we can call *volitionist models* of moral responsibility, assuming the appropriate causal link between the agent and outcome has been established, then if the agent *desires* the outcome, *intends* to bring about the outcome, and *foresees* that his doing the action will cause the outcome to occur, then the agent is morally responsible for the outcome.

In philosophy, models broadly similar to the kinds of volitionist models encountered in social psychology have also been proposed (see Levy & McKenna 2009 for a discussion). However, in addition, there is another family of accounts of moral responsibility that is highly influential in philosophy, but has not been developed much in psychology. These "deep self" accounts of moral responsibility provide a unique vantage point for understanding how neuroscience affects moral responsibility judgments, so we will now sketch the motivation and structure of deep self models.

There are many different kinds of deep self accounts of moral responsibility in the philosophical literature (see Frankfurt 1971; Smith 2008; Watson 1975; see Wolf 1990 for a seminal discussion). What these accounts all have in common is that they draw a basic distinction within the set of an agent's conative attitudes, that is, the set of her desires, wants, values, and other motivationally relevant states. More specifically, deep self models distinguish between conative attitudes that are "surface" and those that are "deep." When a person performs an action, there are invariably certain *surface attitudes* that help to explain why the action was performed—states such as desires and intentions. These mental states are quite *specific*, that is, they are directed at a particular action at a particular time, and *temporary*, that is, they typically arise before the action and dissipate once the action is performed. In addition to surface attitudes such as desires and intentions, however, people also have *deep attitudes* that are more fundamental and important. This is reflected in the fact that we ordinarily use terms such as "values," "cares," and "core commitments" to refer to these kinds of attitudes. Deep self theorists disagree about what makes these states more central and significant, with one theory positing that these states bear a distinctive connection to practical reasoning (Watson 1975), while another theory emphasizes a role for higher order attitudes that endorse one's first-order motives (Frankfurt 1971). But setting these differences aside, these theorists agree that a person's deep attitudes are the very essence of who she is as a practical agent, the *self* that underlies all her actions, and thus these attitudes should play a central role in how she is assessed for what she does. Theories of moral responsibility in psychology, such as the volitionist theories discussed earlier, tend to emphasize the role of surface attitudes in people's judgments of moral responsibility. On this view, a person is morally responsible for an action if she has the appropriate desires and intentions. Deep self theories, in contrast, claim that in addition to surface attitudes, deep attitudes also make important contributions to moral responsibility judgments, in ways to be detailed below.

In a mentally healthy person who is not under duress or constraint, deep attitudes, surface attitudes, and actions will usually be in harmony. That is, people tend to perform actions based on (surface) desires and intentions that are for the most part in agreement with their own underlying (deep) values and core commitments. But there are a number of factors—such as ignorance, coercion, constraints, irresistible impulses, addiction, and the like—that can cause an agent's deep attitudes to diverge from her surface attitudes and her actions. In these cases, our judgments about the agent's moral responsibility appear to be highly sensitive to the content of the agent's deep attitudes, thus providing critical evidence for the deep self view.

Harry Frankfurt's example of willing and unwilling addicts illustrates this point (Frankfurt 1971). Consider two addicts, both of whom have an irresistible desire to use a narcotic. The "unwilling addict" *rejects* his addiction, and desires that his desire to use the narcotic be extinguished. The "willing addict" *endorses* his addiction, and were his desire to use the narcotic ever extinguished, he would seek to reinstate it. When each addict uses the drug, the surface attitudes that drive his action, e.g., the irresistible desire to use the narcotic, are the same. But there is a strong intuition that the addicts differ in terms of moral responsibility; the willing addict *is* morally responsible for his action while the unwilling addict is *not*, or at least the two addicts differ in their degree of moral responsibility. Volitionist models have difficulty making sense of this difference because the two addicts do not differ in terms of the action-directed psychological states (e.g., desire, intention, foresight) that these models claim are determinative of moral responsibility. Deep self accounts of moral responsibility, in contrast, readily explain the difference in responsibility between the willing and unwilling addict in terms of differences in their respective deep selves. The unwilling addict rejects and thus "stands against" his narcotic-directed desires so he is not morally responsible for the resulting actions. The willing addict endorses and thus "stands with" his narcotic-directed desires so he is morally responsible for the resulting actions.

Using *philosophical* theories of the deep self as a starting point, Sripada (2010; 2011; forthcoming) formulated a *psychological* model of intentionality and responsibility judgments. The key element of the model is a *concordance criterion* that specifies how people use information about deep attitudes on the one hand and information about actions and outcomes on the other hand to arrive at judgments about whether the agent is morally responsible for the action or outcome:

> *Concordance criterion for moral responsibility judgments*: An agent is judged to be morally responsible for an action or outcome to the extent that the action or outcome is judged to be concordant with the agent's deep self.

Sripada's "deep self concordance account" raises a number of questions. For example, how do people decide which of an agent's attitudes are truly deep and which are not? Also, how should the notion of concordance be understood? In particular, it seems we can distinguish *wide* versus *narrow* notions of concordance. Wide concordance requires that the action in question promotes the agent's *overall set* of values, cares, and core commitments. Narrow concordance, in contrast, only requires that the action in question promote *some or other element within* the agent's set of values, cares, and core commitments. Preliminary data suggest that it is specifically the narrow notion of concordance that is relevant to people's moral responsibility judgments (Sripada unpublished). Finally, the Deep Self Concordance Model raises intriguing questions about what happens in cases of "deep conflict" when an agent appears to simultaneously hold diverging deep attitudes. A full discussion of these issues is beyond the scope of this chapter. Indeed, most of the preceding issues are only just beginning to be addressed by philosophers and psychologists, and much further research is required.

Although deep self theory is relatively new to the psychological scene, and many questions about how to understand the approach remain to be resolved, it provides a promising framework for addressing questions about how neuroscience will affect people's view of moral responsibility. The current literature tends to see the presumed conflict between neuroscience and moral responsibility in abstract, metaphysical terms—people perceive that neuroscience undermines moral responsibility because it shows that people's choices are produced by neural-cum-physical mechanisms that are subject to the, presumably deterministic, laws of physics (see Greene & Cohen 2004; Nichols & Knobe 2007). Deep self theory, in contrast, portrays the impact of neuroscience along different, distinctively *nonmetaphysical*, lines. On the deep self view, the tension between neuroscience and moral responsibility arises because the kinds of mechanisms that neuroscience identifies as being the source of our actions, at least in some cases, turn out to be of the wrong sort to ensure that our deep attitudes, that is, our underlying values, cares, and commitments, are appropriately reflected in our actions.

To illustrate this idea, consider a recent experiment by Nadelhoffer and colleagues (in preparation). All subjects in the experiment were told of the case of John Smith, who "got into an argument with a co-worker" and subsequently "pushed the [co-worker] to the ground and struck the [co-worker] despite being physically unprovoked." One third of the subjects were in the "neuroscience" condition and read testimony from a neuroscientist who stated that, based on a detailed examination of *brain-based* information, Smith is in the highest risk category for violently reoffending within 5 years. The remaining subjects were either in the "actuarial" or "psychological" condition, where they read testimony from a statistician and a psychologist, respectively, who, based on their respective non-neuroscientific sources of information, also reported that Smith is in the highest risk category for violently reoffending within 5 years.

Results of the study showed that subjects assigned significantly more punishment to Smith in the neuroscience condition compared with the actuarial and psychological conditions. Moreover, attributions of attitudes to Smith's deep self mirrored the pattern of responsibility, blame, and punishment judgments. That is, people judged that Smith's action was more reflective of his true underlying values and character in the neuroscience condition compared with the other two conditions. The precise reasons that neuroscientific descriptions produced altered perceptions of the deep self are unclear. We speculate that accounts of deviant behavior, when pitched in neuroscientific terms, may be viewed as more credible, or the person may be viewed as more fundamentally and/or permanently affected. These perceptions would lead lay observers to perceive that the person's actions reflect the kind of person whom he truly is. Additionally, people may assume that brain-based disorders have more pervasive and comprehensive effects, so that it is not just the person's outward behavior but also his inner values and core commitments that are disrupted. Further research is needed to test these speculations.

The preceding experiment illustrates that the impact of neuroscience on moral responsibility judgments need not always be mediated by abstract metaphysical doctrines such as determinism or mechanism. Rather, neuroscience's impact on responsibility judgments might, at least in some cases, be mediated by construals about whether the agent's deep self is or is not the source of the person's behavior. In addition, it is noteworthy that in this experiment, there is no obvious reason for subjects to have supposed that Smith's *surface mental states*, that is, his means-end beliefs, surface desires, and intentions, differed across the three conditions of the experiment. Thus, this experiment highlights that neuroscientific explanations might have a relatively *specific* impact on construals of the deep self. In contrast, surface mental states such as desires, means-end beliefs, and intentions—the kinds of action-directed mental states that volitionist theories say are relevant for assessing moral responsibility—may be largely unaffected.

Results from the preceding study extend and nuance the results from the studies we reported earlier (section 2) on how neuroscientific information affects judgments of moral responsibility. These studies also illustrate how deep self theory provides an alternative, complementary framework for studying the impact of advances in neuroscientific knowledge on folk practices of praise and blame. Psychiatric neuroscience is increasingly uncovering the brain-based mechanisms that produce abnormal patterns of behavior in disorders such as depression, mania, schizophrenia, and addiction. Deep self theory predicts that at least some of the impact of this new knowledge on judgments of moral responsibility and blame will be mediated by people's perception of how the disorder affects the status of the person's deep self. In some cases, people will perceive that these disorders sever the usual connection between a person's deep self and her actions, causing her to produce actions that she, *deep down inside*, does not endorse, thus mitigating blame. In other cases, people might perceive that these disorders are associated with a more thoroughly compromised deep self, in which case blame will be enhanced. It will require coordinated research by philosophers and psychologists to test these predictions, to determine what makes people go one way in some cases and the opposite way in other cases, and to evaluate their import for the law and related social institutions.

CONCLUSION

In this paper, we aimed to shed new light on the growing debate among philosophers, psychologists, and legal scholars concerning the potential influence that advances in neuroscience are likely to have on our ordinary understanding of free will and responsibility. We also discussed the results of some new studies that suggest that regardless of whether one believes that neuroscientific discoveries ought to alter our views concerning moral agency, it appears that, descriptively speaking, people view wrongdoers as less morally responsible for their actions when their behavior is described as a product of the brain.[9] That being said, this research only scratches the surface, leaving many questions for further research. But even the research we have carried out so far raises interesting practical and philosophical questions. The fact that people are sensitive to whether and to what extent a person's actions are rooted in his underlying character and values suggests that the law's criteria for determining culpability, which do not include character as a salient factor (e.g., Fletcher 1998), may lead to conflicting intuitions in the minds of jurors, at least when jurors are not given careful instruction.

Our recent studies also illustrate how neuroscience is raising new questions about how we are to conceptualize human agency and about how we judge moral responsibility. Whereas some have argued that neuroscience does not currently pose a threat to notions of moral and legal culpability (see Berker 2009; Morse 2008), others have contended that the whole notion of moral responsibility is challenged by emerging developments in cognitive neuroscience (Greene & Cohen 2004; see also Eagleman 2011). The current studies discussed here do not propose any solution to these difficult normative issues. Whether cognitive neuroscience is poised to usher in a revolution in our understanding of moral responsibility and free will remains to be seen, and that itself is largely an empirical question. In the meantime, we believe that psychologists and philosophers must continue to work collectively in order to better understand the complex relationships between the mind, the brain, and the law.

9. It's worth pointing out that future research needs to explore the possibility that the threat of mechanism as it relates to bypassing is distinct from the threat of mechanism as it relates to the deep self view. After all, if what undermines responsibility is bypassing, then people may be held responsible for shallow desires even if they have no connection to the deep self, at least when the agent has control. In contrast, if what undermines responsibility is lack of connection to the deep self, then people will not be held responsible for shallow desires that have no connection to the deep self. If this is correct, then the bypassing view and the deep self view may actually be *competing* accounts of the gathering data. Although shedding light on this issue is a task for another day, we nevertheless thought it merited mentioning because we have assumed for the purposes of this chapter that the bypassing view and the deep self view are complementary rather than competing.

REFERENCES

Ayer, A. J. 2003. Freedom and necessity. In G. Watson (Ed.), *Free Will*. Oxford: Oxford University Press: 15–23.

Berker, S. (2009). The normative insignificance of neuroscience. *Philosophy and Public Affairs* 37: 293–329.

Caspi, A., & Moffitt, T. E. (2006). Gene-environment interactions in psychiatry: Joining forces with neuroscience. *Nature Reviews Neuroscience* 7: 583–590.

Baumeister, R. F., Masicampo, E. J., & DeWall, C. N. (2009). Prosocial benefits of feeling free: Disbelief in free will increases aggression and reduces helpfulness. *Personality and Social Psychology Bulletin* 35: 260–268.

Chisholm, R. 2003. Human freedom and the self. In G. Watson (Ed.), *Free Will*. Oxford: Oxford University Press: 26–37.

Clarke, R. 2003. *Libertarian Accounts of Free Will*. Oxford: Oxford University Press.

De Brigard, F., Mandelbaum, E., & Ripley, D. 2009. Responsibility and the brain sciences. *Ethical Theory and Moral Practice* 12(5): 511–524.

Dennett, D. 1984. I could not have done otherwise: So what? *Journal of Philosophy* 81: 553–565.

Double, R. 1991. *The Non-Reality of Free Will*. New York: Oxford University Press.

Eagleman, D. (2011, July/August). The brain on trial. *Atlantic Magazine*.

Ekstrom, L. 2000. *Free Will: A Philosophical Study*. Boulder, CO: Westview Press.

Farah, M. J. (2002). Emerging ethical issues in neuroscience. *Nature Neuroscience* 5: 1123–1129.

Feltz, A., Cokely, E., & Nadelhoffer, T. 2009. Natural compatibilism vs. natural incompatibilism: Back to the drawing board. *Mind & Language* 24: 1–23.

Fischer, J. M. 1994. *The Metaphysics of Free Will*. Oxford: Wiley-Blackwell.

Fischer, J. M., Kane, R., Pereboom, D., & Vargas, M. 2007. *Four Views on Free Will*. Oxford: Wiley-Blackwell.

Fischer, J. M., & Ravizza, M. 1998. *Responsibility and Control: A Theory of Moral Responsibility*. Cambridge, UK: Cambridge University Press.

Fletcher, G. P. (1998). *Basic Concepts of Criminal Law*. New York: Oxford University Press.

Frankfurt, H. 1971. Freedom of the will and the concept of a person. *Journal of Philosophy* 68: 5–20.

Green, T. A. 1995. *Freedom and Criminal Responsibility in the Age of Pound: An Essay on Criminal Justice*, 93 Mich. L. Rev. 93(2): 1915–2053

Greene, J. D., & Cohen J. D. 2004. For the law, neuroscience changes nothing and everything. *Philosophical Transactions of the Royal Society of London B* (Special Issue on Law and the Brain) 359: 1775–17785.

Gromet, D. M., Goodwin, G. P., Tang, S., Nadelhoffer, T., & Sinnott-Armstrong, W. P. (2011). *Mind, brain, and character: How neuroscience affects people's views of wrongdoers*. Manuscript in preparation. University of Pennsylvania.

Honderich, T. 1988. *A Theory of Determinism*. Oxford: Oxford University Press.

Kane, R. 1996. *The Significance of Free Will*. New York: Oxford University Press.

Kane, R. 2011. *The Oxford Handbook of Free Will: Second Edition*. Oxford: Oxford University Press.

Levy, N., & McKenna, M. 2009. Recent work on free will and moral responsibility. *Philosophy Compass* 4: 96–133.

Lycan, W. 2003. Free will and the burden of proof. In A. O'Hear (Ed.), *Minds and Persons: Royal Institute of Philosophy Supplement*. Cambridge, UK: Cambridge University Press: 107–122.

Mele, A. 1996. *Autonomous Agents.* Oxford: Oxford University Press.

Morse, S. J. (2008). Determinism and the death of folk psychology: Two challenges to responsibility from neuroscience. *Minnesota Journal of Law, Science and Technology* 9: 1–35.

Nadelhoffer, T., & Nahmias, E. 2007. The past and future of experimental philosophy. *Philosophical Explorations* 10(2): 123–149.

Nadelhoffer, T., Sripada, C, Gromet, D., & Sinnott-Armstrong, W. (in preparation) Neuroscience, Future Dangerousness, and the Criminal Law.

Nahmias, E. 2011. Intuitions about free will, determinism, and bypassing. In R. Kane (Ed.), *The Oxford Handbook on Free Will*. 2nd ed. Oxford: Oxford University Press: 555–576.

Nahmias, E., Coates, J., & Kvaran, T. 2007. Free will, moral responsibility, and mechanism: Experiments on folk intuitions. *Midwest Studies in Philosophy* 31: 214–242.

Nahmias, E., Morris, S., Nadelhoffer, T., & Turner, J. 2006. Is incompatibilism intuitive? *Philosophy and Phenomenological Research* 73(1): 28–53.

Nahmias, E., Morris, S., Nadelhoffer, T., & Turner, J. 2005. Surveying freedom: Folk intuitions about free will and moral responsibility. *Philosophical Psychology* 18(5): 561–584.

Nahmias, E., & Murray, D. 2011. Experimental philosophy on free will: An error theory for incompatibilist intuitions. In J. Aguilar, A. Buckareff, & K. Frankish (Eds.), *New Waves in Philosophy of Action*. New York: Palgrave-Macmillan: 189–216.

Nichols, S., & Knobe, J. 2007. Moral responsibility and determinism: The cognitive science of folk intuitions. *Nous* 41: 663–685.

O'Connor, T. 2000. *Persons and Causes: The Metaphysics of Free Will*. New York: Oxford University Press.

Pereboom, D. 2001. *Living Without Free Will*. Cambridge, UK: Cambridge University Press.

Pizarro, D. A., & Tannenbaum, D. (2011). Bringing character back: How the motivation to evaluate character influences judgments of moral blame. In M. Mikulincer & P. R. Shaver (Eds.), *Herzliya Symposia on Personality and Social Psychology. The Social Psychology of Morality: Exploring the Causes of Good and evil*. Arlington, VA: APA Press.

Schlenker, B. R., Britt, T. W., Pennington, J., Murphy, R., & Doherty, K. 1994. The triangle model of responsibility. *Psychological Review* 101(4): 632–652.

Shaver, K. G. (1985). *The Attribution of Blame: Causality, Responsibility, and Blameworthiness*. New York: Springer-Verlag.

Sinnott-Armstrong, W. 2008. Abstract + Concrete = Paradox. In J. Knobe & S. Nichols (Eds.), *Experimental Philosophy*. New York: Oxford University Press: 209–230.

Smilansky, S. 2000. *Free Will and Illusion*. Oxford: Oxford University Press.

Smith, A. 2008. Control, responsibility, and moral assessment. *Philosophical Studies* 138: 367–392.

Sripada, C. S. Forthcoming. What makes a manipulated agent unfree? *Philosophy and Phenomenological Research.*

Sripada, C. S. 2010. The Deep Self Model and asymmetries in folk judgments about intentional action. *Philosophical Studies* 151: 159–176.

Sripada, C. S. Forthcoming. The deep self and psychology of excuse.

Stace, W. (Ed.). 1960. *Religion and the Modern Mind.* Philadelphia: Lippincott.

Strawson, G. 1986. *Freedom and Belief.* Oxford: Clarendon Press.

Strawson, P. F. 2003. Freedom and Resentment. In G. Watson (Ed.), *Free Will.* Oxford: Oxford University Press: 72–93.

Van Inwagen, P. 1983. *An Essay on Free Will.* Oxford: Oxford University Press.

Vohs, K., & Schooler, J. 2008. The value of believing in free will: Encouraging a belief in determinism increases cheating. *Psychological Science* 19: 49–54.

Watson, G. 1975. Free agency. *Journal of Philosophy* 72: 205–220.

Watson, G. 2003. *Free Will.* 2nd ed. Oxford: Oxford University Press.

Wolf, S. 1990. *Freedom Within Reason.* Oxford: Oxford University Press.

Woolfolk, R. L, Doris, J. M., and Darley, J. M. 2006. Identification, situational constraint, and social cognition: Studies in the attribution of moral responsibility. *Cognition* 100: 283–301.

10

Moralistic Punishment as a Crude Social Insurance Plan

EYAL AHARONI AND ALAN J. FRIDLUND

1. WHY PUNISH? DEFINING THE QUESTION

The theory of natural selection teaches that organisms tend to behave in ways that abet their own relative reproductive success (Williams 1966). This tendency would seem to produce massively selfish behavior—and it often does (Dawkins 1990). Adult lions exhibit infanticide toward cubs born by extra-pair copulations (Pusey & Packer 1994), fetal lambs compete with their littermates for nutrients, thereby degrading their littermates' muscle mass (McCoard et al. 2000), and the praying mantis famously devours her mate after insemination (Howard 1886).

Human behavior, however, seems to offer many exceptions to nature's apparent selfishness. One example is found in the punishment of rule violators. We pay taxes to enable the incarceration of criminals from other jurisdictions. Many of us take time out of our day to vote for candidates for government office who are tough on crime. And although we may initially try our best to evade jury duty, we often take it seriously when our time comes. Political philosopher Rousseau would have identified this type of commitment as an example of the "social contract"—a responsibility of the populace to promote an effective system of government (Rousseau 1762/1993), raising the question of why we would ever assume such a responsibility in the first place.

According to the philosophy of jurisprudence, there are at least two broad reasons to punish at a state level—utilitarian and retributive. From the utilitarian view, articulated by Bentham, punishment should be justified with respect to practical societal goals (1789/1988), such as the aim to protect citizens from future harm. Future harm can be avoided by performing acts that incapacitate or deter dangerous offenders or that deter other prospective offenders from criminal behavior. Strict utilitarian punishment is based on the expected future cost and likelihood of harm, regardless of whether the dangerous individual is morally blameworthy for past actions.

In contrast, from the retributive view, enunciated by Kant, the punishment of criminal offenders is righteous for its own sake, even morally obligatory (Kant 1790/1952). This "categorical imperative" to punish must be upheld for retrospective purposes, regardless of whether the offender is likely to reoffend. It is often referred to as "moralistic punishment" or the "just deserts" philosophy. Attempts to define an explicit purpose of retribution tend to converge on the desire to restore a moral balance, but in doing so, it remains unclear what this moral balance is, why it needs restoration, and most important, how punishment can restore it without slipping either into tautology or a frankly utilitarian goal. Ultimately, proponents of retribution resort to claiming that retribution is self-justified (see Packer 1968).

Although both the retributive and utilitarian punishment philosophies underlie modern jurisprudence, current social science research suggests that the role of retribution is markedly stronger in criminal punishment psychology (Aharoni & Fridlund 2011; Blumstein & Cohen 1980; Bohm 1992; Carlsmith, Darley, & Robinson 2002; Darley et al. 2000; Hamilton & Rytina 1980; Harlow, Darley, & Robinson 1995; McFatter 1982; Rucker et al. 2004; Tyler & Boeckmann 1997; Warr, Meier & Erickson 1983).

Given the prevalence of retributive motives, it would be prudent to understand what purpose retributive punishment serves. One answer could be that it does not serve individual self-interest at all, but springs instead from our fundamental altruistic nature, as a means to promote cooperation within our social group, even at a cost to ourselves. This view, known as *strong reciprocity* (Fehr, Fischbacher, & Gächter 2003; Fehr & Gächter 2002), elides with observations that many human helping behaviors seem to occur with no expectation of direct reciprocity, such as anonymous donations of money or bodily organs (Batson 1998). According to strong reciprocity, our species' unique willingness to enforce third-party retribution is an outgrowth of our deeply engrained altruism.

From an evolutionary perspective, however, the primacy of retribution is somewhat puzzling because it is not clear why we would endorse this stance if did not tend to confer a future practical benefit such as protection from recidivism. Indeed, any punishment requires some cost to impose, and so it would not have been selected unless it tended to return some beneficial outcome. The primacy of retribution is especially vexing in third-party contexts, such as in criminal trials, whereby the punishing party has no direct social ties to the defendant or victim. If we can show that third-party retributive punishment responds to cues that are unique to problems in the evolution of social exchange, this would temper claims that retribution simply is an expression of pure altruism.

2. DOES PUNISHMENT SERVE GROUP INTERESTS?

One functional answer to the question of why third parties are retributive is that retributive punishment serves the interests of our social group in a way that is sustained by the resulting benefits to the group. According to this group selection hypothesis, when a defector violates a collective action by skirting his responsibilities to the group (first-order free riding), a group whose members collectively enforce punishment of the defector will better preserve its cooperative norms than one that does not enforce punishment (second-order free riders), even at large net costs to the individual punisher (Boyd et al. 2003; Gintis et al. 2003). In some versions of the argument, once a group member invokes third-party punishment, the regimen will spread culturally through other members because we so readily mimic and conform with those around us.

It is admittedly an appealing argument that group-beneficial behaviors can spread by way of cultural transmission, but this model suffers from the fact that group selection should facilitate the dispersion, not just of costly punishment, but also of any behavior (Boyd & Richerson 1992). Thus, if a self-interested individual were to enter such a group and compete with his altruistic neighbors for supporters, other group members should favor his proclivity to forgo punishment of the defector. In other words, if enforcing punishment had even slight negative consequences for one's reproductive success over time, then punishers who tended to incur that risk without redeeming a proportional fitness benefit would be at a fitness disadvantage compared with those who punished more conservatively. In doing so, such group-directed traits would be deselected. Thus, when agents of cultural group selection are faced with self-interested decisions about to whom they should conform, the temptation to free-ride makes it difficult to explain how their group-directed punishment could evolve. This is true largely because (a) cultural information itself is only transmitted between individuals, and (b) natural selection operates on the genes of individuals (see Dawkins 1990; Hagen & Hammerstein 2006; Hamilton 1964a, 1964b; Trivers 1971).

These objections need not imply that cooperation must crumble under the weight of second-order free riders. Indeed, mathematical simulation studies confirm that social exchange strategies constrained by self-interest can flourish with high degrees of cooperation even in the presence of one-shot exchanges (e.g., Delton et al. 2011). Over the long term, this "selfish" behavior drives cooperation because, given some degree of uncertainty about our future interactions, it proves generally better for us to risk the small cost of being cheated than to forgo regular, genuine opportunities for reciprocal exchange. Although these findings do not single-handedly rule out cultural group selection, they raise the possibility that other, self-interest-based mechanisms could also motivate our taste for punishment.

3. DOES PUNISHMENT BUY SOCIAL RESOURCES?

As we suggested earlier, a full explanation for third-party punishment would explain why *individuals* would be motivated to bear the cost of punishment. One way of approaching this question is by considering that our punitive sentiments are ultimately driven by legitimate expectations of reciprocity. That is, we typically appear to restrict punishment to situations when it is likely to yield a future personal benefit (Daly & Wilson 1988, 1994; Frank 1988; McCullough 2008; Petersen et al. 2010; Price, Cosmides, & Tooby 2001; Trivers 1971).

Understanding the role of reciprocity in third-party punishment can be aided by models describing human responses in *dyadic* conflicts over a resource. In this research, studies have shown that the "anger" response, which can precipitate punishment, is uniquely sensitive to cues of how much each opponent differentially values the contested resource (Sell 2005). Consider, for instance, a bike theft (a common crime among the college student samples studied in this kind of research). Here, the victim's anger might express to the thief that he is not sufficiently valuing the victim's need for the bike. In this case, the bike is perceived as the object of value, and the victim's anger display is an enactment that can potentially convince or coerce the thief to make amends and return the bike.

In the *third*-party context, the benefit to the punisher may be less obvious. After all, the very definition of "third party" connotes that the actor is a disinterested party. However, at the level of ultimate motives for punishment, such third parties may carry implicit prospects of reciprocation. In some cases, as we argue below, the valued "object" under consideration may be the victim himself. Punishment could thus serve to protect and invest in the victim by signaling that the perpetrator is not sufficiently valuing the victim's welfare. If so, third parties should punish selectively, consistent with predictable expectations of gaining a net benefit. More specifically, reliable perceptions that the victim's welfare is of personal value should increase punishment toward the perpetrator.

As one example of how a victim's value might be assessed, research has shown that men prefer women who exhibit traits associated with high fertility (Li et al. 2002; Symons 1979). Fertility can be evaluated by cues related to age, physical morphology, and sexual availability, and these inform our perceptions of others' attractiveness. Evolutionary theorists have described such cues as representing high "embodied capital" (Kaplan et al. 2001). In forensic settings, researchers have already observed that victim attractiveness inspires increased punishment recommendations (Erian et al. 1998; Thornton 1977). Therefore, it might not be surprising if men use punishment preferentially, to protect female victims who display signs of high reproductive quality. In general terms, moralistic punishment could be a tool used by individuals who have stakes in the welfare of others to protect that social capital. This particular example also illustrates that it is possible to favor victims in ways that are inconsistent with ideals of distributive justice. In a courtroom setting, for example, justice would not be served if jurors consistently showed preferential treatment toward crime victims on the basis of their appearance.

The notion that third-party punishment is tailored to perceptions of the victim's value, though derived from evolutionary considerations, is somewhat compatible with the utilitarian argument that we punish to deter dangerous offenders, except that here we are not motivated to deter everyone equally. Rather, we are principally motivated to deter those who provide generally reliable cues that they threaten the welfare of those whom we personally value the most. These could include individuals with whom we are not yet acquainted but have some nontrivial expectation of interaction. This is not to say that our punitive sentiments always produce the maximally selfish (i.e., rational) outcome. By analogy, a vending machine, though designed for exchange, nonetheless has been occasionally observed to produce free candy.

This social capital theory of punishment diverges from utilitarian punishment in another important respect. Unlike the utilitarian model, the social capital view does not require that punishers be consciously aware of the social functions of their punitive sentiments. Extending our analogy, a vending machine lacks insight into its internal workings and does not consider itself selfish, generous, or even calculating, and yet it makes complex calculated exchanges. Likewise, it is possible that punishers subjectively deny any personal benefits expected from punishment. Nonetheless, such subjective interpretations do not preclude our ultimate reasons for punishment, to which we may have no rational or conscious access (see Aharoni & Fridlund 2011; Hugdahl & Ohman 1977; Tooby & Cosmides 1990). In this sense, social capital theory may be better equipped to explain not utilitarian, but retributive punishment, which attempts to define itself without reference to practical consequences.

Social capital theory can be tested in at least two different ways. First, do more ostensibly valuable victims inspire greater punishment? If so, this would show that these fitness-relevant cost-and-benefit trade-offs are being computed and expressed in third-party punishment.

A second way of testing the social capital theory of punishment is to examine the punishment behavior of individuals who devalue others' welfare generally. This trait of devaluing others' welfare is highly characteristic of individuals with psychopathy (Hare 1993; Mealey 1995). One of the hallmarks of the psychopathic personality is a lack of empathy and a tendency to manipulate and use others for short-term gain. So although psychopathic individuals clearly have the capacity to commodify others for immediate, personal gain (often at the expense of those others' welfare), they appear unable or unwilling to value others' welfare, a behavior that is typical of long-term investment in reciprocity. If individuals high in psychopathic traits exhibit less moralistic punishment toward offenders, this pattern would further validate, *via negativa*, that personal valuation of others' (i.e., victims') welfare may be characteristic of retribution.

3.1. Group Membership as a Resource Cue

A favorable demonstration of the concept that third parties punish offenders more on behalf of more valued victims is evident in a study by Bernhard and colleagues (Bernhard, Fischbacher, & Fehr 2006). Although these authors did not set out to test the social capital theory of punishment, their results were strikingly consistent with it. The authors wondered whether third-party punishment might serve to protect members of one's ingroup, a preference referred to as *parochialism*. According to both group and individual selection theories, such a response shouldn't be surprising; ingroup victims, on average, would tend to have greater expected value to the punisher and the punisher's group than outgroup victims because they are more likely to share social ties and resources and to encounter each other again in the future. However, the group and individual selection theories differ with respect to the offender's group membership. When the offender is not a member of the ingroup, group selection accounts predict zero punishment because outgroup offenders are not expected to obey cooperation norms within the ingroup. For this reason, the authors predicted that "the only condition in which evolution should have favoured altruistic punishment" is when all parties are ingroup members because punishment in this condition should sustain group norms that enhance that group's ability to compete with other groups (Bernhard, Fischbacher, & Fehr 2006: 913).

The social capital theory, in contrast, predicts that any condition in which the victim is an ingroup member would inspire punishment regardless of the offender's group membership. This is because the ingroup victim has some degree of direct, absolute value to the punisher, whereas the offender's potential value is likely to be suspect (by virtue of his offense) regardless of his group membership.

To examine this punitive parochialism, the authors conducted an economic game with indigenous groups in Papua New Guinea. The game was an anonymous, one-shot dictator game with three participants: a dictator or donor, a recipient, and a third party with the power to punish the dictator by way of monetary penalties. The authors controlled each participant's tribe membership; in one condition, the third party hailed from the same tribe as the other two participants; in another condition, from a different tribe; and in two other conditions, from the same tribe as the dictator but not the recipient, and vice versa. The authors found that third parties punish most when the *victim* shares tribe membership with them, whereas the dictator's tribe membership was of less importance (see Fig. 10.1). Even the dictator appears to expect this preferential treatment.

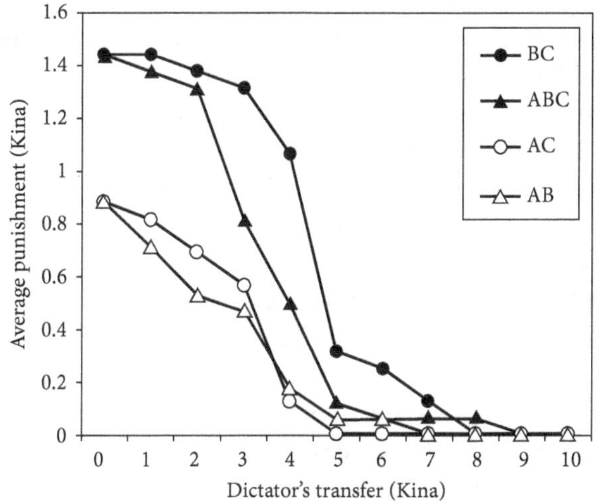

Figure 10.1 Punishment pattern across conditions in the third-party punishment game. The third party spends money (Kina) on punishing the dictator for the violation of an egalitarian sharing norm in all conditions. Punishment expenditures by third parties increase if dictators reduce transfers below the egalitarian sharing norm; punishment is highest in all conditions if the dictator does not share at all. Punishment expenditures are much higher in the ABC condition, where dictator (A), recipient (B), and third party (C) belong to the same group, than in the AB condition (where only the dictator and the recipient belong to the same group) and the AC condition (where only the dictator and the third party belong to the same group). Contrary to predictions, punishment is also much higher in the BC condition (where the recipient and the third party belong to the same group) than in the AB and the AC conditions. (Reprinted by permission from Macmillan Publishers Ltd: Nature. From Helen Bernhard, H., Fischbacher, U., & Fehr, E. [2006]. Parochial altruism in humans. *Nature* 442: 912–915. Copyright 2006.)

Bernhard and colleagues' principal results are directly predicted by the social capital theory: third-party punishment serves to protect victims whom we perceive as most valuable to us.[1] These results are less well predicted by group selection accounts, which also expect that the offender obeys cooperation norms within the ingroup. Nor did participants' responses reflect the most strictly rational choice because participants are aware that the game is anonymous and one-shot, trivializing the possibility of actual future exchange. Finally, this pattern cannot be dismissed as a mere "ingroup bias" because a general ingroup bias should have resulted in more mercy to the ingroup offender. The observed partiality to victims might suggest a punitive function that is unique to these targets.

3.2. Mate Value as a Resource Cue

Although Bernhard's study is compelling, it alone does not allow us to make generalizations about criminal punishment decisions simply because such economic games are limited to low-stakes, normative transactions in which the currency is almost always a windfall with no ultimate cost to the participant. Experimentally measuring higher stakes social exchanges of the criminal sort typically requires a vignette method, which allows the assaying of dangerous risks that may be corporeal in nature. If similar observations result from both economic and vignette methods, we can begin to have more confidence in the findings of either one.

Toward this end, Aharoni (2009) conducted a study in which 78 male University of California Santa Barbara (UCSB) undergraduates were asked to take on the hypothetical role of a trial judge and then to make punishment judgments about offenders who were convicted of a crime (robbery or burglary) in the participant's community. The author aimed to manipulate the victim's value to the punisher by manipulating cues of the victim's *mate* value, reasoning that if punishment tracks victim mate value in opposite-sex pairs, it could be that these punishments serve to protect or impress the more desirable victim. It is also noteworthy that if punishers are influenced by victim mate value, this is not a direct prediction of traditional utilitarian principles, moral norms, or group selection accounts, and would run contrary to the law's explicit stance against consideration of such extralegal factors.

The victim's mate value was designed to be a composite of the victim's facial asymmetry (moderate or low) and her relationship status (available or unavailable). Facial asymmetry was manipulated by distorting photographs of

1. Not all of the patterns in Bernhard's results can be explained by the social capital theory. For instance, all conditions yielded at least some initial degree of punishment. Multiple theories may be necessary to explain the full complexity of punitive behavior.

age-matched female faces that were pre-rated for attractiveness. The symmetry manipulation was chosen because considerable research supports the claim that humans evolved preferences for more symmetrical mates, symmetry being a reliable indicator of immunocompetence and genetic heterozygosity, both of which promote reproductive health (see Fink et al. 2006; Jones et al. 2001; Thornhill & Gangestad 1993). Simply put, we are attracted to opposite-sex others partly because they are reproductively valuable to us.[2] Moreover, we appraise these qualities in others relatively automatically and unconsciously, and we experience them as attraction. It was also assumed that this effect would be strongest when the victim was sexually available. Because it is already widely established that males place a higher premium on physical attractiveness than do women, this study examined male preferences for female victims only.

As predicted, participants punished the offender more harshly when the victim had higher mate value. This difference in severity exceeded an entire year in prison (see Fig. 10.2). Furthermore, when directly asked whether they would be inclined to punish more on behalf of more attractive victims, 75 of the 78 participants emphatically denied this possibility, suggesting that participants are unaware of their partiality to this evolutionarily relevant cue. If the social capital theory of punishment is to be accepted, the mate value study should also be extended to compare same-sex pairings. However, combined with the aforementioned study of parochialism (Bernhard et al. 2006), a pattern appears to emerge: extra-legal factors relevant to the victim's evolutionary fitness appear to sway third-party punishment decisions across both methodologies and culture.

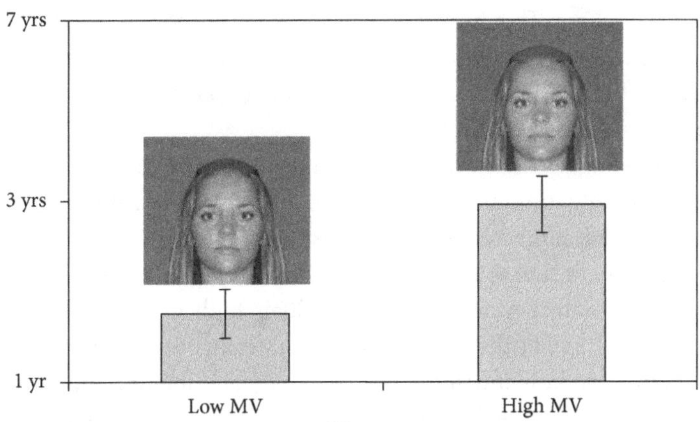

Figure 10.2 Effect of mate value (MV) on recommended prison sentence length, $p < .001$. Error bars represent standard error of the mean.

2. We herein assume heteronormativity on a statistical basis, not a moral or ethical one.

3.3. Punishment Without Social Valuation

A further test of the social capital theory of punishment would do well to show that individuals who tend to undervalue others' welfare exhibit less moralistic punishment. As suggested, individuals high in psychopathic personality traits provide one such example. Using this logic, Aharoni, Weintraub, and Fridlund (2007) assessed 718 UCSB undergraduates for their scores on Lilienfeld's Psychopathic Personality Inventory and recruited 53 of the highest and lowest scorers for a study on punitive decision making.

In the study, participants were asked to make sentencing recommendations for offenders convicted of a homicide as described in an experimental vignette. The authors reasoned that if third-party punishment is a tool that individuals use to protect the welfare of those whom they value, then high psychopathy individuals (HPIs) will fail to show the classic retributive effect in conditions that should rouse it most. Such conditions would incline those of high criminal intent (see Baron & Richardson 1994: 145, 210; Blum West 1985; Geen 1968; Greenwell & Dengerink 1973; Surber 1977; White 1975), in which cues of a perpetrator's intentions would seem to reveal how much or little that perpetrator values the victim's welfare, as research has suggested (Epstein & Taylor 1967; Nickel 1974; Ohbuchi & Kambara 1985; Sell 2005). Importantly, HPIs might also have other, more practical reasons to enforce punishment, such as when they feel *personally* threatened. To exclude this possibility, we independently manipulated the offender's future dangerousness (high or low).

If HPI punishments track the offender's future dangerousness but are insensitive to criminal intent, this would support the argument that HPIs are not retributive punishers. This is exactly what was found. Whereas HPIs' punishment of dangerous offenders was substantial, they did not recommend harsher sentences for the more intentional offenders, unlike their low-psychopathy counterparts (see Figs. 10.3 and 10.4).

These results suggest that when we examine personality traits that are associated with a low valuation of others' welfare, moralistic punishment plummets. And without these ingredients for moralistic punishment, what remains is a form of punishment that is purely instrumental. Yet, given their self-centeredness, perhaps it is unsurprising that individuals high in psychopathy are not retributive. Rather, what the psychopathy result may illustrate is just how surprising it is to learn how much the rest of us care about enforcing punishment of nondangerous intentional offenders. One explanation for this pattern could very well be that, unlike that of psychopathy, typical punishment is based partly on representations of our stakes in others' welfare, such that we punish to protect the welfare of those whom we, at some level, perceive as potentially valuable to us.

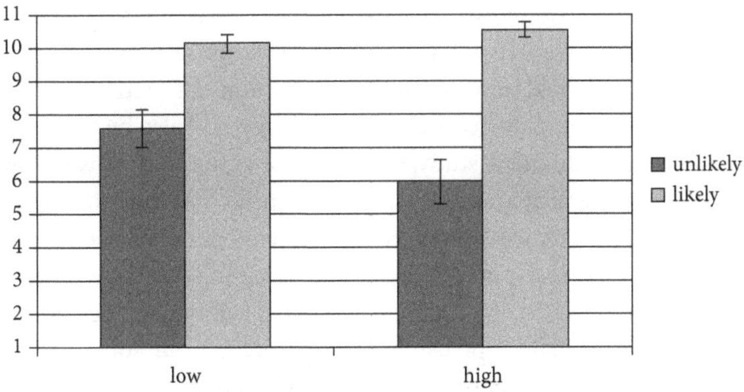

Figure 10.3 Effects of psychopathy level and offender dangerousness on sentence length, $p < .05$. Error bars represent standard error of the mean. (From Aharoni, E., Weintraub, L. L., & Fridlund, A. J. [2007]. No skin off my back: Retribution deficits in psychopathic motives for punishment. *Behavioral Sciences and the Law* 25: 869–889. Available at: http://onlinelibrary.wiley.com/doi/10.1002/bsl.790/abstract.)

4. BROAD IMPLICATIONS

The evidence reviewed above contributes to earlier arguments that one ultimate reason for third-party moralistic punishment could be to garner reciprocity (e.g., Daly & Wilson 1988, 1994; Frank 1988; McCullough 2008; Petersen et al. 2010; Price, Cosmides, & Tooby 2001; Trivers 1971). This interpretation is supported by new evidence that we punish offenders most when their victims carry

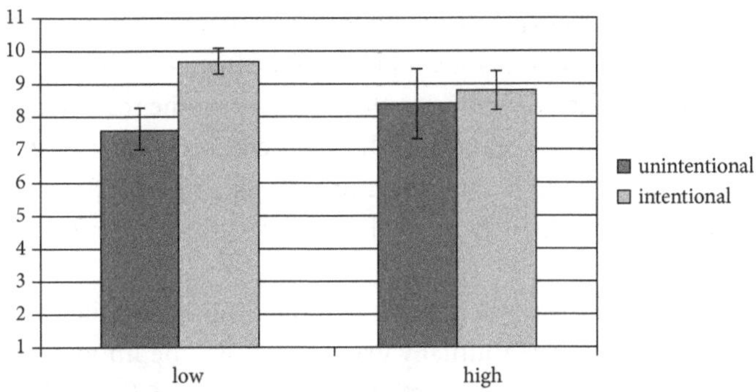

Figure 10.4 Effects of psychopathy level and intent on sentence length, $p < .05$. Error bars represent standard error of the mean. (From Aharoni, E., Weintraub, L. L., & Fridlund, A. J. [2007]. No skin off my back: Retribution deficits in psychopathic motives for punishment. *Behavioral Sciences and the Law* 25: 869–889. Available at: http://onlinelibrary.wiley.com/doi/10.1002/bsl.790/abstract.)

potential long-term value to us, and by the observation that those of us who weakly value others' welfare exhibit less moralistic punishment. In the above studies, this pattern held across multiple definitions of victim value, as displayed both by signs of inclusive group membership and also by high reproductive quality. In the mate-value study, the influence of the victim's value persisted even though most participants denied susceptibility to its influence, suggesting a kind of inadvertent, heuristic responding. Taken together, it seems that when we are prompted to have potential stakes in victims' welfare, we punish in a manner that may tend to track unconscious expectations of long-term reciprocity. This response could plausibly serve to protect our social capital from future harm, earn their favor, or make them indebted to us.

Many details of the social capital theory of punishment have yet to be elaborated. For instance, it will be important to test whether these results generalize to actual judge and jury populations who make real punishment decisions. Thus far, few differences have been observed between the rulings of real and mock judges, according to a meta-analysis including seven studies that directly compared these two groups (Bornstein 1999). Yet studies comparing the punishment decisions of real and mock judges are conspicuously lacking. Judicial expertise and explicit training might potentially neutralize susceptibility to victim-related biases.

Punishment behavior may also be mitigated by changes in the *offender's* prospects for reciprocity. For example, social capital theory would predict that when hearing a heartfelt apology from two similar offenders, we might be more lenient toward the one displaying stronger cues of wealth or power. Such patterns would complement early findings that higher levels of defendants' socioeconomic status were perceived as less blameworthy in mock-jury experiments (e.g., Gleason & Harris 1976).

Furthermore, we must evaluate whether the mechanisms driving third-party punishment are distinct from—or simply emanate from—those motivating victims' punitive sentiments. Speaking to this question, some research has already observed that third parties often punish offenders more harshly than do victims (Fehr & Fischbacher 2004; Green, Burnette, & Davis 2008), a finding that is more consistent with the notion of distinct pressures governing third-party punishment.

Finally, because as a theory of punishment the proposed social capital theory is by no means complete or mutually exclusive, it will be important to examine how it complements likely functions of punishment (McCullough 2008; Petersen et al. 2010), such as the reversal of unfavorable fitness differentials (Price et al. 2001), recruitment of third-party alliances (Frank 1988), and dissuasion of potential enemies (Trivers 1971). A complete theory of punishment will likely identify many aspects of human reciprocity that shape human punitive sentiments.

Our provisional demonstrations of an independent contribution of social capital to punishment motivation do raise an important issue. They point to a potentially stark difference between a natural disposition to punish in accord with evolved, self-interested tendencies and a mandate to punish in accord with society's explicit values, which include the protection of all victims equally, regardless of their personal value to any particular observer.

Confronted by this tension, such a theory could reveal new ways in which punitive biases may already be operating within judicial and juridical sentencing decisions. To date, research has shown that it can be difficult to persuade mock jurors to change their punitive motives (Aharoni & Fridlund 2011; Norris 2000). However, as we learn more about the cues that shape punishment decisions, future prospects for justice reform might consider ways to regulate prejudicial social cues in court proceedings (e.g., perceptions of the victim's appearance) without denying us the aspects of social interaction that humanize our decision making.

In its extreme form, the social capital theory suggests that the legal enterprise of punishment is steered, not by abstract moral truths, but by idiosyncratic intuitions or heuristics that were beneficial to ancestors who were faced with problems of relative survival and reproduction but were entirely unprepared for the complexities of modern social life. This argument should not imply that human punishment behavior is now unchangeable or unmanageable. To the contrary, understanding more fully our punitive sentiments can motivate us to channel them effectively toward pragmatic goals of crime reduction rather than to moralistic and often pyrrhic goals of retribution, which appear to be so vulnerable to the influence of our ancestral heritage.

REFERENCES

Aharoni, E. (2009). Why do we punish? Studies of lay judgments against criminal offenders. Doctoral dissertation, University of California, Santa Barbara.

Aharoni, E., & Fridlund, A. J. (2011). Punishment without reason: Isolating retribution in lay punishment of criminal offenders. *Psychology, Public Policy, and the Law* DOI: 10.1037/a0025821.

Aharoni, E., Weintraub, L., & Fridlund, A. J. (2007). No skin off my back: Retribution deficits in psychopathic motives for punishment. *Behavioral Sciences and the Law* 26(5): 869–889.

Baron, R., & Richardson, D. (1994). *Human Aggression*. New York: Plenum.

Batson, C. D. (1998). Altruism and prosocial behavior. In D. T. Gilbert, S. T. Fiske, & G. Lindzey (Eds.) *The Handbook of Social Psychology, 2* (pp. 282–316). Boston: McGraw-Hill.

Bentham, J. (1988). *An Introduction to the Principles of Morals and Legislation*. New York: Prometheus Books. (Original work published in 1789)

Bernhard, H., Fischbacher, U., & Fehr, E. (2006). Parochial altruism in humans. *Nature*, 442(24): 912–915.

Blum West, S. R. (1985). The seriousness of crime: A study of popular morality. *Deviant Behavior* 6: 83–98.

Blumstein, A., & Cohen, J. (1980). Sentencing of convicted offenders: An analysis of the public's view. *Law and Society Review* 14(2): 223–261.

Bohm, R. (1992). Retribution and capital punishment: Toward a better understanding of death penalty opinion. *Journal of Criminal Justice* 20: 227–236.

Bornstein, B. H. (1999). The ecological validity of jury simulations: Is the jury still out? *Law and Human Behavior* 23(1): 75–91.

Boyd, R., Gintis, H., Bowles, S., & Richerson, P. J. (2003). The evolution of altruistic punishment. *Proceedings of the National Academy of Sciences* 100: 3531–3535.

Boyd, R., & Richerson, P. J. (1992). Punishment allows the evolution of cooperation (or anything else) in sizable groups. *Ethology and Sociobiology* 13: 171–195.

Carlsmith, K. M., Darley, J. M., & Robinson, P. H. (2002). Why do we punish? Deterrence and just deserts as motives for punishment. *Journal of Personality and Social Psychology* 83(2): 284–299.

Daly, M., & Wilson, M. (1988). *Homicide*. New York: Aldine de Gruyter.

Daly, M., & Wilson, M. (1994). Evolutionary psychology of male violence. In J. Archer (Ed.), *Male violence* (pp. 253–288). London: Routledge.

Darley, J. M., Carlsmith, K. M., & Robinson, P. H. (2000). Incapacitation and just deserts as motives for punishment. *Law and Human Behavior* 24(6): 659–683.

Dawkins, R. (1990). *The Selfish Gene*. Oxford: Oxford University Press.

Delton, A. W., Krasnow, M. M., Cosmides, L., & Tooby, J. (2011). Evolution of direct reciprocity under uncertainty can explain human generosity in one-shot encounters. *PNAS* 108(32): 13335–13340.

Epstein, S., & Taylor, S. (1967). Instigation to aggression as a function of degree of defeat and perceived aggressive intent of the opponent. *Journal of Personality* 35(2): 265–289.

Erian, M., Lin, C., Patel, N., Neal, A., & Geiselman, R. E. (1998). Juror verdicts as a function of victim and defendant attractiveness in sexual assault cases. *American Journal of Forensic Psychology* 16(3): 25–40.

Fehr, E., & Fischbacher, U. (2004). Third-party punishment and social norms. *Evolution and Human Behavior* 25: 63–87.

Fehr, E., Gächter, S., & Fischbacher, U. (2003). Strong reciprocity, human cooperation and the enforcement of social norms. *Human Nature* 13: 1–25.

Fehr, E., & Gächter, S. (2002). Altruistic punishment in humans. *Nature* 415: 137–140.

Fink, B., Neave, N., Manning, J. T., & Grammer, K. (2006). Facial symmetry and judgments of attractiveness, health and personality. *Personality and Individual Differences* 41: 491–499.

Frank, R. (1988). *Passions Within Reason: The Strategic Role of the Emotions*. New York: Norton.

Geen, R. (1968). Effects of frustration, attack and prior training in aggressiveness upon aggressive behavior. *Journal of Personality and Social Psychology* 9(4): 316–321.

Gintis, H., Bowles, S., Boyd, R., & Fehr, E. (2003). Explaining altruistic behavior in humans. *Evolution and Human Behavior* 24: 153–172.

Gleason, J. M., & Harris, V. A. (1976). Group dimension and defendant's socio-economic status as determinants of judgments by simulated jurors. *Journal of Applied Social Psychology* 6(2): 186–191.

Green, J. D., Burnette, J. L., & Davis, J. L. (2008). Third-party forgiveness: (Not) forgiving your close other's betrayer. *Personality & Social Psychology Bulletin* 34(3): 407–418.

Greenwell, J., & Dengerink, H. (1973). The role of perceived versus actual attack in human physical aggression. *Journal of Personality and Social Psychology* 26(1): 66–71.

Hagen, E., & Hammerstein, P. (2006). Game theory and human evolution: A critique of some recent interpretations of experimental games. *Theoretical Population Biology* 69: 339–348.

Hamilton, V., & Rytina, S. (1980). Social consensus on norms of justice: Should the punishment fit the crime? *American Journal of Sociology* 85: 1117–1144.

Hamilton, W. D. (1964a). The genetical evolution of social behaviour I. *Journal of Theoretical Biology* 7: 1–16.

Hamilton, W. D. (1964b). The genetical evolution of social behaviour II. *Journal of Theoretical Biology* 7: 17–52.

Hare, R. D. (1993). *Without Conscience*. New York: Pocket Books.

Harlow, R. E., Darley, J. M., & Robinson, P. H. (1995). The severity of intermediate penal sanctions: A psychophysical scaling approach for obtaining community perceptions. *Journal of Quantitative Criminology* 11(1): 71–95.

Howard, L. O. (1886). The excessive voracity of the female mantis. *Science* 8(192): 326.

Hugdahl, K., & Ohman, A. (1977). Effects of instruction on acquisition and extinction of electrodermal responses to potentially phobic stimuli. *Journal of Experimental Psychology: Human Learning and Memory* 3: 608–618.

Jones, B. C., Little, A. C., Penton-Voak, I. S., Tiddeman, B. P., Burt, D. M., & Perrett, D. I. (2001). Facial symmetry and judgments of apparent health: Support for a "good genes" explanation of the attractiveness–symmetry relationship. *Evolution and Human Behavior* 22: 417–429.

Kant, I. (1952). *Kant's Critique of Judgment* (J. C. Meredith, trans.). Oxford: Clarendon Press. (Original work published in 1790)

Kaplan, H. S., Hill, K., Hurtado, A. M., & Lancaster, J. B. (2001). The embodied capital theory of human evolution. In P. T. Ellison (Ed.), *Reproductive Ecology and Human Evolution*. Hawthorne, NY: Aldine de Gruyter.

Li, N. P., Bailey, J. M., Kenrick, D. T., & Linsenmeier, J. A. W. (2002). The necessities and luxuries of mate preferences: Testing the tradeoffs. *Journal of Personality and Social Psychology* 82: 947–955.

McCoard, S. A., McNabb, W. C., Peterson, S. W., McCutcheon, S. N., & Harris, P. M. (2000). Muscle growth, cell number, type and morphometry in single and twin fetal lambs during mid to late gestation. *Reproduction, Fertility, and Development* 12(5–6): 319–327.

McCullough, M. E. (2008). *Beyond Revenge: The Evolution of the Forgiveness Instinct*. San Francisco: Jossey-Bass.

McFatter, R. (1982). Purposes of punishment: Effects of utilities of criminal sanctions on perceived appropriateness. *Journal of Applied Psychology* 67(3): 255–267.

Mealey, L. (1995). The sociobiology of sociopathy: an Integrated Evolutionary Model.

Behavioral and Brain Sciences 18: 523–599.

Nickel, T. (1974). The attribution of intention as a critical factor in the relation between frustration and aggression. *Journal of Personality* 42: 482–492.

Norris, M. R. (2000). A cross-cultural test of the Marshall hypothesis. *Dissertation Abstracts International* 60(7A): 2685.

Ohbuchi, K., & Kambara, T. (1985). Attacker's intent and awareness of outcome, impression management, and retaliation. *Journal of Experimental Social Psychology* 21: 321–330.

Packer, H. L. (1968). *The Limits of the Criminal Sanction*. Stanford, CA: Stanford University Press.

Petersen, M., Sell, A., Tooby, J., & Cosmides, L. (2010). Evolutionary psychology and criminal justice: A recalibrational theory of punishment and reconciliation. In Henrik H øgh-Olesen (Ed.), *Human Morality and Sociality: Evolutionary and Comparative Perspectives*. New York: Palgrave MacMillan.

Price, M. E., Cosmides, L., & Tooby, J. (2001). Punitive sentiment as an anti-free rider psychological device. *Evolution and Human Behavior* 23: 203–231.

Pusey, A. E., & Packer, C. (1994). Infanticide in lions. In S. Parmigiani and F. S. vom Saal (Eds.), *Infanticide and Parental Care* (pp. 277–299). Harwood Academic Press: Chur, Switzerland.

Rousseau, J. J. (1993). *The Social Contract*. In P. D. Jimack (Ed.), *The Social Contract and Discourses*, rev. ed. (p. 203). Rutland, VT: Charles E. Tuttle. (Original work published in 1762)

Rucker, D., Polifroni, M., Tetlock, P., & Scott, A. (2004). On the assignment of punishment: The impact of general-societal threat and the moderating role of severity. *Personality and Social Psychology Bulletin* 30(6): 673–684.

Sell, A. (2005). Regulating welfare tradeoff ratios: Three tests of an evolutionary computational model of human anger. Doctoral dissertation, University of California at Santa Barbara.

Surber, C. F. (1977). Developmental processes in social inference: Averaging of intentions and consequences in moral judgment. *Developmental Psychology*, 13(6): 654–665.

Symons, D. (1979). *The Evolution of Human Sexuality*. New York: Oxford University Press.

Thornhill, R., & Gangestad, S. W. (1993). Human facial beauty: Averageness, symmetry, and parasite resistance. *Human Nature* 4(3): 237–269.

Thornton, B. (1977). The effect of victim's attractiveness in a jury simulation. *Personality and Social Psychology Bulletin* 3(4): 666–669.

Tooby, J., & Cosmides, L. (1990). The past explains the present: Emotional adaptations and the structure of ancestral environments. *Ethology and Sociobiology* 11: 375–424.

Trivers, R. L. (1971). The evolution of reciprocal altruism. *Quarterly Review of Biology* 46(1): 35–57.

Tyler, T. R., & Boeckmann, R. J. (1997). Three strikes and you are out, but why? The psychology of public support for punishing rule breakers. *Law and Society Review* 31: 237–265.

Warr, M., Meier, R., & Erickson, M. (1983). Norms, theories of punishment, and publicly preferred penalties for crimes. *Sociological Quarterly* 24: 75–91.

White, G. F. (1975). Public responses to hypothetical crimes: Effect of offender and victim status and seriousness of the offense on punitive reactions. *Social Forces* 53(3): 411–419.

Williams, G. C. (1966). *Adaptation and Natural Selection*. Princeton, NJ: Princeton University Press.

PART FIVE

The Scope of Justified Punishment

11

Punishing the Addict: Reflections on Gene Heyman

NEIL LEVY

This paper is motivated by a puzzle. Gene Heyman (2009) has recently presented a swathe of evidence for the claim that addicts typically mature out of substance abuse, and they do so in response to incentives. Addicts give up drugs for the same reasons as other people give up wasting too much time playing video games or hanging around the mall: because these activities are incompatible with the responsibilities of adult life. This evidence suggests that one right-wing shibboleth has more than a grain of truth to it: we can respond to addiction by penalizing it, and thereby hope to reduce its incidence. Even the addicted will respond to threats. Addiction is, as Heyman says, a disorder of choice; and choices are responsive to incentives and disincentives.

But this leaves us with a puzzle, or rather a number of interrelated puzzles, which motivate this paper. One puzzle is this: if addiction is a disorder of choice, why is there so little relationship between the legal framework regulating and penalizing drug use and rates of addiction (Degenhardt et al. 2008)? Why have addicts failed to respond to the disincentives of the criminal justice system? Resolving this puzzle, and the other interrelated puzzles surrounding the choices of addicts and their responsiveness to reasons, will require us to reject one of the staples of the moral responsibility literature: that responsiveness to some ordinary incentives is indicative of a capacity to respond to any incentive, such that a failure of response is blameworthy. It therefore has a philosophical, as well as a practical, upshot. I will develop this argument by way of a reflection on Gene Heyman's—rightly influential—recent book, which argues that addiction is a "disorder of choice" (Heyman 2009). Though I believe that Heyman is successful in establishing that addiction is a disorder of choice—in the sense that addictive behavior, the behavior involved in procuring and consuming drugs, is voluntary—this thesis does not entail that addicts can be assisted to give up by simply imposing heavier penalties on their behavior. Although the criminal justice system, and the imposition of sanctions, can play a role in assisting addicts to give up, it will not do so simply by increasing penalties for addictive behavior. In presenting his case that addicts respond to incentives, Heyman neglects the data that show that this responsiveness is unexpectedly patchy and halting. Filling in the picture demonstrates that incentives need to be far better designed if they are to be effective.

1. ADDICTION AND RESPONSIVENESS TO INCENTIVES

Liberal orthodoxy has it that the compassionate approach to the problem of addiction requires us to offer treatment, and not punishment. Addiction is a disease, liberals typically believe, and diseases must be treated and not punished. There was a time, now fortunately long past, when madness was punished, whether to force the person to mend her ways or to drive out evil forces. Just as we came to realize the simultaneous pointlessness and cruelty of punishing the mad, so we must come to realize the pointlessness and cruelty of punishing the addicted. They, too, are sick, and therefore appropriate targets of treatment.

But the evidence Heyman presents confronts the liberal position with a problem. Unlike other mental illnesses (if indeed addiction is, or is a symptom of, a mental illness), addiction responds to incentives. As Heyman points out, it differs from paradigm mental illnesses inasmuch as while many of the *symptoms* of, say, anorexia or obsessive-compulsive disorder respond to incentives, the diseases *themselves* do not. That is, though sufferers from these diseases may be able to suppress or rechannel their symptoms if given appropriate incentives to do so, threats of punishment or promises of rewards do not, by themselves, seem to hold out much hope of curing the disease itself. Addiction seems different.

The great majority of addicts simply mature out of addiction. They give up drugs because they find that consumption is inconsistent with the responsibilities of adulthood (holding down a job, having a partner who relies on you, having children). Addicts themselves report that it is these carrots and sticks that cause them to give up (having a partner, say, entails both carrots and sticks: carrots because you value the relationship and the person, and sticks because someone whom you value has power to shame or criticize you). Further, treatment programs that use incentives are effective with regard to addiction. Heyman cites the work of Steve Higgins, who has successfully used rewards in the form of vouchers in the treatment of cocaine addiction. The vouchers were paid to addicts in return for clean urine tests, with the value of the vouchers increasing over time if the person remained abstinent. The value of the vouchers did not exceed $12 per day, and were sometimes considerably lower than this figure. As Heyman notes, this is probably much less than the addicts were routinely spending on cocaine. Yet the treatment modality was effective in encouraging the majority of subjects to abstain.

These data suggest that incentives, in the form of carrots, are effective in the treatment of addiction. Other data suggest that sticks are also effective. Here Heyman cites programs that drug-tested physicians and airline pilots, who were threatened with loss of their jobs if they failed a drug test. Recovery rates were extraordinarily high. Again, the data suggest that incentives are effective at treating addiction.

Heyman argues that if behavior is responsive to incentives, then it qualifies as voluntary. For him, then, addiction is if not precisely a choice—no one, or virtually no one, chooses *to be an addict*—nevertheless, it is a disorder *of* choice. Although virtually no one chooses to be an addict, the behaviors characteristic of addiction are all themselves chosen. Addiction is not itself a choice because choosing the behaviors symptomatic of the disorder does not entail choosing the disorder, even though choosing those behaviors entails having the disorder. For our purposes here, what matters is the implications of this evidence for punishment. Despite what the liberal consensus might seem to imply, addiction does respond to incentives, including punishments.

It appears, at first glance at very least, that there is no conceptual or practical barrier to responding to addiction with punishment. There is a considerable body of evidence, after all, that criminal behavior can be effectively deterred by punishment. There is strong evidence that the probability of being detected has a deterrent effect, and reasonably persuasive evidence that length of sentence has a deterrent effect on the commission of property crimes (Kennedy 2008). Now, the fact that addiction is responsive to incentives might seem directly to entail that it, too, can be deterred. A standard philosophical approach to moral responsibility can be employed to demonstrate that this is—once again, apparently—the case. This standard approach assesses the responsibility of agents by asking whether the behavior is voluntary, where voluntariness is understood, in the manner of Heyman, as responsiveness to incentives. On this view, an agent acts voluntarily and is therefore responsible for her behavior, if she would act otherwise than she does given appropriate incentives. There is much debate about what kinds of incentives these must be. Clearly, it is not enough that the agent would act otherwise in response to just any incentive. We do not want to say that an agoraphobic voluntarily remains in his house in virtue of the fact that if we set it on fire, he would leave (Mele 1990). Responsiveness to extraordinary incentives is not, by itself, evidence of voluntariness. If, however, he would leave in response to quite ordinary incentives—say for a reward of $100, or in order to avoid his cable TV subscription being cut off—then the behavior is voluntary. It is a difficult question when ordinary incentives become extraordinary, but this is not a question that confronts us here: clearly, the carrots and sticks that have been shown to be effective responses to addiction do count as ordinary incentives. It follows that addictive behavior is voluntary, and responsible.

It follows, further, that we can reasonably hope to encourage abstinence in addicts by penalizing addictive behavior; other things being equal, the heavier the penalties, the greater the reduction in such behavior we can expect. If addicts respond to incentives—and they do—and if, in addition, crimes can be deterred—and they can—then addiction can also be deterred. Some might question this claim on the basis that the responsiveness of addicts to some carrots and some sticks does not entail that they are responsive to *all* incentives, not even all ordinary incentives. But this, many philosophers believe, would be a mistake. Agents can respond to incentives when they have requisite capacities, and capacities are broad in their manifestation conditions. Consider the capacity to play the piano. If I have the capacity to play Mozart on the piano, then I also have the capacity to play any other piece of piano music of comparable or lesser difficulty, whether it is by Mozart or by Bach, or Messiaen. I may not be as good an interpreter of Bach as of Mozart; nevertheless, it would be odd if I were really stumped by the music. Similarly, if I have the capacity to respond to monetary incentives, then I also have the capacity to respond to other incentives of similar or greater value, as long as I recognize them as incentives. As Fischer and Ravizza put it, in their influential account of moral responsibility, "reactivity is all of a piece" (1998: 73): if a mechanism is reactive to *some* incentive to do otherwise, then the mechanism is reactive to *any* incentive to do otherwise. Punishment should therefore be back on the table as a response to addiction.

There is, I think, something right about this claim that addictive behavior can effectively be deterred. Punishment might indeed have some role to play in responding to addiction. There are many difficult questions we would need to answer in designing a punitive response to addiction. For instance, we would need to settle on the behavior that is to be punished. Is it drug use? Perhaps it would be more plausible to punish only procuring drugs, and even more plausible still to punish the crimes that addicts often commit to procure the money for drugs. Nevertheless, there is no in principle reason why we cannot hope to alter some of this behavior by deterrence. Although I think there is something right about this claim, however, I doubt that the imposition of heavier penalties is an effective means of responding to addiction. In fact, I will suggest, punishment will only have a minor role to play in programs designed to reduce addictive behavior. Addicts, I will argue, have special problems with responding to incentives, problems that entail that we cannot justifiably conclude from the fact that they respond to some ordinary incentives that they will respond to the threat of imprisonment.

2. SELF-CONTROL IN ADDICTION

It is well known that addicts have problems with exercising self-control. Addicts are not simply people with unusual preferences; they are people who find it difficult to act on their preferences. One piece of evidence for this claim is the fact that addicts spend time and effort not only in pursuit of their drugs but also in attempts to stop consuming the drug (Ross et al. 2008: 50). This is prima facie evidence of a self-control problem. Longitudinal studies have shown that inability to delay gratification in children is predictive of addictive behavior later in life (Vitaro et al. 1999), suggesting that addiction is caused in part by difficulties with self-control. Other studies suggest that the causal arrow runs in the opposite direction as well, with addiction causing difficulties in deferring gratification: Bickel, Odum, and Madden (1999) found that the discount rates of former smokers were lower than those of current smokers, suggesting either that smoking causes steepness of discount rate or that smokers with reduced discount rates are more likely to quit.

Most relevantly for our purposes, addicts substantially discount rewards that are either delayed in time or have a reduced probability. Drinking alcoholics discount more steeply than nonalcoholics or abstaining alcoholics (Petry 2001). Opioid-dependent subjects discount more steeply than nonaddicts (Madden, Bickel, & Jacobs 1999). Problem gamblers discount more steeply than nongamblers (Ross et al. 2008: 104). Subjects with substance-abuse problems also show difficulties with attention. They are more easily distracted, especially, but not only, by stimuli related to their drug (see Ross et al. 2008: 109–112).

One causal route to failures of self-control in addiction, therefore, goes via discounting mechanisms. We all have a disposition to prefer earlier rewards to later and therefore to discount the latter; in addicts, this disposition seems to be exaggerated. To that extent, their self-control problems are ours magnified. Addicts' difficulties with self-control also proceed via a different mechanism, to which normal subjects are less prone. There is considerable evidence that the motivational salience of rewards can dissociate from their hedonic value (Robinson & Berridge 2003); that is, that we can come to be motivated to pursue (to "want") goods out of proportion to how much pleasure we get from them (from how much we "like" them). The wanting signal seems to be encoded as, or to be caused by, a surge in dopamine from the ventral tegmental area. As the subject habituates to a reward, this dopamine signal tends to attenuate. This attenuation fails to occur with regard to drugs of addiction, and also to gambling rewards, which may explain why their motivational salience increases, even while the degree to which the subject likes the drug tends to fall. This fact makes controlling drug-seeking behavior particularly challenging, given that the signal is highly motivating in ways that bypass consciousness. Dopamine causes a focus on predictors of reward and primes the motor system for action, leading to judgments that are difficult to revise and behavior that is difficult to inhibit (Ross et al. 2008: 154). At the same time as these mechanisms cause judgments and behavior that it would be hard for a well-functioning brain to inhibit, moreover, addiction causes neuroadaptations that weaken the efficacy of the frontal mechanisms that regulate behavior. As Ross and colleagues put it: "[i]n effect, addiction first hijacks the reward system below decks, then commits mutiny on the bridge by sabotaging the cognitive systems that would otherwise check its influence" (2008: 156).

Interestingly, this system responds much more strongly to positive signals than to negative, indicating that reward and punishment are not treated by the brain along a single dimension (Ross et al. 2008: 139–140). This might help to explain why the negative consequences of addiction are often ineffective in motivating addicts to quit. They may need a carrot as well as (or perhaps even instead of) a stick. Ross and colleagues (2008: 180) note that although too little is known about natural recovery (despite its frequency), there is evidence that recovery from alcohol dependence is precipitated by a series of negative events *and* positive rewards. For the effort at abstention to be successful, it must be reinforced. Heyman, on the other hand, claims that the incentives that motivate recovery might be positive or negative (2009: 87). But the programs he cites that use negative incentive, only seem to work because they take advantage of contexts in which plenty of positive incentives are available to reinforce abstinence. These programs involved substance-dependent physicians and airline pilots; the negative incentive was dismissal from employment if a positive drug test was recorded. But the working lives and typical circumstances of people in these jobs are a far cry from the circumstances of more typical drug addicts (Heyman himself cites data showing the close link between addiction and deprivation; 2009: 36–39). There are likely to be plentiful positive reinforcers available in these lives, to reward continued abstention. Programs like these can offer only negative incentives and succeed because they can piggyback on these reinforcers.

I will now argue that the factors outlined above combine to make negative incentives, at least in the form that can be delivered by the justice system as it traditionally works, likely to be ineffective when it comes to the behaviors involved in addiction. Moreover, I will suggest that the remedy suggested above—heavier sentences—at best fails to help, and may actually decrease, the deterrent effect of criminal sanctions.

3. ASYMMETRIES BETWEEN PUNISHMENT AND CHANGE

Criminal sanctions are, almost by definition, delayed and uncertain. That they are heavily delayed is an almost inevitable feature of our criminal justice system: we require that offenses be proved before sanctions are applied, and this requires a lengthy trial. Moreover, there are usually significant delays before the trial owing to the heavy case loads of courts and lawyers. Heavier sentences for drug use (or for other addictive behaviors) have the effect of increasing delays because we rightly require more convincing evidence and stricter procedures before we subject individuals to heavy sanctions.

As mentioned above, prison sentences and other sanctions do have a deterrent effect on crime. But this deterrent effect has a rapidly diminished utility, as a function of delay and uncertainty. If uncertainty of punishment lowers the costs of being caught (calculated as the disutility of the punishment multiplied by the probability of its being inflicted) below the benefits of the crime to the individual, then rational individuals will be more likely to commit it. But criminals differ from the standard rational individual of economic theory in a way that makes them more likely to commit crimes as the probability of punishment decreases: they discount the value of future costs and benefits at a much higher rate than economic theory counsels. In fact, human beings are hyperbolic discounters: they do not discount the value of future contingencies at a steady rate, as classical economics hold that we ought (to take into account uncertainties of delivery and changes in circumstances), but instead discount the future in a manner that shifts as competing rewards become available (Ainslie 2001), with heavier discounting of delayed rewards when they conflict with immediately available rewards. Hyperbolic discounting is especially pronounced in juveniles; as we mature, our discount curves tend to flatten. But criminals have higher discount rates than controls, and more sharply bowed curves than noncriminals (Katz et al. 2003; Wilson & Herrnstein 1985). It seems that uncertainty in the delivery of costs and benefits can dissociate from delays in their delivery as far as discounting is concerned, but uncertainty seems to increase discount rates to a greater extent for those with more bowed discount curves for delay than for those without (Ross et al. 2008: 98–102). As a consequence of their higher discount rate, criminals will value near-term rewards rather more, relative to delayed costs, than will other people. These facts ensure that delayed and uncertain punishment is relatively ineffective at deterring crime.

But worse is to come. A steep discount rate entails that the subject will value delayed and uncertain punishments less than will controls and therefore will value more immediate rewards relatively more. A hyperbolic discount function, however, entails that subjects will have inconsistent preferences. They will often find themselves preferring, and therefore choosing, immediate rewards when they are available, even though they prefer the delayed or uncertain reward most of the time. That is, people with discount functions like this not only have different preferences from other people, they also have great difficulties in pursuing what they themselves value. They have difficulty in exercising control over their own behavior. This makes it especially difficult to effectively deter criminal behavior. These problems increase greatly with addicts because they have even steeper and more bowed discount curves than other criminals. Further, as we saw, the frontal mechanisms that are involved in inhibition of responses are inefficient in addicts. The spike in dopamine caused by predictors of the opportunity to consume a drug primes the motor system for action and thereby produces a prepotent response that addicts will have difficulty in inhibiting. Not only will addicts tend to judge that they ought to consume, or engage in the behaviors necessary to consumption, when rewards are nearby in time; even when they judge that they ought to refrain, they will have difficulty in acting on their judgment. They suffer from a double whammy of self-control problems, one diachronic (affecting their ability to judge consistently across time) and one synchronic (affecting their ability to act on their judgments).

These facts do not entail that addicts are insensitive to punishment, or even that the threat of punishment cannot be effective in motivating them to change their behavior. One response to the facts just presented, then, is to ratchet up the punishments. Perhaps we can deter addictive behavior by genuinely draconian sentencing. Actually, this kind of approach is unlikely to work, for reasons already mentioned. Increasing the severity of punishments tends to increase delay and uncertainty over their delivery; because delay and uncertainty cause the punishment to be discounted, and especially heavily by addicts, the increase in severity may actually make the deterrent less, rather than more, effective. Of course, we could attempt to restrict the procedural checks that ensure only the genuinely guilty be subjected to heavy penalties. Doing so would entail obvious moral costs because it would likely involve subjecting the innocent, or at any rate the less guilty, to such sanctions. It may, in any case, be impractical. Juries and judges are typically reluctant to impose heavy sentences without due process, and constitutional protections may lead to legislation implementing draconian responses being struck down. As Kleiman (2009: 3) notes, "severity is incompatible with swiftness and certainty."

4. CARROTS AND STICKS

In some ways, the considerations just sketched deepen the puzzle with which we began. If heavier sentences are unlikely to be effective in deterring addictive behavior because addicts are relatively insensitive to delayed and uncertain punishments, then how do we explain Heyman's evidence? Doesn't he effectively demonstrate that addiction is a disorder of choice, inasmuch as it responsive to rewards and punishments? The puzzle diminishes when we note that addicts are less sensitive to costs than benefits: the rewards of abstinence may be more motivating than the costs of criminal sanction. However, the stick may be a necessary part of the recovery story, as Ross and colleagues suggest. Even though criminal sanctions may play little or no part in the recovery of addicts, more everyday sanctions, in the form of lost opportunities, loss of jobs or relationships, probably are significant. That leaves the puzzle intact.

The puzzle dissolves when we recognize that the rewards and costs that succeed in motivating recovery are relatively immediate and certain. For instance, the threat of dismissal could be carried out on the spot in response to a positive drug test in the case of those programs targeting substance-dependent pilots and physicians. Because these sanctions are delivered outside the context of the judicial system and do not involve the deprivation of liberty, those subject to them had fewer procedural protections against them and could be more certain that, and when, they could be delivered. Similarly, the vouchers that rewarded Higgins' subjects were delivered quickly and certainly. In natural recovery, rewards may be a little more delayed and a little less certain—which may help account for the stuttering success of addicts' initial attempts to abstain on their own. Nevertheless, these rewards are delivered relatively rapidly and certainly. The rewards of a successful relationship, or of parenting (a common precipitator of recovery [Carlson 2006]) are incremental, and delivered on a daily basis.

Accordingly, we find that judicial programs that deliver rapid and certain sanctions for addictive behavior are successful at deterring it. Because rapid and certain punishments must be small, these programs deliver small punishments; despite the relative triviality of the sanction, they succeed in motivating abstention. Consider the drug-testing and imprisonment program implemented in Hawaii (Kleiman 2009: 34–40). This program was targeted at probationers who were routinely drug tested. Nearly 20% of drug tests were positive. A positive test could trigger revocation of probation and a long prison sentence (between 5 and 10 years, on average). But the probationers knew that their probation officers did not have the time and resources to write up every violation; in addition, they were reluctant to take heavy-handed action in response to what was, after all, a relatively minor breach of their probation conditions. Even if the probation officers decided to take a hard line and make an example of some of their clients, and the judiciary supported them, any punishment would be delayed and uncertain. A probationer would fight a long sentence and would insist upon, and receive, representation. Probation would be revoked, if it happened at all, only after lengthy hearings.

The solution hit upon by Judge Alm, newly appointed to the Hawaiian judiciary, was to institute a system of swift and certain sanctions for every breach.

Swift and certain sanctions cannot, for good moral and legal reasons, be harsh sanctions. A positive drug test resulted in a few days in jail—a sentence too short to be worth fighting. Positive drug tests fell dramatically, despite the fact that it was the worst offenders who were put on the program (i.e., those with a higher than average number of previous violations). Moreover, most of those who received a penalty for one violation did not violate a second time. Overall, the rate of positive tests for those in the program fell by 93% (Rosen 2010). A stick was effective in altering addictive behavior, in part because the penalty was delivered swiftly and certainly.

The Hawaiian program was not designed in a manner that allows us to draw any definitive conclusions about the role of carrots in encouraging abstention. It is worth remarking, however, that its success seems to be due, in part, to the legitimacy of the sanctions in the eyes of those on whom they were imposed (Rosen 2010). Sanctions that are delayed, and especially sanctions that are uncertain, are likely to seem unfair to those who suffer them; they will seem, and to some extent be, arbitrary, inasmuch as the punished will know that things might have gone differently, in ways that were not under her control. But swift and certain penalties are not arbitrary in this manner; they follow surely on violations of certain conditions, and those in the program knew this beforehand. They therefore saw the sanctions as fair. To that extent, the program was not all stick.

More direct evidence comes from other initiatives that combined carrot and stick. Consider the project implemented in High Point, North Carolina, targeting crack dealers (Kleiman 2009: 45–48). Police put together dossiers of evidence sufficient to charge and convict the 20 men responsible for most of the dealing. They then called the dealers in and gave them three sets of messages. Members of the local community told them that the dealing had to stop, but that they were willing to help them find alternative employment. The social services offered them a range of different ways of assisting them: job training, dental work, and so on. Finally, police showed them the evidence against them and an arrest warrant that required only a judge's signature. Prosecution, they were told, was certain if they continued to deal. But if they quit, they would be assisted. The initiative closed down the High Point street drug market, and did so despite lowering, not raising, the number of arrests for dealing.

The High Point program was targeted at dealing by people who may not have been addicts. Nevertheless, the kinds of programs effective for crime more generally are very likely to be the most effective strategies for reducing addictive behavior, too. Both criminals in general and addicts in particular discount the future heavily, so the costs of the behavior that we aim to deter, and the benefits of abstentions, must be swiftly delivered. Because uncertainty is (for many purposes) equivalent to delay, and because uncertainty of sanction delegitimizes it in the eyes of those who are subject to it, penalties and rewards must be delivered with a high probability, contingent on behavior. And because addicts, in particular, are more responsive to reward then to costs, sticks are likely to be less effective than carrots; complementary sticks and carrots may be required to deter addictive behavior.

CONCLUSION

Liberal orthodoxy holds that addiction is a disease and therefore ought to be treated rather than punished. Conservatives argue that addictive behavior is chosen and therefore may properly be punished if society disapproves of it. I think that the evidence shows that neither of these views is quite correct, at least in the form in which they are typically advanced. Unless we have a very expansive definition of "treatment"—which includes penalties for slips—the liberal position is wrong: addictive behavior, including the consumption of the drug itself, can be changed by incentives, positive and negative. (It is worth noting, however, that many people with substance abuse problems also suffer from comorbid mental illnesses, which greatly complicates the picture. Responding to them may require standard treatment in addition to, or sometimes instead of, positive and negative incentives.) But the conservative position is also wrong, inasmuch as it is usually taken to imply that the best way of responding to addiction is with heavier penalties. Severity introduces delay and uncertainty. It may actually lead to an increase in the behavior it seeks to deter, both by delegitimizing the system in the eyes of those it punishes and by reducing the actual and (to an even greater extent) the perceived expected disutility of engaging in that behavior.

The conservative position draws strength from the philosophical analysis of capacities, plus the empirical data presented by Heyman. Because addicts do respond to ordinary incentives, but capacities are general-purpose, we can properly infer that punishments can be fairly meted out to them. But the view that capacities are perfectly general-purpose itself needs to be rethought in the light of all the evidence. Negative and positive rewards are not treated alike by the brain and are differentially motivating for the addict. Distant or delayed rewards that would motivate a normal subject may fail to motivate the addict, even though the addict is perfectly capable of recognizing these incentives when they are nearer in time or more certain in their application. It is a mistake to model the capacities upon which they act on the capacities of the rational agent of economic theory, whose discount function is exponential and who treats uncertainty mathematically. The capacities of such an agent might be perfectly general, but the capacities of real people are not, and the capacities of addicts least of all. If we want to know how broad is the domain of incentives to which they respond, we must look to the data, not to thought experiments.

There is good reason to discourage addictive behavior. Addiction is often (though not always) bad for the addict herself and for those around her. Even in low doses, most of these substances are harmful. It has often been noted that many of the worst consequences of addiction are not directly the product of the drugs themselves, but rather of the fact that they are illegal. Because they are illegal, there are large profits to be made by those who import and distribute them, and this accounts for much of the violence associated with drugs. Because they are illegal, they are ingested in unsafe conditions, and this accounts for much of the adverse health consequences associated with them (ironically, the addictive drugs that are, respectively, mostly associated with violence and with adverse health outcomes, irrespective of their illegality, are both legal). We may reasonably hope to deter addictive behavior, including the consumption of the drug, and remove many of the problems associated with illegality by attaching small but swift and certain sanctions to addictive behavior. Whether we ought to do so—whether this approach is preferable to simply repealing the legislation that controls these drugs, for instance—is a large and difficult question, which I have not addressed here. It is very probable, however, that swift and certain sanctions would at the very least be a vast improvement on our current practices.

REFERENCES

Ainslie, G. 2001. *Breakdown of Will*. Cambridge, UK: Cambridge University Press.

Bickel W. K., Odum A. L., Madden G. J. 1999. Impulsivity and cigarette smoking: Delay discounting in current, never, and ex-smokers. *Psychopharmacology* 146: 447–454.

Carlson, B. E. 2006. Best practices in the treatment of substance-abusing women in the child welfare system. *Journal of Social Work Practice in the Addictions* 6: 91–115.

Degenhardt, L., Chiu WT, Sampson N, et al. 2008. Toward a global view of alcohol, tobacco, cannabis, and cocaine use: Findings from the WHO World Mental Health Surveys. *PLoS Medicine* 5: e141.1053–1067.

Fischer, J. M., & Ravizza, M. 1998. *Responsibility and Control: An Essay on Moral Responsibility*. Cambridge, UK: Cambridge University Press.

Heyman, G. 2009. *Addiction: A Disorder of Choice*. Cambridge, MA: Harvard University Press.

Katz, L., Levitt, S. D., & Shustorovich, E. 2003. Prison conditions, capital punishment, and deterrence. *American Law and Economics Review* 5: 318–343.

Kennedy, D. M. 2008. *Deterrence and Crime Prevention: Reconsidering the Prospect of Sanction*. London: Routledge.

Kleiman, M. 2009. *When Brute Force Fails*. Princeton, NJ: Princeton University Press.

Madden, G. J., Bickel, W. K., & Jacobs, E. A. 1999. Discounting of delayed rewards in opioid-dependent outpatients: Exponential or hyperbolic discounting functions. *Experimental and Clinical Psychopharmacology* 7: 284–293.

Mele, A. R. 1990. Irresistible desires. *Nous* 24: 455–472.

Petry, N. M. 2001. Delay discounting of money and alcohol in actively using alcoholics, currently abstinent alcoholics, and controls. *Psychopharmacology* 154: 243–250.

Robinson, T. E., & Berridge, K. C. 2003. Addiction. *Annual Review of Psychology* 54: 25–53.

Rosen, J. 2010. Prisoners of parole. *New York Times Magazine*, January 8.

Ross, D., Sharp, C., Vuchinich, R. E., & Spurrett, D. 2008. *Midbrain Mutiny: The Picoeconomics and Neuroeconomics of Disordered Gambling.* Cambridge, MA: MIT Press.

Vitaro F., Arseneault L., & Tremblay R. E. 1999. Impulsivity predicts problem gambling in low SES adolescent males. *Addiction* 94: 565–575.

Wilson, J. Q., & Herrnstein, R. 1985. *Crime and Human Nature.* New York: Simon & Schuster.

12

Free Will, Responsibility, and the Punishment of Criminals

FARAH FOCQUAERT, ANDREA GLENN, AND ADRIAN RAINE

INTRODUCTION

The idea that our actions may not be as free as we perceive them to be raises questions not only of how we perceive our everyday behavior but also of how we perceive behavior that is considered unacceptable according to societal standards. If immoral or criminal behavior is the combined result of one's biological makeup and environment, and potentially some added randomness, should individuals be held responsible for their aberrant behavior? Should they be punished for their actions? How should we, as a society and from an ethical point of view, deal with individuals who are almost inevitably destined for immoral and criminal behavior? Might we eliminate desert-based accounts of punishment because neuroscience shows us that free will doesn't exist, as argued by Greene and Cohen (2010)? Two questions inevitably arise: (1) Is it morally defensible for society to take a predominantly punitive approach to crime and recidivism involving mass incarceration? (2) Do we have more to gain from a different approach? We propose a long-term approach that focuses on (early) prevention, rehabilitation, and the humane treatment of offenders, rather than an approach involving massive incarceration without adequate rehabilitation and treatment.

In this chapter, we start with a brief section on the specific contributions made by neuroscience and physics to the philosophical debate on free will. Is it possible that no human action escapes the dictates of biology, environment, and randomness? Might we have reasons to believe that the current criminal justice system relies on an impoverished notion of intentional behavior as its marker for criminal responsibility? In reply to these kinds of questions, we proceed with a case study on psychopathy. Although psychopaths appear to have the rational capacities needed for criminal responsibility, and hence are prima facie responsible, they might nevertheless be excused based on their impaired emotional or moral processing. Psychopaths suffer from brain impairments in the very regions that underlie the emotional processing that is necessary for moral development in normal individuals. Next, we ask ourselves if a similar line of argument (and brain science data) applies to other cases, such as individuals with antisocial personality disorder and those with substance abuse. Even if one is not willing to give up on the notion of truly voluntary behavior, and we might have every reason not to do so, there nevertheless remains a wealth of scientific data that urge us to reconsider our current approach to crime and punishment. In the last section of this chapter, we argue for a more humane treatment of offenders, which should at the very least involve (a) the abandonment of massive incarceration as a solution to crime; (b) the guaranteed personal, physical, and mental well-being of incarcerated individuals; and (c) the integration of choice in terms of an offenders' punishment and rehabilitation trajectory.

According to several authors, recent advances in the neurosciences suggest that free will does not exist (e.g., Haggard, 2005; Libet et al., 1983, 2004; Soon et al., 2008; Wegner, 2003). The famous experiments by Benjamin Libet suggest that our actions are initiated by unconscious brain processes before we become consciously aware of them. Libet and colleagues (1983) found that the onset of the "readiness potential" (i.e., a negative brain potential that originates from the supplementary motor area, a brain region that is involved in motor preparation) preceded the conscious intention to act by several hundred milliseconds. In his experiment, the participants' initial conscious intention to act was measured with the use of a clock. Participants were instructed to look at the clock and recall the position of a spot of light that revolved on it at the exact time that they became aware of "wanting" to act. This time point was then compared with the actual time of the voluntary motor act (muscle activity measured by electromyogram) and the onset of the readiness potential that is evoked before each motor act (brain activity measured by electroencephalogram). In this experiment, the onset of the readiness potential preceded the conscious intention to act by several hundred milliseconds, hence suggesting that voluntary movements are initiated by unconscious brain processes. Although controversial, several scientists and philosophers have interpreted this work as suggesting that free will is an illusion. The experiments were independently repeated by several other scientists, but of course the critique can still be made that the readiness potential merely reflects nonspecific preparatory brain processes (e.g., paying attention to the experiment) and doesn't imply anything specifically related to voluntarily choice or movement, or that measuring inaccuracies on behalf of the participants are responsible for the results. Indeed, as Mele argues (2009), whether or not our conscious intentions play a causal role in our corresponding actions, and whether or not free will is an illusion, cannot be determined based upon the studies by Libet and colleagues. As Mele concludes in *Effective Intentions* (2009, 161): "Scientists have not shown this. Nor has anyone shown that there are no effective intentions."

A more recent experiment by Soon and colleagues (2008) appears to have circumvented these critiques by investigating the brain activity that occurs before making a choice between one of two different motor actions (i.e., using your right or left finger to press a key). This experiment illustrated that the outcome of this choice can be encoded in brain activity in frontal and parietal regions up to 10 seconds before becoming aware of one's decision. Whereas previous studies could easily be contested by arguing that potential inaccuracies in the behavioral measurement of the decision time in such short time delays could lead to misjudgments about the relative timing of brain activation and one's conscious intentions, a time window of 10 seconds appears a lot less threatened by these kind of errors. Also, the fact that the recorded brain activity entails a "neural signature" of the outcome of one's choice, before one is aware of one's choice, appears to rebut the critique that what is measured are mere nonspecific preparatory brain processes. In this functional magnetic resonance study (fMRI), participants were asked to freely decide between one of two buttons (one operated by the left index and the other by the right index) and press it immediately. A stream of letters was presented to the participants while lying in the scanner and making their decision to press the left or right button. To measure the exact time point at which their decision (between left or right) was consciously made, participants had to memorize the letter that was presented to them at this time. The key question of this study was whether there was any brain activity that predicted the participant's choice ahead of time. They found that two brain regions, the frontopolar cortex and a region in the parietal cortex, reliably predicted whether the participant would choose the left rather than the right finger and vice versa before their conscious choice. Apparently, this predictive neural signal preceded the conscious motor decision by up to 10 seconds. Moreover, this study was recently replicated using more accurate scanning methods (Bode et al., 2011). The Soon (2008) study was criticized because the prediction accuracy was in fact only slightly above chance (about 60%) (Roskies, 2010). The same critique can be made regarding the more recent study. However, a recent study by Fried and colleagues (2011) directly recorded brain activity in individual neurons about 1500 milliseconds before the participants reported making the decision to move. Interestingly, the researchers could predict the timing of the decision at 700 milliseconds before conscious awareness with more than 80% accuracy. At least for voluntary motor acts, the latter studies do suggest that there is very little room left for consciously driven choice or "free will" in the brain. However, these studies cannot inform us about more complex behavior and the complex decisions that we typically find important in our day-to-day lives. Moreover, studies like these do not extrapolate to our conscious awareness of more distal intentions and how these might play a causal role in our corresponding intentional behavior. Indeed, there may well be "effective intentions," or at the very least "effective distal intentions" (Mele, 2009). A further question, however, is whether effective intentions leave any room for free will. Effective intentions can indeed lead to reason-responsive behavior, but does this entail free will (i.e., the ability to act or choose differently at a given point in time)?

Some philosophers have argued that free will can be traced back to indeterministic quantum processes deep in our brain. All biological organisms, including human brains, are governed by the law of physics, both classical and quantum. Although classical physics is determinist, quantum physics is indeterminist. Quantum mechanics shows us that indeterminism is part of the microscopic and macroscopic world. However, indeterminism does not imply absence of causation. It implies the presence of nondeterministic causal processes (López-Corredoira, 2009). Moreover, Koch and Hepp (2009) argue that although the brain does obey the laws of quantum mechanics, as do all biological organisms, it doesn't seem to exploit any of its special features. In terms of the objects that humans interact with, it seems that quantum indeterminacy doesn't matter, and operationally speaking, we can act as if determinacy rules the world. The same applies to the brain and its neural networks and the neurons that constitute these networks. "While nervous systems—like anything else—obey quantum mechanics, the collective effects of all these molecules frenetically moving about [are] to smear out any quantum indeterminacy. At the cellular level, neurons look to be firmly governed by classical physics" (Koch, 2009, 44). Koch and Hepp (2011) argue that quantum computations are unlikely to play a role in the functioning of our nervous system (a) because it is unclear what the computational advantage over classical physics would be, evolutionarily speaking (e.g., we can explain higher brain functions such as visual awareness by resorting to computational neuroscience models of neural networks involving thousands of (realistic) neurons, without invoking quantum mechanics), and (b) because the brain is a hot and wet environment such that, because of decoherence, any macroscopic quantum superposition would rapidly be eliminated.

According to Koch (2009), our brains and the many neural networks that compose it, and the many neurons that compose those networks, are subject to deterministic chaos. An infinitesimally small change in any of the building blocks of these neural networks could lead to radically different outcomes in functional activation. In fact, "given the nonlinear and cooperative nature of such neural networks, their behavior is chaotic to a high degree" (Koch, 2009, 37). It is in principle possible that tiny quantum fluctuations deep in the brain are amplified by deterministic chaos and influence behavior. However, such deterministic chaos doesn't leave room for free will. It does tell us that we cannot accurately predict the future state of affairs. At present, there is no evidence for quantum effects on the macroscopic level, and no definite need to invoke these, because traditional computational neuroscience models can explain higher brain functions. Moreover, even if quantum effects did account for indeterminacy at the macroscopic level, which of course cannot be ruled out, this would not imply any evidence for the existence of free will. It would bring only indeterminacy into our everyday behavior, not voluntary choice. Suppose that our behavior (i.e., the macroscopic level) is indeed determined by our brain processing, which is itself determined by our genetics, environments, and the interactions between them. Does this preclude voluntary choice or free will? This has been the subject of much debate. Determinism can be defined as follows: "the metaphysical thesis that *facts of the past, in conjunction with the laws of nature, entail every truth about the future*" (McKenna, 2009). Free will has been defined in a variety of ways within this debate. A neutral definition of free will could read as follows: "*the unique ability of persons to exercise control over their conduct in the fullest manner necessary for moral responsibility*" (McKenna, 2009). The debate itself is not the focus of our chapter, but we will briefly and very generally summarize the main positions. The discussion is mostly centered on moral responsibility and how one needs a concept of "voluntary choice/control" or "free will" in order to save this concept. According to incompatibilists (i.e., libertarians, hard determinists, and hard incompatibilists), free will is not compatible with determinism (e.g., Clarke, 2000; Greene and Cohen, 2004; Kane, 1999; Wegner, 2002). *Libertarians* argue that because at least certain individuals behave freely and are responsible for at least some of their behavior, determinism must be false. *Hard determinists* argue that because of the deterministic processes that are at work, free will is an illusion. *Hard incompatibilists* argue that both determinism and indeterminism (e.g., quantum physics) pose a threat to free will. According to hard incompatibilists, to have "*control over one's conduct*" implies that an individual has the ability to act differently at a given point time (i.e., has freedom of alternatives) or has the capacity for agency (i.e., is the *ultimate* source of his/her actions), or both (McKenna, 2009). For example, if at any given point in time, we *could not have acted differently* (unless the facts of the past or laws of nature would have been different), then an individual cannot be held responsible for her behavior. In contrast, compatibilists argue that free will is compatible with determinism. Many compatibilists refer to an individual's ability for reason-responsive behavior in order to allow for "*control*" over one's conduct and hence moral responsibility (e.g., Dennett, 1984; Fischer and Ravizza, 1998; see also chapter 6 of this volume). Reason responsiveness generally entails that individuals who are unresponsive to appropriate rational considerations do not act of their own free will (e.g., individuals with obsessive-compulsive disorder or schizophrenia), whereas agents who *are* responsive to a range of rational considerations do act of their own free will (McKenna, 2009). So, compatibilists claim that although determinism may be true, it is still compatible with moral responsibility. A great deal of the debate seems to be fueled by a fear of losing too much when potentially denying the existence of free will and thus moral responsibility. Much of the discussion between compatibilists and incompatibilists has focused on the question of whether free will is either impossible or empirically plausible (i.e., whether or not moral responsibility can be saved), regardless of whether determinism is true (Vihvelin, 2011).

SCIENCE AND CRIMINAL RESPONSIBILITY

Biology and physics, and their interactions with the environment, are not different for normal versus mentally disordered individuals. If free will does not exist, then individuals with problematic antisocial behavior are, similarly to normal individuals, not responsible for their personality, intelligence, and other factors that reflect the functioning of their brain. Whereas some individuals are predisposed to engage in antisocial behavior, others are predisposed to abide by the law because of features such as good inhibition, strong emotional empathy, and the ability to learn moral rules at a young age. If free will does not exist, all behavior is ultimately determined by our biology and environment and the physical laws that govern us. All of us make choices that are influenced by a variety of factors, such as our personality, our emotions, and our reasoning skills, which are a result of how our brain functions. On their own, or in combination with specific environmental triggers, such factors may predict aggressive, immoral, and criminal behavior to a greater or lesser degree. Suppose that free will doesn't exist. What would this entail for the current criminal justice system and what would it mean in terms of punishment? Should we change the way the justice system works and how prisons are run today? Suppose that our behavior is indeed ultimately reducible to our brain functioning, which in turn is the result of our biological makeup, our previous and current environmental influences and triggers, the interactions between these, and potentially some added randomness. Can we assume that an individual has control over these factors and how they shape one's intentional mental states and, hence, one's behavior?

The fact that free will is "not an underlying general foundation for legal responsibility doctrines and practices" (Morse, 2007, 203) is not problematic in of itself. It is correct; free will doesn't come into play in the current law's view of the person and his responsibility. In fact, the only way in which today's criminal justice system can be consistent is if one does not enter free will into the debate. If one does enter the concept of free will, and along with it today's scientific knowledge on free will and human behavior, our criminal justice system could collapse. The law is right in assuming that individuals are "conscious and intentional creatures who act for reasons," but the problem is that the story doesn't end there. An individual's "conscious intentional actions" do not arise out of nowhere. The law's view of personhood tells an overly simplistic story, and the current legal system ignores our advancing scientific knowledge when it holds people, including those with mental disorders, responsible merely on the basis of their intentional mental states.

It might not be easy or even wise to give up on the notion of intentional action as somehow expressing an individual's truly voluntary behavior and to replace it with that of a deterministic process that is the end result of one's biology, environment, and some added randomness, leaving no room whatsoever for voluntary control. We will not deal with this issue at present. Instead, we will proceed with an approach that might be more acceptable to those who do not wish to give up on the notion of intentional actions as voluntary behavior. Even if we wish to hold onto the notion of criminal responsibility as it is envisioned today, there is a magnitude of available scientific evidence that urges us to reconsider our current approach to crime and punishment. For example, let's have a look at what brain science tells us about the psychopath. Severe psychopaths are typically capable of rational intentional action in the sense envisioned by Morse (2007). Hence, should they be held fully responsible?

THE PSYCHOPATH'S BRAIN

Neuroscience research is beginning to uncover the brain regions that are likely important for appropriate moral behavior. These regions include the amygdala, ventromedial/orbitofrontal prefrontal cortex, angular gyrus (superior temporal gyrus), and posterior cingulate. Some of these same brain regions have been found to function abnormally in antisocial and psychopathic individuals (Glenn and Raine, 2008; Raine and Yang, 2006). The first region mentioned, the amygdala, is a region that is involved in emotional responsiveness; proper functioning of the amygdala at an early age is important for youth to be able to learn to associate their harmful actions with the signals that another individual is in distress, making it a crucial region for moral socialization (Blair, 2006). Brain imaging studies have observed both structural and functional differences in the amygdala in psychopathy. For example, reduced volume of the amygdala has been reported in psychopathic individuals (Yang et al., 2009a). Reduced activity in the amygdala has been observed in psychopathic individuals during the processing of emotional stimuli (Kiehl et al., 2001), during fear conditioning (Birbaumer et al., 2005), during a socially interactive game (Rilling et al., 2007), and during an affect recognition task (Gordon et al., 2004).

The next region, the orbitofrontal cortex, is located in the frontal lobe, just behind the eyes. The frontal lobe was one of the first brain regions to be identified in early studies of antisocial and aggressive individuals (Goyer et al., 1994; Raine et al., 1994, 1997, 1998). Similar findings have been observed in psychopathic individuals (Müller et al., 2008; Yang et al., 2005, 2009b). The orbitofrontal/ventromedial region is the subregion most commonly implicated in psychopathy. It is important in decision making and is thought to be the region that integrates emotional signals from regions such as the amygdala into decision-making processes. Structural brain imaging studies have found gray-matter reductions in the orbitofrontal cortex in psychopathic individuals (de Oliveira-Souza et al., 2008; Tiihonen et al., 2008; Yang et al., 2009a). Reduced functioning of the orbitofrontal cortex has also been observed during both cognitive and emotional tasks (Birbaumer et al., 2005; Kiehl et al., 2001; Kiehl et al., 2004; Müller et al., 2003; Rilling et al., 2007). Reduced activity in the ventromedial prefrontal cortex has also been observed in criminal psychopaths when evaluating pictures of moral violations (Harenski et al., 2010). Overall, a recent meta-analysis of 43 structural and functional imaging studies of antisocial, violent, and psychopathic individuals revealed a significant association with structural and functional reductions in the right orbitofrontal cortex (Yang and Raine, 2009).

Although the amygdala and orbitofrontal cortex are the regions most consistently implicated in the development of psychopathy, research in psychopathic individuals demonstrates differential functioning in the angular gyrus (posterior superior temporal gyrus) and the posterior cingulate. Reduced gray matter volume (Müller et al., 2008) and concentration (de Oliveira-Souza et al., 2008) in the angular gyrus (posterior-superior temporal gyrus) have been observed, and reduced functioning has been observed during a semantic processing task in psychopathic individuals (Kiehl et al., 2004). In the posterior cingulate, cortical thinning has been observed psychopathic individuals (Yang et al., 2009a). Reduced functioning in this region has been observed in psychopaths during an affective memory task (Kiehl et al., 2001). Both the posterior cingulate and angular gyrus are involved in aspects of social cognition that are important to moral decision making and have been found to be active in studies of moral judgment (Greene et al., 2001, 2004). Activity in these two regions, in addition to the orbitofrontal cortex and the amygdala, has been found to be reduced in individuals scoring higher on the interpersonal aspects of psychopathy during moral decision making (Glenn et al., 2009). The interpersonal features involve manipulativeness, cunning, superficial charm, and deceitfulness. Reduced functioning in these regions may indicate dysfunction of the complex social processes listed above (e.g., self-referential thinking, emotional perspective taking, recalling emotional experiences to guide behavior, and integrating emotion into social cognition) important for interpersonal interactions central to behaving morally. Reduced functioning in these regions may suggest a failure to consider how one's actions affect others, a failure to consider the emotional perspective of the harmed other, or a failure to integrate emotion into decision-making processes.

The studies mentioned here represent only a fraction of the findings that have been observed in antisocial and psychopathic individuals. Brain imaging studies have observed abnormalities in many other brain regions as well. Similar findings have also been observed in antisocial youth, suggesting that differences in the brain can be observed from an early age. In sum, strong evidence supports the idea that the brains of psychopathic and antisocial individuals function differently from those of individuals without these traits.

How do these differences arise? Brain functioning is influenced by a variety of factors. The first source of variation between individuals is genes. Genes facilitate the development of the structure and organization of the brain. Throughout the lifespan, genes continue to affect brain functioning through their effect on neurochemical signaling mechanisms in the brain such as hormones and neurotransmitters. Environmental factors can influence gene expression and alter neurotransmitter and hormone levels, thereby influencing brain functioning. Environmental conditions and events early in life can also affect the development of brain structures and networks and therefore have a significant, long-lasting effect on brain functioning. Behavioral and molecular genetic studies have provided substantial evidence for genetic influences on antisocial and aggressive behavior (Popma and Raine, 2006) and psychopathy (Blonigen et al., 2003; Taylor et al., 2003). The general consensus from behavioral genetics studies is that genetic factors account for approximately 40% to 60% of the variance, although in younger children, the estimate appears to be higher, extending up to 80% heritability (Viding et al., 2005). Several molecular genetics studies have begun to explore which genes may be associated with psychopathy. To date, polymorphisms of approximately eight genes have been studied, and most findings have yet to be replicated (e.g., Fowler et al., 2009; Ponce et al., 2008; Sadeh et al., 2010). Several of these polymorphisms have been associated with neurotransmitters that are associated with reward or stress systems of the brain (e.g., dopamine, serotonin, or endocannabinoid systems). One example is the serotonin transporter gene (*SLC6A4*). There are a number of parallels between findings from the serotonin transporter gene polymorphism and findings from psychopathy (Glenn, 2011), including the finding that individuals who are homozygous for the long version of the serotonin transporter gene (5-HTTLPR) show significantly reduced amygdala responses to emotional expressions relative to those with the short-form polymorphism (Brown and Hariri, 2006). This demonstrates how genes may predispose for criminal behavior via their effects on brain functioning.

Environmental factors are very diverse and include conditions of the prenatal environment, birth complications, exposure to toxins, socioeconomic status, parenting style, maltreatment, trauma, and more. Many environmental factors have been linked to the development of psychopathy and antisocial behavior; some appear to only have an effect when combined with a particular biological risk factor. Environmental factors can influence gene expression and neurotransmitter and hormone systems to change brain functioning. Obstetric factors such as birth complications, prenatal nicotine, and the presence of minor physical anomalies (MPAs) have been associated with antisocial behavior; MPAs such as low-seated ears or adherent ear lobes have been associated with pregnancy complications and are considered to be indicators of fetal neural maldevelopment near the end of the first trimester (Firestone and Peters, 1983). Arseneault and colleagues (2000) showed that MPAs measured at age 14 years predicted violent but not nonviolent delinquency at age 17 years; these effects were independent of childhood physical aggression or family adversity. In another study, an increased level of MPAs was associated with recidivistic violent criminal behavior (Kandel et al., 1989). Extensive evidence on prenatal nicotine exposure has established that children who are exposed to maternal smoking during pregnancy are at increased risk for later antisocial behavior that extends over the life course (Wakschlag et al., 2002). Specifically, prenatal exposure to nicotine has been linked to childhood externalizing behavior, conduct disorder, delinquency, and adult criminal and violent offending (e.g., Brennan et al., 1999, 2002). Fetal alcohol exposure also significantly increases the risk for antisocial behavior in children, adolescents, and adults (Fast et al., 1999; Olson et al., 1997). Exposure to toxins has also been linked to antisocial behavior. Studies of prison inmates have found that hair levels of manganese, lead, and cadmium were significantly higher in violent offenders than in nonviolent offenders or controls (Masters et al., 1998). Environmental lead exposure has been associated with aggressive behavior in children, adolescents, and adults (Needleman et al., 1996; Thomson et al., 1989). Burns and colleagues (1999) found that schoolchildren from a lead-smelting community had increased externalizing behavior problems, when controlling for other variables. It has been suggested that metal toxins may be related to antisocial behavior because they can affect neurotransmitter levels (Liu and Wuerker, 2005).

Finally, several aspects of the home environment have been linked to psychopathy and antisocial behavior. Gao and colleagues (2010) found that poor parental bonding (lack of maternal care and low paternal overprotection) and childhood physical abuse (measured retrospectively via self-report) were associated with increased psychopathy scores in adulthood. Furthermore, a small sample of children who were separated from their parents in the first 3 years of life were significantly more psychopathic at age 28 years than children who were not separated from their parents (Gao et al., 2010). In other studies, childhood abuse and neglect have consistently been found to be associated with psychopathy in psychopathic prisoners compared with nonpsychopathic prisoners (Marshall and Cooke, 1999), in substance-abusing adolescents (O'Neill et al., 2003) and adults (Bernstein et al., 1998), in delinquent boys (Krischer and Sevecke, 2008), and in a community sample (Lang et al., 2002). Prospectively, victims of childhood abuse and neglect have been found to exhibit significantly higher psychopathy scores in adulthood than controls who had not been abused (Weiler and Widom, 1996). Overall, evidence suggests that a variety of genetic and environmental factors contribute to the development of psychopathic traits via their influence on brain functioning. The next question becomes, if factors beyond the individual's control contribute to alterations in brain functioning, which result in poor learning, reduced empathy, and impaired decision-making abilities, should the individual be held responsible for her antisocial actions?

THE PSYCHOPATH'S RESPONSIBILITY

In US criminal law, there are two generic excusing conditions: lack of rational capacity and compulsion (Morse, 2011a). Compulsion may be at work either externally (e.g., a threat) or internally (e.g., addiction). In case of offenders with mental or substance abuse disorders, the internal criterion applies if the disorder leads to such strong internal desires that these render an individual unable to (fully) control his behavior. Although we recognize that the individual acted intentionally, "we might think that it is unfair to ask him to control himself because it will be so difficult to do so" (Morse, 2011a, 379). Similarly, if an individual has a substantial loss of rationality because of to her mental disorder, we might think it is unfair to hold this individual (fully) responsible for her behavior. Hence, in order to compromise responsibility, a mental disorder must either result in (a) a substantial loss of rationality (cognitive defect), or (b) a lack of control (control defect). Indeed, the "moral basis for the insanity defense is that in some cases mental disorder affects the defendant's capacity to act rationally or to control his behavior" (Morse, 2011b, 926).

Although in many cases of mental disorder, such defects will be absent, there are several examples in which such impairments nevertheless seem likely (e.g., psychopathy, substance abuse disorders, and paraphilias). For example, Stephen Morse (2008, 2011) has argued that severe psychopaths should be civilly committed rather than punished because these individuals lack moral rationality. Morse (2008) argues that a severe psychopath is not morally responsible because "[t]he psychopath is not responsive to moral reasons" (Morse, 2008, 208). According to Morse, the best reasons an individual has for not violating others include an understanding of the wrongness of the act and a capacity to empathize with the pain of possible victims, which can then stop him from acting badly. When a person lacks the capacity for empathy and doesn't understand the point of morality, he has no access to the "most rational reasons to behave well" (2008, 208). Hence, when a psychopath's behavior involves moral concerns, she is not responsible. Although the psychopath may have instrumental or cognitive rationality, she lacks "moral rationality." Moreover, Morse argues that offenders with "lesser but still substantial psychopathy should qualify for mitigation" (2011b, 931). His overall view is that a partial excuse should be available for those cases in which offenders, although not substantially lacking in rational and control capacities, may nevertheless suffer from nonculpably, substantially *compromised* rational and control capacities. This reflects the view that rationality ranges along a continuum rather than being either present or absent. Morse also argues that in most cases in which a control test (i.e., Was the offender able to control his behavior?) seems attractive or necessary, the situation can be better explained by referring to the underlying cognitive problem: "[p]eople who are out of touch with reality may have trouble controlling themselves in the sense that they cannot be guided by reason, but irrationality is the problem" (2011b, 929). According to Morse, in cases involving individuals with substance abuse disorders and paraphilias, there is no general rationality impairment, but rather an inability to access good reason when they are "in the throes of peak desire or craving" (2008, 211). This means that when these individuals are not in the peak of desire or craving, they do have intact rational capacity and thus have the capacity to take the necessary steps to prevent future deviant behavior, for example, by entering treatment programs.

Contrary to this view, Caplan (2006) has argued that alcohol addicts suffer from "chronic" impaired autonomy, hence impaired rational decision making, owing to the nature of their disease and the underlying brain impairments. Research has shown that a variety of factors can influence susceptibility to addiction, including genes (e.g., Thanos et al., 2011) and environmental factors (e.g., Enoch, 2011), which may influence the development and functioning of the brain. Addiction impairs brain functioning in such a way that it enhances one's motivational drive for the drug and at the same time weakens one's control over this drive; addicted individuals are typically unable to appropriately weigh delayed rewards, which further undermines their ability to break free from their addiction (Volkow et al., 2011). Their rationality and subsequent control over their behavior are in effect impaired because of their disease and the underlying brain impairments. Hence, these individuals should, at the very least, be considered for partial excuse or mitigation. The preliminary neurobiological evidence on individuals with acquired pedophilia portrays a similar story of impaired brain functioning potentially leading to impulse control and impaired moral rationality (Devinsky et al., 2009).

As brain science progresses, we may come to discover more and more about the brain abnormalities associated with various mental disorders, and how these may affect an individual's rational and control capacities. Such knowledge is crucial. How do we know for sure that the severe psychopath or the severe addict is not (fully) responsive to moral or rational reasons? The brain science, in combination with psychiatric assessments, tells us (see above). The psychopath's lack of empathy or conscience is the result of neurodevelopmental brain abnormalities (Gao et al., 2009; Raine et al., 2010). If one argues for civil commitment in the case of the severe psychopath suffering from a neurodevelopmental brain disorder that impairs his moral reasoning, then a similar line of argument might hold for the less severe psychopath, or for other criminals with various structural and functional brain impairments in the prefrontal cortex that lead to impaired reasoning (Yang and Raine, 2009).

Research on the psychopathy construct suggests that psychopathic traits exist on a dimension in the population, meaning that there is not a qualitatively distinct "severe psychopath" that we can declare to be free of moral responsibility (e.g., Edens et al., 2006). Similarly, brain structure and functioning vary by degree, meaning that there is no distinct threshold by which we would declare "impairment." Admittedly, arbitrary distinctions can be helpful in many cases as a way to categorize individuals for intervention by society. The point here is that an individual who is mildly predisposed to commit crime may be better able to regulate her behavior most of the time and therefore commit less frequent or less severe crime, but the fact remains that the "moral rationality" of this individual is still compromised to some degree, meaning that in the instances in which she does commit a crime, it seems inaccurate to say that the individual is fully responsible.

Although Morse (2008) frames his account of the severe psychopath's criminal responsibility, or lack thereof, in terms of impaired moral reasoning, we argue that the hard evidence ultimately relies on the fact that brain abnormalities underlie the psychopath's impaired moral reasoning. Although behavioral findings of impaired moral reasoning may already guide us in the right direction, the brain science provides us with additional evidence that potentially makes a given case much stronger (Baum, *in press*; Greely, 2011). Indeed, scientifically sound brain science evidence has the *potential* to make certain aspects of criminal cases more objective and less prone to subjective interpretation (e.g., in case of psychiatric diagnoses). The US Supreme Court has acknowledged on several different occasions that psychiatry is not an exact science and that there exists much dispute and disagreement among different mental health professionals about diagnoses (Morse, 2011). Neurobiological evidence has the potential to aid substantially in resolving such disputes and pinpointing the appropriate diagnosis. Moreover, provided that the science is reliable, it opens up a range of new possibilities for the law (e.g., detecting signals of bias with fMRI) (see Greely, 2011).

A similar line of argument can be made regarding less severe psychopaths, criminals without psychopathic traits, and offenders suffering from substance abuse or paraphilias. All these individuals have been found to have brain abnormalities that likely lead to impaired reasoning, moral or otherwise. It might be argued that this impairment is "chronic" in the case of psychopaths, and merely momentarily induced in the case of certain other offenders. However, is there a difference between an individual behaving badly because a brain impairment causes him to be irrational all of the time and an individual behaving badly because a brain impairment causes him to be irrational at that particular time? For the behavior in question, does it matter that the irrationality is chronic or not?

Rather than focusing on drawing "artificial" distinctions between who is blameworthy and who is not, and focusing our efforts on long prison sentences that do not involve treatment and mass-incarceration strategies, we have good reasons to focus on (1) how we can reduce the biological and environmental risk factors that lead to crime, (2) how we can effectively treat individuals after the fact, and (3) how we can treat offenders in a way that is humane and that also protects society. We think the important question is not, "Are they responsible and should they be punished?" but instead, "What can we do to fix this problem?" In the next section, we discuss how a more humane treatment of offenders, involving alternative sanctions and adequate mental health treatment, can provide important steps in the right direction.

HUMANE TREATMENT OF OFFENDERS

According to Greene and Cohen, "our operational legal principles exist because they more or less adequately capture an intuitive sense of justice" (2010, 233). Indeed, "at least in theory, and mostly in practice, our criminal justice system assumes that no one should be blamed and punished unless the agent deserves blame and punishment" (Morse, 2008, 208). If the aim of the criminal justice system is to be just and fair, then it should take the current scientific progress seriously and start thinking about reform. One of the main things that seems to follow is that mass incarceration and prison sentences without adequate treatment programs for individuals with mental disorders are to be avoided, both from a scientific and ethical perspective. Even if one does not agree that free will is an illusion, the current data show us that mass incarceration might not be the best route to success in terms of reducing crime. "In fact, if anything, the evidence suggests that the experience of imprisonment might have a criminogenic rather than a specific deterrent effect" (Durlauf and Nagin, 2011, 21). Although the data suggest that general deterrence (i.e., the threat of punishment has an effect on the population at large) can reduce crime, the data also suggest that specific deterrence (i.e., the way an individual reacts to her actual experience of imprisonment) may enhance criminal behavior. More research is needed to further substantiate both claims, but the likelihood that imprisonment is criminogenic in nature should be given sufficient attention. Nagin and colleagues (2009) rigorously reviewed the existing data. If one only considers the five studies that involved a randomized design, comparing offenders who received a prison sentence with offenders who received a community-based sanction, the empirical evidence points more toward a criminogenic effect than a preventative effect of prison sentences. The authors do mention that the evidence is weak because it involves a limited number of studies, and many of the estimates were not significant.

In reference to the potentially criminogenic nature of prisons, Durlauf and Nagin (2011) point to the possibility that some offenders might find imprisonment not that bad after all, which might encourage rather than deter future crime. They also point to the possibility that prisons function as "schools for crime" in which offenders can learn "the tricks of the business" and become more successful offenders (e.g., Steffensmeier and Ulmer, 2005). Serving prison time might also strengthen an offenders' resentment against society and hence encourage further crime (Sherman, 1993), or it might strengthen an offenders' defiant personality (Matsueda, 1992). Importantly, serving prison time inevitably leads to stigmatization. About 95% of prisoners are eventually released back into society. A major problem that prisoners face upon reentry is that their time spent in prison has eroded their life both professionally (lack of training, loss of skills, limited or no employment opportunities), and privately (family and friends, emotional support networks in general, housing opportunities). Stigmatization acts as an indirect, enduring form of punishment that further aggravates the situation. Not surprisingly, then, recidivism rates are extremely high. In fact, it has been shown that imprisonment is counterproductive in terms of rehabilitation and reintegration in society for low-level offenders and for those in need of special care (e.g., individuals with mental health and substance abuse problems) (United Nations, 2007). Although it is often argued that only incapacitation can offer adequate security, in today's society in which prisons lack the necessary resources to provide adequate care and opportunities for rehabilitation, prison terms often aggravate recidivist behavior, and thus raise rather than diminish crime rates (United Nations, 2007). Moreover, prisons pose a huge cost to society in terms of buildings, staff, and care, as well as in terms of consequential costs upon reentry into society. According to Nagin and colleagues (2006), imprisonment costs on average $30,000 per person-year for adults, and for juveniles, it can exceed $100,000. Also, the long-term costs of imprisonment on offenders' family members and communities are often neglected.

From an ethical and philosophical-scientific point of view, a lot can be said against current mass-incarceration practices and the lack of adequate mental health treatment in today's prisons. What does need to be dealt with from an ethical point of view is (a) the adequate protection of society, (b) the feelings and worries of victims, and (c) the humane treatment of offenders. Although punishment may be a necessary component when providing a solution to (a) and (b), it is paramount that one realizes that this need not involve incarceration. We will not discuss (a) in this chapter, but instead direct the reader to a very interesting approach suggested by Durlauf and Nagin (2011), which argues for more policing and less severe punishment, and point to the importance of early intervention in preventing and reducing crime (e.g., Gao et al., 2010; Heckman et al., 2010; Raine et al., 2003). We will spend a large proportion of this last section on (c) because, in agreement with the aim of this volume, we wish to address the way in which our current system needs to be changed. Nevertheless, before proceeding, we wish to stress that the worries and needs of victims are of the utmost importance. We believe that restorative justice programs offer potentially promising ways to address these. Restorative justice approaches to crime are based on the belief that all the relevant parties need to be actively involved in resolving the existing conflict and addressing its consequences. They have the broader aim of enhancing social capital and promoting tolerance through the implementation of a relational and peaceful approach to conflict resolution.

When faced with today's prison policies, and the US prison system in particular, the humane treatment of offenders forces us to consider two main issues: the abandonment of massive incarceration as a solution to crime, and the guarantee of personal, physical and mental well-being of those individuals who are incarcerated, which among other things implies that individuals with mental disorders need to be placed in secure mental health facilities and not in prison. From an ethical perspective, and specifically from the perspective of nonmaleficence, it can be forcefully argued that imprisonment should be limited to those cases for which no other effective alternatives exist. For the first time in the history of the United States, the number of incarcerated individuals has reached more than 1 per 100 adults at any given time (Pew Center on the States, 2008). For a limited number of severe offenders, violent offenders in particular, incapacitation (imprisonment or secure mental health facilities) remains the only viable option. Incapacitation can be appropriate for offenders who pose a continuous high risk for committing serious offences and for whom imprisonment provides the only acceptable risk-minimizing strategy. However, in many and perhaps most cases, adequate control can be administered through alternative sanctions (e.g., house arrest, electronic monitoring, supervised community service). If less restrictive alternatives achieve the same level of effectiveness in reducing recidivism rates, then those alternative sanctions are to be preferred and need to be implemented. If the goal is to prevent future crime, then current research suggests that community-based sanctions work, at the very least, as well as imprisonment (e.g., Martin, 2003). In general, because of today's overcrowded prisons and the lack of available resources to provide adequate care, community-based sanctions are much less conducive to human rights violations than imprisonment and should therefore be the preferred option for most offenders provided that the rights of victims are upheld and the safety and concerns of society at large addressed. Similarly, imprisonment is much more likely to involve some type of infringement of human dignity compared with community-based sanctions. Moreover, community-based sanctions that include adequate treatment programs offer a better prospect for rehabilitation and reducing recidivism rates in offenders with mental health and substance abuse issues compared with imprisonment (United Nations, 2007). Hence, from a public health perspective, society can only benefit by establishing effective community-based sanctions. Public health policies have a commitment to promote health generally and a commitment to improve the health of those who are systematically disadvantaged.

The United Nations Principles for the Protection of Persons with Mental Illness hold that all individuals who are mentally ill have a basic right to the best available health care and should be treated with humanity and respect for the inherent dignity of the human person. In general, if incapacitation is necessary, offenders with mental health and substance abuse issues should not be held in prisons, but rather should be treated in secure mental health facilities. Prisoners with mental health and substance abuse problems are, owing to the lack of available care and in general inappropriate place of confinement (e.g., drugs are often freely available inside prisons, and adequate treatment options are lacking), a systematically disadvantaged group. The rates of mental ill health among prisoners are higher than for similar groups in the general population, and the overall incidence rate is high. Overcrowding, boredom, and inadequate care in prisons often lead to mental health problems or exacerbates exiting ones. More than half of the prisoners in the United States suffer from mental ill health (Bureau of Justice Statistics, 2006).

The high incidence of mental health problems in US prisons is, to a large extent, due to the federal deinstitutionalization of mental health facilities in the 1960s, which resulted in the massive closing of public mental health facilities without available alternatives at the community or state level. This led to the massive incarceration of the mentally ill in the criminal justice system. Bloom refers to this as the abandonment of the seriously mentally ill to jails and prisons and points to a much-needed expansion and rebuilding of available inpatient psychiatric care in the community, which forms the "backbone of modern acute psychiatric services" (2010, 732). Alarmingly, in the United States, only 1 in 3 state prisoners, 1 in 4 federal prisoners, and 1 in 6 jail prisoners report receiving treatment during their incarceration (Bureau of Justice Statistics, 2006; Kuehn, 2007). A recent review of psychiatric care in European prison systems mentions that none of the 24 countries that were included provided regular national statistics on the frequency of mental health disorders in prisoners or on the availability or frequency of psychiatric treatments (Dressing and Salize, 2009). According to the authors, there is a risk for mental health issues remaining undetected in many European prison systems, mainly because of the inadequacy of mental health screening upon prison entry. It is therefore not unlikely that in many European countries, prisoners with mental health issues do not receive adequate treatment. Again, this is alarming from both a human rights perspective and a public health perspective, especially considering the fact that a recent study found that offenders with mental health and substance abuse issues are more likely to face multiple incarcerations compared with offenders without such issues (Baillargeon et al., 2009).

Also alarming is the number of prisoners with mental health issues in the United States who are subject to solitary confinement, often for many years. For example, Lovell (2008) reports that 45% of supermax residents suffer from serious mental illness. Solitary confinement, either in so-called supermax prison systems or in separate units within a regular prison, can have especially adverse effects on prisoners with mental health disorders (Metzner and Fellner, 2010). This kind of confinement for mentally ill offenders is in disagreement with numerous ethical principles, including nonmaleficence, beneficence, dignity, equality, and fairness, as well as with an individual's basic human rights. Moreover, research studies point to increased recidivism after immediate release from supermax prisons (e.g., Lovell et al., 2007; Mears and Bales, 2009).

As concluded by Vandevelde and colleagues based upon their analysis of the Belgian case: "mentally ill offenders are better off with a treatment model incorporating elements of security, than with a security model incorporating elements of treatment" (2011, 76). They argue for better and profound mental health screening upon prison entry, more possibilities for mental health treatment for offenders, and sufficiently competent and well-trained staff members who know how to deal with this particular population.

Imagine we are given the opportunity to recreate society without knowing what our place will be in that society, without knowing if we will end up being a prison ward, a judge, a victim, or an offender? Would we create a world in which imprisonment is the only option available or create a world in which we can choose between two or more options, for example, one being imprisonment and the other being community-based sanctions? Similarly, imagine not knowing whether we would end up being a prison ward, a judge, a victim, or an offender with substance abuse. Would we create a society in which imprisonment is the only option, or a society in which the offender can choose between imprisonment on the one hand and court-mandated substance abuse treatment on the other hand? Would we prefer having a choice or having no choice? And if we did have a choice, would we want our options to be as humane as possible? Would we prefer a world in which a person who is predisposed to committing crime is punished harshly for his actions and given little or no opportunity for rehabilitation, or a world in which offenders are treated humanely and given the opportunity to receive treatment? Would we want to have more options (provided these options are morally justified) or fewer?

If offenders with mental health and substance abuse problems are given the option of entering into a community-based corrections program that involves intensive mandatory treatment rather than being sentenced to prison, then one could argue that treatment in this sense constitutes quasi-coercion. Quasi-coercion is a controversial issue according to many experts; some even describe it as an abuse of human rights. Others merely view it as a solution to drug-related crime. Although to some, quasi-coercion negates an individual's right to autonomous decision making, it has been defended by others as potentially enhancing autonomy. Autonomy is one of the most important concepts in contemporary medical ethics. It refers to an individual's capacity for self-determination or self-governance and implies that our choices are our own and do not result from any kind of external pressures. Caplan (2006) argues that mandatory psychopharmacological treatment for substance abuse, rather than being an assault on an individual's autonomy, can function to increase the autonomy of individuals with substance abuse problems. Individuals who are severely addicted are coerced by their addiction in the sense that addiction limits their capacity for self-determination and, hence, autonomous decision making. With treatment of their addiction for finite periods of time, the capacity for self-determination can be restored, and treatment can thus be seen as augmenting or restoring the person's autonomy rather than restricting or neglecting it.

In line with Caplan's (2006) view on autonomy and addiction, Epright (2010) has argued that the autonomy of individuals who suffer from psychotic disorders may be temporarily compromised if the goal is to preserve the patient's capacities for autonomy and rational choice. According to Epright, research shows that psychotic disorders negatively affect the brain areas and processes that are necessary for rational deliberation and the ability to predict and evaluate future events, as well as general intelligence. Therefore, psychotic disorders negatively affect an individual's capacity for autonomous decision making. Treatment results in the restoration of the individual's current autonomy and the safeguarding of the individual's future autonomy.

Certain individuals with mental disorders or substance abuse issues may not be competent to fully understand the nature of their disorder and the need for treatment, but these individuals can nevertheless be competent to make informed choices about many other things in life. For example, Moser and colleagues (2004) have shown that prisoners with mental health issues are capable of making an informed choice within prison settings about whether or not they wish to enroll in a research study. We therefore argue that, rather than coercing an individual, the option of quasi-compulsory drug treatment endows the offender with a choice—a choice between either accepting quasi-compulsory drug treatment as an alternative to imprisonment or serving time in prison. It is a restrained choice, and some would argue that one cannot autonomously choose between both options and will likely be pressured into choosing quasi-compulsory drug treatment to avoid spending time in prison.

Even if we assume that a choice between imprisonment and quasi-compulsory outpatient drug treatment cannot be made fully autonomously, does this mean that we should not offer it? Aren't many, if not most, of our choices heavily constrained by situational factors and thus not fully autonomous? The reasons given by the offenders that could be interpreted as indicative of coercion were to avoid boredom, to appear cooperative in hope of receiving better treatment, to meet new people, and to help others (Moser et al., 2004). If we reflect on this for a moment, then we might ask ourselves: aren't those the very same reasons that motivate us, you and me, with respect to our day-to-day behavior and decision making? There is a huge and important difference between coercion, which is obviously morally problematic, and offering a choice between imprisonment and quasi-compulsory treatment. In fact, rather than experiencing it as coercive, receiving the option has been viewed as an opportunity by many offenders.

Recent studies suggest that quasi-compulsory treatment is as effective as voluntary treatment (provided in the same facilities) in reducing crime and substance use. A European study on quasi-compulsory treatment promisingly found that offering treatment to substance-dependent offenders is an effective alternative to imprisonment, both in terms of reducing substance abuse and crime and in improving health and social integration, with better results even in the long run (Schaub et al., 2010). Although more research is definitely needed (Brown, 2010), several US studies involving drug courts show similar promising results in terms of reductions in drug use and crime (Belenko, 2001; Kuehn, 2007; Stevens et al., 2005a, 2005b). Similarly, preliminary evidence shows that mental health courts are associated with longer periods of nonrecidivism (McNiel and Binder, 2007) and that mental health courts are moderately effective in reducing recidivism and enhancing clinical outcomes (Sarteschi et al., 2011). If effective in reducing criminal behavior, then drug and mental health courts are to be preferred from an ethical point of view.

CONCLUSION

The current legal system ignores our advancing scientific knowledge when it holds individuals responsible merely on the basis of their intentional mental states. It tells an overly simplistic story of personhood and, in doing so, fails to adequately address the rights of incarcerated individuals with mental disorders. Moreover, it lends itself to a criminal justice system in which mass incarceration without adequate rehabilitation and treatment is the predominant "answer" to crime. More and more research suggests that mass incarceration is not the best solution to crime. Rather than putting all our efforts into an incarceration/protection model, we could gain a lot by redirecting our efforts toward a treatment/protection model involving effective alternative sanctions. Much can be gained by limiting our appeal to incarceration.

REFERENCES

Arseneault, L., Tremblay, R. E., Boulerice, B., Seguin, J. R., and Saucier, J. F. (2000). Minor physical anomalies and family adversity as risk factors for violent delinquency in adolescence. *American Journal of Psychiatry*, 157, 917–923.

Baillargeon, J., Binswager, I. A., Penn, J. V., Williams, B. A., and Murray, O. J. (2009). Psychiatric disorders and repeat incarcerations: The revolving prison door. *American Journal of Psychiatry*, 166, 103–109.

Baum, M. L. (in press). The monoamine oxidase A (MAOA) genetic predisposition to impulsive violence: Is it relevant to criminal trials? *Neuroethics*. DOI 10.1007/s12152-011-9108-6.

Belenko, S. (2001). *Research on Drug Courts: A Critical Review*. New York: The National Center on Addiction and Substance Abuse at Columbia University.

Bernstein, D. P., Stein, J. A., and Handelsman, L. (1998). Predicting personality pathology among adult patients with substance use disorders: Effects of childhood maltreatment. *Addictive Behaviors*, 23, 855–868.

Birbaumer, N., Viet, R., Lotze, M., Erb, M., Hermann, C., Grodd, W., et al. (2005). Deficient fear conditioning in psychopathy: A functional magnetic resonance imaging study. *Archives of General Psychiatry*, 62, 799–805.

Blair, R. J. (2006). Subcortical brain systems in psychopathy. In C. J. Patrick (ed.), *Handbook of Psychopathy*. New York: Guilford, pp. 296–312.

Blonigen, D. M., Carlson, S. R., Krueger, R. F., and Patrick, C. J. (2003). A twin study of self-reported psychopathic personality traits. *Personality & Individual Differences*, 35, 179–197.

Bloom, J. D. (2010). "The incarceration revolution": The abandonment of the seriously mentally ill to our jails and prisons. *Journal of Law, Medicine & Ethics*, 38, 727–734.

Bode, S., He, A. H., Soon, C. S., Trampel, R., Turner, R., and Haynes, J. D. (2011). Tracking the unconscious generation of free decisions using ultra-high field fMRI. *PLoS One*, 6, e21612.

Brennan, P. A., Grekin, E. R., and Mednick, S. A. (1999). Maternal smoking during pregnancy and adult male criminal outcomes. *Archives of General Psychiatry*, 56, 215–219.

Brennan, P. A., Grekin, E. R., Mortensen, E. L., and Mednick, S. A. (2002). Relationship of maternal smoking during pregnancy with criminal arrest and hospitalization for substance abuse in male and female adult offspring. *American Journal of Psychiatry*, 159, 48–54.

Brown, R. T. (2010). Systematic review of the impact of adult drug-treatment courts. *Translational Research*, 155, 263–274.

Brown, S. M., and Hariri, A. R. (2006). Neuroimaging studies of serotonin gene polymorphisms: exploring the interplay of genes, brain, and behavior. *Cognitive, Affective, and Behavioral Neuroscience*, 6, 44–52.

Bureau of Justice Statistics (2006). Special Report: *Mental Health Problems of Prison and Jail Inmates.*

Burns, J. M., Baghurst, P. A., Sawyer, M. G., McMichael, A. J. and Tong, S. L. (1999). Lifetime low-level exposure to environmental lead and children's emotional and behavioral development at ages 11–13 years: The Port Pirie Cohort Study. *American Journal of Epidemiology*, 149, 740–749.

Caplan, A. (2006). Ethical issues surrounding forced, mandated, or coerced treatment. *Journal of Substance Abuse Treatment*, 31, 117–120.

Clarke, R. (2000). Modest libertarianism. *Philosophical Perspectives*, 14, 21–45.

Dennett, D. (1984). *Elbow Room: The Varieties of Free Will Worth Wanting*. Cambridge, MA: MIT Press.

de Oliveira-Souza, R., Hare, R. D., Bramati, I. E., Garrido, G. J., Ignácio, F. A., Tovar-Moll, F., et al. (2008). Psychopathy as a disorder of the moral brain: Fronto-temporo-limbic grey matter reductions demonstrated by voxel-based morphometry. *NeuroImage*, 40, 1202–1213.

Devinsky, J., Sacks, O., and Devinsky, O. (2009). Kluver-Bucy syndrome, hypersexuality, and the law. *Neurocase*, 16, 140–145.

Dressing, H., and Salize, H. J. (2009). Pathways to psychiatric care in European prison systems. *Behavioral Sciences and the Law*, 27, 801–810.

Durlauf, S. N., and Nagin, D. S. (2011). Imprisonment and crime. Can both be reduced? *Criminology & Public Policy*, 10, 13–54.

Edens, J. F., Marcus, D., Lilienfeld, S. O., and Poythress, N. G. (2006). Psychopathic, not psychopath: Taxometric evidence for the dimensional structure of psychopathy. *Journal of Abnormal Psychology*, 115, 131–144.

Enoch, M. A. (2011). The role of early life stress as a predictor for alcohol and drug dependence. *Psychopharmacology*, 214, 17–31.

Epright, M. C. (2010). Coercing future freedom: Consent and capacities for autonomous choice. *Journal of Law, Medicine & Ethics*, 38, 799–806.

Fast, D. K., Conry, J., and Loock, C. A. (1999). Identifying fetal alcohol syndrome among youth in the criminal justice system. *Journal of Developmental and Behavioral Pediatrics*, 20, 370–372.

Firestone, P., and Peters, S. (1983). Minor physical anomalies and behavior in children: A review. *Journal of Autism and Developmental Disorders*, 13, 411–425.

Fischer, J. M., and Ravizza, M. (1998). *Responsibility and Control: An Essay on Moral Responsibility*. Cambridge, UK: Cambridge University Press.

Fowler, T., Langley, K., Rice, F., van de Bree, M. B. M., Ross, K., Wilkinson, L. S., et al. (2009). Psychopathy trait scores in adolescents with childhood ADHD: The contribution of genotypes affecting MAOA, 5HTT and COMT activity. *Psychiatric Genetics*, 19, 312–319.

Gao, Y., Glenn, A. L., Schug, R. A., Yang, Y., and Raine, A. (2009). The neurobiology of psychopathy: A neurodevelopmental perspective. *Canadian Journal of Psychiatry*, 54, 813–823.

Fried, I., Mukamel, R., and Kreiman, G. (2011). Internally generated preactivation of single neurons in human medial frontal cortex predicts volition. *Neuron*, 69, 548–562.

Gao, Y., Raine, A., Chan, F., Venables, P. H., and Mednick, S. A. (2010). Early maternal and paternal bonding, childhood physical abuse and adult psychopathic personality. *Psychological Medicine*, 40, 1007–1016.

Glenn, A. L. (2011). The other allele: Exploring the long allele of the serotonin transporter gene as a potential risk factor for psychopathy. A review of the parallels in findings. *Neuroscience & Biobehavioral Reviews*, 35, 612–620.

Glenn, A. L., Raine, A., and Schug, R. A. (2009). The neural correlates of moral decision-making in psychopathy. *Molecular Psychiatry*, 14, 5–6.

Glenn, A. L., and Raine, A. (2008). The neurobiology of psychopathy. *Psychiatric Clinics of North America*, 31, 463–475.

Gordon, H. L., Baird, A. A., and End, A. (2004). Functional differences among those high and low on a trait measure of psychopathy. *Biological Psychiatry*, 56, 516–521.

Goyer, P. F., Andreason, P. J., Semple, W. E., and Clayton, A. H. (1994). Positron-emission tomography and personality disorders. *Neuropsychopharmacology*, 10, 21–28.

Greely, H. T. (2011). Reading minds with neuroscience: Possibilities for the law. *Cortex*, 47, 1254–1255.

Greene, J., and Cohen, J. (2004). For the law, neuroscience changes nothing and everything. *Philosophical Transactions of the Royal Society B-Biological Sciences*, 359, 1775–1785.

Greene, J., and Cohen, J. (2010). For the law, neuroscience changes nothing and everything. In M. J. Farah (ed.), *Neuroethics: An Introduction with Readings*. Cambridge, MA: MIT Press, pp. 232–258.

Greene, J. D., Nystrom, L. E., Engell, A. D., Darley, J. M., and Cohen, J. (2004). The neural bases of cognitive conflict and control in moral judgment. *Neuron*, 44, 389–400.

Greene, J. D., Sommerville, R. B., Nystrom, L. E., Darley, J. M., & Cohen, J. (2001). An fMRI investigation of emotional engagement in moral judgment. *Science*, 293, 2105–2108.

Haggard, P. (2005). Conscious intention and motor cognition. *TRENDS in Cognitive Sciences*, 9, 290–295.

Harenski, C. L., Harenski, K. A., Shane, M. S., and Kiehl, K. A. (2010). Aberrant neural processing of moral violations in criminal psychopaths. *Journal of Abnormal Psychology*, 119, 863–874.

Heckman, J., Malofeeva, L., Pinto, R., and Savelyev, P. (2010). *Understanding the Mechanisms Through Which an Influential Early Childhood Program Boosted Adult Outcomes*. Chicago: University of Chicago Press.

Kandel, E., Brennan, P. A., Mednick, S. A., and Michelson, N. M. (1989). Minor physical anomalies and recidivistic adult criminal behavior. *Acta Psychiatrica Scandinavica*, 79, 103–107.

Kane, R. (1999). Responsibility, luck and chance: Reflections on free will and indeterminism. *Journal of Philosophy*, 96, 217–240.

Kuehn, B. M. (2007). Mental health courts show promise. *Journal of the American Medical Association*, 297, 1641–1643.

Kiehl, K. A., Smith, A. M., Hare, R. D., Mendrek, A., Forster, B. B., and Brink, J. (2001). Limbic abnormalities in affective processing by criminal psychopaths as revealed by functional magnetic resonance imaging. *Biological Psychiatry*, 50, 677–684.

Kiehl, K. A., Smith, A. M., Mendrek, A., Forster, B. B., Hare, R. D., and Liddle, P. F. (2004). Temporal lobe abnormalities in semantic processing by criminal psychopaths as revealed by functional magnetic resonance imaging. *Psychiatry Research*, 130, 27–42.

Koch, C. (2009). Free will, physics, biology and the brain. In N. Murphy, G. F. R. Ellis, and T. O'Connor (eds.), *Downward Causation and the Neurobiology of Free Will*. Berlin: Springer, pp. 31–52.

Koch, C., and Hepp, K. (2011). The relation between quantum mechanics and higher brain functions: Lessons from quantum computation and neurobiology. In R. Y. Chiao, L. M., Cohen, A. J., Leggett, W. D., Phillips, and C. L. Harper Jr. (eds.), *Visions of Discovery: New Light on Physics, Cosmology and Consciousness*. New York: Cambridge University Press, pp. 584–600.

Krischer, M. K., and Sevecke, K. (2008). Early traumatization and psychopathy in female and male juvenile offenders. *International Journal of Law and Psychiatry*, 31, 253–262.

Lang, S., af Klinteberg, B., and Alm, P. O. (2002). Adult psychopathy and violent behavior in males with early neglect and abuse. *Acta Psychiatrica Scandinavica*, 106, 93–100.

Libet, B., Gleason, C. A., Wright, E. W., and Pearl, D. K. (1983). Time of conscious intention to act in relation to onset of cerebral activity (readiness-potential). The unconscious initiation of a freely voluntary act. *Brain*, 106, 623–642.

Libet, B. (2004). *Mind Time: The Temporal Factor in Consciousness*. Cambridge, MA: Harvard University Press.

Liu, J., and Wuerker, A. (2005). Biosocial bases of aggressive and violent behavior: Implications for nursing studies. *International Journal of Nursing Studies*, 42, 229–241.

Lopéz-Corredoira, M. (2009). Quantum mechanics and free will counter-arguments. *NeuroQuantology*, 7, 449–456.

Lovell, D. (2008). Patterns of disturbed behavior in a supermax population. *Criminal Justice and Behavior*, 35, 985–1004.

Lovell, D., Johnson, L. C., and Cain, K. C. (2007). Recidivism of supermax prisoners in Washington State. *Crime & Delinquency*, 53, 633–656.

Marshall, L. A., and Cooke, D. J. (1999). The childhood experiences of psychopaths: A retrospective study of familial and societal factors. *Journal of Personality Disorders*, 13, 211–225.

Martin, G. (2003). The effectiveness of community-based sanctions in reducing recidivism. *Corrections Today*, February.

Masters, R. D., Hone, B. and Doshi, A. (1998). Environmental pollution, neurotoxicity, and criminal violence. In J. Rose (ed.), *Environmental Toxicology*. London: Gordon and Breach, pp. 13–48.

Matsueda, R. (1992). Reflected appraisal, parental labeling and delinquency: Specifying a symbolic interactionist theory. *American Journal of Sociology*, 97, 1577–1611.

McKenna, M. (2009). Compatibilism. In Edward N. Zalta (ed.), *The Stanford Encyclopedia of Philosophy*. Available at: http://plato.stanford.edu/archives/win2009/entries/compatibilism/.

McNiel, D. E., and Binder, R. L. (2007). Effectiveness of a mental health court in reducing criminal recidivism and violence. *American Journal of Psychiatry*, 164, 1395–1403.

Mears, D. P., and Bales, W. D. (2009). Supermax incarceration and recidivism. *Criminology*, 47, 1131–1166.

Mele, A. R. (2009). *Effective Intentions: The Power of Conscious Will*. Oxford and New York: Oxford University Press.

Metzner, J. L., and Fellner, J. (2010). Solitary confinement and mental illness in U.S. prisons: A challenge for medical ethics. *Journal of the American Academy of Psychiatry and the Law*, 38, 104–108.

Morse, S. J. (2007). The non-problem of free will in forensic psychiatry and psychology. *Behavioral Sciences & the Law*, 25, 203–220.

Morse, S. J. (2008). Psychopathy and criminal responsibility. *Neuroethics*, 1, 205–212.

Morse, S. J. (2011a). Genetics and criminal responsibility. *TRENDS in Cognitive Sciences*, 15, 378–380.

Morse, S. J. (2011b). Mental disorder and criminal law. *Journal of Criminal Law & Criminology*, 101, 885–968.

Moser, D. J., Arndt, S., Kanz, J. E., Benjamin, M. L., Bayless, J. D., Reese, R. L., Paulsen, J. S., and Flaum, M. A. (2004). Coercion and informed consent in research involving prisoners. *Comprehensive Psychiatry*, 45, 1–9.

Müller, J. L., Gänßbauer, S., Sommer, M., Döhnel, K., Weber, T., Schmidt-Wilcke, T., et al. (2008). Gray matter changes in right superior temporal gyrus in criminal psychopaths: Evidence from voxel-based morphometry. *Psychiatry Research: Neuroimaging*, 163, 213–222.

Müller, J. L., Sommer, M., Wagner, V., Lange, K., Taschler, H., Roder, C. H., et al. (2003). Abnormalities in emotion processing within cortical and subcortical regions in criminal psychopaths: Evidence from a functional magnetic resonance imaging study using pictures with emotional content. *Biological Psychiatry*, 54, 152–162.

Nagin, D. S., Cullen, F. T., and Jonson, C. L. (2009). Imprisonment and reoffending. *Crime and Justice: A Review of Research*, 38, 115–200.

Nagin, D. S., Piquero, A. R., Scott E. S., and Steinberg, L. (2006). Public preferences for rehabilitation versus incarceration of juvenile offenders: Evidence from a contingent valuation survey. *Criminology and Public Policy*, 5, 627–652.

Needleman, H. L., Riess, J. A., Tobin, M. J., Biesecker, G. E., and Greenhouse, J. B. (1996). Bone lead levels and delinquent behavior. *Journal of the American Medical Association*, 275, 363–369.

Olson, H. C., Streissguth, A. P., Sampson, P. D., Barr, H. M., Bookstein, F. L., and Thiede, K. (1997). Association of prenatal alcohol exposure with behavioral and learning problems in early adolescence. *Journal of the American Academy of Child and Adolescent Psychiatry*, 36, 1187–1194.

O'Neill, M. L., Lidz, V., and Heilbrun, K. (2003). Predictors and correlates of psychopathic characteristics in substance abusing adolescents. *International Journal of Forensic Mental Health*, 2, 35–45.

Pew Center on the States (2008). Report: *One in 100: Behind Bars in America 2008*. Pew Charitable Trusts.

Ponce, G., Hoenicka, J., Jimenez-Arriero, M. A., Rodriguez-Jimenez, R., Aragues, M., Martin- Sune, N., et al. (2008). DRD2 and ANKK1 genotype in alcohol-dependent patients with psychopathic traits: association and interaction study. *British Journal of Psychiatry*, 193, 121–125.

Popma, A., and Raine, A. (2006). Will future forensic assessment be neurobiologic? *Child and Adolescent Psychiatric Clinics of North America*, 15, 429–444.

Raine, A., Buchsbaum, M. S., and Lacasse, L. (1997). Brain abnormalities in murderers indicated by positron emission tomography. *Biological Psychiatry*, 42, 495–508.

Raine, A., Buchsbaum, M. S., Stanley, J., Lottenberg, S., Abel, L., and Stoddard, J. (1994). Selective reductions in prefrontal glucose metabolism in murderers. *Biological Psychiatry*, 36, 365–373.

Raine, A., Lee, L., Yang, Y., and Colletti, P. (2010). Neurodevelopmental marker for limbic maldevelopment in antisocial personality disorder and psychopathy. *British Journal of Psychiatry*, 197, 186–192.

Raine, A., Mellingen, K., Liu, J., Venables, P., and Mednick, S.A. (2003). Effects of environmental enrichment at ages 3–5 years on schizotypal personality and antisocial behavior at ages 17 and 23 years. *American Journal of Psychiatry*, 160, 1627–1635.

Raine, A., Meloy, J. R., Bihrle, S., Stoddard, J., Lacasse, L., and Buchsbaum, M. S. (1998). Reduced prefrontal and increased subcortical brain functioning assessed using positron emission tomography in predatory and affective murderers. *Behavioral Sciences & the Law*, 16, 319–332.

Raine, A., and Yang, Y. (2006). Neural foundations to moral reasoning and antisocial behavior. *Social, Cognitive, and Affective Neuroscience*, 1, 203–213.

Rilling, J. K., Glenn, A. L., Jairam, M. R., Pagnoni, G., Goldsmith, D. R., Elfenbein, H. A., et al. (2007). Neural correlates of social cooperation and non-cooperation as a function of psychopathy. *Biological Psychiatry*, 61, 1260–1271.

Roskies, A. (2010). How does neuroscience affect our conception of volition? *The Annual Review of Neuroscience*, 33, 109–130.

Sadeh, N., Javdani, S., Jackson, J. J., Reynolds, E. K., Potenza, M. N., Gelernter, J., et al. (2010). Serotonin transporter gene associations with psychopathic traits in youth vary as a function of socioeconomic resources. *Journal of Abnormal Psychology*, 119, 604–609.

Sartechi, C. M., Vaughn, M. G., and Kim, K. (2011). Assessing the effectiveness of mental health courts: A quantitative review. *Journal of Criminal Justice*, 39, 12–20.

Schaub, M., Stevens, A., Berto, D., Hunt, N., Kerschl, V., McSweeney, T., Oeuvray, K., Puppo, I., Santa Maria, A., Trinkl, B., Werdenich, W., and Uchtenhagen, A. (2010). Comparing outcomes of "voluntary" and "quasi-compulsory" treatment of substance abuse dependence in Europe. *European Addiction Research*, 16, 53–60.

Sherman, L. (1993). Defiance, deterrence and irrelevance: A theory of the criminal sanction. *Journal of Research in Crime and Delinquency*, 30, 445–473.

Soon, C. S., Brass, M., Heinze, H. J., and Haynes, J. D. (2008). Unconscious determinants of free decisions in the human brain. *Nature Neuroscience*, 11, 543–545.

Steffensmeier, D., and Ulmer, J. T. (2005). *Confessions of a Dying Thief: Understanding Criminal Careers and Illegal Enterprise*. New Brunswick, NJ: Aldin Transaction.

Stevens, A., Berto, D., Heckmann, W., Kerschl, V., Oeuvray, K., Ooyen van, M., et al. (2005a). Quasi-compulsory treatment of drug dependent offenders: An international literature review. *Substance Use & Misuse*, 40, 269–283.

Stevens, A., Trace, M., and Bewley-Taylor, D. (2005b) Reducing drug related crime: An overview of the global evidence. *Beckley Foundation Drug Policy Programme, Reports*, 1–10.

Taylor, J., Loney, B. R., Bobadilla, L., Iacono, W. G., and McGue, M. (2003). Genetic and environmental influences on psychopathy trait dimensions in a community sample of male twins. *Journal of Abnormal Child Psychology*, 31, 633–645.

Thanos, P. K., Gopez, V., Delis, F., Michaelides, M., Grandy, D. K., Wang, G.-J., Kunos, G., and Volkow, N. D. (2011). Upregulation of cannabinoid type 1 receptors in dopamine D2 receptor knockout mice is reversed by chronic forced ethanol consumption. *Alcoholism: Clinical and Experimental Research*, 35, 19–27.

Thomson, G. O., Raab, G. M., Hepburn, W. S., Hunter, R., Fulton, M., and Laxen, D. P. (1989). Blood-lead levels and children's behavior-results from the Edinburgh Lead Study. *Journal of Child Psychology and Psychiatry*, 30, 515–528.

Tiihonen, J., Rossi, R., Laakso, M. P., Hodgins, S., Testa, C., Perez, J., et al. (2008). Brain anatomy of persistent violent offenders: More rather than less. *Psychiatry Research: Neuroimaging*, 163, 201–212.

United Nations (2007). *Handbook of Basic Principles and Promising Practices on Alternatives to Imprisonment*. New York: United Nations (Criminal Justice Handbook Series).

Vandevelde, S., Soyez, V., Vander Beken, T., De Smet, S., Boers, A., and Broekaert, E. (2011). Mentally ill offenders in prison: The Belgian case. *International Journal of Law and Psychiatry*, 34, 71–78.

Viding, E., Blair, R. J., Moffitt, T. E., and Plomin, R. (2005). Evidence for substantial genetic risk for psychopathy in 7-year-olds. *Journal of Child Psychology and Psychiatry*, 46, 592–597.

Vihvelin, K. (2011). Arguments for incompatibilism. In Edward N. Zalta (ed.), *The Stanford Encyclopedia of Philosophy*. Available at: http://plato.stanford.edu/archives/spr2011/entries/incompatibilism-arguments/.

Volkow, N. D., Baler, R. D., and Goldstein, R. Z. (2011). Addiction: Pulling at the neural threads of social behaviors. *Neuron*, 69, 599–602.

Wakschlag, L. S., Pickett, K. E., Cook, E. C., Benowitz, N. L., and Leventhal, B. L. (2002). Maternal smoking during pregnancy and severe antisocial behavior in offspring: A review. *American Journal of Public Health*, 92, 966–974.

Wegner, D. M. (2002). *The Illusion of Conscious Will*. Cambridge, MA: MIT Press.

Wegner, D. M. (2003). The mind's best trick: How we experience conscious will. *TRENDS in Cognitive Sciences*, 7, 65–69.

Weiler, B., and Widom, C. S. (1996). Psychopathy and violent behavior in abused and neglected young adults. *Criminal Behavior and Mental Health*, 6, 253–271.

Yang, Y., and Raine, A. (2009). Prefrontal structural and functional brain imaging findings in antisocial, violent, and psychopathic individuals: A meta-analysis. *Psychiatry Research*, 174, 81–88.

Yang, Y., Raine, A., Colletti, P., Toga, A. W., and Narr, K. L. (2009b). Abnormal temporal and prefrontal cortical gray matter thinning in psychopaths. *Molecular Psychiatry*, 14, 561–562.

Yang, Y., Raine, A., Lencz, T., Bihrle, S., Lacasse, L., and Colletti, P. (2005). Volume reduction in prefrontal gray matter in unsuccessful criminal psychopaths. *Biological Psychiatry*, 15, 1103–1108.

Yang, Y., Raine, A., Narr, K. L., Colletti, P., and Toga, A. W. (2009a). Localization of deformations within the amygdala in individuals with psychopathy. *Archives of General Psychiatry*, 66, 986–994.

INDEX

Note: Page numbers followed by an italicized *n* indicate text in footnotes.